# FREEDOM OF INFC
# SOCIAL SCIENCE RESEARCH DESIGN

This multidisciplinary volume demonstrates how Freedom of Information (FOI) law and processes can contribute to social science research design across sociology, criminology, political science, anthropology, journalism and education. Comparing the use of FOI in research design across the United Kingdom, the United States, Australia, Canada and South Africa, it provides readers with resources to carry out FOI requests and considers the influence such requests can have on debates within multiple disciplines. In addition to exploring how scholars can use FOI disclosures in conjunction with interview data, archival data and other datasets, this collection explains how researchers can systematically analyse FOI disclosures. Considering the challenges and dilemmas in using FOI processes in research, it examines the reasons why many scholars continue to rely on more easily accessible data, when much of the real work of governance, the more clandestine but consequential decisions and policy moves made by government officials, can only be accessed using FOI requests.

**Kevin Walby** is Associate Professor of Criminal Justice at the University of Winnipeg, Canada. He is the author of *Touching Encounters: Sex, Work and Male-for-Male Internet Escorting* and the co-author of *Municipal Corporate Security in International Context* as well as *A Criminology of Policing and Security Frontiers*. He is the co-editor of *Access to Information and Social Justice: Critical Research Strategies for Journalists, Scholars and Activists*; *Brokering Access: Power, Politics and Freedom of Information Process in Canada*; *The Handbook of Prison Tourism*; *Corporatizing Canada: Making Business Out of Public Service*; *National Security, Surveillance, and Terror: Canada and Australia in Comparative Perspective*; *Policing Cities: Urban Securitization and Regulation in a 21st Century World* and *Corporate Security in the 21st Century: Theory and Practice in International Perspective*. He is co-editor of the *Journal of Prisoners on Prisons*.

**Alex Luscombe** is a PhD Candidate in criminology at the University of Toronto, Canada. He has published widely on issues of policing, corruption, secrecy and Freedom of Information law in Canada and beyond. His past research has appeared in *Social Forces*, *British Journal of Criminology*, *Sociology*, *International Political Sociology*, *Canadian Journal of Criminology & Criminal Justice*, *Policing & Society*, *Criminology & Criminal Justice*, as well as a number of other academic journals and edited volumes. He serves on the editorial board of *Criminological Highlights*, a University of Toronto publication aimed at providing criminal justice practitioners with an accessible overview of recent criminological research. He is also a Junior Fellow at the University of Toronto's Massey College.

# Routledge Advances in Research Methods

For more information about this series, please visit: www.routledge.com/
Routledge-Advances-in-Research-Methods/book-series/RARM

# FREEDOM OF INFORMATION AND SOCIAL SCIENCE RESEARCH DESIGN

*Edited by Kevin Walby and Alex Luscombe*

Routledge
Taylor & Francis Group

LONDON AND NEW YORK

First published 2020
by Routledge
2 Park Square, Milton Park, Abingdon, Oxon OX14 4RN

and by Routledge
52 Vanderbilt Avenue, New York, NY 10017

*Routledge is an imprint of the Taylor & Francis Group, an informa business*

*British Library Cataloguing-in-Publication Data*
A catalogue record for this book is available from the British Library

*Library of Congress Cataloging-in-Publication Data*
A catalog record has been requested for this book

ISBN: 978-1-138-34573-7 (hbk)
ISBN: 978-1-138-34574-4 (pbk)
ISBN: 978-0-429-43771-7 (ebk)

Typeset in Bembo
by Integra Software Services Pvt. Ltd.

# CONTENTS

# CONTRIBUTORS

**Dr. Hannah Bows** is an Assistant Professor in Criminal Law at Durham Law School (Durham University). Her research spans the areas of violence, gender and ageing. Her recent research includes studies examining homicide and sexual offences against people aged 60 and over in the UK and a current project analysing stalking. She is the incoming Chair of the British Society of Criminology Victims Network and founder of the International Network for Research into Violence Against Older Women.

**Ciara Bracken-Roche** is an SSHRC Postdoctoral Fellow at the University of Ottawa. Her primary research programme analyses the contribution of unmanned aerial systems to the rapid expansion of security, policing and commercial surveillance in Canada. Her research agenda focuses on the relationship between governance and technology, and the social implications of technocratic governmentality. Her work has been published in journals such as *Geopolitics*, *Geographica Helvetica*, *Feminist Journal of Art and Digital Culture* and the *Journal of Unmanned Systems*, in addition to numerous book chapters and policy reports. Bracken-Roche completed her PhD in the Department of Sociology at Queen's University in 2017, funded by the SSHRC Talent Program. She completed her MA (Politics) at the University of Warwick and her BSc (International Relations) at the University of Toronto. Bracken-Roche also has a long history of service within her academic communities, most recently founding a Postdoctoral Association at the University of Ottawa, which has secured benefits and employee status for Postdoctoral Fellows.

**John R. Campbell** is Reader in Sociology and Anthropology at University of London. Following anthropological research on international development in Africa, John Campbell has undertaken research on war, refugees and statelessness in the Horn of Africa and he has written on asylum-related litigation in British courts. The issues in this paper emerged from recent work he has undertaken including *Nationalism, Law and Statelessness: Grand Illusions in the Horn of Africa* (Routledge, 2014) and *Bureaucracy, Law and Dystopia in the United Kingdom's Asylum System* (Routledge, 2017).

**Giancarlo Fiorella** is a doctoral candidate at the Centre for Criminology & Sociolegal Studies at the University of Toronto. He has an M.A. in Sociolegal Studies and a B.A. in Criminology from York University. His dissertation work is focused on the role that pro-government civilian groups play in protest repression in Venezuela. Giancarlo is also an investigator and trainer for Latin America at Bellingcat, an award-winning open-source investigation organisation.

**Pierce Greenberg** is an Assistant Professor of Sociology in the Department of Cultural and Social Studies at Creighton University. His primary research agenda examines environmental inequality in rural communities. Prior to entering academia, he worked as a journalist for two years–where he developed an interest in public records requests. He has organized public records workshops for sociologists at two conferences: the annual American Sociological Association meeting and a meeting of the Association of Humanist Sociology. His work has been published in *Rural Sociology, Environmental Sociology, Social Science Research, Society and Natural Resources*, and other peer-reviewed journals.

**Sean Holman** is an award-winning investigative reporter, digital media innovator and Associate Professor of Journalism at Mount Royal University in Calgary. In 2012, his reporting was recognised with a special mention in J-Source's Canadian Newsperson of the Year competition for "using new and emerging media technologies to expand the number of journalistic voices in this country and to redefine the relationship between journalists and citizens." Holman, who holds as a master's degree in journalism from Carleton University, also produced and directed the Cable Public Affairs Channel documentary Whipped: the secret world of party discipline. Since joining Mount Royal in 2012, his research has focused on the usage and history of Freedom of Information in Canada. He is now continuing that research as a PhD candidate at the University of Birmingham's Department of History.

**Emily J.M. Knox** is an Assistant Professor in the School of Information Sciences at the University of Illinois at Urbana-Champaign. Her research interests include information access, intellectual freedom and censorship, information ethics, information policy, and the intersection of print culture and reading practices. Emily recently edited *Trigger Warnings: History, Theory Context*, published by Rowman & Littlefield. Her book, *Book Banning in 21st Century America*, was also published by Rowman & Littlefield and is the first monograph in the Beta Phi Mu Scholars' Series. Emily received her Ph.D. from the doctoral programme at the Rutgers University School of Communication & Information. Her master's in library and information science is from the iSchool at Illinois. She also holds a B.A. in Religious Studies from Smith College and an A.M. in the same field from The University of Chicago Divinity School. Emily serves on the boards of the Freedom to Read Foundation and the National Coalition Against Censorship.

**Debra Mackinnon** is a post-doctoral associate in the Department of Geography at the University of Calgary. She received her PhD from Queen's University in 2019. Her research interests include surveillance, governance and regulation, smart cities and IoT, urban policy mobility, political economy and qualitative methods. Her dissertation Mundane Surveillance: Tracking Mobile Applications and Urban Accounting in Canadian Business Improvement Areas explored the adoption, mobility and legitimisation of asset management applications in Canadian cities. Her current research focuses on smart cities, urban governance, precursory technologies and partnerships.

**Shannon M. Oltmann** is an Assistant Professor in the School of Information Science at the University of Kentucky. Her research interests include censorship, intellectual freedom, information policy, public libraries, privacy and qualitative research methods. She has presented her research at academic conferences such as the Information Ethics Roundtable, the Annual Conference of the Association for Information Science & Technology, the iConference and the International Congress on Qualitative Inquiry. Her work has been published in the *Journal of the American Society for Information Science and Technology*, *Library Quarterly*, *Public Libraries Quarterly*, *Collection Management*, *Libri* and *Library and Information Science Research*. She is writing a book on intellectual freedom in libraries.

**Chris Peterson** is a researcher at MIT's Center for Civic Media and a member of the Board of Directors at the National Coalition Against Censorship. He has been mapping information access since 2009, and has mapped banned books using data from the Kid's Right to Read Project. In 2012, he partnered with MuckRock and the Boston Globe to launch an FOIA campaign requesting book challenges from every public school and library in Massachusetts. Peterson earned his S.M. in Comparative Media Studies at MIT and his B.A. in Critical Legal Studies at the University of Massachusetts, Amherst. He is a Fellow at the National Center for Technology and Dispute Resolution and former Research Assistant at the Berkman Center for Internet and Society at Harvard.

**Christine Pich** is a PhD Candidate in Sociology at Carleton University. Her doctoral research, which incorporates provincial-level Freedom of Information requests as a research method, focuses on the recognition of occupational diseases through Ontario's workers' compensation system and how the dynamic and contested boundaries between "known" and "unknown" complicate these decision-making processes. Her methodological research interests also include developing approaches to understanding complexity in social phenomenon, as seen through her co-authored publication The Challenge of Complexity: Reflections on Researching an Organizational Change Initiative Promoting Equity and Inclusion in the City of Ottawa featured in the edited volume *Toward Equity and Inclusion in Canadian Cities: Lessons from Critical Praxis-Oriented Research* (McGill-Queens University Press, 2017). She has taught qualitative research methods at Carleton University.

**Mike Sheaff** is Associate Professor in Sociology at the University of Plymouth, UK. With a BA in Psychology, an MA in Industrial Relations, and PhD in Industrial & Business Studies, his teaching and research interests have spanned health, work and employment, and organisations. He has been leading programmes for Sociology, and contributed to teaching on health profession programmes (related to his 2005 book, *Sociology & Health Care*, Open University Press). Mike's academic interests have been accompanied by a range of external governance roles. These include being a trustee of local charities and active in community organisations, a member of his trade union national executive committee, an elected member of a city council and Non-Executive Vice-Chair of an NHS Primary Care Trust. This variety of experience, including sensitive roles, contributed to the development of his interest in secrecy as an obstacle to accountability.

**Keith Spiller's** research focuses on the social consequences of surveillance and monitoring, with an emphasis on the impact of governmental regulatory policy. His recent book examines new forms of public duty mandated by the UK Counter Terrorism and Security Act (2015) and its bearing on the educational sector. Presently, his research concentrates on the project *Desecuritising Higher Education* (Joseph Rowntree Charitable Trust), which reviews Prevent Duty policies and guidance within HE providers across the UK. He has also published work on eBorders, money laundering, CCTV, lifelogging, the Prevent Strategy and the impacts of security regimes on organisations and individuals.

**Ian Warren** is a Senior Lecturer with research interests spanning numerous criminological subject areas. He has written widely on comparative criminology, illicit drug regulation, the use of technology to prevent crime, the relationship between surveillance and privacy and the relationship between crime and sport.

**Andrew Whiting** is a Senior Lecturer in Security Studies at Birmingham City University. His research to date spans two main areas: first, investigating discursive representations of security issues such as terrorism and cyber-threats and, second, exploring the impact of UK counter-terrorism policies and practices within UK Higher Education. Currently, Andrew is serving as the Principal Investigator on a research project entitled *Desecuritising Higher Education* (supported by the Joseph Rowntree Charitable Trust) that is investigating the encroachment of counter-terrorism policy into UK Higher Education. Andrew's research has been published in journals including *Perspectives on Terrorism*, *The European Journal of International Security*, *Critical Studies on Terrorism* and *Global Society* and with publishers including Routledge, Springer and most recently Palgrave Pivot (2019) as part of a co-authored book written with Imran Awan and Keith Spiller.

**Ben Worthy** is Lecturer in Politics at Birkbeck College, University of London. He is the author of *The Politics of Freedom of Information: How and Why Governments Pass Laws that Threaten their Power.*

**Toerien van Wyk** is a PhD candidate in the ARC Laureate Program in Comparative Constitutional Law at Melbourne Law School. Her interests are in comparative constitutional law, fundamental rights and access to information. Before joining the Laureate Program, Toerien was a Co-Director of the South African History Archive (SAHA) and the Coordinator of SAHA's Freedom of Information Programme (FOIP). SAHA is an independent human rights archive dedicated to documenting, supporting and promoting greater awareness of past and contemporary struggles for justice through archival practices and outreach, and the utilisation of Freedom of Information laws. Toerien has extensive experience in the use of Freedom of Information laws as a means of expanding on the boundaries of access to information and has presented on this experience in various forums. Toerien is an admitted attorney with a Baccalaureus Legum degree (LLB) from the University of South Africa as well as a Master of Laws: Human Rights Law degree (LLM) obtained, with distinction, from the University of Johannesburg. Toerien has experience in many facets of human rights law and has also previously worked as a human rights researcher and as a lecturer.

# ACKNOWLEDGEMENTS

Kevin Walby thanks his colleagues in the Department of Criminal Justice at the University of Winnipeg and everyone at the Centre for Interdisciplinary Justice Studies (CIJS). Thanks to Bilguundari Enkhtugs, Joanne DeCosse and Crystal Gumieny for their assistance as well.

Alex Luscombe thanks his colleagues at the Centre for Criminology and Sociolegal Studies at the University of Toronto and at Massey College for their invaluable feedback and support. He also thanks his partner Melissa, without whom none of this would be possible.

We dedicate this book to all those who have fought for FOI laws in their home country. They are the force that makes this research possible.

# FOREWORD: THINKING ABOUT ACCESS

In legislative terms, Freedom of Information (FOI) laws have been a huge success, with more than 100 appearing in various forms across the world. The struggle to pass legislation is seen as a "kind of morality play" and a test of the credibility of a government's radicalism (Wald, 1984, p. 649). Symbolically, they embody the public's moral right to know what's happening, and are frequently seen as a signal of a government's willingness to allow the light in.

Once in place, ATI laws can be powerful tools of political accountability. Across the world, openness laws have helped remove corrupt leaders and triggered systematic change across a range of areas, from exams systems in Thailand to MPs' expenses arrangements in the United Kingdom. Politicians' complaints are perhaps a testament to their strength and the anticipated reactions and fears they can create.

Yet, ever since the passing of major legislation since the 1960s onwards, there have been questions about how well they work in reality. On a day-to-day basis, ATI laws can be a micro-tool for securing personal interests and righting wrongs. They also offer a means of accessing information about services, schools and sanitation. But how well do they work at the "street level" for the citizen?

Tracing the processes and effect of ATI laws is hard. FOI laws are also plagued with difficulties. This is partly about the sheer scope of laws that frequently reach police forces, parliaments and public libraries. Even in well-established FOI regimes, response rates can be low and records of use or outcomes sparse.

As Berliner et al.'s (2018) study of Mexico has shown, much remains to be known about requesters and the mixture of public and micro-political private motives that drive them. Squaring this with how their actions then interact with the bureaucratic request system is even more problematic. The process from initial use to outcome remains somewhat of a black box, and ideas of supply and demand oversimplify a complex process. There is often a long and uncertain chain between request and response (Roberts, 2015). Researchers have sought a range of ways to try to peer inside the black box, from big data analysis and interviews, to surveys and detailed case studies.

Using access laws themselves to assess laws has grown in popularity. Early approaches included Price's (2005) testing of the functioning and timeliness of New Zealand's Official Information Act and Lidberg's comparison of Australian and Swedish openness laws (2006). In 2006, the Open Society Justice Initiative (2006) tested laws across 14 countries at national level with standardised requests. Roberts systematically made FOI requests to a specific UK department (2009), while Access Info Europe used a similar approach using the European Union's access to documents legislation in 2014.

Requests have been deployed in experimental form to measure the simple working of the Act, to test for its potential impact and to assess levels of legal compliance or "concordance" with the "spirit" of the law (Grimmelikhaujsen & Meijer, 2014; Richter & Wilson, 2013, p. 181). Request-based studies have now tested laws at a whole range of institutions and levels of government, from village councils and police forces to the European Union, and across the world from the UK to Uruguay.

Different approaches have been used to get at the functionality. Some request-based studies measure, for example, the timeliness of responses and success of the system as a whole. Others have also examined the equity of FOI systems, testing for biases and partiality. To give a flavour of these, Lagunes (2007) used Mexico's FOI Act to see if implied connections to certain influential families had an effect on responses, with this and a later follow-up study by Lagunes and Pocasangre (2017) finding little evidence of partiality. Michener and Rodrigez (2015) replicated the approach in Brazil when looking for possible bureaucratic bias based on requester identity. In the US, Cuillier (2010) looked at whether different approaches in the tones of requests themselves, labelled "honey versus vinegar," led to different results. Ben-Arron et al. (2017) tested peer-conformity among North Carolina County-level local government bodies, using open access law responses to see if one authority's openness then influenced others to do the same. Studies as far apart as Germany and Uruguay have used requests to reveal gender bias and differences in request results (Grohs & Knill, 2017; Rodríguez & Rossel, 2018).

One big question around the politics of openness is how or if FOI enables greater political involvement: does it have a "ripple effect" and work as a "leverage" right to access other social goods (Darch and Underwood, 2010)? Using India's Right to Information law, Peisakhin (2010) and Peisakhin and Pinto (2012) explored how requests could speed up quotidian, but vital, bureaucratic procedures such as voter registration, while Shankar et al. (2011) look at corruption and access to India's landmark rural poverty reforms.

Overall, the approaches have given us a vital insight into how and whether laws function, in terms of the basic compliance and spirit, and the extent to which there is "street-level" latitude and bias, for good or ill (Wilson, 2015). They have also illustrated some of the limitations, both as a political tool and basis for experimental design. Use can be hampered by the same practical problems that users face: low response rates, delay and poor compliance. Nevertheless, these experiments have shed light on whether FOI works, while also generating insights into gender, bias and practical problems.

There is, as ever, a final word of warning. As this collection shows, using laws in this way is not easy. It requires careful planning, design and experimentation. It also needs time and often raises ethical questions around use. But it can undoubtedly allow us to see how, when and whether FOI laws work.

Ben Worthy,
Department of Politics, Birkbeck,
University of London
March 12, 2019

# INTRODUCTION

## Freedom of Information and research design in international perspective

*Kevin Walby and Alex Luscombe*

## Introduction

Freedom of Information (FOI) laws are important features of governments in most societies today (Michener & Bersch, 2013; Schudson, 2015; Wasike, 2016; Worthy, 2017). FOI affords citizens a legal right to access information that is being privately held and sometimes strategically concealed by state agencies. The purpose of enacting FOI laws in a country or jurisdiction is to enhance transparency and accountability in government. Citizens in countries with FOI laws can use this democratic right to learn more about the practices of government that affect everyday life. In most FOI regimes, there are laws in place at each level of government and its associated public bodies (Arnold, 2014; Clement, 2015; Holsen, 2007; Jiwani & Krawchenko, 2014). Despite the usefulness of FOI requests, most academics, especially outside of journalism, have yet to take advantage of this powerful tool in their research. This is an unfortunate oversight. FOI requests comprise a novel source of data that can inform research endeavours in ways that more traditional strategies, like surveys or analysis of public reports, cannot. At the core of this volume is the argument that FOI comprises a powerful tool for data collection and should be embraced more fully by social scientists when conducting research on government.

*Freedom of Information and Social Science Research Design* sets out to achieve five major objectives. First, the volume will provide readers with resources to help them carry out their own FOI requests. FOI is more difficult than many people assume. Unfortunately, scholars who set out to use FOI are likely to find it difficult to identify resources to help them through the process. Often times research reports will make note that data was obtained through FOI, but the messy process that went into *accessing* that data is often glossed over. By having scholars reflect in-depth on the process of using FOI in their diverse research endeavours and countries, we hope to offer new and experienced users of FOI alike a set of resources to help guide them through the often times chaotic process of brokering access.

Second, the volume will explore FOI and the influence such access requests can have on disciplinary debates. The data one obtains from FOI is qualitatively different than the information one accesses through public reports like press releases and other official publications. Relying strictly on the latter is likely to skew both the questions that we ask about the work of state institutions and the answers we generate. This is not to say that FOI is a *superior* source of data, nor is it to suggest that every research project on government ought to use FOI. The point is rather that in cases where FOI data would be relevant to a particular research project, opting not to use it (in the absence of some meaningful alternative, like direct insider access to records) is likely to impact the nature of the results.

Third, the volume will address how scholars can use FOI disclosures in conjunction with interviews, archival records and other sources of data. While we believe that FOI is a legitimate means of producing social scientific data, it has as many limitations as any other tool of inquiry. By combining FOI with other forms of data in mixed-methods projects, many of its weaknesses can be overcome. And by generating novel data, it can also fill gaps and weaknesses in the methods it is combined with.

Fourth, the volume will showcase how scholars can conduct FOI requests and analyse FOI disclosures in a rigorous and systematic way. Many of the contributors in this volume, for example, have used FOI to generate large multi-institutional datasets that allow for comparisons across contexts, issues and time periods. Doing so involves filing tens, sometimes hundreds, of FOI requests and negotiating with officials in each agency to gain access to information. As the chapters in this volume show, making sense of this information is no less difficult. Analysing FOI disclosures requires systematic use of the same methods used to analyse any other social scientific data.

Finally, *Freedom of Information and Social Science Research Design* will examine why many scholars continue to rely on more traditional forms of data when much of the information available about governance, including the more clandestine but highly consequential decisions and policy manoeuvres government officials make, can often only be accessed using FOI. While a greater number of scholars worldwide are beginning to tap into the potential of FOI in their research, it is still far from "mainstream" in most disciplines.

A diverse group of scholars – some of whom contributed to this volume – have now used FOI requests to conduct rigorous, social scientific research on a range of government issues and programmes (Bows, 2017; Brown, 2009; Cuillier & Piotrowski, 2009; Jiwani & Krawchenko, 2014; Lee, 2005; Savage & Hyde, 2014). Building on this literature, the chapters in *Freedom of Information and Social Science Research Design* examine topics such as how FOI protocols originated and have changed over time, how FOI processes can be conducted effectively, how government employees bury the traces of their work to forego lengthy processes of divulging data, as well as how the media and the public respond to the presentation of the results of FOI requests in published reports. At a more practical level, the volume addresses how scholars can use FOI disclosures in conjunction with interview data, archival data, survey data, official statistics and other more conventional data types. The chapters in this volume also showcase how scholars analyse the results of FOI disclosures using established quantitative and qualitative techniques.

FOI laws are being implemented in countries around the globe (Ackerman & Sandoval-Ballesteros, 2006; Byrne, 2003; García-Tabuyo, Sáez-Martín, & Caba-Pérez, 2016; Hazell, 1989; Lagunes, 2009; Michener, 2015; Shepherd, Stevenson, & Flinn, 2010). Situating the rise of FOI and its implications for social science research in international perspective is a main goal of this volume. This does not mean, however, that all FOI laws are created equal. FOI laws vary from jurisdiction to jurisdiction, meaning there is also variation in how social scientists can use FOI as a tool to produce data (Luscombe, Walby, & Lippert, 2017). While more and more countries are adopting FOI laws, many regimes are at the same time trying to weaken or hollow out the laws they have (Birkinshaw, 2010a, 2010b; Halstuk & Chamberlin, 2006; Roberts, 2000). The wide array of FOI laws out there underscores the need to study how FOI works in different countries, particularly in a subnational and international comparative perspective, and adopting such a perspective is what makes this volume unique.

The chapters in this collection consider FOI not just in relation to themes of access and transparency but also the power to control information. Government departments have a vested interest in keeping some information concealed, and there are a variety of exemption clauses in the various FOI Acts that permit them to do so (Cherry & McMenemy, 2013; Cramer, 2018; Cuillier, 2010; Katz, 1969; Kimball, 2012; Roberts, 2002; Walby & Larsen, 2012, 2011). As Thomas (2019) has shown in the context of the UK, FOI decisions are almost always made in the interests of secrecy rather than disclosure. Government agencies claim to make the decision by "balancing" public and state interests, but in practice, the decision-making process centres around the value of secrecy rather than the potential value of disclosure. Government departments increasingly collect, process and store information in ways that mimic security and intelligence agencies (Monahan & Fisher, 2015; Pozen, 2005; Rappert, 2012; Sheaff, 2017), and this has major implications for issues of access, disclosure and FOI (Cuillier & Pinkleton, 2011; Michener & Bersch, 2013). As many of the chapters in this volume show, the power to control information always mediates the access that researchers can reap.

Although there are other edited volumes on FOI (Brownlee & Walby, 2015; Cuillier & Davis, 2010; Davis & Splichal, 2000; Larsen & Walby, 2012), *Freedom of Information and Social Science Research Design* is the first text to explicitly address the relationship between FOI processes and social science research design from a multi-disciplinary and comparative perspective. On the whole, there exist few publications on the importance of FOI for social research, on how to practically engage in FOI as a research method, and on broader issues of FOI governance, accountability and justice. Material obtained through FOI and reported on in the media has long been a driving force behind key public debates and of resistance to troubling government practices and processes in civil society. Academics, however, seem to have been slow to take up FOI in their research endeavours, both as an empirical focus and a method. It is our hope that *Freedom of Information and Social Science Research Design* will shape how critical scholarship is conducted in the social sciences, and will change the way sociologists, criminologists, historians, political scientists and others approach research methods and design.

## Layout of the volume

The chapters in this volume engage a range of topics related to FOI and research design in international perspective. Showcasing the increasingly global relevance of FOI laws for researchers worldwide, the chapters in this volume span a range of countries, including the United States, South Africa, United Kingdom, Canada, Australia, and South America.

In Chapter 1, Knox, Oltmann, and Peterson reflect on their use of FOI requests to research censorship in schools, libraries and other public institutions across the United States (US) as part of their larger Mapping Access Project. They begin the chapter with a rough overview of the history of federal and state FOI laws in the US followed by a discussion of the increasing popularity of FOI in academic research. Although FOI still has a way to go before it is fully embraced as a legitimate (and perhaps one day mainstream) social scientific method, they argue it is an important and powerful tool that scholarly researchers ought to adopt. In their research on state censorship practices, they admit that they never would have been able to gain access to the data they needed were it not for FOI. In the latter half of the chapter, Knox et al. offer practical guidance on how to file an FOI request in the US, providing tips on everything from identifying the right agency, to how to frame the request in writing, to the kind of responses one can expect, to how to avoid what they call "FOI harassment." Although FOI requests can be difficult, Knox et al. stress that the "rich data that one can receive in return" is always worth it.

In Chapter 2, we head to South Africa. Toerien van Wyk writes on the intersection of FOI and archives by reflecting on the use of FOI by the South African History Archive (SAHA), a non-profit anti-Apartheid initiative based in Johannesburg, Gauteng. Using South Africa's FOI law, the *Promotion to Access to Information Act*, SAHA aims to document and promote awareness of current and historic struggles for justice in post-Apartheid South Africa. Using SAHA case studies, Van Wyk reflects on the messiness and complexity of how South Africa's FOI law operates in action. Using theories of information and access, she lays out the different ways of framing a request for information (as a general request for information, as a request for a particular record-as-object or as both) under South Africa's FOI regime and the various challenges associated with each.

In Chapter 3, Keith Spiller and Andrew Whiting consider the United Kingdom's (UK) Freedom of Information Act (FOIA) as a tool for academic research. After reflecting on the value and limitations of the UK's FOIA as an academic research tool, the authors set out to locate the FOIA within a broader framework of digitalisation and highlight some of the challenges that researchers using FOI may face as a result of this trend. FOI-based research, the authors argue, although challenging, is a valuable means of producing potentially democratising and politically impactful academic research on government.

In Chapter 4, Mike Sheaff discusses his experiences of using FOI to research governance and decision-making processes, also in the context of the UK. FOI requests, Sheaff argues, are an especially powerful tool for researching government where "official accounts" are limited in what they reveal. Sheaff describes this as a critical approach to using FOI, in that it allows researchers to cut through the idealised representations of the state into the backstage of government practices. When used in this more critical manner, Sheaff argues that FOI can help researchers hold states accountable by making decision-making processes both more visible and intelligible in novel ways. In a time of diminishing public trust in state institutions, Sheaff argues that this kind of more critical use of FOI is crucially important.

In Chapter 5, Ian Warren brings the discussion to Australia. He argues that FOI is underused for scholarly research on government in Australia – specifically criminological research – in large part because of the extensive powers granted to federal and state governments to block FOI requests and, in the case of disclosure, redact records to the point of revealing very little. Next to countries like Canada, Warren declares Australia's FOI regime comparably weak. Criminal justice agencies like the Victoria Police find no shortage of ways to block disclosures and the appeals process tends to offer little in the way of remediation. Although not unique to Australia, the rise of public–private contracts in the Australian criminal justice system only makes matters of accessing info through FOI more difficult. Moving forward, Warren calls for greater reflection on FOI in the Australian context. In particular, he calls for more empirical research about how FOI operates within particular criminal justice contexts in Australia, as well as for more work on how criminologists in Australia are actually using FOI for their work, if at all.

In Chapter 6, Ciara Bracken-Roche reflects on her use of FOI requests in Canada, specifically how she used a combination of FOI and interviews to research the growing civil and commercial market for drones in that country. Due to the heavily redacted nature of FOI disclosures on government use of drones, Bracken-Roche turned to interviews in search of a fuller understanding of the phenomenon. Bracken-Roche shows how the results of FOI requests paired well with interviews, but also generated new methodological challenges. In some cases, for example, stakeholders appeared hesitant or even unwilling to agree to an interview having perceived her as the culprit of numerous FOI requests on their agencies. In order to overcome these and other obstacles associated with using FOI in scholarly research, Bracken-Roche underscores the need for both reflexivity and flexibility in research design.

In Chapter 7, Pierce Greenberg examines the use of FOI requests to research protest policing. Greenberg is writing from the US, where he argues very few academics are using FOI to collect data for research. As he argues, most protest policing scholars rely on media coverage and interviews with protest participants as data, but such "sources rarely involve behind-the-scenes details on policing strategies and intentions" that one can find in records disclosed through FOI. Greenberg argues in favour of triangulation in use of FOI requests. He reflects on his own research using FOI to obtain access to protest-related records from the Seattle Police Department. He shows how FOI can be used to advance studies of protest policing that use protest event analysis and case studies.

In Chapter 8, Debra Mackinnon reflects on her use of FOI to research the public–private policing partnerships in Canada enabled through Business Improvement Areas (BIAs). Public–private partnerships, particularly in the realm of policing and security, can be exceptionally difficult to research due to their cagey nature and nebulous relationship to most public access and accountability laws. Driven to research these tricky institutional arrangements, Mackinnon finds ways to make FOI work. Engaging with actor network theory, Mackinnon conceptualises FOI as an "oligoptic technology" that can afford researchers a partial but still useful means to trace and reveal complex, networked relations between public–private actors. Exploring the scope of public records, she reflects on how FOI can be used as a partial, albeit imperfect, "entry way" into public–private policing partnerships.

In Chapter 9, Christine Pich writes on her use of FOI requests to obtain documents from Archives of Ontario and Ontario's Workplace Safety and Insurance Board for her research on knowledge contestations around occupational disease recognition and standards of proof. Similar to Bracken-Roche's study of drones, Pich opts to combine FOI with in-depth interviews in what she calls a "multi-method qualitative research design." Pich's decision to incorporate FOI into her research design was serendipitous rather than planned. Encountering barriers to accessing data in the Archives of Ontario, she turned to FOI. Her ability to add FOI into her research design was possible because of the "openness and flexibility" of the qualitative research process. Pich also challenges the idea of triangulation. She argues that triangulation, which generally assumes that multiple data sources come together to reach some deeper, singular truth, does not accurately characterise qualitative research involving use of FOI.

In Chapter 10, Kevin Walby and Alex Luscombe conceive of FOI requests in social research as a way of accessing data that governments do not proactively disclose and of rethinking the repertoires of empirical social science more broadly. Specifically, Walby and Luscombe examine how content analysis, discourse analysis, metaphor analysis and social network analysis can be used by researchers to make sense of the records they obtain through FOI. Like any social science data, FOI records do not speak for themselves but instead must be systematically analysed using established techniques. Walby and Luscombe argue that the choice of data analysis technique should be determined by the type of FOI data one receives and by the particular research question they are trying to answer.

In Chapter 11, John R. Campbell reflects on his use of the UK's FOIA to gain access to insider records and go "beyond official discourse" in his research on the Home Office's processing of asylum applications through the so-called "language analysis." He describes how the Home Office could refuse to comply with FOI requests on the subject of asylums by invoking claims about threats to national security. Exploring the parameters of the national security state, Campbell further finds that his efforts to dispute the Home Office's use of national security to block access were not sufficiently investigated by accountability agents, raising questions about the efficacy of processes of appeal in this country.

In Chapter 12, Hannah Bows reflects on tips, tricks and barriers to using FOI for research in the UK. Bows used FOI to obtain records from 49 police forces across the UK on rape and sexual assault, stalking and homicide. Bows discusses the use of FOI requests to research these issues in three phases: designing the request, accessing the data and analysing the data. As Bows shows, each of these phases involves navigating and overcoming barriers to access. At the design stage, researchers need to use the correct terminology to get at internal records, which can be difficult to figure out beforehand. One of the greatest reasons for delays, Bows argues, is that FOI coordinators do not understand what is being asked for in a request. At the accessing stage, researchers have to overcome lengthy delays, steep cost estimates and redactions. At the analysis stage, researchers have to deal with complicated and inconsistent document formats and missing information. Rather than cause to avoid FOI, Bows underscores the need for researchers to overcome these and other barriers through strategic planning and creative brokering.

In Chapter 13, Sean Holman examines the history of FOI law as a product of the "right to know" discourse that emerged in postwar US and Canada. He shows how, in postwar Canada and US, increasing public concern over governments growing in both size and secrecy fuelled a demand for information that was eventually operationalised through FOI law. In the lead up to passing FOI laws, he argues there was also a growing distrust of government. In general, people believed that the information government proactively released was "somehow compromised" and potentially even deceptive. In conclusion, Holman argues that the same demand for information and accountability that fuelled the passing of FOI laws "may be receding in favour an emotional demand for certainty" that has brought with it "the seduction of authoritarianism." For Holman, the way out of this downward trend is for scholars, journalists, activists and anyone else who cares about government transparency to re-advocate the importance of information as the "currency of democracy."

Finally, in a postscript, Giancarlo Fiorella reminds us that not all countries have passed, or even have aspirations to pass, FOI laws. Venezuela, for instance, where Fiorella conducts most of his research, is one of these countries. Working at the intersections of activism, academia and investigative journalism, Fiorella highlights the issues of data starvation that such countries suffer from, but also the power of open-source investigations to partially fill the void that the lack of public access laws creates. Rather than working separately, Fiorella stresses the need for FOI researchers to pay greater attention to the work of open-source investigators, whose methodological advancements in verification and theories of power and information have much to offer those using FOI.

## References

Ackerman, J. M., & Sandoval-Ballesteros, I. E. (2006). The global explosion of freedom of information laws. *Administrative Law Review, 58*(1), 85–130.

Arnold, J. (2014). *Secrecy in the sunshine era: The promise and failures of U.S. open government laws.* Witchita: University Press of Kansas.

Birkinshaw, P. (2010a). *Freedom of information: The law, the practice and the ideal.* Cambridge: Cambridge University Press.

Birkinshaw, P. (2010b). Freedom of information and its impact in the United Kingdom. *Government Information Quarterly, 27*(4), 312–321.

Bows, H. (2017). Researching sexual violence against older people: Reflecting on the use of freedom of information requests in a feminist study. *Feminist Review, 115*(1), 30–45.

Brown, K. J. (2009). COUNTERBLAST: Freedom of information as a research tool: Realising its potential. *The Howard Journal of Criminal Justice, 48*(1), 88–91.

Brownlee, J., & Walby, K. (Eds.). (2015). *Access to information and social justice: Critical research strategies for journalists, scholars, and activists.* Winnipeg: Arbeiter Ring Publishing (ARP) Books.

Byrne, M. (2003). Freedom of information in the post-communist world. *Problems of Post-Communism, 50*(2), 56.

Cherry, M., & McMenemy, D. (2013). Freedom of information and 'vexatious' requests: The case of Scottish local government. *Government Information Quarterly, 30*(3), 257–266.

Clement, D. (2015). Freedom of information in Canada: Implications for historical research. *Labour / Le Travail, 75*, 101–131.

Cramer, B. W. (2018). Old love for new snoops: How exemption 3 of the freedom of information act enables an irrebuttable presumption of surveillance secrecy. *Communication Law and Policy, 23*(2), 91–124.

Cuillier, D. (2010). Honey v. vinegar: Testing compliance-gaining theories in the context of freedom of information laws. *Communication Law and Policy, 15*(3), 203–229.

Cuillier, D., & Davis, C. N. (2010). *The art of access: Strategies for acquiring public records.* Los Angeles: Sage Press.

Cuillier, D., & Pinkleton, B. E. (2011). Suspicion and secrecy: Political attitudes and their relationship to support for freedom of information. *Communication Law and Policy, 16*(3), 227–254.

Cuillier, D., & Piotrowski, S. J. (2009). Internet information-seeking and its relation to support for access to government records. *Government Information Quarterly, 26*(3), 441–449.

Davis, C. N., & Splichal, S. L. (Eds.). (2000). *Access denied: Freedom of information in the information age.* Boise: Iowa State University Press.

García-Tabuyo, M., Sáez-Martín, A., & Caba-Pérez, M. D. C. (2016). Mandatory versus voluntary disclosures: Drivers of proactive information provision by local governments in Central America. *Information Development, 32*(4), 1199–1215.

Halstuk, M. E., & Chamberlin, B. F. (2006). The freedom of information act 1966–2006: A retrospective on the rise of privacy protection over the public interest in knowing what the government's up to. *Communication Law and Policy, 11*(4), 511–564.

Hazell, R. (1989). Freedom of information in Australia, Canada and New Zealand. *Public Administration, 67*(2), 189–210.

Holsen, S. (2007). Freedom of information in the UK, US, and Canada. *Information Management Journal, 41*(3), 50–55.

Jiwani, F., & Krawchenko, T. (2014). Public policy, access to government, and qualitative research practices: Conducting research within a culture of information control. *Canadian Public Policy, 40*(1), 57–66.

Katz, J. M. (1969). Games Bureaucrats play: Hide and seek under the freedom of information act. *Texas Law Review, 48*, 1261–1284.

Kimball, M. B. (2012). Shining the light from the inside: Access professionals' perceptions of government transparency. *Communication Law and Policy, 17*(3), 299–328.

Lagunes, P. (2009). Irregular transparency? An experiment involving Mexico's freedom of information law. SSRN Working Paper Series.

Larsen, M., & Walby, K. (Eds.). (2012). *Brokering access: Power, politics and freedom of information process in Canada*. Vancouver: University of British Columbia Press.

Lee, R. (2005). The UK Freedom of Information Act and social research. *International Journal of Social Research Methodology, 8*(1), 1–18.

Luscombe, A., Walby, K., & Lippert, R. (2017). Brokering access beyond the border and in the wild: Comparing freedom of information law and policy in Canada and the United States. *Law & Policy, 39*(3), 259–279.

Michener, G. (2015). Assessing freedom of information in Latin America a decade later: Illuminating a transparency causal mechanism. *Latin American Politics and Society, 57*(3), 77–99.

Michener, G., & Bersch, K. (2013). Identifying transparency. *Information Polity, 18*(3), 233–242.

Monahan, T., & Fisher, J. A. (2015). Strategies for obtaining access to secretive or guarded organizations. *Journal of Contemporary Ethnography, 44*(6), 709–736.

Pozen, D. E. (2005). The mosaic theory, national security, and the freedom of information act. *Yale Law Journal, 115*, 628–679.

Rappert, B. (2012). States of ignorance: The unmaking and remaking of death tolls. *Economy and Society, 41*(1), 42–63.

Roberts, A. (2000). Less government, more secrecy: Reinvention and the weakening of freedom of information law. *Public Administration Review, 60*(4), 308–320.

Roberts, A. (2002). Administrative discretion and the Access to Information Act: An "internal law" on open government? *Canadian Public Administration, 45*(2), 175–194.

Savage, A., & Hyde, R. (2014). Using freedom of information requests to facilitate research. *International Journal of Social Research Methodology, 17*(3), 303–317.

Schudson, M. (2015). *The rise of the right to know: Politics and the culture of transparency, 1945–1975*. Harvard: Harvard University Press.

Sheaff, M. (2017). Constructing accounts of organisational failure: Policy, power and concealment. *Critical Social Policy, 37*(4), 520–539.

Shepherd, E., Stevenson, A., & Flinn, A. (2010). Information governance, records management, and freedom of information: A study of local government authorities in England. *Government Information Quarterly, 27*(4), 337–345.

Siltanen, J., Willis, A., & Scobie, W. (2008). Separately together: Working reflexively as a team. *International Journal of Social Research Methodology*, *11*(1), 45–61.

Thomas, O. D. (2019). Security in the balance: How Britain tried to keep its Iraq War secrets. *Security Dialogue* (online first).

Walby, K., & Larsen, M. (2011). Getting at the live archive: On Access to information research in Canada. *Canadian Journal of Law and Society*, *26*(3), 623–634.

Walby, K., & Larsen, M. (2012). Access to information and freedom of information requests: Neglected means of data production in the social sciences. *Qualitative Inquiry*, *18*(1), 31–42.

Wasike, B. (2016). FOIA in the age of Open.Gov: An analysis of the performance of the Freedom of Information Act under the obama and bush administrations. *Government Information Quarterly*, *33*(3), 417–426.

Worthy, B. (2017). *The politics of freedom of information: How and why governments pass laws that threaten their power*. Manchester: Manchester University Press.

# PART 1

# Freedom of Information and research design

## The foundations

# 1

# DESIGNING RESEARCH USING FOI REQUESTS IN THE USA

*Emily J.M. Knox, Shannon M. Oltmann and Chris Peterson*

## Introduction

One of the most difficult aspects of conducting social scientific research is collecting data. Data collection can, of course, be accomplished through many different methods. Surveys, interviews and observations are just a few examples of methods that are often used in the social sciences. It should be noted, however, that these methods can be quite difficult to employ since they involve the willingness of people to participate. Laypersons are often surprised at the small number of responses compared to the number of surveys sent out or the effort involved in getting a few dozen people to be interviewed on a topic. This can be even more difficult when the topic is sensitive.

Our research focuses on censorship and restricting access to information – actions that few people will ever admit to. In the United States, research indicates that challenges (i.e., requests to remove, relocate or restrict library or school materials) take place in different types of communities – large and small, liberal and conservative – across the country. Researchers often state that the ubiquity of challenges is one of the most perplexing aspects of working in public libraries and schools – one never knows when a book or other item might be challenged or what kind of material might be targeted (Schrader, 1997). Another common, though less widely publicised, method of censorship is to restrict access to information through the use of Internet filters in publicly supported institutions. Filters are often used by public institutions to comply with the Children's Internet Protection Act (CIPA), which was signed into law in the United States in 2000. However, many public schools and libraries misinterpret the law and use filtering as a classroom management tool or a means to curb access to legally protected materials (Batch, 2014; Peterson, Oltmann, & Knox, 2017).

In the U.S., the American Library Association (ALA) collects information on book challenges and conducts an annual survey of public school libraries that includes information on filtering. The ALA's Office for Intellectual Freedom (ALA-OIF) is the primary national body that collects book challenge statistics. All information is self-reported because the ALA values protecting the privacy and confidentiality of reporting institutions; meanwhile, no geographical information regarding challenges is released. It is also assumed that these reported cases account for only a small fraction of the overall number of challenge cases that happen in the United States.

Our research project, called Mapping Information Access (mappinginfoaccess. org), has three primary goals. First, the project is intended to provide a comprehensive, accessible geographic overview of censorship in the United States over the past five years. Second, it explores the similarities and differences among how community institutions provide access to information during the same period. Third, it investigates similarities and differences among the communities in order to determine if certain characteristics lead to restricted access to information in public institutions.

The project aims to be a systematic investigation into how information is restricted (or censored) in public institutions across the United States. As noted, people who restrict access to information rarely see themselves as censors but as protectors of society or the local community. This means that obtaining data about current censorship practices can be quite daunting. It is not information that is usually volunteered. In light of this, we have turned to Freedom of Information (FOI) laws to gather information about censorship in public institutions across the U.S. This chapter gives an overview of FOI laws in the U.S., demonstrates how social science researchers can use FOI processes as a research tool, offers best practice guidelines on how to design FOI-based research projects and describes how to actually use FOI requests in the U.S. at both the state and federal levels.

## History of Freedom of Information laws in the United States

The Freedom of Information Act (FOIA) first became law in the United States in 1966. John Moss, a Democratic Congressman from the state of California, originally proposed the legislation in 1955 in response to the increase in government secrecy practices in the Cold War (Electronic Frontier Foundation, 2012). Of particular interest is that the original report to congress was titled "Clarifying and Protecting the Right of the Public to Information and for Other Purposes," as one might assume that "other purposes" was referring to research. The bill passed both the Senate and House (the latter with a 307–0 vote), but it was not supported by Democratic President Lyndon B. Johnson.

Johnson signed the bill, with his signing statement noting:

> This legislation springs from one of our most essential principles: a democracy works best when the people have all the information that the security of the

nation will permit. At the same time, the welfare of the nation or the rights of individuals may require that some documents not be made available. As long as threats to peace exist, for example, there must be military secrets, a citizen must be able in confidence to complain to his government and to provide information just as he is – and should be – free to confide in the press without fear of reprisal or being required to discuss or reveal his sources.

*(The White House, 1966)*

According to Thomas Blanton (2006), Bill Moyers, an aide to the president and originally an opponent to the legislation, eventually became one of its proponents and wrote the original signing statement, though President Johnson refused to include some of Moyer's more supportive language.

Following the passage of the national law, all 50 states plus the District of Columbia passed their own FOI laws. Generally, the laws work in the same way: a member of the public (defined by the law) makes a written request to review non-classified government documents. However, the laws have various levels of efficacy. This is most clearly seen in the varying deadlines for responses in the laws. For example, the North Carolina public records law does not include a time limit for response while the Illinois Freedom of Information Act requires a response within 5 days after receiving the request (Oltmann, Knox, Peterson, & Musgrave, 2016). Some laws provide an appeals process if the requestor finds fault with the government agency's response. It should be noted that these issues regarding deadlines and appeals have implications for research, as administrative bodies in states without timely response requirements may never respond to a request at all.

## FOI in journalism and research

Journalists were among the first stakeholders to push for FOI laws in the US and have long used FOI in their work. The *New York Times* published an article on how its reporters employ the law in a July 2018 *Times Insider* column (Lucas, 2018). Over the previous year, the *Times* had published a series of articles that centred on misdeeds by the then-head of the US Environmental Protection Agency, Scott Pruitt. All news stories were based on information received through FOIA requests, as described in the column; one can surmise that the "steady drumbeat" of negative stories led to Pruitt's resignation in June, 2018. Lucas (2018) writes:

And when a public agency denies a FOIA request, or under certain other circumstances, the law allows journalists and newsrooms to appeal. If that appeal is also denied or delayed, they can sue – and *The Times* is not afraid to do so. In fact, a 2017 report from the FOIA Project found that from 2001 to 2016, *The Times* filed at least 36 FOIA lawsuits, more than any other media organization.

*(para. 8)*

As Lucas (2018) notes, because the stories that they write using FOIA are often high stakes, they must consider whether the ensuing lawsuit would be prudent. None of the authors of this chapter have been involved in such a lawsuit over public records but it is a possibility.

Lucas (2018) also mentions "triangulating" information to boost the efficacy of a news article, a method that will be further discussed below:

> One of the ways FOIA becomes most valuable, Mr. [Eric] Lipton said, is by combining the information he has requested and received under the law with what has been released to other reporters, non-profits or anyone else requesting information about the same thing, as he did for the story about offshore drilling regulations.
>
> *(para. 16)*

FOI for academic research has been a topic of discussion for many years but, for various reasons, is still seen as an unusual research method. For example, Mike Forrest Keen (1992) argues that FOIA gives sociologists and other researchers "unparalleled access to the working of one of our most pervasive and influential formal organizations, the federal government" (p. 46). This is true not only of the federal FOIA, but also of FOI laws more generally. Raymond Lee (2001) reviewed the use of FOIA by social scientists for research data. He notes that social scientists originally used FOIA to find out what was in their own personal intelligence files. Lee argues for "the utility of moving away from seeing the FOIA as a source of personal records or as providing a window on government and toward seeing it more generally as a tool for studying bureaucratic organizations" (p. 384). He also suggests that FOIA can be understood as a kind of archival repository for researchers.

In his article arguing for the efficacy of FOI in research, Pierce Greenberg (2016) states that social researchers should make FOI requests a routine part of their research. He posits four different areas that are suitable for FOI: archival research, evaluation and triangulation with other data, case studies and organisational research. Greenberg also mentions some limitations that will be discussed below, including reluctance on the part of institutions to respond. Kevin Walby and Alex Luscombe (2017) present a typology for evaluating the quality of research that uses FOI data. These criteria, based on Sarah Tracy's work, are: worthy topic, rich rigor, sincerity, credibility, resonance, significant contribution, ethics and meaningful coherence. Walby and Luscombe offer concrete interpretations for applying each criterion to FOI research. They also note, however, that they "have been belittled on numerous occasions by researchers who argue that ATI/FOI data is 'unscientific'" (p. 548). It is hoped that this chapter will add to the ongoing effort to demonstrate that not only is FOI research legitimate, but also that it is, in fact, sometimes the only method for obtaining data to effectively answer certain research questions.

## Why use FOI in research?

Like all research, the most important thing to consider is what method (or methods) will answer the research question (see Savage & Hyde, 2014). It may be possible – but more difficult – to answer one's question without using FOI laws. This was the case for the authors of this chapter. Our research focuses on how public libraries and public schools in the US restrict access to information. In particular, we focus on filtering software that is placed on computers when public administrative governing boards use E-Rate, the Universal Service Program for Schools and Libraries administered by the Federal Communications Commission's Universal Service Fund ("E-rate," 2011). Note that if institutions employ E-Rate, they are required by law to filter. Questions about public institutions' use of E-Rate and filtering are often part of general surveys of libraries and schools. However, these questions are usually dichotomous; they simply ask whether the institution uses E-Rate filtering or not.

Dichotomous questions tell us nothing about the nature of these filters: Where do they come from? What information do they filter? How much do they cost? More specifically, we wanted to see the documents themselves: black- and white-lists of sites that are restricted or accessible, contracts with filtering companies and the names of the companies themselves. This more granular information could only come from the school and library administrations and was not available through regular data-gathering channels. Although the authors sent emails asking for this information to administrations, those emails were generally ignored. It was only through the force of law, i.e., by citing the applicable state FOI legislation, that we were able to obtain responses to our research questions.

Issues of finances and censorship are often controversial, and administrators sometimes need to be legally compelled to release information that might paint them in a poor light. We received some pushback when we asked for this documentation from public administrations. Even though these were all tax-supported institutions, many administrations wanted to argue that this information could not be made public. This argument, however, is not legally supported, and administrators are required to respond to FOI requests. Thus, when seeking information that might be sensitive, controversial or unflattering to the institution in question, FOI requests may be the best approach; sometimes, compelling information release (through the use of FOI law) is more effective than a simple email or phone call.

## How to use FOI laws in research

There are several steps involved in using FOI laws for research. These include finding the appropriate governing body, finding the appropriate person to address in the governing body and carefully wording the request. Although it might seem straightforward, in fact, each of these steps comes with its own challenges.

## *Finding the governing body*

Finding the appropriate governing body or administrative agency can be easy or difficult, depending on the research question(s). For example, at the federal level in the US, there is a website (foia.gov) dedicated to helping citizens make FOIA requests. The website includes a flowchart for determining when a FOIA request is needed and which federal agency to contact. The site allows users to search for information on agency websites and FOIA libraries before making a request. Next, there is a link to a website that sorts federal agencies by topic. For example, if you want information about student loans, the link takes the user to the Federal Student Aid office of the U.S. Department of Education. Therefore, you would know that a FOIA request on student loans would be handled by the Department of Education. Questions about foodborne illnesses, however, might be handled by one of three agencies: the Centers for Disease Control and Prevention, the Food Safety and Inspection Service or the US Food and Drug Administration. In the case of foodborne illness, more information is needed to identify the correct governing body to which to address a FOIA request.

US states have idiosyncratic FOI laws. However, it is generally easy to find state agencies via search engines and advocacy organisation like the National Freedom of Information Coalition (nfoic.org). For example, North Carolina has FAQ online related to understanding public records access. The FAQ states that

> a request to any employee in a government office is sufficient to get access to records in that office. However, it is the custodian of public records who is specifically required to allow those records to be inspected. The public official in charge of an office is designated to be the custodian of records for that office.

It is up to the researcher to consult records like these before conducting a request in a particular state jurisdiction.

## *Making the request*

One of the most difficult aspects of using FOI for research is tailoring the request (see also van Wyk, this volume). There is often a desire to ask for as much as possible, to ensure that the researcher will get the information they need. However, it is best to be specific and tailor one's request. These requests should be made in writing. In keeping with the idiosyncrasies of local bureaucracies, sometimes this means filling out a form while other agencies require an email. There are several FOI generators online that are helpful for figuring out what legal information should be included in each request.

Requests generally have four sections. First, the request should list the appropriate statute. For example, in Illinois, one would cite the Illinois Freedom of Information Act, 5 ILCS 140. Next is the document request. The more specific the better. Third, the request should provide an overview of fees. Since different public bodies charge different amounts, it is best to give a minimum amount charged that would trigger additional communication. For example, one of the authors asked for communication from the administrative agency if the cost will be more than $25.00. Finally, the request should have a time period for response that is in keeping with the state's law. For example, a request might ask for a reply "within 5 business days" in Illinois and "as promptly as possible" in North Carolina. It is not surprising that this is fairly straightforward; however, there are many problems that can pop up when using FOI for research. Often, sending the request is the easiest part of the process, but analysing the variety of responses could be a research study in its own right.

## Responses to requests

We have a combined 20 years' experience of using FOI for research purposes and have encountered almost every type of response in our research. Responses vary depending on the nature of the administrative unit, its financial resources and the strength of the pertinent governing FOI law. One of the most important things to keep in mind is that once a request is made, even though it has the force of law behind it, one is now in the idiosyncratic realm of people and systems. As Luscombe and Walby (2017) note, "the mundane and bureaucratic workings of FOI are more multi-faceted and less linear than one might expect" (p. 379). The authors received responses that ranged from a terse "No" to a long description of the respondent's health problems (as justification for not sending the information) to a simple email with the requested files attached. Once a request is sent, there is no way of knowing exactly what one will receive, but some generalisations can be made.

### Who responds?

Responses to FOI requests can vary widely. Sometimes responses come from an administrative assistant while other times they come from an attorney. Since the authors sent requests to public libraries, they sometimes received responses from the local volunteer who answers the general library email address and opens the library for a few hours per week. Often these volunteers would reply that they simply did not have time to gather the responsive materials for the request. In other instances, the requests were sent to the administrative body's attorney. Responses from attorneys varied. Sometimes, they would offer legal reasoning for not sending responsive materials, such as trying to claim that a public library was not a government agency and hence not subject to FOI laws. Other times, the request was simply directed to the attorney, who would answer in full. Most often, however, the designated public records administrator would send full responses to our requests.

## What do they send?

The responses one receives also vary based on the requests. What is most important here is to note that the responses to FOI requests can occasionally verge on the hostile. For example, the lead author recently sent a FOI request to a public school system in Virginia. This state's FOIA law says that

> all public records shall be open to citizens of the Commonwealth, representatives of newspapers and magazines with circulation in the Commonwealth, and representatives of radio and television stations broadcasting in or into the Commonwealth during the regular office hours of the custodian of such records.
>
> *(Code of Virginia § 2.2–3704)*

The school administration refused to send the requested documents since the author is not a citizen of Virginia. It should be noted that the Virginia FOIA Council, a state agency, recommends that out-of-state requests be treated the same as in-state requests, especially since one can easily just ask a Virginia citizen to make the request for them. Indeed, this is what the first author had to do to obtain the needed documents. However, rather than sending the materials electronically, the school administration sent the Virginia citizen a USB drive and CD-ROM, that were then sent via USPS to the author. These extra steps and delays amounted to small hurdles meant to frustrate the requests for documents.

The actual documents sent can also vary considerably. Each administrative body interprets the request differently. For example, the authors have been sent 500 pages and two pages in response to the same request sent to different agencies. As Savage and Hyde (2014) note, FOI requests often "produce large amounts of data, particularly if the same request is submitted to a large number of authorities or agencies" (p. 309).

## When do they send it?

This can also vary, not only according to local laws, but also in keeping with resources available with the administrative body. As noted, public institutions are not always run by bureaucrats but, at least for some public libraries, by volunteers. If there is a dedicated FOI officer or an attorney, responses will generally be sent in a timely manner. However, if the request is controversial or detailed, it might be delayed. Often someone at the administrative unit will send an email or call if there will be a delay.

It should be noted that response times are highly subject to local laws. For example, the FOI law in the state of Alabama does not have a time limit for responses. In effect, then, the administrative body never has to respond to a request. Furthermore, in Alabama, there are no repercussions for not responding. An institution can simply delay replying indefinitely and still, technically, be within compliance of the law. This will vary from state to state, based on the relevant laws. There is a timeframe of 20 business days for federal FOI requests in the U.S., but many federal agencies are unable to meet this requirement.

If time is a factor for research, then FOI requests must be carefully considered. In certain jurisdictions, researchers are more likely to receive some sort of response in a timely manner, but in others, one might not receive anything. It is also quite common to receive requests for extensions. For example, researchers might send a request to a state that requires response within 10 business days. The agency then responds within 10 days for additional time to gather documents. It is recommended that researchers build time for these communications into their data collection timelines.

In general, receiving responses to FOI requests is a bit of a gamble. If you are sending many requests out at one time to different agencies or public bodies, it will be difficult to estimate when documents will be received. You may encounter security spins (efforts to redirect or reshape claims and practices), security stalls (slowing down the transfer of information) or security shutdowns (which are a complete blockage of information) (see Lippert, Walby, & Wilkinson, 2016 for more on these tactics). However, this does not mean that FOI should not be used for research purposes. As stated above, sometimes, it is the only way to answer one's research questions. In such cases, the unique aspects of using FOI should be built into the overall research design with adequate time made for responding to individual problems with requests and time allowed for potentially delayed documents.

## The problem of FOI harassment

FOI harassment is a subject that has been increasingly discussed in the news over the past few years. What is most important about FOI harassment is the goal of the harasser: the focus is not necessarily on receiving particular documents, but on overwhelming the agency with requests which, of course, have the force of law behind them. FOI harassment has made some government agencies more cautious about handling FOI requests.

The following is an illustrative case of FOI harassment: in 2013, Megan Fox complained to the administration of the Orland Park (Illinois) public library that a patron was using pornography at one of the public terminals. After writing a letter and attending a board meeting, Fox requested that the library change their filtering policies. Fox asked for an immediate response and the counsel for the board recommended that she file FOI requests to find answers to her questions. What followed was probably not what the attorney intended:

> Over the next 11 months Fox and [her colleague] DuJan filed 133 FOIA submissions, containing 742 distinct document requests, and at least 34 complaints with the Illinois Attorney General's Public Access Bureau alleging transparency law violations by library staffers. Their FOIA requests

for documents ranged from records of incidents involving patron complaints about individuals accessing pornographic websites to information
on library policies, personnel, and spending, to asking why one member
of the board wore red to every meeting.

*(Peet, 2016)*

The Orland Park library was overwhelmed by these requests and eventually had
many of them dismissed. In response, one of the Illinois library consortia,
Reaching Across Illinois Library System (RAILS, found at railslibraries.info),
started a FOIA hotline to help its members with responding to FOIA requests.
Researchers must be aware of ongoing harassment issues when they send
requests to administrations. Because of FOI harassment, it is important to tailor
one's request appropriately and be respectful in communications; plus, doing so
will increase the likelihood of receiving the desired documents.

## Conclusion

As demonstrated in this chapter, FOI requests are a research method that more
people should consider incorporating into their research designs. In fact, it is
sometimes the only method that will provide answers to one's research questions. As with any research method, there are a variety of factors that must be
considered. Perhaps, the most important is that although FOI requests are sent
to a somewhat faceless administrative body, they are reviewed and responded to
by people. A person gets attached to the request and the researcher is no longer
dealing with a faceless bureaucracy. The person reviewing the request will put
their own stamp on the response. This can make research using FOI requests
a bit of roller coaster ride. However, like others in this volume, we contend
that these interactions are worth the aggravation for the rich data that one can
receive in return.

## References

Batch, K. R. (2014). Fencing out knowledge: Impacts of the Children's Internet Protection
   Act 10 years later. *American Library Association*. Retrieved from www.ala.org/offices/
   sites/ala.org.offices/files/content/oitp/publications/issuebriefs/cipa_report.pdf
Blanton, T. (2006, July 4). Freedom of information at 40: LBJ refused ceremony, undercut
   bill with signing statement. Retrieved from https://nsarchive2.gwu.edu//NSAEBB/
   NSAEBB194/index.htm
Electronic Frontier Foundation. (2012, October 9). History of FOIA. Retrieved from
   www.eff.org/issues/transparency/history-of-foia
E-rate: Universal service program for schools and libraries. (2011, May 24). Retrieved from
   www.fcc.gov/consumers/guides/universal-service-program-schools-and-libraries-e-rate
Greenberg, P. (2016). Strengthening sociological research through public records requests.
   *Social Currents, 3*(2), 110–117.

Keen, M. F. (1992). The Freedom of Information Act and sociological research. *The American Sociologist, 23*(2), 43–51.

Lee, R. M. (2001). Research uses of the US Freedom of Information Act. *Field Methods, 13* (4), 370–391.

Lippert, R. K., Walby, K., & Wilkinson, B. (2016). Spins, stalls, and shutdowns: Pitfalls of qualitative policing and security research. *Forum: Qualitative Social Research, 17*(1).

Lucas, J. (2018, July 22). How Times reporters use the Freedom of Information Act. *The New York Times*. Retrieved from www.nytimes.com/2018/07/21/insider/information-freedom-reporters-pruitt.html

Luscombe, A., & Walby, K. (2017). Theorizing freedom of information: The live archive, obfuscation, and actor-network theory. *Government Information Quarterly, 34*(3), 379–387.

Oltmann, S. M., Knox, E. J. M., Peterson, C., & Musgrave, S. (2016). Using open records laws for research purposes. *Library & Information Science Research, 37*(4), 323–328.

Peet, L. (2016). Judge dismisses final lawsuit between Orland Park PL, Bloggers. *The Library Journal*. Retrieved from www.libraryjournal.com/?detailStory=judge-dismisses-final-lawsuit-between-orland-park-pl-bloggers

Peterson, C., Oltmann, S. M., & Knox, E. J. M. (2017). The inconsistent work of web filters: Mapping information access in Alabama public schools and libraries. *International Journal of Communication, 11*, 4583–4609.

Savage, A., & Hyde, R. (2014). Using freedom of information requests to facilitate research. *International Journal of Social Research Methodology, 17*(3), 303–317.

Schrader, A. M. (1997). Why you can't "censorproof" your public library. *Public Library Quarterly, 16*(1), 3–30.

The White House. (1966, July 4). Statement by the president upon signing S. 1160. Retrieved from https://nsarchive2.gwu.edu//NSAEBB/NSAEBB194/Document%2035.pdf

Walby, K., & Luscombe, A. (2017). Criteria for quality in qualitative research and use of freedom of information requests in the social sciences. *Qualitative Research, 17*(5), 537–553.

# 2

# ACCESSING INFORMATION IN SOUTH AFRICA

*Toerien van Wyk*

## Introduction

"Amandla Awethu" (power to the people) is a popular rallying cry used in South Africa during the struggle against Apartheid. Well over two decades after South Africa became a truly democratic nation in 1994, the question arises whether the people now hold the power they fought for. There are many ways of looking at the extent to which ordinary South Africans have, or have not, been empowered since 1994. Undoubtedly, however, the extent to which information is accessible is one important consideration in trying to make that determination. This is because of the strong connection between knowledge and power.

Of course, power is always contested and subject to challenge. Therefore, it should not be surprising that information accessibility is also never a state that is achieved, but is rather itself a ground of contestation (Harris, 2009). This chapter describes the use of access to information laws in South Africa, focusing, in particular, on such use by a non-profit, non-governmental organisation that uses it in support of struggles for social justice: the South African History Archive ("SAHA").[1] SAHA is an independent human rights archive. Initially established in the late 1980s as an anti-Apartheid struggle archive, today SAHA collects and makes accessible records related to both past and ongoing struggles for justice. Since the *Promotion of Access to Information Act* (PAIA), Act 2 of 2000, came into effect, in 2001, SAHA has, through its Freedom of Information Programme, been using, advocating around and providing training on PAIA. SAHA is also a founding member of the Access to Information Network ("the Network") and contributes to the Network's annual report on the state of access to information in South Africa.[2]

This chapter is divided into three parts. The first part provides a description of the legal framework for accessing information in South Africa. It also details some of the methods used, within this framework, by South Africans seeking to access information. The second and third parts focus on one particular method for seeking access, namely, requests for information made in terms of PAIA. In particular, the second part describes a South African High Court decision with implications for the requirements for a PAIA request description. It further connects requirements for request descriptions arising out of this judgement with Michael Buckland's conceptualisation of the three main uses of the term "information" in Information Science scholarship (Buckland, 1991). Using Buckland's three categories as a lens, this part also describes three types of request description: description in terms of the knowledge the requester is seeking to acquire; description in terms of the thing that holds the information the requester is seeking to acquire; or description in terms of both knowledge and thing. This part of the chapter also notes some specific ways in which descriptions can be made richer, including through reference to time periods and specific locations, persons or functions. The third part illustrates the discussion in the second part by describing some of SAHA's prior request descriptions and the outcomes of those requests. With respect to each of the three request types, an example is provided of a request that resulted in access as well as an example of a request that did not (at least, not in full). This juxtaposition allows for reflection on how other factors, such as the existence of an affordable, functioning enforcement mechanism, impact access.

## Methods for addressing information gaps

When it comes to accessing information in South Africa, the most important legal provision is section 32 of the South African Constitution ("the Constitution") which reads as follows:

> (1) Everyone has the right of access to
> (a) any information held by the state; and
> (b) any information that is held by another person and that is required for the exercise or protection of any rights.
> (2) National legislation must be enacted to give effect to this right, and may provide for reasonable measures to alleviate the administrative and financial burden on the state.

In compliance with section 32(2), the South African Parliament has enacted PAIA. This makes PAIA a potentially very important legal instrument in someone's search for information. PAIA provides, in line with international trends, procedures for the making of formal requests for recorded information ("records"), and outlines when access to information may be refused and how decisions can be appealed (Riegner, 2017, p. 337). Unlike most freedom of information legislation in other jurisdictions in the world, but in keeping with section 32(1)(b) of the Constitution, PAIA provides procedures not just for requesting information held in state hands, but also for requesting information held in private hands.

PAIA itself contains no record-creation duties. In other words, PAIA creates no obligation to record information, just a duty to disclose pre-recorded information, unless exceptions to disclosure provided for in PAIA apply. Record creation duties are however contained in a plethora of other, sector-specific legislation. This includes duties arising from provisions in the *Companies Act*, Act 71 of 2008, the *Consumer Protection Act*, Act 68 of 2008, the *Electronic Communications and Transactions Act*, Act 25 of 2002 and hundreds more (Van Wyk, 2016, pp. 101–109). Many of these pieces of legislation also have disclosure requirements, mandating that relevant, primarily (though not exclusively) public, institutions ensure certain records are proactively accessible without the need for a formal PAIA request. Some institutions also do this voluntarily, an example being the decision by the eThekwini Municipality, in KwaZulu-Natal, to make air quality (air pollution) data automatically publicly accessible.[3] PAIA recognises this need for proactive disclosure, and requires, in section 15, that public entities provide an annual list of categories of information that are proactively available from them (whether voluntarily or in terms of other legislation) to the Minister of Justice. Section 52 of PAIA allows for private entities to voluntarily do the same, on a periodic basis. The Minister in turn has a duty to publish the lists from public entities in the Government Gazette, and a discretionary choice to do so if lists are received from private entities. In the latest version of a relevant entity's section 15 or 52, a notice must also be included in that entity's so-called "PAIA manual." A PAIA manual, prescribed by sections 14 and 51 of PAIA, is a guidebook that PAIA mandates be created and published. The PAIA manual must outline the structure of the relevant entity and provide specific detail with respect to how to submit information requests ("PAIA requests") to that entity. This would include, for instance, the name and contact details of the person responsible, day-to-day, for the processing of PAIA requests.

In theory, then, the starting point when looking to access information is not PAIA. The openness and transparency envisioned both by the Constitution and PAIA itself would see information, critical to the exercise or protection of fundamental rights and public interest issues, being accessible without the need for a request (see also section 1 of the Constitution and section 9 of PAIA). This means that the starting point for anyone seeking access to this kind of information should be automatically, publicly accessible records; and the PAIA Manual should be a source of information about how these records can be accessed. For an information seeker who is also lucky enough to be part of the 40% of South Africans with Internet access, the first step in a search for information would probably be a visit to a website (if there is one) of the public or private entity holding the information they need (Shapshak, 2017). According to many community activists, attending training with SAHA on using PAIA, however, the starting point is usually a visit to the local library or municipal notice boards (South African History Archive, 2016). Some will approach an entity they believe may hold information that they need by directly and personally asking for information, either telephonically or physically at the entity's offices. If, in such a situation, the information a person is seeking to access is held by a government department or entity, but is not accessible without a PAIA request, section 19 of PAIA requires that public officials assist the individual with making the request. In reality, however, activists are often sent from pillar to post without any real assistance. While a request in terms of PAIA clearly ought to be a measure of last resort, a failure to ensure that there is proactive disclosure and that PAIA manuals are available, compliant with legislative requirements, up-to-date and user-friendly may in fact result in the use of PAIA requests as a first option.

This raises a further question regarding whether using PAIA requests, as a first option or as part of a range of methods, results in access to information. Although the PAIA manual ought to be facilitating requests, the South African Human Rights Commission finds that compliance with section 14 of PAIA remains low (South African Human Rights Commission, 2016, p. 4 and 52). This finding is supported by numerous other reports of low levels of compliance with request provisions of PAIA (*Access to Information Network Shadow Report* 2016, 2017). The reality is that ordinary people, in the absence of legal training or the resources to take legal action to enforce compliance, often give up on PAIA altogether as a tool for access. Often community activists wind up relying on expert, non-profit organisations to help them access the information they need. Journalists tend to rely on whistle-blowers. Researchers collect other kinds of data.

As PAIA is nevertheless somewhat successfully relied on as a means of access by certain sectors of South African society, particularly non-profit organisations, investigative journalists and political parties, this chapter will look more closely at its use in practice (Calland, 2017). Drawing on SAHA's experiences, PAIA request descriptions will be discussed in greater detail. As will become clear from the subsequent discussion, accurate PAIA request description is not sufficient alone to guarantee access, but it does play an important role.

## Ways of formulating request descriptions

PAIA is clear that what it gives access to is "records," that is, information that has been recorded in some form or another, rather than "information" as such (see the definition of "record" in section 1 of PAIA). This is narrower than the formulation in the Constitution itself, which allows for access to "information" without any qualification; as has been noted in a minority dissenting decision of the Constitutional Court (*My Vote Counts NPC v Speaker of the National Assembly and Others* (CCT121/14) [2015] ZACC 31 (September 30, 2015), par 100). In formulating a request description, PAIA requires a requester to provide "sufficient particulars to enable an official … to identify the record or records requested …" (section 18(2)(a)(i) of PAIA). Section 18 of PAIA therefore requires that a requester provide an accurate enough description of the information they seek to enable a competent and efficient information officer to identify records that contain requested information. It does not, however, set up the naming of specific records as a requirement. Even when a record is named in a request description "the label is *per se* unimportant" as Sutherland J. noted in *Afriforum NPC v Deputy Information Officer of the Presidency and Others* Unreported (7376/14) [2015] ZAGPPHC 933 (October 30, 2015) ("the Afriforum case," par 10).

In the Afriforum case, the Applicant had requested:

> THE PRESIDENTIAL HANDBOOK – in particular those parts dealing with travel benefits, travel arrangements, private holidays, expenses in respect of private holidays and the use of the presidential aircraft, owned by the South African Air Force in respect of private holidays.
>
> *(the Afriforum case, par 2)*

Sutherland J. held that the key issue was whether the requester had given sufficient information to enable officials in the Office of the Presidency to determine which existing record holds that information. Specifically, the court held, that what was being sought was:

> ... whatever "record" that exists that contains the information about how the "... travel benefits, travel arrangements, private holidays, expenses in respect of private holidays and the use of the presidential aircraft, owned by the South African Air Force in respect of private holidays" of the President and Deputy-President are conferred on them.
>
> *(the Afriforum case, par 10, emphasis added)*

The difference between what the court referred to as the "label" and what it referred to as just "information about ..." can also be described as the difference between what Buckland refers to as "information-as-knowledge" and "information-as-thing" (Buckland, 1991). Buckland identifies three main ways in which the word "information" gets used in academic literature in the field of Information Science. The word gets used, first, to identify the process of transference of knowledge, as in the phrase "to inform" – what Buckland refers to as "information-as-process." It is, second, also used to refer to the knowledge that is transferred – what Buckland refers to as information-as-knowledge. And, third, it is used to refer to objects that retain or hold information-as-knowledge – what Buckland refers to information-as-thing. This classification of ways in which the word "information" gets used is helpful for describing how PAIA request descriptions get formulated.

As noted, what PAIA gives access to are records, that is, information-as-thing. Presumably that is because what PAIA ultimately aims to ensure is that information-as-knowledge is transferred (information-as-process) from the requestee to the requester. PAIA envisions the transference as occurring when information-as-knowledge has been recorded (information-as-thing). While a detailed discussion of access through records will not be attempted here, it is worth noting that such a model for information transference, by way of information-as-thing, requires that there be concomitant record-creation and record-keeping duties. Within this frame, of transference of information-as-knowledge by the medium of information-as-thing, a requester can describe what she is seeking either in terms of the knowledge she is interested in, in terms of the material thing that holds the information she wants, or both.

The Afriforum case provides an example of the mixed approach. The Applicant in that case both identified the record (or "thing") they were seeking to access, and described the underlying information (or "knowledge") they were seeking to have transferred to them. That is to say, the requester noted, in the request description, that they were seeking access to information about travel and holiday benefits that accrue, at state expense, to the President and Deputy President of South Africa, *and* that this information would be in "the Presidential Handbook." The court held in that case, that the test for determining what a specific request should be understood to be asking for is "what the applicant could reasonably be understood to have asked for" (the Afriforum case, par 18).

In the Afriforum case itself, it had come to light, through correspondence following the submission of the request, that what the Applicant had been seeking to access was a copy of the record on which reliance had been placed in authorising *past* expenses of the kind described in the request. A record entitled "the Presidential Handbook" did exist, but it was a draft document intended to regulate the authorisation of *future* expenses of the kind described in the request. The relevant record authorising past expenses of the kind described in the request was in fact a record of a cabinet policy decision (the Afriforum case, paras 12, 16 and 17). Applying its own test, the court found that the Applicant's description could be reasonably understood, by a reasonable official, as referring to the draft Presidential Handbook, rather than the record of the cabinet policy decision. In light of this, the court found that the Applicant could not pursue that specific request further in order to gain access to the record of the policy decision. If the Applicant wanted to further pursue the record related to past decisions about presidential expenses, they would have to submit a new request, describing or naming that record (the Afriforum case, paras 10 and 26).

One important implication of the decision in the Afriforum case therefore is that request descriptions need to be as rich as possible. From the judgement in the above matter, it appears that it was through subsequent correspondence, and not from the request description itself, that it became clear the Applicant had been seeking to access a record that had applied during a specific time-period. The record the Applicant had named in the request applied at a different time to the time-period the Applicant was interested in. The Applicant in that matter might have avoided an understanding of the request as being a request for the Presidential Handbook specifically, had the request provided more detail about the time-period in relation to which information-as-thing was sought. Requests should therefore not only name the information-as-thing (record), but also, if possible, give a description of the information-as-knowledge (the knowledge the requester is seeking to gain). Further, the description of the information-as-knowledge should be as detailed as possible. Requests can be made richer not only by describing, where possible, the time-period to which the information requested relates, but also by describing, if relevant, locations it relates to or specific persons or functions it relates to (Young & Razzano, 2008, p. 24).

The Applicant in the Afriforum case chose to describe the information they were seeking (information-as-knowledge) *and* to name the record (information-as-thing). This is, however, not the only way to formulate a request. The test, as formulated in the Afriforum case, would allow for a range of request description formulations, provided it would be reasonably possible for a deputy information officer to identify a record that holds the information. It is important to note, however, that the relevant person who needs to be able to identify the record is the *deputy information officer* (the Afriforum case, paras 10 and 26). A deputy information officer is someone specifically appointed, under PAIA, from within an organisation to ensure compliant processing of PAIA requests. A deputy information officer is someone with inside knowledge of the organisation the request is directed at. They know what kinds of records their institution produces and what kinds of information it records, have access to other officials within that organisation, are able to make enquiries with colleagues within relevant internal departments, and can find out whether the requested information is recorded, and if so, in which record. In other words, the information need not be described accurately enough for any reasonable *person* to be able to locate it, but accurately enough for any reasonable, *suitably qualified, official* to be able to locate it using the resources at their disposal. While this places some burden on the requester to be as accurate as they can, it also places an onus on the officials to use the knowledge and resources at their disposal to process the request as best they can.

## Using PAIA in practice

Requests made by SAHA provide excellent examples of the range of formulations of request descriptions, under PAIA, and the range of responses to those formulations. Unfortunately, there is no one way to formulate a request description that will ensure access is granted. That is because there are several factors, not least of which are political will and available resources, that mediate compliance and therefore access (*Access to Information Network*, 2017, p. 29; Colin Darch and Peter Underwood, 2010, pp. 9–10 and 109–110). Even with a clear and accurate description and with the necessary institutional will, PAIA requests may still be denied in order to protect other rights and interests, such as someone else's right to privacy. Access refusals must however be made with reference to specific provisions in Chapter 4 of PAIA, which makes provision for protection of these other rights and interests. In addition, sections 25 and 56 of PAIA require reasons be provided as to why the relevant section in Chapter 4 is believed to be applicable.

## Request descriptions with information-as-thing

Often request descriptions deal with information "as-thing," providing the name or title of the record that holds the information a requester is seeking to access (Buckland, 1991). This is what SAHA did when it requested a "current water use licence" for the only nuclear power station in South Africa, Koeberg Power Station.[4] Knowing that the information it was seeking, about how water use at Koeberg is regulated, must, in terms of provisions in the *National Water Act*, Act 36 of 1998, be recorded in a "water use licence," SAHA specified the record it was seeking to access. The request resulted in access being granted.

An equally specific request made by SAHA for a copy of a report on the cost of relocating the South African Parliament, however, resulted in a denial of access.[5] In his state of the nation address in 2016, then President of South Africa, Jacob Zuma, suggested South Africa could save on unnecessary expenses if Parliament and the seat of national government (the Executive) were located in the same city rather than in two cities, over a thousand kilometres apart, as they currently are (Gqirana, 2016). But this was not the first time such a suggestion had been made; the professional services company KPMG had, as early as 1997, provided a report to then President, Nelson Mandela, on the cost of relocating Parliament (*Mail and Guardian*, 1997). SAHA requested copies of the report that had been commissioned by the Presidency, from both the President's office and KPMG. SAHA could make the request to a private company like KPMG, because PAIA, unlike most freedom of information legislation elsewhere in the world, allows for requests to non-state actors. Requests to non-state actors however must be for information that is needed to exercise or protect some other right that the requester holds (section 50 of PAIA). This threshold requirement actually arises from the similar wording in section 32(1)(b) of the Constitution. Part 3 of PAIA, in which section 50 can be found, aims to give legislative effect to section 32(1)(b) of the Constitution. The Presidency denied access, claiming no copy of the report could be located. KPMG also denied access, but on different grounds, arguing that granting access would lead to the disclosure of third-party confidential information.[6]

These two differing results from requests that both described information-as-thing illustrate how different factors, such as third-party rights, can have an impact on the outcome of a request. The former of the two requests illustrates something further as well. The Presidency's response to SAHA sheds light on the fact that the President had requested the report in his capacity as president of the African National Congress (ANC), and not in his capacity as President of the Republic of South Africa. While time-consuming, clarity arising out of responses to requests can in some instances, ultimately, assist a requester with locating the information they are after. When the request is to a state institution (such as the Presidency) and the other body that holds the information is also a state institution, PAIA requires that the first state institution transfer the request to the second state institution for processing (section 20 of PAIA). There is no similar provision when the information is held by a non-state actor (like the ANC), or if the request was in the first place made to a non-state actor (like KPMG). In such circumstances, a requester that wishes to pursue the information further will have to submit a new request. SAHA did not pursue this request further.

## Request descriptions with information-as-knowledge

When requesters do not know the name or title of the record that holds the information they are seeking to access, their request description will refer to information "as-knowledge" (Buckland, 1991). That is, the information the requester is after will be described, but the exact record holding that information will not be named. This is what SAHA did when it was seeking to assist an individual who wanted to determine whether a testament that had surfaced after the death of a parent was authentic.[7] In order to have the testament's authenticity independently confirmed by a forensic expert, verified signature specimens were required for comparison. SAHA requested, on behalf of this individual, copies of signature specimens from the commercial bank the deceased had banked with while still alive. The bank granted access to records containing signature specimens, which SAHA's client was then able to hand over to a forensic expert. This request serves as an example of a request to a non-state actor that resulted in access. Data on requests to state-entities suggest that access is often granted to personal information, when it has been requested by the person the information pertains to (Darch & Underwood, 2010, p. 57). As PAIA essentially treats the personal information of a deceased person, for the first 20 years after their death, as the personal information of the deceased's next-of-kin, this response by the bank seems to fit with trends seen in requests to state-entities. Unfortunately, the scarcity of data on decisions regarding requests made to private entities prevents similar credible trends analysis in relation to requests to private entities (*Access to Information Network*, 2016, p. 4).

A similarly framed request for information-as-knowledge that SAHA filed on behalf of a community activist, for information about a decision to close two railway stations, was less successful.[8] The request description simply asked for records that would provide information regarding a decision to close the two railway stations (stations that served communities on the outer skirts of the city of Johannesburg). The Passenger Rail Agency of South Africa (PRASA) failed to provide any response to the request, resulting in the request being deemed refused (also known as a "mute refusal") (section 27 of PAIA). Similarly, no response was provided to SAHA's appeal against the deemed refusal, submitted to the Minister of Transport, resulting in the appeal being deemed dismissed as well (section 77(7) of PAIA). With no Information Regulator in place, and very limited funding for litigation, SAHA was unable to further pursue this request.

These two different responses to request descriptions that described information-as-knowledge illustrate the role of administrative efficiency in ensuring access. The latter of the two requests also illustrates the urgent need for South

Africa's Information Regulator to be made fully functional, especially considering the affordability of this enforcement mechanism as compared with the high costs of judicial enforcement (Adeleke, 2016, p. 71). While the Chairperson and Members of the Information Regulator were appointed already in September 2016, and while the office is seemingly being set up, it is not yet at the time of writing, in early 2019, operational.

## Request descriptions with information both -as-knowledge and -as-thing

Sometimes, descriptions both describe the information sought, as-knowledge, as well as name the records, as-thing, believed to hold that information. This is what SAHA did when it submitted a request to the City of Tshwane in support of the work of a partner organisation working for environmental justice. The request description asked for:

Copies of any and all records relating to the "future generation" (or "sale" and/or "lease") of the Pretoria West and Rooiwal Power Stations including but not limited to:

1. Records detailing the valuation of both the Pretoria West and Rooiwal Power Stations, as required in terms of the provisions of the Municipal Asset Transfer Regulations, issued in terms of the Municipal Finance Management Act, 2003 (MFMA), and the outcomes of such valuations;
2. Proof of public consultation on the "future generation" (or "sale" and/or "lease") of the Pretoria West and Rooiwal Power Stations specifically including:
   a. Invitations to all such consultations [which may take the form of: letters, emails, printouts of text or sms messages or screenshots of invitation over social media (e.g. Facebook or Twitter)];
   b. Attendance registers for all such consultations;
   c. Agendas for all such consultations; and
   d. Minutes for all such consultations.
3. Records detailing progress with regard to the timeline for the "future generation" of the aforementioned power stations, as detailed in the Council's resolution dated November 27, 2014 … [which records may take the form of internal office memos, emails or other records of communications between relevant stakeholders].

The request description not only describes the project SAHA was seeking to access information about, but also details the aspects of that project with regard to which SAHA was seeking to access information. The description also names types of records believed to be likely to hold the information sought. To ensure the deputy information officer was armed with enough information to determine which records held the information SAHA was after, SAHA also referenced a resolution of the City and attached copies of the relevant pages of that resolution to the request. The City failed to respond in a timely manner to SAHA's request, resulting in the request being deemed refused (a mute refusal). The request was however ultimately successful. After the submission of an appeal against the deemed refusal and communication with the City, all of the information requested was released to SAHA.[9]

Another example of a request description framed as both information-as-knowledge and information-as-thing is a request by SAHA to the National Department of Environmental Affairs. SAHA was seeking to access records that would reveal internal policies of the Department aimed at regulating conflicts of interest. The request description was (as with the request to the City) a combination of a detailed explanation of the information SAHA was after, as well as an itemised list of specifically named records SAHA felt might hold that information. The Department released certain records but denied that others even existed. In line with provisions in PAIA, the Department's deputy information officer however also provided an affidavit to this effect (section 23 of PAIA).[10] Section 23 of PAIA provides that, if all reasonable steps were taken to search for a requested record and the record cannot be found, or it is determined the record does not exist, the requester must be provided with an affidavit or affirmation to this effect. The affidavit or affirmation must indicate what steps were taken to search for the record and must note specifically whether the record could not be found or does not in fact exist.

The different outcomes to the similar approaches to request descriptions highlight the role that record-creation and record-keeping play in ensuring access to information through PAIA. In both instances, deputy information officers could locate the records containing the information SAHA was seeking to access. In the latter instance, however, not all the information SAHA was seeking to access was recorded and access could therefore not be granted in full.

## Conclusion

This chapter set out to describe the use of access to information laws in South Africa, focusing in particular on such use by SAHA. This description has illustrated that information access is subject to contestation, and that an access request is influenced by multiple factors (see Luscombe and Walby's (2017) application of the actor-network theory to access to information for a useful theoretical perspective on this contestation over access).

The first part of the chapter provided a description of the legal framework for accessing information in South Africa. It noted that the South African Constitution gives express recognition to a fundamental right of access to information. The emphasis in the second and third parts of the chapter was on PAIA, as the legislation enacted to give direct effect to the constitutional right of which requests for information can be made. In particular, the second part of the chapter notes the High Court decision in the Afriforum case on the test for determining what a specific request should be understood to be asking for. The court found that what is decisive is what "the applicant could reasonably be understood to have asked for" (the Afriforum case, par 18).

When viewed through the lens of Buckland's categorisation of the ways in which the term "information" is used in Information Science scholarship, request description can be conceptualised in three ways. First, a request description can be a description of the knowledge the requester is seeking to acquire. Second, a request description can be a description, or naming, of the thing (or record) that holds the information sought. Third, a request description can combine description of the knowledge sought with description, or naming, of the thing (record) that holds that information. There may be a variety of reasons why one might rely on a particular formulation for the request description. Irrespective of which formulation is used, the decision in the Afriforum case has methodological implications for request descriptions, as it connotes a need to provide rich descriptions. The chapter notes that descriptions, particularly of the knowledge sought to be acquired, can be enriched through the provision of details about specific time-periods, locations, persons, or functions to which the information relates. SAHA's practice, as described in part three, also indicates that use can be made of other records (or extracts thereof) of the organisation to which the request is directed. That is to say, if possible, reference can be made within a request description to a record of the requestee-organisation in order to provide further clarification as to the information sought.

Part two of the chapter also highlights the fact that officials processing requests have a duty to process those requests using the knowledge and resources at their disposal. The legal and constitutional role fulfilled by such officials requires that they be suitably qualified. The positions they fill provide them with inside knowledge of the organisation the request is aimed at. This knowledge and skill must be applied to request descriptions to determine what the requester is asking for.

The third part of the chapter illustrated the discussion in the second part by describing some of SAHA's prior request descriptions and the outcomes of those requests. With respect to each of the three request types, an example was provided of a request that resulted in access as well as an example of a request that did not (at least, not in full). This juxtaposition allowed for reflection on the impact on access of factors external to the request description. In particular, it highlighted the fact that third-party rights, such as someone else's right to privacy, can impact the outcome of a request. Further, administrative efficiency, including record-creation and record-keeping practices, will influence the ultimate outcome of requests. Finally, and arguably most urgent currently in South Africa, this chapter highlights the importance of an affordable, functioning, enforcement mechanism in ensuring access to information.

## Notes

1  For more on the work of SAHA, visit www.saha.org.za/and http://foip.saha.org.za/.
2  For more information about the Access to Information Network, visit http://foip.
   saha.org.za/static/south-africa2. To access the Network's Shadow Reports, visit
   http://foip.saha.org.za/static/paia-reports-and-submissions.
3  See the department's webpage for air pollution monitoring, available online at:
   www.durban.gov.za/City_Services/health/Environmental_Health_Services/Pages/
   Air-Pollution-.aspx (accessed: 18-03-2018).
4  For more on SAHA's request for information about water-use at the Koeberg Power
   Station and to access the released records, see http://foip.saha.org.za/request_tracker/
   entry/sah-2015-esk-0001 (accessed 13-05-2018).
5  For more on SAHA's request to the Presidency for a copy of the report on the cost of
   relocating the South African Parliament, see http://foip.saha.org.za/request_tracker/
   entry/sah-2016-pre-0001 (accessed 13-05-2018).
6  For more on SAHA's request to KPMG for a copy of the report on the cost of
   relocating the South African Parliament, see http://foip.saha.org.za/request_tracker/
   entry/SAH-2016-KPM-0002 (accessed 13-05-2018).
7  For more on SAHA's request for verified signature specimens, see http://foip.saha.
   org.za/request_tracker/entry/SAH-2015-NEG-0001 (accessed: 13-05-2018).
8  For more on SAHA's request for information about the decision to close two railway
   stations, see http://foip.saha.org.za/request_tracker/entry/sah-2017-prs-0002
   (accessed: 13-05-2018).
9  For more on SAHA's request for information related to the Pretoria West and Rooiwal Power Stations, or to access the released records, see http://foip.saha.org.za/
   request_tracker/entry/sah-2015-cot-0001 (accessed: 01-06-2018).
10 For more on SAHA's request for copies of policies related to conflicts of interest, see
   http://foip.saha.org.za/request_tracker/entry/sah-2016-dea-0002 (accessed: 01-06-2018).

## References

Access to Information Network. (2016). *Access to information network shadow report*. Retrieved
   from http://foip.saha.org.za/static/paia-reports-and-submissions.
Access to Information Network. (2017). *Access to information network shadow report*. Retrieved
   from http://foip.saha.org.za/static/paia-reports-and-submissions.
Adeleke, F. (2016). The role of the right to information in the contestation of power in
   South Africa's constitutional democracy. *Southern African Public Law*, *31*(1), 54–72.
Buckland, M. K. (1991). Information as thing. *Journal of the Association for Information Science
   and Technology*, *42*(5), 351–360.
Calland, R. (2017). Access to information and constitutional accountability: Ruffling fea-
   thers in South Africa. *VRÜ Verfassung und Recht in Übersee*, *50*(4), 367–389.
Darch, C., & Underwood, P. (2010). *Freedom of information and the developing world: The citi-
   zen, the state and models of openness*. Oxford: Chandos Publishing.
The Doors of Learning Shall be Opened! (2016). South African history archive. Retrieved
   from www.saha.org.za/news/2016/June/the_doors_of_learning_shall_be_opened.htm.
Gqirana, T. (2016, February 15). ANC welcomes Zuma's 'bold' proposal to move Parliament. *News24*. Retrieved from www.news24.com/SouthAfrica/News/anc-welcomes-
   zumas-bold-proposal-to-move-parliament-20160215.
Harris, V. (2009). From gatekeeping to hospitality. In K. Allan (Ed.), *Paper wars: Access to information in South Africa* (pp. 201–213). Johannesburg, South Africa: Wits University Press.
Luscombe, A., & Walby, K. (2017). Theorizing freedom of information: The live archive,
   obfuscation, and actor-network theory. *Government Information Quarterly*, *34*(3), 379–387.

Pretoria set to take Parliament. (1997, September 5). *Mail and Guardian*. Retrieved from https://mg.co.za/article/1997-09-05-pretoria-set-to-take-parliament.

Riegner, M. (2017). Access to information as a human right and constitutional guarantee. A comparative perspective. *VRÜ Verfassung und Recht in Übersee, 50*(4), 332–366.

Shapshak, T. (2017, July 19). South Africa has 21 million internet users, mostly on mobile. *Forbes*. Retrieved from www.forbes.com/sites/tobyshapshak/2017/07/19/south-africa-has-21m-internet-users-mostly-on-mobile/#100c013b1b2d.

South African Human Rights Commission. (2016). *The promotion of access to information annual report 2014–2015*. Johannesburg, South Africa: Author. Retrieved from www.sahrc.org.za/index.php/sahrc-publications/paia-annual-reports.

Van Wyk, T. (2016). Don't blame the librarian if no one has written the book: My vote counts and the information required to exercise the franchise. *Constitutional Court Review, VII*, 97–154.

Young, C., & Razzano, G. (2008). PAIA workshop guide: A guide to requesting information in terms of the Promotion of Access to Information Act 2 of 2000 (PAIA). *South African History Archive*. Retrieved from http://foip.saha.org.za/uploads/images/Chapter_Two.pdf.

# 3

# UK EXPERIENCE OF FREEDOM OF INFORMATION AS A METHOD OF ENQUIRY

*Keith Spiller and Andrew Whiting*

> *... there really is no description of stupidity, no matter how vivid, that is adequate. I quake at the imbecility of it.*
>
> (Blair, 2011, p. 516)

## Introduction

Thus reflected Tony Blair in evaluating the impact of introducing the policy that began the right to use Freedom of Information requests (FOIs) in the UK. Blair had led a landslide victory in the national elections of 1997 and the establishment of a freedom of information law began with a pledge made in the Labour Party election manifesto – *New Labour New Britain*. Upon electoral victory, the manifesto pledge developed into the white paper *Your Right to Know* where the Government committed to this law as part of their wider commitment to constitutional reform that included decentralising power, individual rights and open government (Chancellor of the Duchy of Lancaster, 1997). Within three years, the white paper had formed the basis of the Freedom of Information Act (FOIA) that came into force in 2000. However, the major aspect of the law – right of access – did not actually come into effect until January 1, 2005. By 2005, the FOIA was a fully functional law and provided public access to information held by UK public authorities.

The coverage of the FOIA includes over 100,000 public authorities (Briskinshaw, 2010, p. 313) and guarantees access to information in the public interest. This is achieved, first, through the obligation to respond to written requests for information and, second, via the obligation to publish certain information as part of a "publication scheme." The most recent Cabinet Office statistics record 46,681 FOI requests across central government in 2017 (Cabinet Office, 2018, p. 1). Yet, despite this wealth of potential information, there appears to be a dearth of academic research using FOIA as a means to gather data and in turn to address pressing UK social and political issues (Brown, 2009).

This chapter considers the FOIA as a viable tool for academic research. To date, journalist, campaigners or concerned consumers have been at the forefront in using FOIs to gain access to information on issues as diverse as politicians' expenses, the cost of policing a royal event or the levels of food hygiene in restaurants. Our chapter begins by considering the value of FOIs as a scholarly research tool. Second, the chapter considers some of the limitations to using FOIs in research. Third, we locate the FOIA within a broader process of modernising digital information and highlight challenges faced by researchers using FOIs. Fourth, we review the effective use of FOIs in research. Finally, we offer some observations from a nascent research project of our own that is using FOIs as a key methodological approach. The chapter concludes by stressing the usefulness of the FOIA for researchers to produce democratising and politically impactful research.

## The FOIA as a research tool

To date, there has been a coterie of commentators that have examined the value of the FOIA for research purposes (Michener & Worthy, 2018; Rodríguez & Rossel, 2018). Notable is Johnson and Hampson (2015) who investigate the practice of crime prevention in British policing. Having identified what appeared to be an emphasis on using the British Crime Survey to identify "crime hot spots," they utilised FOIs to verify how such identification was taking place. The information that guided this approach was "Police-created, Police-held and Police-owned" data (p. 250). Yet through FOIs, the information had to be shared with outside researchers, thus revealing the potential for FOIs to provide access to information that had previously been "off limits" or difficult to access. As it was designed to do, the FOIA makes officialdom (read governmentality) more transparent and accountable to those subject to such forms of power (read citizens/researcher).

FOIs have been used by the media, NGOs and other groups to effect accountability (Worthy, 2012). Examples include the use and abuse of parliamentary expenses – where politicians were discovered to be exploiting funds allocated for specific roles or activities; for instance, financial assistance for MPs to buy a second home near parliament with the intention to make it easier for politicians to attend parliament. In some cases, the homes were being let for profit which counters the intent of the funding (The Telegraph, 2012). Hazell, Bourke, and Worthy's (2012) evaluation of the impact of FOIs upon Parliament found that the Act has "helped make UK Parliament even more transparent and more accountable," albeit these are positives not fully reflected in public understanding, participation or trust (p. 918). Worthy (2012) argues that few politicians use FOI in the pursuit of information or accountability. Parliamentary Questions, he attests, are the investigation method of choice for politicians – they are reluctant, or slow, to use alternative forms of enquiry. Equally, it is unusual for members of the government to question the government – either using Parliamentary Questions or FOIs. As Worthy finds, during the period of 2005–2009 when the Labour party was in power in the UK, the party making the most FOIs were the Conservatives, making about 40% of all parliamentary FOIs, compared to Labour's 16%. However, when Labour lost power in 2010 and the Conservatives formed a coalition government, Labour's rate of FOIs jumped to 64% of all requests and the Conservatives dropped to 11%. Yet to offer some perspective on how FOIs are used, MP requests rarely exceed 2% of all the requests received by governmental departments (Worthy, 2012).

## Broader challenges and limitations

While the FOIA was passed into law amidst a discourse of transparency and open government, Brown (2009) reminds us that FOIs might not always be received in that spirit. The possibility that an FOI is viewed as a "confrontational" tool is a real possibility. This is a possible dilemma facing researchers, particularly in light of ethical board approval tensions in university settings (Charlesworth, 2012). Walby and Luscombe (2018) have drawn attention to and questioned the need for FOIs to receive ethical approval given that these requests are concerned with organisational practice and not individuals. It is the job of the government agency to remove any identifying or potentially identifying information (Savage & Hyde, 2014, p. 310) and if releasing the information would unavoidably identify someone, this is grounds for exception (Johnson & Hampson, 2015). Nevertheless, it is unlikely that this should provide an avenue of explanation for why FOIs are not applied more readily by researchers (see also Warren, this volume) – in short, compliance is unlikely to be viewed as a significant deterrent.

There may be a growing trend where controversial or challenging research is being viewed through a defensive lens; for example, FOIs seeking sensitive information – in our experience, this has often been the case with responses to information regarding counter-terrorism or immigration policies. Organisations can and do present a bureaucratic conservatism, or risk-adverse approach in how they respond to such requests (Spiller, Awan, & Whiting, 2018). Yet, and perhaps more pressing, there is a lack of engagement by universities with FOIs as a research tool, illustrated by the fact that doctoral and MA courses rarely include FOIs in research method classes.

Compounding this defensive perception towards FOIs is the fact that it is the world of journalism that has made most frequent use of the FOIA and in this domain there is a tendency to frame these reports as "exposés." This is at the very least misleading, if not also outright damaging for the perception of FOIs, first, because the information by its very nature is publicly available, and second, because the process is simply about drawing the information into the public realm. Granted, how the information may be collected, analysed and presented can at times be experimental, inventive as well as enlightening, but this is not information that was secretly extracted from an organisation, no matter how secretive it may be. Monahan and Fisher (2015) provide insight into how defensive difficulties can be circumvented by using tools such as FOIs to make initial contact. They consider "perceptions of threat" and how organisations may initially view the researcher in terms of the potential damage they could pose to their organisation (for example, exposing trade secrets). There are of course other tactics available to organisations to hinder or dissuade requests (Luscombe & Walby, 2017; Sikka, 2017). Alongside swamping requestors, organisations may also rest behind legal exceptions or frustrate requests with additional demands for clarity. This is not to suggest all such responses are a defensive tactic; indeed, discrepancies in response may not be surprising as requests can demand specific information that requires specialist knowledge to accurately access the information held. Added to this are legal pressures on FOI staff to return data within the 20-day limit. As a result, staff may be less focused on the detail of the information requested and more concerned with meeting the time constraints (see Richter & Wilson, 2013). Furthermore, requests are dependent on the proficiencies and experience of the responder. There is variance in how organisations respond to initial questions. For example, when we asked for the amount of referrals made by an organisation, some respondents detailed exact numbers, while others stated that due to the information being a "security issue," they could offer no response. FOI requests as we have found are open to interpretation by those tasked with responding to the requests.

## Modernising digital information

Richter and Wilson (2013) argue that FOIs are part of a wider information modernisation agenda, where the collection, analysis and transparency of influential data were revamped to provide reassurances to the public that governmental authorities were acting in a legal and acceptable manner. Key to their work was uncovering the variance in how local authorities dealt with the FOI Act. Organisations are conscious of their responsibility in providing information, but are also mindful to comply and not face legislative enquiry for essentially not doing their role correctly. There is a "performative quality" to FOIs where citizens ask questions and organisations are obliged to respond. Richter and Wilson argue that rather than informing citizens of their rights and illuminating how governments may be held to account, the process is further evidence of individualisation, where the citizen becomes a customer rather than exercising their civil rights. One could add this may be exacerbated by how local governments are failing to engage with citizens because the emphasis remains on meeting their legislative duty and rarely does the process go any deeper. As we have experienced, responses often do not go beyond the cursory or the bare minimum of what is expected. However, where we disagree with

Richter and Wilson is that this is about using rights correctly and availing of the methods available to the researcher. In that regard it goes beyond the performative (but this is not to suggest it always excludes it), the aim as we see it is about knowledge generation and gaining insight through the rights available to the researcher.

It is also worth remembering that researcher's findings, when working for public universities or on a government grant, may also be subject to a FOI request – therefore, confidential information may affect ethical concerns for the researcher, but also this has potential ramifications for those supplying the information. Monahan and Fisher (2015) consider how researchers should be aware that many organisations "research" researchers before interacting with them. Organisations may review the researchers' previous publications in an effort to predict what they are likely to argue and what impact their analyses might have on their organisation (also see Spiller, 2016). This of course should not prevent the organisation from fulfilling their duties; nevertheless, it will more than likely influence their overview. More specifically, if the research takes a critical perspective of the activities of the organisation, then requests for information will be looked upon less favourable (Berg, 2009). These types of responses add to the burden of the researcher attempting to make contact and, in the case of difficult-to-access organisations, contribute to the dilemma of how best to approach them in a way that ensures access.

An example of the challenges faced by researchers can be viewed in the dilemma once faced by Sterling University in Scotland, where a team looking into the marketing of cigarettes and the attitudes of teenagers to smoking was subject to a FOI. The interview data and other material were requested first by a law firm, and when challenged by the research team and the ICO (UK's Data Protection Authority), it was established that the law firm was making the request on behalf of their client Philip Morris – a giant in the tobacco industry. The University argued the information they held was confidential and that the teenage respondents had offered their comment in good faith. The university researchers further argued the research data they had found would be unlikely to gain acceptance if the tobacco industry had commissioned the research. This to a large degree is the crux of FOI and transparency – all information should be available to those who request it, whether it be a citizen or a customer. In relation to the Sterling case, Philip Morris withdrew their request for information, but there remain ethical concerns for university researchers or those working with information that has clear economic value and/or health or other implications.

## Effective FOI requests for research purposes

In our research, we have found that while organisations respond to requests, the quality and detail offered can be variable (discussed below). This certainly does not negate the value of FOIs as a research tool but does highlight the attention needed in forming questions that will prompt accurate and informative responses. For example, FOIs allow for very effective comparative analysis between data held across similar authorities, thus allowing the researcher to ask identical questions across a specific sector to prompt considerations of how, for example, a new governmental policy has been enacted. However, while FOIs are often useful in this sort of comparative endeavour, their value in providing *explanations* for a new policy or why a policy has been enacted in a particular way is likely to be less forthcoming.

What can be debilitating for the researcher and the research data produced is the quality of the FOI and the quality of the response from the organisation. The former includes elements the research team can mitigate against by ensuring that their request is focused and unambiguous (see Information Commissioner's Office, 2019b). While this is never a precise science, asking direct questions with clear parameters should reduce the possibility of questions being ignored or perceived as unanswerable. Indeed, having a realistic agenda that is attentive to the likelihood of specific information being available should be a consideration for any researcher. This, of course, needs to be balanced against the comprehensibility of the request so that a non-subject specialist (which those responding to the FOI may very well be) can understand, locate and provide the information. While working in this manner can be productive, it has also faced accusations of "research on the cheap," where responses generate information that informs similar or comparable research publication. Breathnach, Riley, and Planche (2011) warn of using FOI in the name of thriftiness, such as medical researchers compelling fellow institutions to impart data relevant to their research, all with the intention of expanding findings for the purpose of publication. That said, there are protections for such information; section 22 of the FOIA, for instance, allows potential withholding of information until a planned publication date.

The quality of the response, however, is outside of the researchers' hands and can be a frustration to the process of data generation and collection. Sometimes, even where the researcher has been diligent in how they have constructed the request, they will find that the information they received is inconsistent with what was requested or has not been provided in the expected format. The former of these concerns can often be resolved with an informal contact from the researcher or in more extreme cases, a formal appeal (in the UK, this is made via the Information Commissioner Office (ICO)). Differentiations in the presentation of the information received can create hindrances. For example, as we have found in our work, when institutions are asked to provide details on the number of staff that had received a particular type of training, responses included raw numbers, percentages and more ambiguous phrases such as "all frontline staff." These responses are not immediately helpful but do offer some insight into how those tasked with responding to requests are dealing with them and indeed it does offer a response that can be followed up on for further information (in this instance, the number of frontline staff at the institution).

## FOIA for us

In this chapter, we have highlighted a number of challenges and limitations that appear when researchers use the FOIA as a data generation technique. The literature suggests FOIAs can be a hindrance to organisations, yet for investigative journalists, to cite one example, they have proven to be powerful tools for generating information that is both newsworthy and in the public interest. In moving toward a conclusion, we wish to stress the benefits the FOIA has provided our nascent research project on issues of British national security.

The project we refer to is one that is examining a particular aspect of the UK Prevent Strategy often referred to as the "Prevent Duty." The Prevent Strategy is one part of the UK's larger counter-terrorism strategy that aims to "stop people becoming terrorists or supporting terrorism" (Home Office, 2018, p. 31). In 2015, this was expanded to place a statutory duty (the Prevent Duty) on a series of public authorities meaning that they must pay "due regard to the need to prevent people from being drawn into terrorism" (*Counter Terrorism and Security Act*, 2015). Among other things, this meant that public authorities must report activity that may encourage radicalisation and/or support terrorism. The remit of the strategy covers state-funded organisations, such as hospitals, schools, prisons and local authorities.

In our study, we have placed the focus upon UK Higher Education (UKHE), specifically with a view to understanding how higher education providers are implementing the strategy and what actions they have taken. The institutions we have focused on share many similarities, such as publicly accessible webpages detailing their approach to this new duty and how they are implementing it. However, within the webpages what becomes immediately apparent are discrepancies – be they how the strategy has been interpreted, the language used or how HE providers have understood and implemented this duty. As a result, we have undertaken a structured analysis about Prevent Duty policies and guidance within UKHE to establish in greater detail what the Duty actually looks like across the sector and where and in what form sameness and divergences exist.

The approach we have taken in this study is to send an FOI to 160 UKHE providers, which includes universities, colleges and performing arts centres. In the FOI, we have asked for details on how providers have acted to respond to their duty; how many staff they have trained as well as who they have trained and how they have trained them; what non-public facing (or in-house) information and guidance has been produced about the strategy; and finally, the amount of referrals that have been made in relation to those suspected of extremism, radicalisation or terrorism. The project is in its very early stages and we began sending FOIs to UKHE institutions in November 2018. To date, we have had responses from 158 of the 160 institutions we sent requests to. The vast majority of these responses came within the expected 20 days and where delays did occur, we often received a pre-emptive email informing us the reply would be late. The high response rate and speed with which we received this data is promising, although at the time of writing there were still two responses outstanding that have well surpassed the 20 day limit despite informal prompts on our part.

We must be careful to note that the methodological decisions a researcher makes are often dependent on the information they are seeking and/or their skill set. However, when comparing the expediency of FOIs versus alternatives such as interviews that often include a long process of organisation, conduct, transcription, analysis and write-up, there are clear benefits and efficiencies. Indeed, an added advantage of FOI responses is that they can come ready categorised. Assuming all questions in the FOI have been answered, they can be quickly coded and compared. It is the promptness of FOI data generation and its ready-made organisation that make it such a powerful research tool with potential to get to the heart of pressing social issues.

At the same time, as we have found in our initial reviews of the data, there are still many challenges to be faced, first in chasing up those non-responses. This requires a high degree of organisation and patience keeping track of who has not responded and engaging in a dialogue to ensure we receive/received the data. Second, we received generic and obfuscating responses to some of our questions. Clearly, this is the most sensitive area of our FOI but the discrepancy across the responses is quite telling as the majority *did* provide an answer (surmising it is in the public interest) and yet a significant minority refused the same questions either citing exemptions concerning national security or potential identification of individuals.

Third, as this kind of response has served to highlight, there was some anxiety on our part about constructing the questions to be asked in the FOI. We agonised for a long time on what we would ask and how we would ask it, concluding that seven questions would be reasonable. Any more than this we thought ran the risk of not receiving detailed responses – and therefore there was pressure to be precise. Interestingly, Fowler, Agha, Camm, and Littlejohns (2013) found in their review of published academic papers using FOIs as data sources, on average, 86 FOIs were made per published paper and of those FOIs made, they usually contained five questions. Selecting the "right" questions is no different to many research situations, as the question is often the key to unlocking a new discovery. Equally as our FOIs began to produce replies and generate data, another anxiety manifested in relation to how we would eventually present this research for publication. Pressing here is whether we identify those institutions that have responded with substandard information (as we are legally entitled to do). In "naming and shaming" would we be overstepping our role as researchers and becoming adjudicators? Or, would this be consistent with our role? This is a dilemma we continue to wrestle with.

## Conclusion

In this chapter, we began with the hesitancy and fears that FOIs have presented for those who have implemented this technique by offering an overview of such work within a UK context. We have also drawn on how this is a "modern" tool that can and should be used in the way it was intended – as a tool to increase transparency and provide a data platform to tackle pressing social issues. Finally, we have described how our emerging project is availing of this tool and some of the initial findings and conundrums it has presented. What we are keen to stress is our belief that the FOIA is a valid and apt tool for the researcher.

Luscombe and Walby (2017, p. 384) talk of the "precariousness" of FOI networks and their functioning; each part must work to ensure a successful FOI. When one element ceases, then the FOI grinds to a halt, for example, a non-response or not answering a question due to "security issues." Thus, "creatively handling unexpected barriers" is a methodological component to FOIs (Luscombe & Walby, 2017, p. 379) and this is certainly something we have experienced with more ambiguous and less precise responses such as the aforementioned, "all frontline staff." Yet, these challenges of data collection are similar to many other forms of research, but what the FOI offers above many of these is a clear means of "studying-up" (Lippert, Walby, & Wilkinson, 2015). What Lippert, Walby, and Wilkinson refer to here is getting access to those hard to reach or secretive governmental agencies that methodological approaches such as interviews or participant observation often struggle to do. To use more traditional methods, often detailed knowledge of the organisation, its structure and its management levels are needed to identify gatekeepers or those with authority for the relevant information, but this information is not always available (McClean, 2010; Morrill, Buller, Buller, & Larkey, 1999). While the institutions we have looked at in our own research project are not those typically thought of as the secretive kind, the material we are requesting is potentially sensitive and often engenders something of a "chilling effect" (Spiller et al., 2018). FOIs have not only given us swift access to these institutions, but also to information surrounding contemporary and politically contentious policies about counter-terrorism.

More importantly, perhaps, is that FOIs have the potential to study down or study sideways. In our experience when studying fellow institutions and requesting responses from other UK universities, studying sideways has very much been the case. Our requests have not had a focus on secretive information and indeed having a working insight into how UK universities function does alleviate some of the difficulties we may have had in, as mentioned above, looking for gatekeepers or knowing who to question. Nevertheless, FOIs have allowed us to gain factual responses to the activities undertaken by the universities and provided a clear overview of how these institutions exercise their responsibilities.

The clear benefit to the information generated through FOIs is that it supplements, expands or strengthens findings through the added detail they present. As mentioned, it is also a tool of relative immediacy as the 20-day rule of response can stimulate a viable dataset with a speed that can be rarely replicated in other research approaches. However, the most important benefit of the FOIA for researchers returns us to the Act's original intention: transparency. As our opening quote attests, Tony Blair regrets his role in introducing the FOIA. However, the Act has empowered citizens and researchers to source information, as well as helping to increase accountability of these authorities and central Government. The information produced from FOIs can further our knowledge of how publicly funded organisations operate and how they enact Government policy, all of which provides a better sense of how the state functions and gives us a fuller insight into, for example, the formal extension of counter-terrorism into the public sector. Indeed, as we have demonstrated, the FOIA can be used to hold organisations to account or conduct research on the cheap, but can also be used to produce data and further knowledge in ways valuable to academic research.

# References

Berg, B. L. (2009). *Qualitative research methods for the social sciences* (7th ed.). Upper Saddle River, NJ: Pearson Prentice Hall.

Blair, T. (2011). *A journey*. London: Hutchinson.

Breathnach, A. S., Riley, P. A., & Planche, T. D. (2011). Use of freedom of information act to produce research on the cheap. *British Medical Journal, 343*, d6129.

Briskinshaw, P. (2010). Freedom of information and its impact in the United Kingdom. *Government Information Quarterly, 27*(4), 312–321.

Brown, K. J. (2009). COUNTERBLAST: Freedom of information as a research tool: Realising its potential. *The Howard Journal of Criminal Justice, 48*(1), 88–91.

Cabinet Office. (2018). *Freedom of information statistics in central government for 2017*. Retrieved from https://assets.publishing.service.gov.uk/government/uploads/system/uploads/attachment_data/file/704094/foi-statistics-annual-2017-bulletin__1_.pdf

Chancellor of the Duchy of Lancaster. (1997). *Your right to know*. London: Cabinet Office.

Charlesworth, A. (2012). Data protection, Freedom of Information and ethical review committees. *Information, Communication & Society, 15*(1), 85–103.

*Counter Terrorism and Security Act* 2015, c. 6. London: The Stationary Office.

Fowler, A. J., Agha, R. A., Camm, C. F., & Littlejohns, P. (2013). The UK Freedom of Information Act (2000) in healthcare research: A systematic review. *BMJ Open, 3*(11), e002967.

*Freedom of Information Act* 2000, c. 36. London: The Stationary Office.

*Freedom of Information Act (Scotland) Act* 2002, asp. 13. London: The Stationary Office.

Hazell, Robert, Gabrielle Bourke, and Benjamin Worthy. (2012). Open house? Freedom of information and its impact on the UK parliament. *Public Administration, 90*(4), 901–921.

Home Office. (2018b). *Contest: The United Kingdom's strategy for countering terrorism*. Retrieved from https://assets.publishing.service.gov.uk/government/uploads/system/uploads/attachment_data/file/716907/140618_CCS207_CCS0218929798-1_CONTEST_3.0_WEB.pdf

Information Commissioner's Office. (2019a). *What information do we need to publish?* Retrieved from https://ico.org.uk/for-organisations/guide-to-freedom-of-information/publication-scheme/

Information Commissioner's Office. (2019b). *How to access information from a public body.* Retrieved from https://ico.org.uk/your-data-matters/official-information/

Johnson, D., & Hampson, E. (2015). Utilising the UK Freedom of Information Act 2000 for crime record data: Indications of the strength of records management in day to day police business. *Records Management Journal, 25*(3), 248–268.

Lippert, R. K., Walby, K., & Wilkinson, B. (2015). Spins, stalls, and shutdowns: Pitfalls of qualitative policing and security research. *Forum Qualitative Sozialforschung/Forum: Qualitative Social Research, 17*(1).

Luscombe, A., & Walby, K. (2017). Theorizing freedom of information: The live archive, obfuscation, and actor-network theory. *Government Information Quarterly, 34*(3), 379–387.

McClean, T. (2010). Who pays the piper? The political economy of freedom of information. *Government Information Quarterly, 27*(4), 392–400.

Michener, G., & Worthy, B. (2018). The information-gathering matrix: A framework for conceptualizing the use of freedom of information laws. *Administration & Society, 50*(4), 476–500.

Monahan, T., & Fisher, J. A. (2015). Strategies for obtaining access to secretive or guarded organizations. *Journal of Contemporary Ethnography, 44*(6), 709–736.

Morrill, C., Buller, D. B., Buller, M. K., & Larkey, L. L. (1999). Toward an organizational perspective on identifying and managing formal gatekeepers. *Qualitative Sociology, 22*(1), 51–72.

Richter, P., & Wilson, R. (2013). 'It's the tip of the iceberg': The hidden tensions between theory, policy and practice in the management of Freedom of Information in English local government bodies – Evidence from a regional study. *Public Money & Management, 33*(3), 177–184.

Rodríguez, R. P., & Rossel, C. (2018). A field experiment on bureaucratic discretionary bias under FOI laws. *Government Information Quarterly, 35*(3), 418–427.

Savage, A., & Hyde, R. (2014). Using freedom of information requests to facilitate research. *International Journal of Social Research Methodology, 17*(3), 303–317.

Scottish Information Commissioner's Office. (2017). *FOI in the UK: Difference between the Scottish and UK FOI Acts.* St Andrews: Scottish Information Commissioner.

Sikka, P. (2017). Using freedom of information laws to frustrate accountability: Two case studies of UK banking frauds. *Accounting Forum, 41*(4), 300–317.

Spiller, K. (2016). Experiences of accessing CCTV data: The urban topologies of subject access requests. *Urban Studies, 53*(13), 2885–2900.

Spiller, K., Awan, I., & Whiting, A. (2018). 'What does terrorism look like?' university lecturers' interpretations of their Prevent duties and tackling extremism in UK universities. *Critical Studies on Terrorism, 11*(1), 130–150.

The Independent. (2011). Exclusive: Smoked out: Tobacco giant's war on science - Philip Morris seeks to force university to hand over confidential health research into teenage smokers. Retrieved from www.independent.co.uk/news/science/exclusive-smoked-out-tobacco-giants-war-on-science-2347254.html

The Telegraph. (2012). Expenses scandal: 27 MPs let one home and claim for another. Retrieved from: www.telegraph.co.uk/news/newstopics/mps-expenses/9619022/Expenses-scandal-27-MPs-let-one-home-and-claim-for-another.html

Walby, K., & Luscombe, A. (2018). Ethics review and freedom of information requests in qualitative research. *Research Ethics, 14*(4), 1–15.

Worthy, B. (2008). The future of freedom of information in the United Kingdom. *Political Quarterly, 79*(1), 100–108.

Worthy, B. (2012). A powerful weapon in the right hands? How members of parliament have used freedom of information in the UK. *Parliamentary Affairs, 67*(4), 783–803.

# 4

# USING FOI TO EXPLORE GOVERNANCE AND DECISION-MAKING IN THE UK

*Mike Sheaff*

## Introduction

This chapter considers use of Freedom of Information (FOI) legislation in researching decision-making by those in authority within a context of declining public trust in elites and simultaneous demands for greater transparency. The focus here is on the use of FOI as a tool for social research, and its relationship with investigative journalism. The chapter begins with a summary of the use of FOI in UK social research, before introducing examples of FOIA requests by others, including journalists. This is followed with an account of my own use of FOI to explore decision-making in a failed public service contract in the UK. A concluding discussion considers the potential for using FOIA as a tool for research beyond the collection of information, to support a more critical exploration of decision-making within state organisations, with some final comments on the relationship between social research and investigative journalism.

The British state has a long history of secrecy. In 1971, the Labour Minister Richard Crossman described secrecy as the, "real English disease and in particular the chronic ailment of the British Government" (Crossman, 1971). This tradition was challenged in 1998 with the publication of a Government White Paper, *Your Right to Know*, which proclaimed:

> Openness is fundamental to the political health of a modern state. This White Paper marks a watershed in the relationship between the government and people of the United Kingdom. At last there is a government ready to trust the people with a legal right to information.
>
> *(Chancellor of the Duchy of Lancaster, 1998)*

This resulted in the UK Freedom of Information Act 2000, which came into effect in 2005. An estimated 121,000 requests were made in the first year of the Act's operation (Colquhoun, 2010); non-central government bodies received about 87,000 of these, of which approximately 60,000 were submitted to local authorities (Colquhoun, 2010). Seeking disclosure through FOIA requests in the UK involves up to five stages:

1.  Request for disclosure to a public authority
2.  Request for Internal Review by the public authority
3.  Complaint to Information Commissioner (resulting in a Decision Notice)
4.  Appeal to Information Rights Tribunal (Lower Tier)
5.  Appeal to Information Rights Tribunal (Upper Tier) (on points of law only)

Despite the promise of openness, of 46,681 FOI requests received by central governmental bodies in 2017, 17,309 were withheld in full or in part. In 29% of cases, this was due to the cost exceeding the allowable limit, and 2% were judged vexatious or repetitious. The remaining 12,643 (68%) were withheld on the grounds that one or more of twenty-three statutory exemptions applied (Cabinet Office, 2017). Some exemptions are absolute, but most are qualified, meaning that a decision not to disclose is subject to a public interest test. Forty seven percent of the 12,643 FOIA requests received by central government in 2017 were refused on the grounds that the information sought was deemed to be "personal data" and consequently exempt under s40 (Cabinet Office, 2017). I return to this issue below, as the boundary between personal and collective responsibility can be complex. Before considering the determination of "public interest," the following section reviews examples of UK research in which FOIA has been used.

## Accessing information: FOIA and social research in the UK

There are now many examples of such research, but referring to an observation by Brown (2009), Savage and Hyde (2014, p. 303) note suggestions "that researchers are yet to fully appreciate the value of FOIA to empirical research in the fields of social science and law." A common feature of existing research is the collection of comparative data across public authorities, including Savage and Hyde's (2014) study of whistle-blowing. This involved requests to 48 food safety regulatory bodies to identify whether the regulators were receiving whistle-blowing disclosures, and what action resulted from such disclosures. Savage and Hyde (2014, p. 309) note, "FOIA request are particularly useful where comparisons are sought to be drawn between various public authorities. By using a standardised FOIA request, data obtained from public authorities can be standardised."

Similarly, Johnson and Hampson (2015) sent FOIA requests to police forces in England as part of a larger research study of criminal activity among EU migrants. Over a fifteen-month period, 43 forces were asked to disclose information relating to criminal charges, the type of crime and the nationality and age of the alleged offenders. While noting limitations, the authors' overall conclusion was that "access afforded by the FOIA is valuable. Research conducted would not have been possible without this formal mechanism to obtain the required data; results received have been useful, interesting and informative" (Johnson & Hampson, 2015, p. 263).

In the context of social work research, Murray (2013) investigated free access to leisure centres for children in care through requests to all 152 local authority children's services in England. Results showed a differential provision, "with fewer than half of councils (48%) currently providing free leisure passes" (Murray, 2013, p. 1347). Murray also comments on limitations in use of FOIA, including difficulties in asking extensive questions and probing responses, and potentially a reluctance by some authorities to comply (although this was not experienced in this study). Murray (2013, p. 362) concludes "these limitations notwithstanding, there are many advantages associated with using Freedom of Information requests. It is suggested that it be considered a suitable way to elicit data across a range of social work topics." A review of use of FOIA requests in research involving the English NHS described the number of studies as "relatively few" (Fowler, Agha, Camm, & Littlejohns, 2013, p. 6). Sixteen studies conducted between 2005 and 2013 had requested disclosure on a diverse range of issues, including litigation, surgical provision, funding for rarer cancers, laboratory provision, pharmaceutical safety and midwifery discipline. These studies involved a total of 1732 requests, with a median of 86 per paper, and the review noted, "questions were being asked across a cross-section of the NHS" (Fowler et al., 2013, p. 4).

Use of FOIA in UK research has prompted discussion on ethical implications, particularly relating to informed consent, confidentiality and anonymity. Use of FOIA may increase response rates – one study achieved an 83% response rate using FOIA compared to 11% when informal request letters were sent (cited in Fowler et al., 2013) – raising the question of whether use of a statutory tool in this way is ethically justified. In the context of clinical research, objections have been that "researchers [are] using the Act to compel hospitals to provide data to further their research" (Breathnach, Riley, & Planche, 2011). The fundamental concern is whether use of a statutory entitlement to obtain data strikes against the ethical principle of informed consent to participate in research, since "national and international guidance states that participation in research must be voluntary." The authors argue consideration should be given to "the ethical and resource implications of compelling colleagues to participate in research, even if such compulsion is permitted in law" (Breathnach et al., 2011, p. 1).

This objection deserves attention, but context is important. The concerns arose in the context of FOIA requests from a tobacco company for research data on smoking and young people from a British University, and the authors' own experiences of attempts to disclose hospital research data. Conducting research without consent can be considered in some ways analogous to covert research, about which the British Sociological Association's Statement of Ethical Practice observes:

There are serious ethical and legal issues in the use of covert research but the use of covert methods may be justified in certain circumstances.... Researchers may also face problems when access to spheres of social life is closed to social scientists by powerful or secretive interests.

*(British Sociological Association, 2017, para 14)*

On confidentiality and anonymity, Savage and Hyde (2014) suggest that Freedom of Information requests "fall outside the traditional dichotomy between primary and secondary research," as although it involves publicly available data, this status is achieved solely as a consequence of the researcher's requests. They suggest this has prompted concern from some ethics committees, defining the data as primary data generated by the researcher. However, Savage and Hyde argue there is an important difference:

In the FOIA scheme the responsibility for cleansing the data of personal information lies with the public authority to which the request is made. The data provided in response to a FOIA request should not contain information that identifies any person, living or dead. If this is not possible then the request should be refused by the public authority. Therefore, research conducted through FOIA requests will not pose ethical issues in the same way as research where data is gathered directly by the researcher.

*(Savage & Hyde, 2014, p. 310)*

The examples described above used FOIA requests as a form of survey technique, directed towards collecting cross-organisational comparative data. In this chapter, I consider its use in ways more analogous to qualitative research, involving follow-up questions and probing that raise ethical issues beyond those discussed by Savage and Hyde (2013). This is a method more frequently adopted by journalists, politicians and citizens. Here, requests have been prompted by suspicions that information is being concealed to protect the organisation and individuals from potentially embarrassing revelations, or to avoid public scrutiny of decisions. Three examples are described in the next section, considered in the context of "personal privacy" and "private spaces."

## Freedom of Information versus personal privacy: the 2009 MP's expenses scandal

An early conflict in the UK between transparency and privacy developed following FOIA requests by journalists and others for details of allowances claimed by members of parliament. The request was rejected on the grounds that the information was the "personal data" of the subject, a position maintained following internal review. The journalist appealed to the Information Commissioner, and there followed a highly protracted communication between the IC and HoC lasting eighteen months. In a Decision Notice issued in June 2007, the Information Commissioner sum-marised the view of the House of Commons authority:

> It considered the information to be exempt under section 40(2) of the Act because it was personal data about the MP concerned. The House maintained that disclosure would breach the requirement of the first Data Protection Prin-ciple that personal data be processed fairly and lawfully (Information Commis-sioner DN FS50070469, para 6) ... disclosure of this information in the detail sought would compromise the privacy of the MP and his or her family and that there can be personal security risks in disclosing where a MP lives.
>
> *(para 10)*

In contrast, the Information Commissioner took the view:

> ... the link with holding public office is clear. If individual MPs had not been elected to carry out their role as public representatives they would not be entitled to claim the related expenses.... It is only because such costs are considered to be expenses arising from the holding of public office that they are subject to reimbursement from the public purse.
>
> *(para 32)*

The House of Commons authority appealed to the Tribunal on several requests, which upheld the Information Commissioner's decision, concluding that there is, "a balance between competing interests broadly comparable, but not identi-cal, to the balance that applies under the public interest test for qualified exemp-tions under FOIA" (The Corporate Officer of the House of Commons v Information Commissioner and Norman Baker MP, EA/2006/0015 & 0016, para 90). An appeal by the House of Commons to the High Court was unsuc-cessful. Confirming that there are circumstances where public office is involved when it may be fair to reveal personal information under FOIA, the court upheld the earlier instruction to disclose the material with appropriate redac-tions. In Spring of 2009, leaks from some of the documents began to appear in the media, including revelations about £116,000 claimed by the Home Secretary for a "second home" that was her family residence. It seemed that while disclos-ure of MPs' expenses, "followed a four-year campaign by journalists using FOI laws ...(these) worked alongside a very old-fashioned form of information provi-sion, a leak" (Worthy, 2014, p. 27). As BBC journalist Martin Rosenbaum commented, subsequent more extensive revelations by the *Daily Telegraph*,

> would not have happened without the FOI Act, that is clear. Yet they are actually based on a leak, not legally-enforced disclosure. So some of today's revelations may be as much about leaking, or "chequebook jour-nalism," as about freedom of information.
>
> *(Rosenbaum, 2009)*

Another interpretation of these later reports, unlike the early leaks, views them as a departure from conventional journalism.

> Those initial leaks, based on a sample of the redacted data, conformed to the traditional journalistic model of identifying scandalous individuals, rather than reporting expenses more systematically. Yet those working on the redacted data thought that the abuses they were processing were systemic and not to be easily identified as "fingering" corrupt individuals.
>
> *(Ruppert & Savage, 2011, p. 75)*

Those involved in leaking the un-redacted material consequently demanded wholesale publication, a condition refused by several newspapers, until "the Daily Telegraph, with its unusually large corps of political journalists thought it could devote the resources to allow a comprehensive treatment" (Ruppert & Savage, 2011, p. 76). Importantly, this included details of private addresses, which would have been redacted under the High Court judgement. As this would have removed information that enabled revelations about MP's claims for different accommodation addresses, the BBC's Martin Rosenbaum noted at the time: "the Telegraph today argues that without these addresses, the newspaper would not have been able to shed light on some of the questionable practices it reveals" (Rosenbaum, 2009).

Publication of the un-redacted details sold to the *Daily Telegraph* had significant repercussions, with resignations by Ministers and the House of Commons Speaker, and criminal investigations into eight parliamentarians, four of whom were jailed. The scandal reached the scale that it did, to a considerable extent because "personal information" that would have been redacted, notably MP's addresses, was leaked. How far individuals in positions of authority can reasonably expect typical expectations of privacy to apply to them is a question to which I return. Before this, the next section considers two examples where the British government refused disclosure of information on the grounds that official deliberations on sensitive issues needed to be conducted in a "private space."

## "Private spaces" for official deliberations: use of the government veto

In common with most FOI systems, the UK allows a government veto on disclosure, creating a rare opportunity for the executive to over-rule a judicial decision. The first use of this provision came in the wake of the invasion of Iraq, with a request from a citizen, Dr. Christopher Lamb, for disclosure of Cabinet minutes and meeting records from March 2003. These concerned the provision of legal advice by the Attorney-General on military action against Iraq. The Cabinet Office refused disclosure on public interest grounds, arguing the need for confidentiality surrounding policy development and ministerial communications. The Information Commissioner subsequently identified significant public interest factors favouring disclosure:

> These included the gravity and controversial nature of the decision to go to war against another country and the particular public interest in transparency given the controversy surrounding the Attorney General's legal advice on the legality of the military action in question. The Commissioner did not consider that the information in the public domain sufficiently enabled the public to scrutinise the manner in which the decision was taken and took the view that disclosure of the Minutes was necessary to understand that decision more fully.
>
> *(Information Commissioner, 2009, p. 8)*

The Cabinet Office appealed to the Tribunal, which by 2–1 majority decided that on balance the public interest favoured disclosure of the minutes. The Tribunal described this as:

> an exceptional case, the circumstances of which brought together a combination of factors that were so important that, in combination, they created very powerful public interest reasons why disclosure was in the public interest. It was this that led the majority of the panel to conclude that they were at least equal to those in favour of maintaining the exemption.
>
> *(Information Commissioner, 2009, p. 11)*

On February 23, 2009 Jack Straw, Secretary of State for Justice, issued a "veto" certificate under section 53(2) of the Act to overrule this decision. Essentially, his argument was that Cabinet discussions need the protection of a "private space" to allow free and frank debate:

> Dialogue must be fearless. Ministers must have the confidence to challenge each other in private ... To permit the commissioner's and the tribunal's view of the public interest to prevail would, in my judgement, risk serious damage to Cabinet government – an essential principle of British parliamentary democracy.
>
> *(Ministry of Justice, 2009)*

A similar argument was employed in applying the veto to documents relating to the Coalition Government's re-organisation of the NHS in 2011–2012. Here the request was submitted by a politician, John Healey MP, a former Labour health spokesperson. A focus was upon requests for disclosure of a Transitional Risk Register (TRR), created as part of the Department of Health's (DH) risk assessment of the proposed changes. DH refused on the grounds that "disclosure would or would be likely to inhibit the free and frank provision of advice."

Mr. Healey requested an internal review. DH maintained its refusal but changed the justification, suggesting the requested information was exempt from disclosure as it was concerned with the formulation and development of government policy. This is also a qualified exemption, and DH maintained its position that the public interest favoured non-disclosure.

Mr. Healey complained to the Information Commissioner (IC), who in accepting the risk register was potentially exempt went on to consider the public interest test. Against Healey's claim that there was a public interest at issue, as disclosure would allow greater scrutiny of the government's plans, DH claimed disclosure would jeopardise success of the policy through inhibiting frank discussion. Concluding the arguments were finely balanced, the IC judged the information should be disclosed, explaining:

> … there is a very strong public interest in disclosure of the information, given the significant change to the structure of the health service the government's policies on the modernisation will bring. There has also been widespread debate amongst the general public, commentators, experts and those who work in the NHS…. Disclosure would significantly aid public understanding of the risks related to the proposed reforms and it would also inform participation in the debate about the reforms.
>
> *(ICO DN FS50390786, para 31)*

DH appealed the decisions to the Information Tribunal, which accepted "a safe space is required for government to formulate and develop policy," but argued the significance of this would change over time (para 59). A former Cabinet Secretary and the DH Permanent Secretary advised the Tribunal that disclosure would inhibit thinking and consequently damage sound policy-making. The Tribunal rejected this reasoning, commenting, "there was no actual evidence of such an effect" (para 66), citing research by the Constitution Unit at University College London that found little evidence that FOIA has what is described as a "chilling effect" on discussion.

DH's position was described by the Tribunal as, "tantamount to saying that there should be an absolute exemption for risk registers at the stages the registers were requested in this case" (para 73). By establishing the relevant exemption as qualified, Parliament had made it subject to a public interest test, and the Tribunal concluded that the public interest justified disclosure:

> … the NHS reforms were introduced in an exceptional way. There was no indication prior to the White Paper that such wide ranging reforms were being considered. The White Paper was published without prior consultation. It was published within a very short period after the Coalition Government came into power. It was unexpected. Consultation took place afterwards over what appears to us a very short period considering the

extent of the proposed reforms…. Even more significantly the Government decided to press ahead with some of the policies even before laying a Bill before Parliament (para 85)…. We find the weight we give to the need for transparency and accountability in the circumstances of this case to be very weighty indeed.

*(para 89)*

The Tribunal decision was published on April 5, 2012, and on 8 May was over-ruled by the Secretary of State for Health, vetoing disclosure. He explained that, "there is already a considerable amount of material in the public domain on risks involved in the reform programme," suggesting, "there was a significant risk" that "disclosure of the TRR at this time would in fact have distorted debate and understanding" (Information Commissioner, 2012, p. 28). The Information Commissioner's subsequent report to Parliament noted:

> The previous three occasions on which the veto has been exercised related to the disclosure of Cabinet material under FOIA. The Commissioner would wish to record his concern that the exercise of the veto in this case extends its use into other areas of the policy process. It represents a departure from the position adopted in the Statement of Policy and therefore marks a significant step in the Government's approach to free-dom of information.
>
> *(Information Commissioner, 2012, pp. 19–20)*

Both these examples concerned attempts to disclose how decisions were made by government, and the evidence used to inform the outcomes. Social and institutional practices, rather than the alleged wrongdoing of individuals, provide the focus. While the example of the MP's expenses is significant for establishing a balance between protection of personal information, transparency and public accountability, requests for the Iraq war legal advice and the NHS risk register perhaps offer examples of more direct relevance for social researchers.

## Using FOIA to research a contracting failure

For three decades, British governments have pursued policies favouring the con-tracting of public services to external organisations. "Government outsourcing and contracting has become a very significant part of the delivery of central and local government services throughout the world. The UK Government spends £251.5 billion per year on outsourcing and contracting" (House of Commons Public Administration Committee Constitutional Affairs, 2018). Despite this rep-resenting approximately one-third of public spending, it can be difficult to sub-ject these contracts to effective scrutiny.

This became apparent with the collapse of several high-profile contractors, seemingly unanticipated by the relevant public authorities. A lack of awareness of Southern Cross's financial difficulties until its collapse in 2011 was repeated on an even larger scale with Carillion in 2018. Holding around 420 public sector contracts, "by value, Carillion was central government's sixth largest supplier in 2017" (National Audit Office, 2018, p. 6). This included facilities management, catering, road and rail maintenance, accommodation, consultancy and construction. Since 2013, the Cabinet Office regularly raised with Carillion its delayed payments to sub-contractors, but, "the scale of the losses announced on July 10, 2017 came as a surprise to the Cabinet Office as it contradicted previous discussions with Carillion and market expectations" (NAO, 2018, p. 7). Although the Cabinet Office subsequently "took steps to improve its information about Carillion's financial health," the company went into compulsory liquidation in January 2018. Interserve, a company employing "45,000 staff in the UK working on £2bn worth of government contracts" went into administration in March 2019. The GMB trade union claimed Interserve received public contracts valued at £660m "in the run-up to going into administration, in an apparent repeat of the Carillion fiasco" (Brignall, 2019).

One of the obstacles to gaining better knowledge and understanding of these episodes is the exclusion of public service contractors from Freedom of Information legislation. This is the subject of considerable debate in Britain, with the Information Commissioner recently urging that, "Freedom of information legislation should be extended to enable greater transparency in the delivery of public services. This would promote democratic accountability but also act as a driver for improving contractual oversight and service delivery" (Information Commissioner, 2019). FOIA does, nevertheless, apply to the contracting public authorities themselves. Drawing upon my own research using FOIA to study a contracting failure, this section describes elements of the experience, including opportunities it presents and obstacles that can be encountered (Sheaff, 2017, 2016). Attention to the latter relates my experiences to potential pitfalls encountered in FOIA research described by Lippert, Walby, and Wilkinson (2016). First, I provide a contextual background to my own study, the origins of which did not lie in a conventional research proposal, but through a role I held as a Non-Executive Director in an NHS Primary Care Trust (PCT) in South West England.

## Setting the scene: "hierarchies of credibility"

In 2010, the newly elected Coalition Government's plans for NHS reorganisation involved abolition of existing organisations – including PCT's and Strategic Health Authorities (SHA's). As previously noted, the plans generated widespread controversy, in part because the implementation of change (including "clustering" of PCT's and SHA's) began prior to the proposals gaining parliamentary approval (on which, see also House of Lords, 2013). The pace of change was rapid, with little opportunity for meaningful challenge. In a letter to the Chair of our PCT "Cluster" in June 2011, I explained my concerns, concluding, "Unlike previous NHS reorganisation, 'clustering' has not been subject to Parliamentary scrutiny, which arguably means we have greater responsibilities in our role of Non-Executive Directors to contribute to achieving public confidence in future arrangements."

The tempo of change continued, with the government's reforms intended to promote competition across health and social care. The "Cluster" Chair had substantial NHS experience, having been a chief executive of a Strategic Health Authority, and subsequently Chair of a social enterprise delivering an NHS contract, Secure Healthcare Ltd (SHL). I enquired about the governance arrangements for this organisation. My interest was stimulated having learned of it being awarded a £130,000 start-up grant by the Department of Health, winning a £5 million contract with Wandsworth PCT to provide health services at Wandsworth Prison, but collapsing little more than two years later in September 2009 with debts of over £1.5 million. My questions to its former Chair were forwarded to the South West SHA, and my PCT Chair was asked by the SHA Chair to discourage me from pursuing my concern. I was described as causing "disruption" to the NHS reorganisation.

In response, in September 2011, I wrote to the SHA, copying local MPs, explaining why I believed this episode, "reveals important insights into how decisions have been made at different levels within the NHS ... from which there are important lessons that we should be prepared to learn." The SHA forwarded my letter to the Appointments Commission (AC), the body responsible for appointing NHS Non-Executive Directors, which established a review into my concerns. The subsequent report gave particular attention to the SHL contract, with an overall assessment that "the underlying reason for the failure of SHL were typical reasons for business failure" (Appointments Commission, 2011, p. 11). In so far as reasons were explored, responsibility was directed at subordinate organisational levels. SHL's bid team were judged to have "let down the company," and Wandsworth PCT was criticised for demonstrating "poor procedures and many failings in management." Very different assessments were made of those in more senior roles. The investigation concluded that problems experienced by SHL "were addressed by the management of the company as they arose; without success as it turns out." Strong endorsement is given to processes for approving DH funding, described as "thorough, independent, open and externally reviewed," and subject to, "due diligence from the outset."

This report was described by the AC chief executive as "supported by robust evidence" and "well argued," and by the SHA Chair as "very detailed," "thorough" and "rigorous." The SHA Chair informed local MPs that having taken "two months to complete and involved the review of over 450 pages of documents from 45 personal and organisational reference sources," the review had concluded my concerns were "completely unfounded." In response, I used the NHS complaints procedure to argue my concerns were not adequately addressed. This too was dismissed, and an appeal to the Parliamentary & Health Service Ombudsman met the response that as a "personnel" matter, it was outside their jurisdiction. My member of parliament requested a meeting with me and the Health Minister to discuss the contract, but was told:

> You ask that I meet with you and Mr Sheaff to discuss his continuing concerns. I regret I have to decline … there is nothing I can usefully add to the various independent investigations that have been conducted on this matter … I regret that Mr Sheaff continues to have concerns over this matter, but am of the view that we have devoted as much attention to his concerns as can reasonably be expected under the circumstances.
>
> *(Correspondence to Oliver Colvile MP, February 2014)*

This response from a government minister illustrates what Becker described as a "hierarchy of credibility," wherein, "participants take it as given that members of the highest group have the right to define the way things really are" (Becker, 1967, p. 241). Perceptions "that those at the top have access to a more complete picture of what is going on than anyone else," align with views, that, "Members of lower groups will have incomplete information, and their view of reality will be partial and distorted in consequence." A consequence is that, "any tale told by those at the top intrinsically deserves to be regarded as the most credible account obtainable of the organizations' workings" (Becker, 1967, p. 241). My move in role from participant to researcher was prompted by Becker's recognition that

> credibility and the right to be heard are differentially distributed through the ranks of the system. As sociologists, we provoke the charge of bias, in ourselves and others, by refusing to give credence and deference to an established status order, in which knowledge of truth and the right to be heard are not equally distributed.
>
> *(Becker, 1967, p. 242)*

"Truth" is inevitably contested, and my goal was twofold. First, to use FOIA requests relating to the collapse of SHL to go beyond official accounts, taking the opportunity to engage in what Laura Nader described as "studying-up" to uncover behaviour in "powerful institutions and bureaucratic organisations" (Nader, 1969/1972, p. 292). For this, I drew upon Diane Vaughan's concepts of organisational deviance and routine non-conformity, involving deviation "from both design goals and normative standard or expectations" (Vaughan, 1999, p. 273). Alongside this, I wanted to explore opportunities for using FOIA disclosures as a route for uncovering an example of what Vaughan terms "clean-up work," through which organisations seek to "prevent incidents of routine nonconformity from being publicly defined as mistake" (Vaughan, 1999, p. 287).

## Official accounts and information disclosures

Over a period of more than eighteen months, I made twenty three requests to nine public authorities, including the SHA, DH, two NHS Trusts, the Appointments Commission and the Cabinet Office. Nine of the requests were followed by requests for internal reviews, of which two continued to appeals to the Information Commissioner and the Information Rights Tribunal. This process contributed to my experiences of "stalls" (Lippert et al., 2016), where information was disclosed through a very slow and frequently protracted process. Nevertheless, by providing new insights, several disclosures prompted further requests to other organisations. Through gradually piecing these together, an alternative perspective emerged to that offered in official accounts. Illustrative examples are provided here to present an alternative representation of the demise of SHL, directing attention upwards in the organisational hierarchy rather than to those at more junior levels. The first concerns the official assessment that problems "were addressed by the management of the company as they arose," whereas SHL's bid team "let down the company." SHL's accounts are cited as evidence of the organisation's financial stability:

> A review of the accounts of Secure Healthcare Ltd for the first year of its operation show a solvent organisation with sufficient resources to meet its liabilities … There was no immediately obvious sign of the difficulties that later arose in making payments to creditors at this point.
>
> *(Appointments Commission, 2011, p. 11)*

A different picture is revealed from FOIA disclosures by two NHS Trusts to which SHL sub-contracted services.

By March 2008, nine months into the contract, SHL's debts to these Trusts amounted to £532,822.75. Twelve months later, this had risen to £556,222.00 (over one-tenth of the contract's total value), and to £648,565 by the time SHL collapsed in September 2009. It appears none of this was known to Wandsworth PCT, which from April 2008 had been making advance payments to SHL, in contravention of financial procedures. After further advance payments, on July 21, 2008 SHL informed the PCT, "we do not have sufficient funds to cover our July payroll."

In the same month, SHL was awarded a government loan of £400,000, "to bid for and deliver upcoming prison healthcare contracts." £259,000 was drawn down, and subsequently written off. The Cabinet Office responded to a FOIA request with a statement that the decision on the loan "included a review of previous accounts, financial systems, and cashflow forecasts." But SHL's first and only set of accounts were not approved until February 5, 2009. On the previous day, the Department of Health awarded SHL a grant of £380,000 for a new training campus. Yet, seven months later, on 9th September, the SHL

Board received a report from its chief executive, disclosed by DH in response to a FOIA request. This advised the Board of:

> serious liquidity issues … A number of factors have contributed to the current crisis position. It is clear we have had poor financial information to track our progress and limited cost controls … our cost control and management data has been poor from day one … The grant and loan income injections masked the overspending … The Wandsworth cost over-runs were not addressed.

Writing about the training campus, SHL's Board was informed: "We went ahead with [this] development without a tested business plan."

Some of the most significant data obtained through FOIA disclosures concerned the role of the Department of Health, revealing a considerably closer relationship with SHL than is suggested in official accounts. One document records two payments totalling £220,770 made as part of a "service level agreement" between DH and SHL. These included costs of seconding a DH employee to SHL as a "project manager." As these figures did not correspond with SHL's accounts, I requested an internal review, receiving details of three more payments. These amounted to £2,205,882.50, with the final payment – of £1,457,882.50 – made twelve days before SHL went into liquidation. According to subsequent correspondence with a government Health Minister, the first reference in DH's own records to SHL's debts was on September 14, 2009, just two days before its collapse. Despite this, the official investigation into my original questions about DH funding concluded: "The means by which applications were assessed and due diligence conducted from the outset … was thorough, independent, open and externally reviewed. An investment committee was put in place that had responsibility for approving investments independently of the Department" (Appointments Commission, 2011, p. 6).

In her analysis of organisational failure, Vaughan uses the term "structural secrecy" to describe: "the way that patterns of information, organizational structure, processes and transactions, and the structure of regulatory relations systematically undermine the attempt to know and interpret situations in all organisations" (Vaughan, 1996, p. 238). In the case of SHL, disclosed data revealed that neither the PCT nor DH had knowledge of SHL's debts until it was on the very brink of collapse. Together with failures in information flow, correct procedures were not always followed. "Normalization of deviance" is a concept used by Vaughan to describe a gradual process of adopting unacceptable practices which, in the absence of negative consequences, become the norm. Examples in this episode are advance payments made by the PCT to SHL, and the apparent lack of rigour shown by government in awarding grants, a loan and establishing a "service level agreement." The context for this was the government's enthusiasm for establishing a market within healthcare, and an audit review commissioned by one of the two sub-contracting NHS Trusts refers to, "considerable enthusiasm from DH downwards for a social enterprise model of care." Documents such as these provide valuable insights into decision-making, and the role of culture alongside organisational structures in inhibiting more rigorous scrutiny.

There is no cause to believe errors and omissions in the official investigation were deliberate in any way. Its assessment was based upon documents that were in the public domain. Only through use of documents released in response to FOIA requests could an alternative account be constructed. Without this, the hierarchy of credibility afforded protection to a deeply flawed analysis. This prompted a second strand in my research, in an attempt to explore processes of concealment achieved through "clean-up work."

## Lifting the veil on "clean-up work"

Becker urged social researchers to "doubt everything anyone in power tells you" (Becker, 1998, p. 91). This is not founded upon personal mistrust, but his view that, "institutions always put their best foot forward in public ... social organization gives them reasons to lie" (Becker, 1998, p. 91). One consequence, as he had written earlier, is that

> by refusing to accept the hierarchy of credibility, we express disrespect for the entire established order. We compound our sin and further provoke charges of bias by not giving immediate attention and "equal time" to the apologies and explanations of official authority.
>
> *(Becker, 1967, pp. 241–242)*

In a sense, I sought to turn this on its head, giving attention to processes used by those in authority to marginalise discrepant voices. And it was within this focus of the research that I met some of the greatest obstacles to disclosure, including examples of "shutdown" (Lippert et al., 2016).

At an early stage, the SHA declined to communicate with me other than through a lawyer, who maintained my concerns were without basis. In October 2012, he explained, "My Client is satisfied that the concerns you raised have been fully investigated and that they are unfounded." In December, he reiterated, "You make reference ... to the concerns you raised regarding Secure Healthcare. As I stated in my email of 2 October, my Client is satisfied that such concerns have been fully investigated and that they are unfounded." Seeking a better understanding of how my concerns had been handled, I submitted FOIA requests for three documents created at the time I informed the SHA of my concerns, in September 2011. These included the transcript of a telephone conference call involving the SHA Chair and my PCT Chair and a letter from the SHA Chair to the Appointments Commission.

The SHA informed me that all relevant documents were with the lawyer, to whom I should submit my request. I did so, but no information was disclosed.

The lawyer told me the letter could not be found, and when I asked what search had been conducted, he wrote, "You have been informed that the letter you were seeking cannot be found. That is the end of the matter" (April 12, 2013). This experience came closest to what Lippert et al. (2016) describe as "shutdown," involving a permanent locking of information, but I requested an internal review, handled by the SHA's Information Officer who was more helpful. The telephone transcript, with some redactions, was disclosed to me, a matter of days before the SHA was abolished, following a decision by the Information Officer to treat my request as a subject access request under the Data Protection Act. He considered that the conversation about me was my own personal data, to which I was entitled. On the letter I was told,

> I have reviewed our files and we cannot find a copy of (the) letter … I think the quickest and easiest way to find if the letter is held in archive would be a FOI request directly to the Department of Health.

This was to present one of the most challenging responses to my FOIA requests, resulting in appeals to the Information Commissioner and the Information Rights Tribunal. The outcome of my request to the DoH was summarised in the Tribunal's judgement:

> DoH provided a heavily edited copy, which contained almost nothing of substance. It relied on s.40(1), as regards the personal data of MS and s.40(2) as to the personal data of three third parties. It modified its position to a limited extent when complying with MS's request for an internal review by removing redactions relating to matters that were clearly not personal data.
>
> *(Sheaff and The Information Commissioner & the Department of Health,*
> *EA/2014/0005)*

Included in the respondent's bundle for the hearing was a statement from the former SHA Chair urging non-disclose of the redacted sections: "we clearly expect the Secretary of State to firmly protect us and our reputations in the proper execution of our duties as leaders within the NHS." While noting the "the entirely legitimate purposes of MS's quest for greater transparency and accountability," the Tribunal upheld the Information Commissioner's decision:

> The ICO found that, as to MS and three individuals named in the letter, it contained their personal data. Whilst the letter was concerned with performance of their public functions, the professional reputations of two of the third parties were engaged. Disclosure would be unfair, hence would breach the first data protection principle so that the first condition for application of the absolute exemption was satisfied (see FOIA s.40(3)(a)(i)). It would be unfair because the letter was marked "Private and

confidential" and referred to matters affecting professional reputations and none of the third parties would have reasonably expected its content to be disclosed to the general public.

*(Sheaff and The Information Commissioner & The Department of Health, EA/2014/0005)*

The Tribunal also explained,

> there is a general expectation that internal staff matters will remain confidential. We do not accept the distinction made by MS between disciplinary issues and other expressions of opinion as to staff members nor the argument that public office holders are not entitled to the same protection of personal data as employees. We find that all concerned reasonably expected that the matters referred to would remain confidential within a limited circle of senior personnel.

In some respects, the construction of a body of information as being "personal," and thereby exempt from disclosure, suggests an example of what is described by Lippert, Walby and Wilkinson (2016, p. 5) as "spins": "an effort to redirect or reshape the meaning of particular claims, observations and practices." Elsewhere (Sheaff, 2019) I refer to this as framing, having consequences not only for disclosure but also contributing to a fragmentation and diminution of accountability. An example relating to the SHA Chair's letter illustrates how the framing of information can place it beyond disclosure. The ICO Decision Notice made reference to redactions under s40(1), as this involved my own personal data. Individual's personal data is exempt from disclosure through FOIA, being accessible instead through a subject access request under the Data Protection Act. I submitted such a request. Disclosure was however refused by DH, which explained:

> The DPA prevents us from disclosing to you any personal data which is not yours. It also prevents us from breaching any duty of confidentiality owed to any other individuals involved … The first bullet point expresses a viewpoint held by another individual at the time of writing and therefore is also their personal data. The Department cannot disclose this without breaching the confidentiality of the individual concerned and consequently disclosure is refused.

*(Department of Health, January 3, 2014)*

Although insights were provided, it proved far more difficult to use FOIA to explore this example of "clean-up work" than to examine decision-making concerning the failed contract itself. A significant barrier was the relationship between FOIA and the DPA in the UK, where there has been a notable rise in numbers of FOIA disclosure refusals on the grounds that the material involves "personal data" (Sheaff, 2019).

## FOIA as a tool for critical social research

The boundary between "personal" and "public" information lay at the heart of the dispute over the disclosure of MP's expenses. As noted previously, although it would not have been possible without FOIA disclosures, eventually it was a "leak" to journalists that allowed wrongdoing to be brought to the attention of the public. Journalism, as Weber discussed in The Profession and Vocation of Politics, can be undervalued, playing as it does a vital role for scrutiny in a democratic society. It can contribute to unveiling "cover-storying," a term used by Luscombe to refer to, "one mechanism used by state actors to inhibit publics from learning the true nature of their plans, intentions and activities" (Luscombe, 2018, p. 402). Many sociologists might claim a similar role, illustrated in a comment by Keen introducing his FOI-research of FBI surveillance of sociologists: "the struggle for democracy, tolerance, and the freedom of speech and dissent, necessary for the creative discovery of a vibrant sociological imagination, is a never-ending one which cannot be left untended" (Keen, 2004, p. 207).

Shared commitment does not imply a uniform approach. An obvious difference might be that of ethical considerations. As a discussion on reporting of the Watergate scandal noted, "That documents may be of use to social scientists is one conclusion, but the cultural norms and ethics governing access to documents are quite different for social scientists and for journalists" (Levine, 1980, p. 628). A century after Weber's observation that, "it is the irresponsible pieces of journalism that tend to remain in the memory because of their often terrible effects" (Weber, 1919, cited in Lassman & Spiers, 1994, p. 332), we learned of revelations in the UK of journalist "phone-tapping", illustrated notoriously in the case of Millie Dowler. Transgressions of ethical boundaries need not be as egregious to draw an apparent division between journalism and social research. Writing under a pseudonym, "a journalist working in a senior position in the UK media" emphasises the status of journalism as an art in arguing, "too many reporters these days confuse the use and management of Freedom of Information requests – and the endless back and forth with the Information Commissioner that often follows – for investigative journalism." He suggests a quasi-legal "new style journalism" focuses on revealing secret documents and of railing against "redactions," but which erodes "the all-important art of contact management: of building a reliable and sympathetic network who will share gossip and, ultimately, leak you information." He adds,

> too often journalists these days are as expert in the details and mechanisms of FOI law as they are in taking a key contact out for one more pint than he or she might deem sensible. This is bad for democracy and for the

fourth estate because the FOI Act gives officials the framework to delay and even deny the publication of stuff it doesn't want to get out. There is no such framework to stop the handing over of a brown paper envelope under a pub table.

*(Jenkinson, 2007)*

Writing in the US in the 1960s about what he referred to as depth journalism, Copple describes, "digging out facts beneath the surface. There is no opinion in truly investigative reporting. It resembles a scientific approach" (Copple, 1964, p. 19). A similar point was made in another, later, US account, describing an increasingly prominent trend during the preceding decade with the rise of investigative reporting, as being, "the merger between social science methodology" creating "a new genre called precision journalism" (Weaver & McCombs, 1980, p. 477). A classic example of investigative journalism was Bernstein and Woodward's exposure of the Watergate scandal published by the *Washington Post*, and recounted in All the President's Men. Levine (1980), describing their methods as "more than muckraking," suggests it "deserves the accolade of art, but there was, in addition, a distinct method to their approach" (Levine, 1980, p. 626). Noting the challenge of drawing together "the mass of disconnected pieces of information," Levine puts social research and investigative journalism within the same camp: "The self-conscious emphasis on controlled and disciplined observation and inference distinguishes the professional researcher from the ordinary citizen" (Levine, 1980, p. 627).

Since then, several commentators have written of a "decline of investigative reporting" (e.g. Centre for Investigative Journalism, 2018). Others, while detecting "some reasons to be optimistic," describe investigative journalism as being "in a fragile state in the UK" (Lashmar, 2013, pp. 37–38). My own research caused me to consider how some of the methods of investigative reporting might align with sociological inquiry, to develop a more critical analysis of state organisations in ways that focused on social and institutional practices. Because these are expressed, through the actions of individuals, I met obstacles when disclosure of information was refused on the grounds that it was "personal." These were not insurmountable, and the MP's expenses case law established that public officials must expect greater scrutiny than private citizens. Piecing together disparate pieces of information from different organisations presented challenges familiar to both social science and journalism.

My interest is in exploring how FOIA might be used to go beyond collecting cross-organisational comparative data to contribute more in-depth analysis of the operation of secrecy (see also Greenberg, this volume). A recent discussion on institutional transparency in the UK notes differences between FOI and transparency programmes more generally. While the former are generally reactive, "depending upon pressure groups and the public to identify and request information, transparency seeks to be proactive" (Moore, 2018, p. 420). Drawing on the work of Simmel, Moore suggests visibility is not the same as intelligibility, and with increasing amounts of data available, the presumption is "that individuals are best placed to sift the information and decide its uses" (Moore, 2018, p. 427). Ultimately, she suggests,

> 21st-century transparency is more likely to calcify than reduce the gap between the public and the state. Refocusing the policy and academic debate to make this a thoroughgoing concern must be the chief task of a new sociology of institutional transparency.
>
> *(Moore, 2018, p. 428)*

There is potential for FOIA research to contribute both to visibility and intelligibility, with opportunities to learn from use of FOIA by journalists, to create innovative approaches to examining processes of decision-making beyond the gathering of information. This may be very different to many traditional models of social research, and there can be legitimate concerns about the impact on relationships between the researcher and the public authorities, but these are part of wider sets of relationships, including service users, employees and taxpayers. At a time when many western democracies are experiencing a loss of public trust in traditional institutions, research of this type could make an important contribution to public debate and understanding. Faced with multiple responsibilities, ethical duties are owed not only to the organisation being researched. As acknowledged in a framework for research ethics published by the British Economic and Social Research Council:

> Much social science research has a critical role to play in exploring and questioning social, cultural and economic structures and processes (for example relating to patterns of power and social inequality, and institutional dynamics and regimes that disadvantage some social groups over others, intentionally or not). Such research results may have a negative impact on some of the research participants/organisations.
>
> *(Economic & Social Research Council, 2012, p. 28)*

FOIA offers one route for gaining access to information in these circumstances. Writing in a North American context, Luscombe, Walby, and Lippert (2017) employ the term "feral lawyer" to describe citizen-researchers operating in the field of FOI, who are not lawyers but end up "bargaining, arguing, and appealing in ways familiar to formally trained legal practitioners" (Luscombe et al., 2017, p. 260). Yet just as Jenkinson (2017) warned, journalists not to be seduced into thinking this is journalism, it represents one element of a research process. The capacity of FOIA research to explore these matters will require not only knowledge of the law but also of the organisations involved. This can attune the researcher to the types of questions to be asked and of whom. My own research would not have been possible without the experiences and insights I gained when unsuccessfully attempting to raise questions within the NHS. "Insider" knowledge of this type may rarely be available directly, but opportunities for collaboration between researchers and others with such knowledge might be fruitful. Trade unions, whistle-blowers, campaign groups and others could be involved in developing a co-operative research focus and approach. FOIA research of this type may not produce quick results, but has a real potential to contribute to a strengthening of transparency and accountability.

## References

After Carillion: Public Sector Outsourcing and Contracting' Seventh Report of Session 2017–19, HC 748. 9 July 2018. London: House of Commons.

Appointments Commission. (2011). Review of the appointment of xxxx as chair of xxxx trust.

Becker, H. (1967). Whose side are we on? *Social Problems, 14*(3), 234–237.

Becker, H. 1998. *Tricks of the trade: How to think about your research while you're doing it.* Chicago: University of Chicago Press.

Breathnach, A. S., Riley, P. A., & Planche, T. D. (2011). Use of Freedom of Information Act to produce research on the cheap? *British Medical Journal, 343*.

Brignall, M. (2019). Interserve given 'public contracts worth £660m in run-up to collapse'. *The Guardian.* 18 March 2019.

British Sociological Association. (2017). Statement of ethical practice for the British Sociological Association. British Sociological Association.

Brown, K. J. (2009). Freedom of information as a research tool: Realising its potential. *The Howard Journal, 48*(1), 88–91.

Cabinet Office, FOI Statistics Bulletin. (2017). Retrieved from https://assets.publishing. service.gov.uk/government/uploads/system/uploads/attachment_data/file/704094/ foi-statistics-annual-2017-bulletin__1_.pdf

Campaign for Freedom of Information. (2009). Press notice, concern over new freedom of information exemptions.

Centre for Investigative Journalism. (2018). Tradecraft and ideas. Retrieved from https:// tcij.org/about-cij/history/

Chancellor of the Duchy of Lancaster. (1998). Your right to know. White Paper. London: The Stationery Office.

Colquhoun, A. (2010). The cost of freedom of information. Constitution Unit, University College London. Retrieved from www.ucl.ac.uk/constitution-unit/research/foi/ countries/cost-of-foi.pdf

Copple, N. (1964). *Depth reporting.* Englewood Cliffs, NJ: Prentice Hall.

Crossman, R. (1971). The real English disease. *New Statesman.* 24 September, p. 1.

Economic & Social Research Council. (2012). Framework for Research Ethics (FRE) 2010 updated September 2012. ESRC.

Fowler, A. J., Agha, R. A., Camm, C. F., & Littlejohns, P. (2013). The UK Freedom of Information Act (2000) in healthcare research: A systematic review. *BMJ Open,* e002967.

House of Lords. (2013). The pre-emption of Parliament. Select Committee on the Constitution 13th report of session 2012–13. London: The Stationery Office.

Information Commissioner. (2009). House of Commons Ministerial veto on disclosure of Cabinet minutes concerning military action against Iraq Information Commissioner's Report to Parliament. The Stationery Office HC622.

Information Commissioner. (2012). Ministerial veto on disclosure of the Department of Health's Transition Risk Register: Information Commissioner's Report to Parliament. The Stationery Office.

Information Commissioner (2019). The Information Commissioner's written evidence to the Public Administration and Constitutional Affairs Committee's inquiry into sourcing public services: Lessons learned from the collapse of Carillion. Information Commissioner's Office.

Johnson, D. & Hampson, E. (2015). Utilising the UK Freedom of Information Act 200 for crime record data: Indication of the strength of records management in day to day police business. *Records Management Journal, 25*(3), 248–268.

Keen, M. (2004). *Stalking sociologists: J Edgar Hoover's FBI surveillance of American sociology.* New Brunswick: Transaction Publishers.

Lashmar, P. (2013). From the Insight Team to Wikileaks, the continuing power of investigative journalism as a benchmark of quality news journalism. In P. J. Anderson, G. Ogola, & M. Williams (Eds.), *The future of quality news journalism.* New York: Routledge, 47–64.

Lassman, P., & Spiers, R. (Eds.). (1994). *Weber: Political writings.* Cambridge: Cambridge University Press.

Levine, M. (1980). Investigative reporting as a research method: An analysis of Bernstein and Woodward's All the President's Men. *American Psychologist, 35*(7), 626–638.

Lippert, R., Walby, K., & Wilkinson, B. (2015). Spins, stalls, and shutdowns: Pitfalls of qualitative policing and security research. *Qualitative Social Research, 17*(1).

Luscombe, A. (2018). Deception declassified: The social organisation of cover storying in a secret intelligence operation. *Sociology, 52*(2), 400–415.

Luscombe, A., Walby, K., & Lippert, R. K. (2017). Brokering access beyond the border and in the wild: Comparing freedom of information law and policy in Canada and the United States. *Law & Policy, 39*(3), 259–279.

Ministry of Justice. (2009). Exercise of the executive override in respect of the decision of the Information Commissioner FS50165372 as upheld by the decision of the Information Tribunal EA/2008/0024 & EA/2008/0029. Statement of Reasons.

Moore, S. (2018). Towards a sociology of institutional transparency: Openness, deception and the problem of public trust. *Sociology, 52*(2), 416–430.

Murray, C. (2013). Sport in care: Using freedom of information requests to elicit data about looked after children's involvement in physical activity. *British Journal of Social Work, 43*(7), 1347–1363.

Nader, L. (1969/1972). Up the anthropologist: Perspectives gained from studying up. In D. Hymes (Ed.), *Reinventing anthropology.* New York: Random House.

National Audit Office. (2018). *Investigation into the government's handling of the collapse of Carillion.* London: Cabinet Office.

Rosenbaum, M. (2009, June 10). Two Government plans FOI restrictions. *BBC Open Secrets.* Retrieved from www.bbc.co.uk/blogs/opensecrets/2009/06/government_plans_foi_restrictions.html

Ruppert, E. & Savage, M. (2011). Transactional politics. *The Sociological Review, 59*(2), 73–92.

Savage, A., & Hyde, R. (2014). Using freedom of information requests to facilitate research. *International Journal of Social Research Methodology, 17*(3), 303–317.

Sheaff, M. (2016). On the frontline: Challenging secrecy in the NHS through research. *Discover Society.*

Sheaff, M. (2017). Constructing accounts of organisational failure: Policy, power and concealment. *Critical Social Policy*, *37*(4), 520–539.

Sheaff, M. (2019). *Secrecy, privacy and accountability: Challenges for social research*. Cham, Switzerland: Palgrave Macmillan.

UK Supreme Court. (2015). Judgment: R (on the application of Evans) and another (Respondents) v Attorney General (Appellant). UKSC 21. On appeal from (2014) EWCA Civ 254.

Vaughan, D. (1996). *The challenger launch decision*. Chicago, IL: University of Chicago Press.

Vaughan, D. (1999). The dark sides of organizations: Mistake, misconduct and disaster. *Annual Review of Sociology*, *25*, 271–305.

Weaver, D. H., & McCombs, M. E. (1980). Journalism and social science: A new relationship? *The Public Opinion Quarterly*, *44*(4), 477–494.

Worthy, B. (2014). Freedom of information and the MPs' expenses crisis. In J. Van Heerde-Hudson (Ed.), *The political costs of the 2009 British MPs' expenses scandal*. London: Palgrave Macmillan.

# PART 2

# Freedom of Information and research design

Disciplinary applications

# 5

# FREEDOM OF INFORMATION AND AUSTRALIAN CRIMINOLOGY

*Ian Warren*

## Introduction

Despite aiming to promote increased transparency and accountability across all aspects of public administration, there have been only a few references to Freedom of Information (FOI) in Australia's three leading criminological journals since 1980.[1] Most are raised in the context of general arguments about other criminal justice issues, and there is a lack of empirical scrutiny of FOI processes as they apply directly to the criminological field. While this is clearly a crude measure of the extent FOI is used in Australian criminology, this chapter argues it is a symptom of a general lack of understanding of the potential value of FOI for research, which in turn compromises its use in applied justice research into a range of issues associated with public and private policing (Fairchild, 1994; McGovern & Lee, 2010), judicial administration, sentencing policy (Indermaur, 2012) and corrections.

This chapter also suggests the limited use of FOI in Australian criminological research is a legacy of the considerable discretionary power vested in public agencies to veto FOI requests (Lee, Taylor, & Willis, 2018, p. 8), or heavily redact any information that is authorised for disclosure (Sentas & Pandolfini, 2017, pp. 8–9). This reflects growing criticism about the relationships between Australian police and Federal and state information commissioners, who are sanctioned under FOI and related privacy laws to assist public agencies to develop suitable information management policies (Smee, 2019). The increasingly complex structures of Australian justice administration, which comprise a mix of exclusively government-provided services and public–private partnerships (see also Mackinnon, this volume), can also potentially shield viable claims for the release of information that is useful for criminological research and organisational accountability (see Davids & Hancock, 1998; English, 2005;

Freiberg, 1999). After describing the relevance of Australia's federal and state FOI processes to criminological research, this chapter reviews administrative appeals against adverse FOI decisions in the area of policing to highlight the complexity of this system. These case studies help to contextualise the complex relationship between FOI and contemporary justice administration, and further explain why these procedures are likely to be considered of limited value in Australian criminological research (Lidberg, 2016, p. 76).

## FOI and Australian criminology

FOI is part of a governmental rationality aiming to promote openness and transparency in public administration (Luscombe, Walby, & Lippert, 2017). When first introduced in 1966, Australia's national FOI regime sought to "overturn a deeply entrenched tradition of government secrecy" that characterised public administrative law since federation in 1901 (Paterson, 2015, p. 3). The new generation of FOI reforms, generally referred to as Information Access 2.0, establishes a presumption of disclosure in line with the expansive role of new technologies in contemporary e-government (Lidberg, 2015; Paterson, 2015). In other words, government and bureaucratic information should be publicly available unless an agency can justify non-disclosure under one of many exceptions identified in FOI legislation.

However, in the diverse fields of criminal justice administration, increased transparency often contradicts organisational demands to preserve secrecy and confidentiality. This is particularly evident in complex criminal investigations (Australian Law Reform Commission, 2009), or the areas of national security (Paterson, 2018) and commercial secrecy requirements that are commonly associated with prison privatisation (Freiberg, 1997; Harding, 2018). These countervailing tensions intersect with several related legal areas, including information privacy law (Batskos, 2015a, 2015b), criminal record screening in many government and private employment contexts (Paterson, 2011), and both federal and state human rights legislation (*Minogue v. Dougherty; Minogue v. Trotter*, 2017).

Historically, the number of FOI requests lodged by Australian citizens, businesses and media organisations has been low compared with other nations (Hazell, 1989). This appears to have had potential flow-on effects into the academic sector, where "preventing abuse of government powers and protecting individual privacy and confidentiality by limiting access to and use of … [governmental] data" has produced a complex "regulatory regime [that] inhibits access for researchers" (Adams & Allen, 2014, p. 11). This observation is particularly salient for criminologists, given that the inherent complexities of navigating the highly technical administrative character of the FOI system (Luscombe et al., 2017) can also reinforce the power of justice organisations to use their discretionary powers to deny access to information. Public interest considerations can be formally invoked to protect investigative processes (Australian Law Reform Commission, 2009, p. 75), the identities of suspects, informants, witnesses or victims (Paterson, 2015, p. 487; *Scholes,* 1996), or shield contentious crime reduction strategies from external review (Sentas & Pandolfini, 2017). In other words, the very protections conferred under the law to enable individual privacy and the disclosure or non-disclosure of public sector information in the public interest, however defined (*Clark v. Australian Federal Police*, 2005; McDonagh & Paterson, 2017), can become key mechanisms for blocking FOI claims for viable criminological research purposes. When viewed alongside more stringent university ethics procedures that can add further constraints to the use of government information despite formal agency approval (Walby & Luscombe, 2018), and which often work in conjunction with confidentiality protocols established by justice agencies themselves (Israel, 2004), these developments can have a chilling effect on Australian criminological research more generally (Brown, 2011).

Australian criminology could benefit from more guidance on how best to employ FOI requests alongside other established research procedures. Significantly, generalist doctrinal texts examining FOI in Australia (Paterson, 2015) tend to overlook the nuances of the institutional structures, information flows and particularised ethical requirements in justice and allied fields that impact the broad range of issues examined in criminological research. These nuances offer an important starting point for a more direct criminological engagement with, and critique of, FOI processes in their own right. The next section provides a useful starting point for the critical examination of these issues by outlining Federal and state FOI provisions relevant to the criminal justice sector.

## Relevant FOI provisions

Australian Federal and state public sector organisations are under a positive obligation to publish most forms of information relevant to their activities (see generally Paterson, 2015), which usually appears in publicly released annual reports (for example, see Victoria State Government, 2018). FOI supplements these general reporting requirements by conferring a universal legal right on citizens to access to government documents and have identifiable errors corrected. Applications are usually lodged with a FOI division of the relevant agency (see, for example, Victoria Police, 2018), and individual requests are dealt with by the agency itself, or acting on the advice of a dedicated information commissioner in each jurisdiction (*Freedom of Information Act (Commonwealth)*, 1982, s. 8E; *Freedom of Information Act (Victoria)*, 1982, s. 6I). The Administrative Appeal Tribunal (AAT) can review an adverse decision by a Federal justice agency, while the Victorian Civil and Administrative Tribunal (VCAT) and equivalent bodies hear appeals under state FOI laws.

A presumption of disclosure applies to a variety of government records, regardless of their form as written or electronic text material, maps, plans, photographs, or audio and visual recordings (Paterson, 2015, pp. 101–102). Ultimately, the material's content determines whether it should be fully disclosed, or produced on a qualified basis with exempt information redacted. These issues are decided on a case-by-case basis.

Documents containing information that discloses the business affairs or identities of third parties, that can affect formal legal proceedings or accountability processes, or that might have an adverse impact on "the proper and efficient conduct of an agency's operations," are generally exempt from disclosure (see Paterson, 2015, p. 432 and generally at pp. 321–458). Federal and Victorian FOI laws allow justice agencies to prevent disclosure of material that might reveal official "methods or procedures for preventing, detecting, investigating or dealing with matters arising out of breaches or evasions of the law," or confidential communications between different state, Federal and even international law enforcement agencies (*Freedom of Information Act (Commonwealth)* s. 37(2)(b); *Freedom of Information Act (Victoria)* s. 31(1); *Rees v. Australian Federal Police*, 1999). Information that reveals the "names, addresses, dates of birth and business connections … [and associate] those details with possible criminal investigations," or which contains the personal information of third parties, such as passport details, is also exempt from disclosure (*Clark v. Australian Federal Police*, 2005, para 30). However, documents dealing with alleged breaches of the law by police investigators, or other government and regulatory agencies, are not classified as exempt documents if their disclosure is considered to be in the public interest (*Freedom of Information Act (Commonwealth)* s. 37(2)(b); *Freedom of Information Act (Victoria)* s. 31(2)). Ultimately, the burden is on the public authority to provide a compelling justification for non-disclosure, although it is generally up to individual citizen to pursue these issues through the formal administrative process.

Administrative appeals challenging a justice agency's FOI determination reveal the types of documents commonly considered to warrant public disclosure. For example, the applicant in *Re Wallace v. Australian Federal Police* (2004) sought disclosure of 127 documents in the possession of the Australian Federal Police (AFP) to determine whether or not to plead guilty to charges relating to his alleged involvement in a heroin trafficking operation from Thailand. After inspecting each document, the AAT upheld most exemptions as determined by the AFP, but allowed Wallace access to his personality profile, as well as various excerpts of diary entries, letters, emails and audio recordings that were linked to the warrant applications and several other aspects of the investigative process, including the investigation into the activities of co-conspirators who were convicted in Australia. Diplomatic communications with the British Embassy in Bangkok and Thai police were also released.

*XYZ v. Victoria Police* (2010) involved a claim by a former police officer for a wide range of documents compiled during an internal investigation into irregular gambling activities that raised suspicions of his involvement in corrupt and fraudulent behaviour. The applicant was never criminally charged, but sought to use the FOI process to achieve "total exoneration" and ""expose" the "unlawful" and "improper" ESD (Ethical Standards Division) investigation" (*XYZ v. Victoria Police*, 2010, para 3). This case itemises various types of personal information that were authorised on appeal for full or partial disclosure, including search warrants, log books, documents provided to investigators from other public and regulatory agencies, and communications with the Office for Public Prosecutions. When viewed holistically, the information revealed "some breaches of the law and procedure were committed in the commencement of and during the ESD investigation" (*XYZ v. Victoria Police*, 2010, para 584; see also *Freedom of Information Act (Victoria)* s. 31(2)). However, VCAT also noted the need to balance this issue against the public interest in preserving the confidentiality of material provided to ESD by third parties (McDonagh & Paterson, 2017), including other law enforcement agencies and informants. This point is of significance as:

> ... the human right to freedom of expression incorporates a positive right to obtain access to government-held documents ... [but this] is not an absolute right and can be subject to objective, proportionate and reasonable limitations ... Specifically, the public interest ... must be exercised consistently with this human right.
>
> *(XYZ v. Victoria Police, 2010, para 583)*

This review is a snapshot of the vast number of Australian administrative appeals against FOI decisions by Australian Federal and state police agencies involving material that is not generally on the public record collected for a formal investigative or intelligence purpose. These cases raise concern about the nature of the "gatekeeping" or "veto" functions exercised by FOI officers in police organisations, which shapes a certain vision of the public interest for law enforcement purposes, either independently from, or with the direct sanction of, publicly appointed information commissioners (Smee, 2019) and other external stakeholders, including academic criminologists. This is particularly salient in cases involving the use of new technologies or the implementation of crime prevention policies, where a decision not to release data collected from Automatic Number Plate Recognition systems (Paterson, 2018; Warren, Lippert, Walby, & Palmer, 2013), body-worn cameras (Lee et al., 2018) or crime prevention programmes that disproportionately target minority populations (Sentas & Pandolfini, 2017) can be justified in the public interest, yet at the same time potentially shield highly problematic police practices from independent scrutiny. Similarly, as the next example indicates, a police decision to grant a media organisation's FOI request for a photograph of a convicted violent offender can also be justified in the public interest, despite compelling arguments suggesting this decision served "no useful *Police purpose*" other than "*vilification and daemonization*" of the applicant (*Smith v. Victoria Police (General)*, 2005, para 8, emphasis in original).

## Smith v. Victoria Police (General) *(2005)*

In *Smith v. Victoria Police (General)* (2005), VCAT upheld a decision by the Victoria Police FOI officer to grant a media organisation's request for the applicant's mugshot, without his authorisation. While VCAT acknowledged the decision potentially contravened Victoria's Information Privacy Principles (IPPs) and internal police directives aimed at preventing the disclosure of personally identifying information except to execute accepted law enforcement "functions or activities," including unspecified "community policing functions" (*Information Privacy Act (Victoria)*, 2000, s. 13,[2] cited in *Smith v. Victoria Police (General)*, 2005, para 19), it denied Smith's claim for $100,000 damages and a formal order admonishing Victoria Police and directing it to develop a more informed policy for the distribution of mugshots for publication (*Smith v. Victoria Police (General)*, 2005, para 48).

At the time of the case, Smith was serving a minimum of seven years imprisonment for a series of violent sexual offences committed against elderly women in an outer Melbourne suburb where he also lived. After discovering his image was published by a local newspaper circulated free-of-charge to households in the area (*Smith v. Victoria Police (General)*, 2005, para 41), he lodged a complaint with the Office of the Victorian Information Commissioner (OVIC), arguing this was an "unreasonable disclosure of information relating to the personal affairs of any person (including a deceased person)" that contravened Victoria's IPPs and Victoria Police policies governing personally identifiable information about third parties (*Freedom of Information Act*, 1982, s. 33, cited in *Smith v. Victoria Police (General)*, 2005, paras 29 and 45). Smith claimed the decision had no viable community policing purpose, as he had already voluntarily handed himself in, confessed and had been convicted. He also emphasised publication of the image would have ongoing repercussions "by *linking his physical appearance to the details of the offences* of [sic] which he was convicted" (*Smith v. Victoria Police (General)*, 2005, para 9, emphasis in original), as he "*could now be identified and targeted because of the real possibility for persons to seek their own retribution … [and his] family and associates could also be placed at risk*" (*Smith v. Victoria Police (General)*, 2005, para 47). These claims were supported by a representative of the OVIC, who testified that neither the FOI nor information privacy legislation provided "a blanket exemption for the Police in relation to its law enforcement … or community policing functions" (*Smith v. Victoria Police (General)*, 2005, para 53). In other words, the Victoria Police FOI officer should have given greater weight to the fact that Smith's:

> recorded image was not a matter of public record by virtue of his appearance in open court … [and] was compulsorily provided … as a result of his being charged with a criminal offence.
> (Smith v. Victoria Police (General), 2005, *para 53 emphasis in original*)

Despite these concerns, VCAT supported police arguments that releasing the image was a legitimate exercise of its discretionary authority made in the overall public interest (*Smith v. Victoria Police (General)*, 2005, paras 49–50). While expressing some concern over the practice of releasing mugshots to the media for publication with only the consent of the informant or victim, rather than the subject, VCAT endorsed a very broad notion of public interest that supported an equally imprecise notion of community policing that was presented by the Victoria Police FOI officer. This suggested:

... release of the photograph made people feel safer because they knew the person had been removed from the community and paid the penalty, and publication of a photograph removed any doubt that anyone else committed the offence.

(Smith v. Victoria Police (General), 2005, *para 36)*

In other words, VCAT endorsed non-compliance with Victoria's privacy principles in this case largely based on the seriousness of the offences, and the ill-proven idea that "publicizing the workings of the criminal justice system" in this way "would indicate that justice was done, and ... provide a means of enabling members of the public to feel safer" (*Smith v. Victoria Police (General)*, 2005, para 83). While recognising potential harm to Smith and others who might be affected by this practice in the future, and the lack of reasonable grounds police had for violating the IPPs, there was ultimately little VCAT could do in this case given the image had already been released and published.

## Discussion

Invariably, FOI is used way more than the records of Australian criminological journals tend to reveal. However, realities of contemporary Australian Federal and state justice research suggest a certain degree of trust is arguably more conducive to revealing confidential issues than recourse to the FOI process (Israel, 2004). This is particularly salient for research aimed at questioning formal police policies, given FOI requests for access to visual images or crime data can be readily denied on public interest or privacy grounds. As *Smith* (2005) demonstrates, even discernible individual harms from public disclosure can be validated through the administrative appeals process if police decisions fall loosely within general terminology such as "community policing," "public interest" or "privacy." Thus, the very structure of Australia's Federal and state FOI systems confers considerable discretion on the agencies to determine what these terms mean and how they are enforced, despite the existence of various formal administrative review mechanisms.

The cases described in this chapter all involve claims by individuals for information that is directly relevant to a personal legal claim, or potential harm emanating from a third party's FOI request. Despite the presumption of free and open access to governmental and bureaucratic information under the Information Access 2.0 logic, many countervailing aspects of police practice contradict this aspiration. In a related vein, much research also needs to be done on the role of FOI in the specific contexts of Australian corrections. As with many other areas of Australian public service delivery that are considered to lack adequate public access or accountability structures (English, 2005), prison privatisation generates many new governmentalities of information production (Brady & Lippert, 2016; Sokhi-Bulley, 2011) that are commonly shielded or immunised from conventional FOI processes by legislatively sanctioned commercial and contractual secrecy requirements (Freiberg, 1997; Harding, 2018). Unlike Canada, where FOI requests reveal much about corporate security practices in the sphere of municipal governance (Lippert & Walby, 2014; Walby, Luscombe, & Lippert, 2014), information disclosure in these contexts remains largely untested in Australia. If recent experience in the field of prison administration is an appropriate gauge, legislative and regulatory decisions to open private contracts to greater public scrutiny is a more meaningful approach to information dissemination, public accountability and institutional reform (Carlton & Russell, 2018; Harding, 2018; Kirby, 2000) than the highly individualised FOI structure. However, this approach also has potential costs, as governments can lose the perceived benefits from market competition by automatically renewing service provision contracts (Department of Justice and Regulation and Department of Treasury and Finance (Victoria), 2016), while the practices of information non-disclosure simply evolve from the current FOI structure into something different, yet equivalent.

Two unanswered issues about FOI in Australia remain open for further discussion. The first involves the need for more empirical research into the FOI process that is specific to each discrete justice administration context. The second involves determining with greater empirical precision how the Australian criminological community views and invokes FOI. In both respects, we can take much guidance from the work of Canadian scholars who are leading the way on these issues (Luscombe et al., 2017).

## Notes

1 The search "freedom of information" was conducted in the *The International Journal of Crime, Justice and Social Democracy*, which produced three hits between 2012 and January 2019 (one of which was a Canadian study), the *Australian and New Zealand Journal of Criminology* produced fifteen hits dating back to 1980, which includes two book reviews, one two-page editorial introductions and two studies from Canada, and *Current Issues in Criminal Justice* produced one in 1997 and two in 1999.
2 This legislation was repealed by s. 126 of the *Privacy and Data Protection Act (Victoria)*, 2014.

## References

Adams, C., & Allen, J. (2014). Data custodians and decision-making: A right of access to government-held databases for research? *Australian Institute of Administrative Law (AIAL) Forum, 76*, 11–19.

Australian Law Reform Commission. (2009). *Secrecy laws and open government in Australia: Report no. 112*. Canberra ACT: Australian Government/Australian Law Reform Commission.

Batskos, M. (2015a). Balancing the treatment of 'personal information' under FOI and privacy laws: A comparative Australian analysis part 1. *Australian Institute of Administrative Law (AIAL) Forum, 80*, 28–53.

Batskos, M. (2015b). Balancing the treatment of 'personal information' under FOI and privacy laws: A comparative Australian analysis part 2. *Australian Institute of Administrative Law (AIAL) Forum, 81*, 74–91.

Brady, M., & Lippert, R. K. (Eds.). (2016). *Governing practices: Neoliberalism, governmentality and the ethnographic imaginary.* Toronto: University of Toronto Press.

Brown, D. (2012). The global financial crisis: Neo-liberalism, social democracy, and criminology. In M. Bosworth, & C. Hoyle (Eds.), *What is criminology* (pp. 76–94). Oxford, UK: Oxford University Press.

Carlton, B., & Russell, E. (2018). *Resisting carceral violence: Women's imprisonment and the politics of abolition.* Cham: Palgrave Macmillan.

Davids, C., & Hancock, L. (1998). Policing, accountability and citizenship in the market state. *The Australian and New Zealand Journal of Criminology, 31*(1), 38–68.

Department of Justice and Regulation and Department of Treasury and Finance (Victoria) 2016. *Partnerships Victoria, Port Phillip prison contract extension, project summary.* Department of Justice and Community Safety, Melbourne, VIC. June. Retrieved from www.dtf.vic.gov.au/sites/default/files/2018-01/Partnerships-Victoria-Project-Summary-Port-Phillip-Prison-Contract-Extension.pdf.

English, L. M. (2005). Using public-private partnerships to deliver social infrastructure: The Australian experience. In G. Hodge, & C. Greeve (Eds.), *The challenge of public-private partnerships: Learning from international experience* (pp. 290–331). Cheltenham, UK: Edward Elgar.

Fairchild, P. (1994). The emerging police complex: Hoogenboom and Australian interagency cooperation. *The Australian and New Zealand Journal of Criminology, 27*(2), 111–132.

Freiberg, A. (1999). Commercial confidentiality and public accountability for the provision of correctional services. *Current Issues in Criminal Justice, 11*(2), 119–134.

Freiberg, A. (1997). Commercial confidentiality, criminal justice and the public interest. *Current Issues in Criminal Justice, 9*(2), 125–152.

Harding, R. (2018). *Private prisons and public accountability.* London, UK: Routledge.

Hazell, R. (1989). Freedom of information in Australia, Canada and New Zealand. *Public Administration, 67*(2), 189–210.

Indermaur, D. (2012). Engaging the public in the development of sentencing policy. *International Journal of Crime, Justice and Social Democracy, 1*(1), 27–37.

Israel, M. (2004). Strictly confidential: Integrity and the disclosure of criminological and socio-legal research. *British Journal of Criminology, 44*(5), 715–740.

Kirby, P. (Chair). 2000. *Independent investigation into the management and operations of Victoria's private prisons*, Parts I-II and appendices, Department of Justice and Community Safety, Melbourne, Vic, October. Retrieved from www.corrections.vic.gov.au/utility/publications+manuals+and+statistics/independent+investigation+management+victorias+private+prisons+kirby+report. Accessed 18 Jan 2019.

Lee, M., Taylor, E., & Willis, M. (2018). Being held to account: Detainees' perceptions of police body-worn cameras. *The Australian and New Zealand Journal of Criminology.* Online first.

Lidberg, J. (2016). Information access evolution. Assessing freedom of information in Australia. *Australian Journalism Review, 38*(1), 73–82.

Lidberg, J. (2015). Next generation freedom of information – from 'pull' to 'push': A comparative study. *Australian Journalism Review, 37*(1), 81–90.

Lippert, R. K., & Walby, K. (2014). Municipal corporate security, legal knowledges, and the urban problem space. *Law & Social Inquiry, 39*(3), 720–739.

Luscombe, A., Walby, K., & Lippert, R. (2017). Brokering access beyond the border and in the wild: Comparing freedom of information law and policy in Canada and the United States. *Law & Policy, 35*(3), 259–279.

McDonagh, M., & Paterson, M. (2017). FOI in the balance: The function and role of the public interest test. *Public Law, 2017*(1), 81–98.

McGovern, A., & Lee, M. (2010). 'Cop[ying] it sweet': Police media units and the making of news. *The Australian and New Zealand Journal of Criminology, 43*(3), 444–464.

Paterson, M. (2018). The public privacy conundrum – anonymity and the law in an era of mass surveillance. In J. Lidberg, & D. Muller (Eds.), *In the name of security – Secrecy, surveillance and journalism* (pp. 15–32). London, UK: Anthem Press.

Paterson, M. (2015). *Freedom of information and privacy in Australia: Information access 2.0* (2nd ed.). Chatswood, NSW: LexisNexis Butterworths.

Paterson, M. (2011). Criminal records, spent convictions and privacy: A trans-tasman comparison. *New Zealand Law Review, 1*, 69–89.

Sentas, V., & Pandolfini, C. (2017). *Policing young people in NSW: A study of the suspect targeting management plan*. Sydney, Australia: Youth Justice Coalition NSW.

Smee, B. (2019). Queensland FOI watchdog and police united to block citizens from accessing own data. *The Guardian*. Retrieved from www.theguardian.com/australia-news/2019/jan/17/queensland-foi-watchdog-and-police-united-to-block-citizens-from-accessing-own-data.

Sokhi-Bulley, B. (2011). Government(ality) by experts: Human rights as governance. *Law and Critique, 22*(3), 251–271.

Victoria Police. (2018). Our services: Freedom of information. *Victoria Police Website*. Retrieved from www.police.vic.gov.au/content.asp?Document_ID=669.

Victoria State Government. (2018). *Department of justice and regulation annual report 2017–18*. Victorian Government, Melbourne. Retrieved from www.justice.vic.gov.au/annual-reports.

Walby, K., Luscombe, A., & Lippert, R. K. (2014). Expertise and the professionalisation of municipal corporate security in Canadian cities. In K. Walby, & R. K. Lippert (Eds.), *Corporate security in the 21st century: Theory and practice in international perspective* (pp. 116–133). London, UK: Palgrave Macmillan.

Walby, K., & Luscombe, A. (2018). Ethics review and freedom of information requests in qualitative research. *Research Ethics, 14*(4), 1–15.

Warren, I., Lippert, R., Walby, K., & Palmer, D. (2013). When the profile becomes the population: Examining privacy governance and road traffic surveillance in Canada and Australia. *Current Issues in Criminal Justice, 25*(2), 565–584.

## Legislation

*Freedom of Information Act (Commonwealth)* 1982.
*Freedom of Information Act (Victoria)* 1982.
*Information Privacy Act (Victoria)* 2000.
*Privacy and Data Protection Act (Victoria)* 2014.

## Legal Cases

*Clark v. Australian Federal Police* [2005] AATA 632.
*Minogue v. Dougherty; Monogue v. Trotter* [2017] VSC 724.

*Re Rees v. Australian Federal Police* [1999] AATA 252.
*Re Wallace v. Australian Federal Police* [2004] AATA 845.
*Scholes v. Australian Federal Police* [1996] AATA 347.
*Smith v. Victoria Police (General) and Victorian Privacy Commissioner* [2005] VCAT 654.

# 6

# ACCESSING INFORMATION IN A NASCENT TECHNOLOGY INDUSTRY

## Tracing Canadian drone stakeholders and negotiating access

*Ciara Bracken-Roche*

## Introduction

My research into drone technologies began with a project for the Office of the Privacy Commissioner of Canada (OPC) in 2013, during which I had the opportunity to coordinate and lead a project investigating drones as technologies of surveillance, and the privacy and social implications of these technologies within Canada (see Bracken-Roche et al., 2014). The use of drones for civil and commercial applications in Canada started to expand rapidly in 2013 and existing regulations failed to address many privacy and surveillance concerns introduced with the technologies (OPC, 2013). With the growth of the market, legislation was struggling to adapt, and many civil liberties and privacy advocates – such as the British Columbia Civil Liberties Association (BCCLA) and the Office of the Privacy Commissioner of Canada – began to express concerns with the adoption of these technologies by private and public agencies (Bracken-Roche et al., 2014; Gersher, 2013; Molnar & Parsons, 2013). I became aware, throughout this research, of the ways in which government and industry were cooperating to develop new regulations to govern the civil and commercial use of drones (see Bracken-Roche et al., 2014; Gersher, 2013). A history of inter-agency cooperation around drones in military and policing activities as well as between public and private partners began to reveal itself as I started my own project (see Department of National Defence, A-2005-00283, A-2013-01491). It was this increasing connectedness of public and private agencies that made it clear to me that I needed to investigate who, in fact, was shaping drone development and governance. While the OPC project was incredibly useful in shaping my own research, it was perhaps even more helpful in the way that it introduced me to new research methods.

During the preliminary stage of data collection for this project, I became aware of Access to Information (ATI) and Freedom of Information (FOI) requests as a method, as a way of gaining access to *dirty data*, that is, "information which is kept secret and whose revelation would be discrediting" (Marx, 1984). The outcomes of requests obtained by other researchers and our project team were illustrative of the asymmetric, technocratic governance of drone technologies in Canada (Bracken-Roche, 2016), and pointed me towards the dynamics emerging between public and private organisations in this sector. The use of ATI became an iterative part of my research methodology where initial findings informed interviews, and where interview findings led to further ATI requests that highlighted particular trends. ATI and FOI data lend themselves well to "studying up" – the empirical study of elites (Dafnos, 2012; Walby & Luscombe, 2018) – and were foundational in shaping my research project and informing the other methods that I would employ to study drone stakeholder networks. The data obtained in the early stages of my research highlighted the workings of authority and governance that were shaping drone deployment, policy and technology, and thus, the need to study up. However, the secret nature of these groups resulted in difficulties obtaining full ATI data and so rapport building with respondents was integral for further data collection and will be discussed later in the chapter.

I begin this chapter with a discussion of the literature on access in the fields of policing, security and surveillance in Canada, against which I situate my analysis of Canadian drone networks. Next, I turn to a discussion of the methods used to acquire data and contextualise their relevance in situating the technologies and demonstrating the evolution of a surveillance-industrial complex. Here, I build on the findings from ATI documents that revealed trends that corresponded with or further elucidated interview data. And lastly I discuss the research challenges that emerge when trying to gather data in a small, emerging technological industry as ATI requests can be quite political and must be balanced against the ability to gain access through interviews. These issues can be amplified further when a researcher is "studying up" (Dafnos, 2012; Mukherjee, 2017) due to various power dynamics. These discussions explore the challenges faced by researchers when employing different methodological tools and the need to weigh up various methods when engaging with politically charged research. I conclude the chapter with some final remarks on my own research experience and the need for further discussion on research methods in this area.

## Negotiating access and situating technologies

Negotiating access can be difficult where questions of policing, security and surveillance are being researched, whether the researcher wants to discuss discourses, practices or technologies (see Luscombe, Walby, & Lippert, 2017; Rigakos & Worth, 2011). The difficulties in gaining research access can, in part, be explained by cultures of secrecy that permeate policing and security practices in Canada (Forcese & Roach, 2015; French, 2007; Monaghan & Molnar, 2016) and by the liquidity of the public–private relationships that characterise these practices (O'Reilly, 2010). Across the social sciences, there are many conceptualisations of the intersections between public and private entities in and across states; a few are listed here: the implications of the *state–corporate nexus* are discussed in the context of transnational policing (O'Reilly, 2010); the *mobius ribbon of security* describes the convergence of international and internal security interests by the state with private corporations (Bigo, 2002); and the existence of *public–private policing* networks have been identified from the mid-1990s onwards (Bayley & Shearing, 1996). Further work has been done to create research typologies, such as the work done on corporate security by Lippert, Walby, and Steckle (2013), which add to the methodological rigour in this growing area of work on public–private partnerships. The challenges of data collection, and the ability to negotiate access to information, are compounded by these layered, multi-modal networks that span public–private divides (O'Reilly, 2010).

Therefore, while it might be difficult to know where requests should be directed, ATI and FOI legislation can often act as a valuable tool for researchers. While these mechanisms allow individuals to request information from municipal, provincial and federal levels of government, researchers still face a number of challenges using these tools as institutions can "stymie critical inquiry," where the "balance of access versus secrecy," tips "towards the latter, under the ever-present assumption that secrecy equals security" (Rigakos & Worth, 2011, p. 645). Huey (2009) is hopeful in her assessment of ATI as tools of counter-surveillance and resistance in policing and security research. She reflects on her own research with political advocacy groups to show how ATI helps counteract political power asymmetries that are expressed through surveillance (Huey, Walby, & Doyle, 2006; Monahan, 2006). The value of ATI and FOI requests is becoming increasingly clear in research emerging in the areas of Canadian security studies and critical surveillance research, especially for empirically driven work. The data collected as a result of such requests can be used to inform the direction of a project generally, and to direct or supplement other research methods such as interviews or surveys (Rigakos & Worth, 2011; Walby & Larsen, 2011). ATI data can also act as an insightful alternative to official documents and publications, or crafted responses to researcher's requests in its ability to showcase backstage practices (Monaghan & Walby, 2012; Rigakos & Worth, 2011; Walby & Larsen, 2011).

In my own research, I used Hayes' (2012) notion of the surveillance–industrial complex to discuss the proliferation of drones in Canada which demonstrated a revolving door where the key stakeholders developing, deploying and regulating the technologies move back and forth between roles in government, industry and the military, despite conflicting interests (see Bracken-Roche, 2016, 2018; Gersher, 2013). This echoes much of the existing research on public–private partnerships in the realms of policing and security as discussed above. In Hayes' (2012) conceptualisation, the revolving door speaks to the way stakeholders from different groups move seamlessly from one to another, circulating within a privileged space of power. My research on drones found this pattern primarily with stakeholders moving from government and military agencies to private industry, and sometimes back to government, taking different positions that influenced the development and regulation of drone technologies and policy (Bracken-Roche, 2018). Often the military experience of stakeholders preceded their positions in government and industry, but the movement between these various private and public agencies tended to occur frequently across stakeholders. Through interviews and documents obtained using ATI requests, it became clear that technical expertise was the means by which stakeholders perpetuated a form of technocratic governance around drones (Bracken-Roche, 2016, 2018; Gersher, 2014).

From the way the drone is framed within the context of trade shows (Jackman, 2016) to the broader flows of money that shape the drone market (Hayes, Jones, & Töpfer, 2014), the drone falls into the surveillance–industrial complex by virtue of its technological capabilities, as well as the ways Canadian stakeholders shaping the technologies move seamlessly from military to industry to policy roles and back again (Bracken-Roche, 2016; Gersher, 2013). Wall (2013) argues that while drones are used abroad to pacify foreign others, they are also used domestically to pacify others in the name of security. He states that the drone market is not limited to foreign war zones but is being repurposed as a "domestic security technolog(y)" because the US security state and corresponding security industries see drone technologies as a "dual-use technology" that can be readily deployed across a number of spatial contexts (Wall, 2013, p. 33). This argument is not unique to drones as it also applies to a number of surveillance technologies that are used both domestically and abroad.

The drone space in Canada further highlights the fusion of civilian and military interests globally and within states, "made possible by the 'complementarities' of government and corporate 'needs'" (Ball & Snider, 2013). This space creates a revolving door between industry and government, establishing partnerships at the domestic and international level, that can lead to corporate interests and earnings being prioritised over concern for the public good (Hayes, 2012). There is also a direct consequence of outsourcing the so-called "dual use" civilian and military surveillance tools. Each new surveillance technology is seen as a tool for gathering, transmitting and analyzing data. In responding to risks and threats, surveillance technologies are used to assess situations in both civilian and military scenarios. These developments are associated with new innovations in surveillance technologies, which have become at once cheaper and more sophisticated. Theorists (Feenberg, 2002; Winner, 1980) refute that rationality and expertise are valid reasons for excluding publics and secondary stakeholders from the development of policy and regulations around new technologies.

Accessing existing ATI data collection from other research projects and researchers was invaluable to shaping my project in terms of how significant certain stakeholders were in terms of the political economy of the drone space as well as policy shaping. And being aware of the resistance by government agencies to fulfil ATI and FOI requests on drone technologies was useful in pushing me to broker access to stakeholders by way of other qualitative methods. More significantly, the reluctance of agencies to share information of these seemingly benign technologies and processes made it clear that I needed to pursue the research. The ATI information is a significant piece of the puzzle because the relationships that go on within and between government agencies, as well as with the publics they are trying to govern, are all textually mediated (Smith, 1999, 2005). As opposed to publicly available texts which are seen to represent the frontstage of government – carefully crafted, official discourse – ATI texts reveal more about the backstage of government (Walby & Larsen, 2011). This is significant because even if connections between public and private agencies are known, ATI data can elucidate the extent of interconnectedness. In my own research, the use of ATI in conjunction with other methods allowed me to situate the evolution of the drone as a technology, as well as trace the history of key stakeholders and groups developing and regulating the technologies.

In this sense, I became part of my research because of the iterative nature of negotiating the field and going back and forth from the field with different research methods (see a similar discussion by Mackinnon – this volume; Law, 2004). However, as will be discussed later in the chapter, my use of ATI disclosures and interview data both demonstrated that technical expertise was used to determine who could participate in the regulatory working groups.

## The back and forth: reflective methods

Many key findings that shaped my research were obtained through ATI data. However, based on the data obtained, it became clear that the censorship of documents on the topic of drones was likely and therefore other methods would be required to compliment the ATI findings. This phenomenon is not uncommon in using ATI and FOI (Galison, 2004). And because documents are often redacted, use of ATIs as the only form of data collection is not recommended (Monaghan, 2015). Luscombe et al. (2017) argue that inexperienced users of ATI are unlikely to acquire the information they are looking for due to their high degree of trust in the system and in the "presumed legal expertise of state bureaucrats" (p. 261). Monaghan (2015) and Larsen and Walby (2012) list a number of common issues that arise around ATIs including amberlighting (the tagging of a request or requestor as politically contentious), red filing (where a request is stalled by a Minister or the Prime Minister's Office), time delays and exorbitant costs, lack of depth in the data disclosed and insufficient documentation being passed on to the requester, and redaction. Learning how to broker access and practice "feral law" as per Luscombe et al. (2017) allows researchers to negotiate access effectively and to counter and engage with the bureaucratic and oversimplified FOI process presented by government agencies. Following "textual trails" allows us to better trace the relationships within and between government agencies, as well as between public organisations and private agencies (Walby & Larsen, 2011). Linking up information from ATI data with interviews allowed me to see the extent of the private–public interconnectedness with key events and individuals in the drone industry.

When attempting to access information using ATI and FOI processes, a formal access request for information can be made online by selecting the appropriate department and submitting your query (and paying the fee), or an informal request for access to a previously requested/released data can be made (Government of Canada, 2016). Each type of request has pros and cons, however. Formal requests can be shaped to the needs of a researcher; but this often increases the chance of delays and heavy redactions if the request is topical instead of more generic. An informal request, on the other hand, is beneficial as the documents are usually released with a quicker turnaround and at no cost although they may still have redactions and might not be relevant to the researcher's needs (Vallance-Jones, 2014). When I started my research, I was unaware of the informal request process so I submitted six formal ATI requests to Transport Canada and Innovation, Science and Economic Development Canada which was built on the previously obtained ATI data from DND and on the public reports made available by Transport Canada (c). This practice was not helpful for me initially as it was met with the usual issues surrounding formal ATIs, including time delays and high fees, as well as receiving almost entirely redacted sets of documents when I finally received the data. After learning about informal requests, I acquired seven more ATIs.

Altogether, the thirteen ATIs that I obtained came from the following federal agencies: Transport Canada, the Department of National Defence, Public Safety Canada, the Office of the Privacy Commissioner of Canada, and Innovation, Science and Economic Development Canada. A majority of the ATI requests were sent to Transport Canada as this agency plays a key role in regulating and authorising the operation of drones for civil operations here in Canada. Moreover, Transport Canada has a close relationship with drone industry stakeholders because of their role in the UAV Regulatory Working Group. Therefore, I wanted to target this agency for disclosures in order to see if ATI practices could give me any further insight into the role commercial actors play in the policy process around drones. Innovation, Science and Economic Development Canada (formerly Industry Canada) was included because of the various funding programmes it offers for commercial innovation as well as the fact that it regulates radio spectrum frequencies on which many drones operate. I also obtained informal requests from Public Safety Canada. I did not request information from the Canadian Border Services Agency or the RCMP as a number of colleagues informed me that they were unlikely to fulfil requests on this topic and the average turnaround time fell outside of the acceptable timeline for my project. Much later in my project, I submitted a request to the Treasury Board Secretariat as an interviewee informed me about the Regulatory Cooperation Committee (RCC) which works to fulfil part of the Canadian–U.S. beyond the Border

Partnership mandate. This group works to establish common policy across Canada and the U.S., which includes air regulations and standards. I was hoping to see if there was any cross-border coordination of civil drone operations or policies, but unfortunately the time on my request was extended to the point that I could not include it in my project.

Although there are several other departments and agencies that work with drones in various forms (whether development and innovation, or military operations) and have some regulatory oversight of drones, they were excluded from requests because of their peripheral nature. These include NAV Canada, 1 Canadian Air Division, the Transportation Safety Board and the National Research Council of Canada (NRC). Provincial and municipal agencies were also excluded from the requests as well since my goal was to provide an overall assessment of the development and regulation of the Canadian market and stakeholders as a whole. Recruiting stakeholders from civil liberties groups, industry and policing agencies was relatively easy across the board; however, obtaining access to high-ranking civil servants was much tougher. This difficulty was expected given the limited number of officials who work in the UAS divisions of government departments, their busy schedules and the fact that I was investigating a topic where access to information had been very difficult (something that I was warned about by other colleagues working on drones who were attempting to gain access to government officials, and documents through ATI and FOI requests). However, persistence in liaising and building rapport with industry stakeholders, as well as following up with emails and phone calls, paid off.

I had some informal, off the record conversations that took place with various industry stakeholders when I ran into them at conferences or after running into them when interviewing other stakeholders. These off the record interviews gave me some important thematic insights into various industry attitudes towards information sharing, with many stakeholders saying they withheld access and information to other researchers because they were not contacted directly but instead had to go through the inconvenience of filling an ATI request. These conversations in themselves opened more doors for me as I was able to establish myself as an accessible, open researcher who was really interested in connecting with stakeholders directly, though I did submit numerous ATI requests as well. However, these requests were submitted as a last resort once I had exhausted other avenues to get the information. This was important for accessing information not available via official websites or through interviews. This demonstrates once again, as other researchers have highlighted, that ATI brokering must be done strategically and is never a linear process. It might also be useful to have informants who point you towards information for which you should put in an ATI request. Just as I went back and forth between the data I was obtaining and the methods I was employing, it is important to assess and reassess the value of the methods employed. At times ATI requests can be a counter-productive measure if the researcher does not deploy them carefully or with a full, deep assessment of their field of research first.

While obtaining documents through ATI and FOI requests can often add to, illuminate, or stand in, for other types of data collection, this type of method is often met with resistance (Brownlee, 2015; Monaghan, 2015; Piché, 2012; Walby & Luscombe, 2017). Researchers often need to weigh the complications and nuances of filing FOI requests while also trying to broker access to engage in other qualitative research methods with stakeholders (see Brownlee & Walby, 2015; Walby & Larsen, 2011, 2012; Walby & Luscombe, 2017). Based on the information collected through ATI requests, my research became more concerned with the stakeholder networks around drones in Canada, rather than the privacy and surveillance implications of the technologies themselves. My project became focused on the stakeholder networks shaping the drone space in Canada, asking whether or not there existed a revolving door of stakeholders, demonstrative of the surveillance–industrial complex (Hayes, 2012). Building on this, my primary research question looked at how technocratic governance would introduce problems for shaping these technologies in a way that was sensitive to privacy and surveillance concerns.

## Building on ATI data: situating the drone

The objective of my research, in part, was to assess the role of key stakeholders in shaping the development of civil drone technologies in Canada. Therefore, this required data collection that would identify and trace key stakeholders and the role of particular stakeholder groups in shaping UAS technologies. However, personally identifiable information is not included in ATI documents, nor did I want to mention names in my research, but many documents reflected numbers about general trends in who made up regulatory working groups, and what types of groups and individuals were meeting to discuss the technologies. Assessing the stakeholders' logics is not necessarily possible using documents recovered through ATI requests alone, but the correspondence between stakeholders and inclusion or exclusion of particular groups can be seen in such documents. The role of key agencies involved in the development of regulation within the domestic drone market, I argue, is a key consideration to ascertain what types of logics and rationalities are shaping the adoption of drones in Canada.

ATI disclosures had a few key findings that I identify as critical markers demonstrating the technocratic dominance, characteristic of the surveillance–industrial complex in the Canadian drone market. The first case involves the use of drones for the G8 Summit in Kananaskis in 2002 as part of Operation Grizzly, a joint operation coordinated by policing and military agencies (DND A-2005-00283). This event is now seen as a watershed moment for the drone industry and their use domestically (Bracken-Roche, 2018; Bracken-Roche et al., 2014; Gersher, 2014b), and additionally, it was seen as a foundation for future domestic surveillance operations by joint police and military organisations in the domestic context (Bracken-Roche, 2018; Gersher, 2014a). The second finding, and perhaps the most important one, was the release of a report indicating the composition of the

Transport Canada (TC) UAV Working Group in 2012 (Gersher, 2013; Transport Canada, 2012). It was revealed that the regulatory working group was overwhelmingly stacked with industry stakeholders (over 60% of members were in the aviation or drone industry) while the remaining stakeholders were coming from TC, DND, the Ontario Provincial Police (OPP) and the National Research Council of Canada (NRCC) (Gersher, 2013). In 2016, another report produced by the working group showed that over 60% of group members were still primarily from industry (Transport Canada, 2015).

Building on the findings above as well as simple online searches, it became clear that a majority of the industry and military stakeholders involved in the working group had strong connections to the national drone industry group, Unmanned Systems Canada (USC) (Bracken-Roche, 2018; Gersher, 2014b). Due to the way Canadian regulations are created, this largely meant that up until 2014, there was limited consultation with the public, privacy commissioners, or civil liberties advocates. While many advocacy groups had been seeking consultations with Transport Canada as early as 2012, they were unable to engage in the regulatory process until the recommendations of the TC drone working group made it to the Canada Gazette (Bracken-Roche, field notes, 2015, 2016). The OPC and other civil liberties associations have been involved in the Canada Gazette process for UAS regulations and have given feedback at every opportunity during the Gazette process. Academics also provided feedback as available during Canada Gazette for the latest round of regulations (Thomasen & Bracken-Roche, personal communication, 2017). However, for the most part – and because of the lack of inclusion of individuals without the technical expertise on drones – the outcomes for drone development, deployment and regulation are shaped by a small group of stakeholders, but who may not consider the wider impact of these technologies on democratic values, governance or social control.

Like others conducting ATI research in the areas of policing, security and surveillance, my research has built on Gersher's (2013) findings and employed ATI requests as part of a methodological strategy to trace transformations within the Canadian drone space. However, ATI data "rarely lead to full-picture explanations" of the topic at hand (Monaghan & Walby, 2012, p. 138). This explanation is not only pragmatic in that the information obtained through FOI can be discontinuous, delayed, expensive, exempted and somewhat curated on occasion (see Jiwani & Krawchenko, 2014; Monaghan, 2015; Piché, 2012; Walby & Luscombe, 2017), but can lead to generally linear explanations of reality (Abbott, 2000; Savage & Burrows, 2007). However, as in this case, the data found in ATI documents can ultimately be quite fruitful in revealing trends that correspond with or further elucidate interview data and worked to fill in the gaps where it was not possible to conduct interviews. Therefore, using complementary methods helps fill in the gaps that emerge through one method by employing another (see Savage & Hyde, 2014). This is not simply as a stopgap however, but allows for various governance practices to come to light (Jiwani

& Krawchenko, 2014; Savage & Hyde, 2013; Walby & Larsen, 2012). This negotiating between different methods as and when necessary allows for the researcher to become engaged in reflexive, iterative research that should be the hallmark of critical qualitative research (Walby & Luscombe, 2017). What a lot of ATI disclosures revealed was the coalescence of particular stakeholder groups in driving the development and regulation of the technologies. On the surface, the revelations seen in the ATI documents seem to demonstrate a harmonious alignment between government and industry drone stakeholders. However, the number of industry stakeholders in a working group is not enough to show that technocratic governance exists, nor does it show the nuanced relations that emerge between government and industry. In interviews, however, the tensions between stakeholder groups and the distinctions in their opinions emerged in ways that would not be obvious through the reading of documents alone (Bracken-Roche, 2018).

## The politics of using ATI alongside other research methods

In a small, emerging industry, ATI requests can be quite political and, in my experience, submitting these requests often needs to be balanced against the ability to gain access through other means (whether ethnographic, participant observation, interviews and so forth). Due to the nascent nature of the Canadian drone industry, and the limited number of academics conducting research in the area, I often encountered friction and hostile responses from potential participants when approaching them for the first time. I was often accused of filing excessive ATI requests by stakeholders, yet in many cases, the request was not made by me, which led to them being more guarded which put me in an awkward position. It so happened, that because of the small community of researchers and journalists working in this area, that I often knew who did submit the ATI requests although I never told the stakeholders. When I explained that it was not me who submitted the request, if this was the case, they would usually state that they would have been happy sharing the information directly. As such, the timing and wording of ATI requests, or submitting them at all, became a consideration as I balanced the information retrieved through ATI versus interviews and negotiations with stakeholders to access information without having to go through the formal process. Given the size of the industry, I often collected more data directly from stakeholders as a result of correspondence and rapport building prior to, during and after conferences and interviews rather than through formal access avenues.

The spins – attempts to reshape information, stalls – slowing of information transfer, and shutdowns – permanent withholding of information (Lippert et al., 2013) – characteristic of researching policing and security, can be linked to practices of secrecy and security (Adler & Adler, 2002; Lippert et al., 2013). And in my experience, the stalls and shutdowns manifested in the information (or lack thereof) obtained in ATI requests. When I requested more information or less redaction from the ATIP liaison in respective departments, I was usually informed that information was not secret per se, but that it was linked to personally identifiable information or proprietary information and thus could not be shared. This secrecy, in my mind, validated the extent of the public–private partnerships in the drone space. However, as discussed throughout this chapter, using complimentary research methods such as elite interviews allowed me to "triangulate" the missing information and overcome this research challenge (see Mackinnon and Pich this volume). The spins that Lippert et al. (2013) refer to were not something I encountered with ATI data but, in the traditional sense of the word spin, were something I encountered when interviewing key stakeholders. This primarily was accounted for when individuals would try to reposition relationships and portray public–private partnerships in transparent, economic terms rather than as deeply intertwined and mutually beneficial. Additionally, portrayals of drones as like any other smart, mobile device were popular in spinning the technology away from being new and novel in terms of privacy concerns.

Two political implications that are very real for researchers in this area are amberlighting and red filing. As introduced earlier, these are "techniques of opacity" used to stymy comprehensive and timely disclosure of requested information to researchers (Larsen & Walby, 2012). These types of responses to information requests have, in part, been facilitated by the adoption of advanced software to help various government departments process the requests (ibid.). Ericson's (2007) analysis of western societies purports that they are governed by logics of uncertainty and precaution. This can be seen with ATIs as the need to limit political risks and mitigate uncertainty outweighs other or overrides other democratic values such as access to information (Larsen & Walby, 2012). In my case, I cannot be sure whether amberlighting or red filing occurred but there has certainly been an effort to limit the data released to researchers requesting information on drones (Gersher, 2014b). The excuses or reasons for documents being redacted in the context of my work were often related to personally identifiable information or proprietary information, even when requesting seemingly innocuous data such as records of certificates for drone flights, the type of drone and corporate entity operating it would often be omitted (Bracken-Roche et al., 2014). However, having to be careful about introducing yourself to interviewees in case they have been received an ATIP request in your topic area makes the process of gaining access for interviews or participant observation even more tricky. This can also be compounded by, and often was for me, positionality as I will discuss in the following section.

## Fieldwork challenges

I encountered challenges at almost every stage of my fieldwork which ranged from the logistical to the personal. In terms of the logistical issues that arose during my work, although they were undoubtedly highly political, the stalls and shutdowns with ATI data proved challenging and disheartening. While I am very lucky that I rarely encountered these challenges with respondents, it meant that I needed to make up for lengthy redactions with more data collection with stakeholders, which was both financially costly and time-consuming. My position as a researcher and the resulting dynamics that emerged when I engaged with respondents were not static but varied and changing; this was not just a result of the way interviews vary, but it also depended upon the institution, the interviewee and my own context. Some institutional protocol resulted in much more work to arrange some interviews over others. In most cases, I felt like I could use my positionality to my advantage and play an unassuming and naïve role, or I could use the correct acronyms to show I was in the know about drone technologies. But a few instances made me feel undermined as a researcher, and as a woman researcher. In one case when I emailed a potential respondent, they did not reply to me, but instead emailed my supervisor and department head directly (as instructed in the Letter of Information if they had concerns), even though as per my sampling method for obtaining interviews, this individual had been introduced to me by their own colleagues. To me, this (momentarily) undermined my integrity as a researcher in favour of the greater perceived legitimacy of my supervisor and our department head. While it is always an option for participants to contact these individuals, the fact that I did not hear from the respondent before they initiated contact with others made me very conscious of my positionality as a female researcher and a graduate student. It also felt awkward to me as most referrals from other stakeholders helped establish a friendly rapport with respondents from first contact, so the fact that this individual did not respond to my email or acknowledge its receipt before emailing my supervisor and department head stood out from other interactions.

Another unanticipated aspect of my fieldwork was an intense awareness of my own identity as a result of the way individuals acted towards me as I carried out my research. My own knowledge of drone technologies, the regulations and the various acronyms associated with both of these things gave me the confidence to engage with stakeholders and attend tradeshows. Many individuals recognised my expertise around drones in terms of privacy and policy. A number of the conferences and meetings I attended though were overwhelmingly male-, military-dominated, so my gender and expertise were both a stark contrast to the norm. However, it was not just my identity as a woman that I became more aware of as I started going to conferences and reaching out for interviews, but being a young doctoral student in Sociology also affected my knowledge production. Being a young female scholar from a social science field as opposed to an engineering or science background was met with some confused and even derisive attitudes which complicated some of my interactions. My age, gender and academic discipline were key factors that potential participants considered when deciding whether they would interview, how they spoke with me during interview and sometimes what they communicated with me. The awareness I possessed about drone technologies, however, was a great asset in negotiating these issues. Once I was able to demonstrate a fairly comprehensive knowledge of UAS and the Canadian UAS industry, many individuals spoke with me much more openly. A key element in this was being able to use industry-specific jargon, including numerous complicated acronyms, in conversations, via emails or in person, prior to interviews. The importance of a personal narrative became important in building rapport with my interviewees throughout the project, and it was foundational in order to overcome the secrecy that characterises stakeholder groups.

## Conclusion

Acquiring data and access to the field of surveillance technology within the policing and security context can be challenging at best, and near-impossible at worst. However, it is necessary for researchers to keep studying in this area to situate new technologies, and to highlight the concerns and potential implications associated with them. Where elites operate with secrecy and privacy for security's sake, they ask the public to sacrifice privacy for security and/or access, where protecting economic interests and technological optimism become key facets and in maintaining the surveillance–industrial complex. My research in the Canadian drone space has shown that ATI documents are often foundational in revealing important themes that can shape additional qualitative research. However, there are many challenges that emerge when trying to gather data in a small, emerging technological industry. ATI requests can be quite political and must be weighed against how much information you think you will receive (because of redactions) versus the extent to which submitting these ATIs might impact your ability to gain other types of research access. Issues in gaining access might be amplified for a number of reasons, including but not limited to a researcher's positionality and various power dynamics involved with "studying up." Researchers must be reflexive as they carry out their methods and be willing to negotiate their approach relationally. In my experience, being flexible in the field and adjusting to challenges allowed me to overcome the spins and secrecy associated with the area of research. These discussions explore the challenges faced by researchers when employing different methodological tools and the need to weigh up various methods when engaging with politically charged research. Based on these findings, I argue that researchers need to engage in critical reflexivity throughout their research, not only about the methods they are using and the data they are collecting, but also about their own positionality and their relationships with their research participants. In this way, critical qualitative research can be an incredibly invigorating and rewarding experience, if not also challenging and depleting on a personal level.

At the beginning of this chapter, I discussed literature which discusses gaining access in the context of policing, security and surveillance in Canada. This contextualised my own research, empirically and methodologically, on drone technologies in Canada. While my project did not result in focused ATI requests on military, policing and security in particular, the tracing of the drone and surrounding stakeholders resulted in the need to obtain information from such agencies and interview relevant stakeholders in these areas. ATI data obtained at the outset of my project framed the focus and allowed for an engagement with questions of political economy and technocratic governance in Canada's drone space. Similar to Dafnos' (2012) reflections on ATI on indigenous activism and policing, my research methods have been a reflection of the strength of ATIs, especially to the extent that they were useful in framing my whole research project, but also illustrative of the difficulties in obtaining information around new technologies of security and surveillance due to a risk-based approach employed by government in responding to ATIs. Obtaining tangible, accurate documents that reflect the surveillance–industrial complex requires a focused tracing of agents and technologies, something that is not always possible using ATI because of the problems discussed throughout this chapter. This networked web is particularly complicated by the intersections of public and private agencies and the challenges they pose for access brokering (see Mackinnon, this collection). However, the careful consideration of data that is released in ATI can lead to fruitful research paths which can be equally informative.

## References

Abbott, A. (2000). *Time matters*. Chicago, IL: University of Chicago Press.

Adler, P. A., & Adler, P. (2002). Do university lawyers and the police define research values. In W. C. van den Hoonaard (Ed.), *Walking the tightrope: Ethical issues for qualitative researchers* (pp. 34–42). Toronto: University of Toronto Press.

Ball, K., & Snider, L. (2013). Introduction: The surveillance-industrial complex: Towards a political economy of surveillance? In K. Ball & L. Snider (Eds.), *The surveillance-industrial complex: A political economy of surveillance* (pp. 15–22). London: Routledge.

Bayley, D. H., & Shearing, C. D. (1996). The future of policing. *Law and Society Review*, *30*, 585–606.

Bigo, D. (2002). Security and immigration: Toward a critique of the governmentality of unease. *Alternatives*, *27*(supplement), 63–92.

Bracken-Roche, C. (2016). Domestic drones: The politics of verticality and the surveillance industrial complex. *Geographica Helvetica*, *70*, 285–293.

Bracken-Roche, C. (2018). *Navigating Canadian drone space: A sociological analysis of the stakeholders, narratives, and policy shaping Canadian unmanned systems* (Unpublished Doctoral thesis). Queen's University.

Bracken-Roche, C., Lyon, D., Mansour, M., Molnar, A., Saulnier, A., & Thompson, S. (2014). *Privacy implications of the spread of unmanned aerial vehicles (UAVs) in Canada*. Kingston, Canada: Surveillance Studies Centre. (Research project for the 2013–2014 Contributions Program of the Privacy Commissioner of Canada). Retrieved from www.sscqueens.org/sites/default/files/Surveillance_Drones_Report.pdf

Brownlee, J. (2015). Contract faculty in Canada: Using access to information requests to uncover hidden academics in Canadian universities. *Higher Education, 70*(5), 787–805.

Brownlee, J. & Walby, K. (Eds.). (2015). *Access to information and social justice: Critical research strategies for journalists, scholars and activists*. Winnipeg: Arbeiter Ring Publishing (ARP) Books.

Dafnos, T. (2012). Beyond the blue line: Researching the policing of aboriginal activism using access to information. In M. Larsen & K. Walby (Eds.), *Brokering access: Power, politics, and freedom of information process in Canada* (pp. 209–233). Vancouver: University of British Columbia Press.

Ericson, R.V. (2007). *Crime in an insecure world*. Cambridge: Polity.

Feenberg, A. (2002). *Transforming technology: A critical theory revisited*. Oxford: Oxford University Press.

Forcese, C., & Roach, K. (2015). *False security: The radicalization of Canadian anti-terrorism.* Toronto: Irwin Law Inc.

French, M. (2007). In the shadow of Canada's camps. *Social & Legal Studies, 16*(1), 49–69.

Galison, P. (2004). Removing knowledge. *Critical Inquiry, 31,* 229–243.

Gersher, S. (2013). Canada's domestic regulatory framework for RPAS: A call for public deliberation. *Journal of Unmanned Vehicle Systems, 2*(1), 1–4.

Gersher, S. (2014a). Drone surveillance is increasing in Canada. *Ottawa Citizen.* Retrieved from http://ottawacitizen.com/news/drone-surveillance-is-increasing-in-canada

Gersher, S. (2014b). *Eyes in the sky: The domestic deployment of drone technology & aerial surveillance in Canada* (Unpublished Master's thesis). Carleton University.

Government of Canada. (2016, May 12). Best practices for posting summaries of completed access to information requests. *Treasury Board Secretariat.* Retrieved from www.canada.ca/en/treasury-board-secretariat/services/access-information-privacy/access-information/best-practices-posting-summaries-completed-access-information-requests.html.

Hayes, B. (2012). The surveillance-industrial complex. In D. Lyon, K. Ball, & K. Haggerty (Eds.), *Routledge handbook of surveillance studies* (pp. 167–175). London: Routledge.

Hayes, B., Jones, C., & Töpfer, E. (2014). Eurodrones Inc. (Report for the transnational institute and statewatch). Retrieved from www.statewatch.org/news/2014/feb/sw-tni-eurodrones-inc-feb-2014.pdf.

Huey, L., Walby, K., & Doyle, A. (2006). Cop watching in the Downtown Eastside: Exploring the use of (counter) surveillance as a tool of resistance. In T. Monahan (Ed.), *Surveillance and security: Technological politics and power in everyday life* (pp. 149–165). London: Routledge.

Huey, L. (2009). Subverting surveillance systems: Can access to information mechanisms be understood as counter-surveillance tools? In S. P. Hier, & J. Greenberg (Eds.), *Surveillance: Power, problems, and politics* (pp. 219–243). Vancouver: University of British Columbia Press.

Jackman, A. (2016). Rhetorics of possibility and inevitability in commercial drone tradescapes. *Geographica Helvetica, 71*(1), 1–6.

Jiwani, F. N., & Krawchenko, T. (2014). Policy, access to government, and qualitative research practices: Conducting research within a culture of information control. *Canadian Public Policy, 40*(1), 57–66.

Larsen, M., & Walby, K. (2012). Introduction. In M. Larsen, & K. Walby (Eds.), *Brokering access: Power, politics, and freedom of information process in Canada* (pp. 1–32). Vancouver: University of British Columbia Press.

Law, J. (2004). *After method: Mess in social science research.* London: Routledge.

Lippert, R., Walby, K., & Steckle, R. (2013). Multiplicities of corporate security: Identifying emerging types and trends. *Security Journal, 26*(3), 206–221.

Luscombe, A., Walby, K., & Lippert, R. (2017). Brokering access beyond the border and in the wild: Comparing freedom of information law and policy in Canada and the United States. *Law & Policy, 39*(3), 259–279.

Marx, G. (1984). Notes on the discovery, collection, and assessment of hidden and dirty data. In J. Schneider, & J. Kitsuse (Eds.), *Studies in the sociology of social problems.* (pp. 78–113). Norwood, NJ: Ablex.

Molnar, A., & Parsons, C. (2013, November). *Watching below: Dimensions of surveillance-by-UAVs in Canada.* Block G Privacy and Security Report.

Monahan, T. (2006). Counter-surveillance as political intervention? *Social Semiotics, 16*(4), 515–534.

Monaghan, J. (2015). Four barriers to access to information: Perspectives of a frequent user. In J. Brownlee & K. Walby (Eds.), *Access to information and social justice: Critical research strategies for journalists, scholars and activists* (pp. 53–74). Winnipeg, MB: Arbeiter Ring Publishing.

Monaghan, J., & Molnar, A. (2016). Radicalisation theories, policing practices, and the future of terrorism? *Critical Studies on Terrorism, 9*(3), 393–413.

Monaghan, J., & Walby, K. (2012). Making up 'terror identities': Security intelligence, Canada's integrated threat assessment centre and social movement suppression. *Policing and Society: An International Journal of Research and Policy, 22*(2), 133–151.

Mukherjee, S. (2017). Troubling positionality: Politics of "studying up" in transnational contexts. *The Professional Geographer, 69*(2), 291–298.

O'Reilly, C. (2010). The transnational security consultancy industry: A case of state–Corporate symbiosis. *Theoretical Criminology, 14*(2), 183–210.

Office of the Privacy Commissioner of Canada (OPC). (2013). "Drones in Canada." *OPC.* Last modified November 21, 2013. Online. https://www.priv.gc.ca/en/opc-actions-and-decisions/research/explore-privacy-research/2013/drones_201303/.

Piché, J. (2012). Accessing the State of imprisonment in Canada: Information barriers and negotiation strategies. In Larsen, M. & Walby, K. (Ed.), Brokering access: Politics, power, and freedom of information in Canada (pp. 234–260). Vancouver: UBC Press.

Rigakos, G. S., & Worth, S. R. (2011). Access to information (ATI) as a double-edged sword for critical policing research. *Canadian Journal of Law and Society, 26*(3), 645–652.

Savage, M., & Burrows, R. (2007). The coming crisis of empirical sociology. *Sociology, 41*(5), 885–899.

Savage, A. & Hyde, R. (2013). Local authority handling of Freedom of Information requests: lessons from a research project. *Web Journal of Current Legal Issues, 19*(2).

Savage, A., & Hyde, R. (2014). Using freedom of information requests to facilitate research. *International Journal of Social Research Methodology, 17*(3), 303–317.

Smith, D. E. (1999). *Writing the social: Critique, theory, and investigations.* Toronto: University of Toronto Press.

Transport Canada. (2012). "UAV Systems Program Design Working Group - Phase 1 Final #Report." *Transport Canada*, March. Online. www.apps.tc.gc.ca/Saf-Sec-Sur/2/NPA-APM/doc.aspx?id=10298.

Transport Canada. (2015). Notice of Proposed Amendment: Unmanned Aerial Vehicles. Canadian Aviation Regulations Advisory Council (CARAC), May. Online. http://wwwapps.tc.gc.ca/Saf-Sec-Sur/2/NPA-APM/doc.aspx?id=10294.

UAV Systems. Program Design Working Group. (2012 March). *Transport Canada.* Retrieved from www.apps.tc.gc.ca/Saf-Sec-Sur/2/NPA-APM/doc.aspx?id=10286.

UAV Systems. Program Design Working Group Report. (2016 May). *Transport Canada.* Retrieved from www.apps.tc.gc.ca/Saf-Sec-Sur/2/npa-apm/doc.aspx?id=10588.

Vallance-Jones, F. (2014). National Freedom of Information Audit 2014. Newspapers Canada. Retrieved from https://nmc-mic.ca/sites/default/files/FOI2014-FINAL.pdf.

Walby, K., & Larsen, M. (2011). Getting at the live archive: On access to information research in Canada. *Canadian Journal of Law and Society, 26*(3), 623–634.

Walby, K. and Luscombe, A. (2017). Criteria for quality in qualitative research and use of freedom of information requests in social research. *Qualitative Research, 17*(5), 537–553.

Walby, K., & Larsen, M. (2012). Access to information and freedom of information requests: Neglected means of data production in the social sciences. *Qualitative Inquiry, 18*(1), 31–42.

Walby, K., & Luscombe, A. (2018). Research ethics and freedom of information requests in qualitative research. *Research Ethics, 14*(4), 1–15.

Wall, T. (2013). Unmanning the police manhunt: Vertical security as pacification. *Socialist Studies/études Socialistes, 9*(2), 32–56.

Winner, L. (1980). Do artefacts have politics? *Daedalus, 109*(1), 121–136.

# 7

# USING CONTINUAL FOI REQUESTS TO UNCOVER THE LIVE ARCHIVE

## Tracking protest policing in the USA

*Pierce Greenberg*

## Introduction

Public records requests – or freedom of information requests (FOIR) – allow citizens in the U.S. to access a vast amount of government data, ranging from written reports to large databases under open records laws.[1] Journalists, lawyers and even some activists are adept at obtaining government records via FOIR to enhance their work. But a widespread interest in FOIR has not infiltrated into sociological research – despite a variety of potential usages across subfields and methods (Larsen & Walby, 2012; Savage & Hyde, 2014). This paper illustrates how a specific application of FOIR – using continual and repeated requests – can contribute to research on protest policing.

Protest policing amounts to a form of social control that may result in the repression of certain social movements (Earl & Soule, 2006). In recent years, police departments in the U.S. and abroad have become increasingly militarised – using warzone-grade weapons and equipment in the management of large protest crowds (Wood, 2014). Further, the U.S. has seen a number of nationwide protests in recent years – most notably involving Black Lives Matter, a group that organised in response to several police shootings of unarmed black men and women. As sociologists seek to understand protest policing in the U.S., they may find continual FOI requests increasingly useful for obtaining data collected by police.

This chapter focuses on how continual FOIR can contribute to two major strands of social movements research: (1) protest event analysis, and (2) multi-perspectival case studies of specific movements and protests. Those methods of analysis often rely on limited data sources. For example, researchers often rely on media coverage to count and describe protest events (Earl, Martin, McCarthy, & Soule, 2004). In other cases, scholars may conduct in-depth interviews with movement actors to understand protestor tactics and motivations. But these sources rarely involve behind-the-scenes details on police strategies and intentions, aside from information provided to the press. FOIR provides an opportunity to triangulate data sources and better understand police perspectives.

This chapter begins by reviewing how previous sociologists and academic researchers have used FOIR across subfields and methods. Then, I examine literature on social movement methodologies – and how FOIR could supplement them. Next, I illustrate the utility of FOIR by obtaining protest-related documentation from the Seattle Police Department. While several studies have used protest permits and other government data to examine protest policing, few review the mechanics of public records data collection. Then, I analyse how the documents I obtained could contribute to both protest event analysis and case studies of protest policing. Finally, I discuss the potential limitations of FOIR data.

## Literature review

Sociologists have long criticised government action, but have been somewhat resistant in accessing the "live archive" of government data that is created on a daily basis (Walby & Larsen, 2012, p. 4). Millions of memos, reports, emails, recordings and other public data are produced by a variety of government agencies everyday – and are accessible via public records requests. The U.S. Congress passed the Freedom of Information Act (FOIA) in 1966 following concerns about transparency in federal government agency practices (Roberts, 2006). Citizens may submit requests for records to the government in writing – and many agencies have developed streamlined forms that can be filed and tracked online. The government can withhold information under certain exemptions – including information that may violate personal privacy, reveal trade secrets and interfere with law enforcement investigations.[2] However, a new FOIA reform law, signed by former President Obama in 2016, instructs federal agencies to presume openness and only withhold information where a "foreseeable harm" exists (Sadurni, 2016). The law also directs federal agencies that haven't yet begun streamlining FOIA requests through online portals to do so. Although no significant changes in FOIA law have occurred since 2016, the new Trump administration has denied a record high percentage of FOIA requests (Bridis, 2018). In addition to federal laws, all 50 states and local agencies are required to fulfil public records requests. Outside of the U.S. context, more than 100 countries across the world have open records laws, with varying levels of accessibility (Michener, 2011).

However, few scholars to date have used this valuable resource. In fact, academics only filed 1 percent of all FOIA requests to the Federal Bureau of Investigation in 1999 (Lee, 2001).[3] One potential barrier to a widespread adoption of FOIR may be its association with activists who seek to expose the wrongdoings of powerful governments (Marx, 1972, 1984). Yeager (2006) writes that FOIR data collection falls under "more progressive theories of criminology, such as conflict, radical, or critical perspectives" (p. 500). Gary Marx (1972) also characterises

FOIR as a tool for use in "sacred cow-smashing" (p. 3) muckraking sociology. Further, these scholar-activists espouse the difficulties of obtaining public records data – likely due to the critical nature of their requests (Yeager, 2006). But the activist conception of FOIR vastly limits the breadth of potential applications for FOIR in sociological research. I propose a more pragmatic approach to FOIR – whereby scholars pursue public records for their utility in answering research questions, rather than criticising government institutions (Greenberg, 2016).

Social science scholars in Canada (Larsen & Walby, 2012) and the United Kingdom (Savage & Hyde, 2014) have been most active in theorising and using FOIR as a method for collecting data. For example, Luscombe and Walby (2017) theorise FOI law in three ways: (1) as a live archive, accessible by researchers and the public, (2) a tool for government secrecy and obfuscation and (3) an example of actor-network theory – how micro-processes between actors influence the application of FOI law. These conceptions of FOI law lead to a number of potentially fruitful areas of social research. For example, scholars have examined how interactions between requestors and agency officials differed between police departments in the U.S. and Canada (Luscombe, Walby, & Lippert, 2017). After filing more than a hundred requests, they found that Canadian officials were more likely to negotiate the scope of requests and charge costs for fulfilling requests, while U.S. agency officials were less likely to communicate with formal response letters. While the results were not generalisable to all departments, this study illustrated how interactions between individuals influenced the administration of FOI law and some of the barriers to accessing the live archive of government data.

Scholars have also incorporated public records data into a number of quantitative and qualitative projects (see also Walby and Luscombe, this volume for a review). For example, Walby (2009) uses public records data to help inform in-depth interviews with police. An additional review article shows how FOI meets the criteria for quality in qualitative research (Walby & Luscombe, 2017). Other scholars – mostly historians – have used public records extensively in historical analyses of government action, such as FBI surveillance (Noakes, 1995; Theoharis, 2011). Quantitative applications of public records data are more sparse, but previous work has used FOIR to obtain locations of hazardous coal waste dams to empirically assess whether they are disproportionately proximate to disadvantaged communities (Greenberg, 2017). While these scholars have used FOIR successfully, few studies provide in-depth analyses of FOIR as a data collection method in the U.S. context.

## FOIR and social movements

Social movements research provides an opportunity to demonstrate the usefulness of FOIR due to the field's focus on state actions. McCarthy and Mayer (1977) define social movements as a "set of opinions and beliefs in a population, which represents preferences for changing some elements of the social structure and/or reward distribution of a society" (pp. 1217–1218). Government authorities impact society's reward distribution through various forms of social control (McCarthy & Mayer, 1977). Thus, social movements are often oriented towards the state. Major theoretical paradigms in social movements research reflect the state's centrality to movements. For example, political opportunity theory posits that movements are largely influenced by "exogenous factors" that "enhance or inhibit prospects for mobilization" (Meyer & Minkoff, 2004, p. 1457). While scholars differ in how they conceptualise "political opportunity," the government remains a central actor through mechanisms like repressive tactics and policy changes (Meyer & Minkoff, 2004).

This review focuses on how FOIR can contribute to the study of protest policing. I further centre this study primarily on two social movements methodologies: protest event analysis and case studies. First, research on protest policing often uses protest event analysis to quantitatively examine whether specific claims or movements are more likely to (1) draw a police presence, or (2) result in use of force or arrest (Beyerlein, Soule, & Martin, 2015; Davenport, Soule, & Armstrong, 2011; Earl, Soule, & McCarthy, 2003). FOIR could contribute to protest event analysis by providing a secondary data source to triangulate and validate traditional sources of protest data such as media and newspaper reporting. Second, FOIR expands the realm of qualitative perspectives in case studies by providing police narratives about tactics and priorities. Case studies in social movements research aim to include "thick" descriptions of movement processes and events, which often involve multiple methods, data sources and perspectives (Snow & Trom, 2002). While researchers are likely to speak with movement participants – or even conduct participant observation (Uldam & McCurdy, 2013) – the same kind of access may not be possible with police departments. But FOIR provides the opportunity to investigate interdepartmental workings that could provide supplemental details about the tactics, strategies and priorities used in protest policing.

The institutionalisation of protest may also make FOIR an increasingly valuable data source in protest event analysis. Following a period of contentious protests in the 1960s and 1970s, state agencies formalised rules for managing and policing protests (McCarthy & McPhail, 1998). In turn, protests became a recognised, normal function of democratic society. Therefore, the institutionalisation of protest management within state bureaucracies likely led to the creation of more documentation that could be obtained through FOIR. These sources may consist of permits, after-action reports and other internal communications related to the negotiation or management of protests.

## Counting protest events with FOIR

Social movements research has long sought to measure the occurrence of social movement activity across time and space. Protest event analysis often relies on media accounts like newspaper articles or television coverage as the primary data source. Protest event analysis is a type of quantitative content analysis that codes articles on protest events for some attributes. This data can contribute to long-standing research questions, such as "how national political contexts influence levels of protest mobilization" (Hutter, 2014, p. 336). Recent protest event analyses of policing examine the effect of race (Davenport et al., 2011), religion (Beyerlein, 2016) and familiarity with protestors (Eggert, Wouters, Ketelaars, & Walgrave, 2018) on police presence at protests.

While newspaper articles provide a consistent source of protests, media-based data come with two major limitations: selection and description bias (Earl et al., 2004; Woolley, 2000). Selection bias refers to the internal processes of how newspapers choose to cover certain events (Earl et al., 2004). News agencies make "newsworthy" determinations, often based on the size of the "news hole" in that day's paper. Also, the old news adage "if it bleeds, it leads," applies to the coverage of movements: if protests are violent, they are more likely to be reported (Woolley, 2000). Further, McCarthy, McPhail, and Smith (1996) found that media outlets are more likely to cover events that draw large amounts of protesters. Maney and Oliver (2001) explain the under-coverage of small pro-tests as a result of increased protest institutionalisation since the 1970s. As pro-tests became cemented in the political process, they also became less newsworthy (Maney & Oliver, 2001). Description bias in media sources refers to the selective content and details of what news sources choose to report. If violence or arrests occur at a protest, that "hard news" often takes precedent over "soft news" like the detailed claims of protesters (Earl et al., 2004).

FOIR offers a practical way of obtaining sources that can test the reliability and validity of media counts *and* descriptions of protests. McCarthy et al. (1996) illustrate this approach by filing FOIA requests with three different federal agen-cies that monitor protests in Washington, D.C. They sought an archival record of protest permits to compare against media accounts of protests. The study revealed that the media was biased towards protests that had large numbers of participants or were relevant to issues in the current news cycle (McCarthy et al., 1996). Despite these important findings, few researchers have followed McCarthy et al.'s (1996) lead in seeking out public records. Hocke (1999) and Maney and Oliver (2001) were able to collaborate with police agencies to obtain similar data sources, bypassing the FOIR process. These studies all find a stark underrepresentation of protest events by media sources and urge scholars to pursue multiple data sources in protest event analysis.

In addition to investigating media selection bias, government-held documents could also help examine description bias. While newspapers may report on police presence, documentation may provide additional details about the tactics used by police and protesters. This could help researchers move beyond dichot-omous variables regarding police repression. For example, Earl et al. (2003) create categories of police response based on the presence of repressive tactics described in newspaper articles, but police documents could help provide more specific details about troop deployments. Eggert et al. (2018) illustrate this approach in an analysis of protest policing in Belgium from 2000 to 2010. Data from the Brussels police department allowed them to use both the number of police officers and types of equipment deployed as dependent variables. They found that police's prior knowledge of protest organisers was a strong and significant predictor of an increased police presence (Eggert et al., 2018). Internal data may also reveal undercover or "plainclothes" operations that reporters or other observers may not recognise.

## Police and protester tactics and negotiation

In addition to protest event analysis, FOIR data collection could also help uncover details of protest management for use in qualitative analyses and in-depth case studies. McAdam (1983) explains the importance of analysing the "chess-like" tactical interaction between movement participants and agents of social control. Case studies of protest events "develop thick, detailed, holistic elaborations of selected cases" (Snow & Trom, 2002, p. 149). Analysis of cases also requires a triangulation of methods and data sources because "social reality is too complex and multifaceted to be adequately grasped by any single method" (Snow & Anderson, 1991, p. 151). Police perspectives are also important to understanding movement activity and repression, but access to that data may be prohibitive without FOIR.

Earl and Soule (2006) advocate for a police-centred approach to understanding how and why certain protest events result in repression. They find that "situational threats" to the police are more important predictors of protest repression than broad threats to social elites (Earl & Soule, 2006). They argue for a police-based, or "blue," approach to understanding movement repression – one that considers organisational and institutional characteristics of law enforcement agencies. While police will make some data publicly available online, FOIR provides the opportunity to learn more about departmental characteristics and how police perceive threats.

Protest policing studies often focus on overt repression – such as violence – which has "the virtues of being systematically observable" (Earl et al., 2003, p. 582). But other forms of policing may go unnoticed by media sources or the public. Gillham (2011) refers to the post-9/11 form of policing protests in the U.S. as "strategic incapacitation." Gillham (2011) posits that police have moved past using "negotiated management" techniques for protests and toward "strategic incapacitation." This new policing strategy includes increased surveillance, information sharing among agencies and control of public spaces (Gillham, 2011). These tactics – especially surveillance and information sharing – are mostly covert operations that could be uncovered by FOIR. Many activists use public records requests to examine government surveillance methods. Andrew Hendricks (2014), a self-proclaimed "public documents geek," has uncovered hundreds of documents related to repressive police tactics in Washington state. These documents range from communications between government agencies and businesses (information sharing) to video footage from a Washington State Patrol plane during a May Day protest in 2013 (surveillance) (Hendricks, 2014).

Several scholars have used FOIR to uncover veiled details about movement repression and management. Dafnos (2012) filed records requests to examine how police confront aboriginal movements in Canada. This use of FOIR attempts to "push beyond official rhetoric to examine actual practices" of law enforcement agencies (Dafnos, 2012, p. 214). The documents obtained by Dafnos (2012) displayed how agencies internally framed aboriginal movement protests as national security threats, rather than simple disruptions in public order. Further, the militaristic response to aboriginal movements was in direct opposition to law enforcement's stated protocol on how to handle such incidents (Dafnos, 2012). In another case study, Beehner (2013) used FOIR documents from an activist to examine a local struggle over a bike lane in New York City.[4] Emails obtained through FOIR showed collaboration between local Department of Transportation officials and the "biking lobby" (Beehner, 2013). The use of FOIR in protest case studies of policing and management can often carry a more critical tone. Dafnos (2012) notes how probing for such critical information can invoke institutional resistance. But the results of these requests can enhance "thick" qualitative descriptions of protests and complement other methods of analysing protest events.

In sum, FOIR has the potential to significantly expand the scope of research conducted by social movements scholars. Klandermans and Staggenborg (2002) advocate for avoiding research questions that are based on "the availability of protest event data and methods" because those sources "make it more likely that we will focus on visible protests than on behind-the-scenes cultural or organizational activities" (p. 330). In other words, social movements researchers should not pose questions that only focus on what certain data sources (like news coverage) can answer. The use of FOIR data collection could help shine light on the organisational activities of government agencies and thereby broaden the range of questions posed by social movements research.

## Seattle Police Department protest documentation

While FOIR data collection could be useful in conducting social movements research, the existing literature rarely provides in-depth analyses of (1) how the data collection process works, and (2) potential applications of certain types of government data. The routinisation and institutionalisation of police–protester interactions, as well as concerns for the rights of protesters, has likely increased the documentation of protests created by police departments (McCarthy & McPhail, 1998). In order to illustrate the usefulness of FOIR, I filed a series of requests with the Seattle Police Department (SPD). Seattle was chosen as the site for this study due to its history of high-profile protests, including riots at the 1999 meeting of the World Trade Organization (Gillham & Marx, 2000; Noakes & Gillham, 2007). Seattle is the 22nd largest city in the U.S., and the economic centre of the 15th largest

U.S. metropolitan area. Further, the size of the Seattle Police Department – which has more than 1,400 sworn officers and 580 civilian employees – ensures that it is familiar with receiving and responding to public records requests. Below, I aim to share in-depth details about continual FOIR data collection and demonstrate how it can be applied to protest event analysis and case studies.

## Collecting FOIR data through repeated requests

FOIR data collection is a "process" which extends beyond simply filing requests and receiving documents; records requests involve knowledge of internal processes and effective communication with gatekeepers (Larsen & Walby, 2012). It is important to file requests that refer to specific documents, rather than asking for an unwieldy amount of data such as "all information related to policing of protests in Seattle." Therefore, I began my inquiry by reviewing the Seattle Police Department manual, which is available online. As evidence of protest institutionalisation, the SPD manual contained an entire section titled "Demonstration Management." The policy referred to specific documents called "After Action Reports" and "Event Debrief" forms that officers are required to file after protests. My initial request, filed by email in February 2015, asked for:

> Copies of all After Action Reports and Event Debriefs Forms filed under 'Demonstration Management,' as identified in the Seattle Police Department Manual (Section 14.090-12). Based upon the departmental manual, these documents are believed to be located in the S:drive Demonstration Management folder.

The SPD responded by email four days later, stating that they anticipated having a response in April, roughly seven weeks following the initial request. On April 1, the SPD responded with seven PDF documents. However, the files were not consistent with the documentation that I requested. Instead, the SPD sent me previously released post-protest/demonstration reports from *other* agencies. One of the documents was a previously released report from SPD following May Day protests in 2012. I quickly responded via email and clarified, more specifically, that I wanted documents filed by SPD sergeants and incident commanders following protests in Seattle. I also limited my request to reports filed between January 1, 2014 and March 1, 2015. I received a response to that request on June 3, roughly six weeks after my renewed request.[5]

After receiving the correct documents for the initial timeframe, I then filed an identical follow-up request on July 8 for reports filed between March 1 and July 1. The SPD fulfilled that request on July 23. Two additional requests were filed in October 2015 and January 2016 to complete the data collection. Table 7.1 lists each of the request dates and corresponding response times. End-of-year pressures, request backlogs, administration and personnel changes, or even holidays could influence response times. On average, the four records requests were fulfilled in about seven weeks (50 days).

**TABLE 7.1** FOIR request dates and SPD response times.

| Request Date | SPD Response Time |
| --- | --- |
| 2/9/2015 | 51 days |
| 4/14/2015 | 50 days |
| 7/8/2015 | 15 days |
| 10/9/2015 | 94 days |
| 1/20/2016 | 49 days |

The method of filing repeated, identical requests reduces the burden on administrative personnel and could decrease the chance of an unfulfilled request. Some requestors could err by casting a net (i.e., timeframe) that is too wide. For example, a researcher may request the last 15 years worth of protest reports filed by the police department. But given institutional change and personnel turnover, it may be difficult or impossible for public records officials to obtain those records. The process of making continual requests allows for semi-frequent contact with the agency – and will familiarise them with the request and help them fulfil the request with ease. I chose a roughly 3-month interval so that requests were not incessant. However, it is also fairly normal to file repeat requests weekly or even monthly.

While it was not needed in this case, there are several options for appealing public records disclosure decisions that may be useful for researchers in the U.S. While state laws may differ, Washington state allows two ways for requestors to appeal agencies' decisions to redact or withhold records: (1) a legal challenge filed in local court, (2) a direct appeal to the state Attorney General. The lawsuit option is available for requests of both state and local agencies and places the burden of proof on the state agency to prove that the records met one of the legal exemptions to disclosure. The Attorney General review is only available to requests filed under state agencies (i.e., the Washington State Patrol) – and would not be available for requests for local police departments.

## Data

Overall, the SPD provided 125 pages of documentation that covered 45 protest events during the requested time periods. The "After Action Reports" (AARs) were standardised forms that contained information about planning, staffing, tactics, suggestions, commendations and logistics. Those reports varied in length, with some responses simply consisting of "N/A" or single words. Several of the AARs consisted of longer narratives of the police response to protests. In one case, police filed an AAR for a protest that never materialised – possibly because of bad weather. One document contained numerous comments from police officials about the annual May Day protests in 2014. Several event debrief forms, filed by sergeants, revealed information that largely overlapped with the AARs. These forms ensured that essential information about tactics and planning were effectively communicated to officers policing the event. The event debrief forms all had accompanying AARs, and therefore did not offer much added value to the overall count of protests.

The redaction of large amounts of text or data is a potential limitation of FOIR. One of the key exemptions to open records law is information or data related to police investigations or other intelligence information that may compromise law enforcement activities. Unsurprisingly, the SPD redacted some text, which they interpreted as "specific intelligence information that is essential to effective law enforcement."[6] The department also withheld information related to the prevention, mitigation and response to "criminal terrorism acts." According to the SPD, "disclosure of the information would expose specific vulnerabilities, response plans, and/or endanger citizens/law enforcement personnel."[6] Nonetheless, the documents still contained useful data, which I outline below.

## Comparison with newspaper data

To evaluate the FOIR documents as a source of protest counts for protest event analysis, I cross-referenced the protest events covered by SPD with those reported on in *Seattle Times* Seattle's largest daily newspaper. I performed a database search for articles containing the keywords protes★, rall★, demonstrat★ or riot★.[7] For the purpose of this project, I borrow McCarthy et al.'s (1996) definition of protest events as gatherings of two or more people whom make a public claim that seeks to impact the interests of people or groups beyond those participating (Tilly, 1978). Further, the referenced events had to occur within the SPD's jurisdiction during the same time period as the FOIR requests, January 1, 2014 to January 1, 2016. This search revealed 47 articles, only 15 of which overlapped with the SPD data obtained through FOIR. Therefore, the combined dataset included 77 unique protest events.

One of the strengths of the SPD data is that it provides more frequent counts of protests that occur over a longer period of time. For example, the SPD closely documented protestors who took to the streets in the weeks and months following highly publicised events in Ferguson, Missouri. On November 24, 2014, a grand jury in Ferguson declined to prosecute a police officer who shot and killed an unarmed black teenager. The controversial decision sparked protest events across the country, including in Seattle. *Seattle Times* covered Ferguson-related protests on Nov. 24, Nov. 25 and Nov. 28, several of which resulted in arrests. However, the SPD did not provide any AARs until Nov. 29. But from Nov. 29 to Dec. 15, the SPD documented 11 protests, while *Seattle Times* only covered seven. Table 7.2 shows that the SPD filed more sustained reports on the Ferguson events and the Black Lives Matter movement throughout the data collection period. A similar trend was noted in response to environmental group protests against Shell in the Port of Seattle. The newspaper covered the topic on four occasions, but the SPD filed seven reports.

**TABLE 7.2** Protests covered by SPD report and *Seattle Times*, by movement claim.

| | SPD | Seattle Times | Overlap | Total Unique Events |
|---|---|---|---|---|
| All Protests | 45 | 47 | 15 | 77 |
| Ferguson/Black Lives Matter | 23 | 14 | 9 | 28 |
| Shell Oil Rig protest | 7 | 4 | 2 | 9 |
| Minimum Wage Protest | 0 | 4 | 0 | 4 |
| Other[a] | 15 | 25 | 4 | 35 |

a Sea Appendix A for complete list.

In addition to simply counting protests, these findings also reveal a potential bias in the *type* of protest covered by the SPD. The protests most frequently documented by the SPD are in response to the discriminatory policing of minorities and the U.S. criminal justice system. The Black Lives Matter movement has publicly criticised local police departments amid numerous police shootings of unarmed black men and women. Black Lives Matter protests accounted for 38 percent of the protests covered by *Seattle Times*, compared to 51 percent of the protests documented by the SPD. The newspaper referenced a larger variety of protest types, such as a pro-Palestinian rally, teacher walkouts and marches, and large demonstrations in favour of increasing the minimum wage. This data shows that the largest percentages of protests documented by the SPD are (1) organised by minority groups and (2) target the police. This finding is consistent with Earl and Soule's (2006) assertion that levels of movement repression stem from "situational threats" perceived by police (i.e., criticism of the police), rather than "diffuse threats" such as other anti-establishment goals (p. 149). The disproportionate policing of Black Lives Matter protest may also hold implications for the continued study of racial bias in protest policing (Davenport et al., 2011).

This data suggests that continual FOI requests can be used to (1) assess the validity of newspaper data and contribute to a fuller accounting of protest activity, and subsequently (2) contribute to empirical tests of social movements theories regarding suppression of protests by the state. In sum, the police documents do not constitute a fuller accounting of protests than newspapers, but a combination of FOIR and newspaper data clearly captures a more complete picture of protest activity in Seattle.

## Case study details

The SPD documents also provide law enforcement perspectives that could serve as one of several data sources in a case study. The AARs reveal information about SPD planning and tactics that would likely not be available from other sources. For example, one AAR noted "confusion" over a staffing issue and claimed there "weren't enough resources to control this group" during a March Against Police Brutality. It also referenced officers that were "tired and agitated by the many protest events they had worked, as well as the skirmishes that took place with more aggressive protestors." It is unlikely that police departments would reveal those vulnerabilities in a press release or interview. Another AAR reveals behind-the-scenes police tactics. Following a "Check Your Privilege" protest at the University of Washington, the SPD noted: "For most of the evening, personnel were kept on standby at a distance that was close but out of sight, and they did not need to interfere with this planned event." Therefore, newspaper or other accounts may report a minimal police presence, when troops were actually present but kept "out of sight." The same report notes the presence of Department of Justice monitors at the event – which could influence police action.

Several SPD documents included longer narratives about protest events with more details than the AARs. An 11-page narrative provides a detailed account of a protest involving about 60 people. The commander who filed the report interpreted the event as a "protest against the police under the umbrella of a Ferguson protest" organised by a local anarchist group. The report also noted protestor strategies such as communicating via text messages, having trailing photographers to capture images of confrontation and dispersing into smaller groups. Sections titled "concerns/observations," "successes," "staffing," "challenges," and "outside the box" contained extensive redactions, but some of the text was recoverable. This data revealed that the SPD utilised more than 170 personnel – in addition to support from the Washington State Patrol – for a protest with 60 expected participants. Staffing data was completely redacted in other documents – so this information was not comparable to other protests.[8] The documents also revealed strategies for the deployment of bicycle troops, arrest procedures, and protecting property and roadways.

The reports also give hints at some of the surveillance strategies police use to determine *how* to staff or cover events. For example, the police reports often reference monitoring social media to gauge characteristics of protests. Several reports project the number of participants based on how many Facebook users have joined an event. One report noted that "information surrounding this event on social media was at times inflammatory" – confirming that police also monitor the content of social media postings. These details verify the police emphasis on surveillance that comprises Gillham's (2011) "strategic incapacitation" theory of protest policing.

In sum, the documents obtained via FOIR reveal important police perspectives that may help round out case studies of specific protest events. Many of the documents reference *other* documents that may be useful for more in-depth analyses of particular events. For example, some AARs referred to additional written plans – Incident Actions Plans (IAPs), protest permit applications, roll call briefing notes and database management systems – all types of data that could be obtained through FOIR. There are also other public agencies that are referenced, such as the Washington State Patrol and Seattle Fire Department, which may log information about protests. Therefore, the content of these requests are only a small sampling of the types of data that could be available via FOIR.

## Limitations

FOIR data may be useful to researchers, but, like all data sources, there are several limitations and biases. First, much like newspaper data, police institutions have their own form of selection bias in deciding whether to file reports or record information (Maney & Oliver, 2001). For example, the SPD manual does not define the criteria for what constitutes a "demonstration." A policy does mandate that commanders file AARs whenever a "significant deployment or other unusual circumstances are involved ..." or when directed by a higher authority (SPD Manual 2015). Therefore, the AAR reports do not capture all protest events in Seattle, nor do they necessarily represent all protests with a police presence. Additional information, perhaps gained through interviews with SPD officials, is needed to fully understand the biases in police reports. Researchers may assume that agency responses include all of the requested data that exists. However, there are layers of interpretation and bureaucracy that may impact the response to the request. For example, the first response to my request above yielded irrelevant documents. Scholars may have to be persistent if requests are not correctly interpreted or fulfilled. Cuillier and Davis (2011) offer additional tips for filing effective public records requests.

There are also limitations regarding the temporal scope of FOIR documents. Policies are subject to change, and archival requests may take more time to fulfil. For example, the SPD reports only covered one protest between January 1, 2014 and November 28, 2014. Over the first six months of 2015, the SPD recorded 26 protests. This inconsistency could be due to the tightening of internal reporting policies following the proliferation of Ferguson protests in November 2014. Nonetheless, it may be useful to file consistent, continual requests that cover recent time periods – as I did during 2015.

FOIR data collection may also be difficult to incorporate into comparative and cross-national studies. Researchers are largely beholden to agency gatekeepers who determine what information can be made public – and different gatekeepers may interpret requests differently. For example, Rappert (2012) encountered varying levels of disclosure when filing overlapping requests with multiple agencies. Also, police departments may have different record-keeping procedures that vary in the amount and type of information reported. Finally, FOIR data collection can also be geographically limited in terms of researcher access. Some state-level open records laws require requestors to be residents of the state. From a cross-national research perspective, there may also be varying levels of disclosure or openness between countries (Michener, 2011). As illustrated earlier, the data obtained by Eggert et al. (2018) in Brussels appeared to contain more in-depth details on troop deployments than the data from Seattle. Due to these limitations and biases, FOIR may be best suited for local or state-level research and case studies. These limitations and biases are necessary to consider when conducting FOIR research, but should not deter scholars from attempting to access this valuable source of data.

## Conclusion

This chapter aimed to show how using continual FOI requests can strengthen the methodological toolbox for scholars studying protest policing. Complex questions about the suppression of collective action are best answered by using multiple data sources and methodologies (Klandermans & Staggenborg, 2002). Internal police documents obtained by FOIR can assist in both quantifying the occurrence of protests and adding behind-the-scenes details for in-depth case studies. Further, national interest in protest policing continues amid the proliferation of the Black Lives Matter movement – and other important discussions about policing and race in the U.S. Therefore, FOIR offers a valuable and methodologically flexible source of data for a pertinent area of sociological research. While limitations exist, FOIR data could readily supplement existing data sources, especially in local-level studies.

This study only scratches the surface of potential FOIR uses in social movements and – more broadly – sociological research. Sociologists are not shy about criticising government action and policy, yet few attempt to access the live archive created by the government. Some scholars have posited that sociologists are too polite – or that they view FOIR as only falling under the purview of journalists and lawyers (Keen, 1992; Lee, 2001). Others claim that FOIR is too much of a hassle – and a potential time-suck. But several of these burdens have recently been alleviated by some agencies. During the course of this research, the SPD unveiled a new online portal for FOIR requests that allows the public to easily file requests, track their status and receive records. The adoption of FOIR by more scholars – and the dissemination of research experiences and findings – will help advance methodological discussions of FOIR.

## Notes

1 For this paper, I use the term "freedom of information requests" (FOIR), to be consistent with past work in this field (Greenberg, 2016). Larsen and Walby (2012) point out that "freedom of information" is a misnomer – it implies that information will be made "free" and available. However, researchers with experience in filing open records requests recognise that the "freedom" may oversimplify the process of "brokering access" (Larsen & Walby, 2012).
2 The Department of Justice (2014) provides a full explanation of all exemptions at the federal level.
3 That figure fluctuated between 1 and 6 percent in the preceding five years (Lee, 2001).
4 If presented with FOIR documents from an activist, it may be wise to re-file a similar request to make sure the information is being represented accurately.
5 Scholars often ask whether they should seek institutional review board approval prior to filing public records requests. Walby and Luscombe (2018) lay out a number of reasons why FOIR should be exempt from ethic review boards' purview.
6 Sheila Friend-Gray, Seattle Police Department, email message to the author, June 3, 2015.
7 These keywords are consistent with those referenced by Maney and Oliver (2001).
8 The withholding of police staffing data stands in contrast to the data obtained by Eggert et al. (2018) in Belgium – where police provided complete counts of police staff and equipment used.

## References

Beehner, L. (2013). Cycles of protest: How urban cyclists act like insurgents. *Theory in Action, 6*(2), 52–86.

Beyerlein, K., Soule, S. A., & Martin, N. (2015). Prayers, protest, and police: How religion influences police presence at collective action events in the United States, 1960 to 1995. *American Sociological Review, 80*(6), 1250–1271.

Bridis, T. (2018, March 12). US sets new record for censoring, withholding gov't files. *Associated Press.*

Dafnos, T. (2012). Behind the blue line: Using FOIR in researching the policing of aboriginal activism. In K. Walby, & M. Larsen (Eds.), *Brokering access: Power, politics, and freedom of information process in Canada* (pp. 209–233). Vancouver: University of British Columbia Press.

Davenport, C., Soule, S. A., & Armstrong, D. A. (2011). Protesting while black? the differential policing of american activism, 1960 to 1990. *American Sociological Review, 76*(1), 152–178.

Earl, J., Martin, A., McCarthy, J. D., & Soule, S. A. (2004). The use of newspaper data in the study of collective action. *Annual Review of Sociology, 30*(1), 65–80.

Earl, J., & Soule, S. A. (2006). Seeing blue: A police-centered explanation of protest policing. *Mobilization, 11*(2), 145–164.

Earl, J., Soule, S. A., & McCarthy, J. D. (2003). Protest under fire? Explaining the policing of protest. *American Sociological Review, 68*(4), 581–606.

Eggert, N., Wouters, R., Ketelaars, P., & Walgrave, S. (2018). Preparing for action: Police deployment decisions for demonstrations. *Policing and Society, 28*(2), 137–148.

Ellis, R. (2014). Creating a secure network: The 2001 anthrax attacks and the transformation of postal security. *The Sociological Review, 62*, 161–182.

Gillham, P. F. (2011). Securitizing America: Strategic incapacitation and the policing of protest since the 11 september 2001 terrorist attacks. *Sociology Compass, 5*(7), 636–652.

Gillham, P. F., & Marx, G. T. (2000). Complexity and irony in policing and protesting: The world trade organization in Seattle. *Social Justice, 27*(2), 212–236.

Greenberg, P. (2016). Strengthening sociological research through public records requests. *Social Currents, 3*(2), 110–117.

Greenberg, P. (2017). Disproportionality and resource-based environmental inequality: An analysis of neighborhood proximity to coal impoundments in Appalachia. *Rural Sociology, 82*(1), 149–178.

Hendricks, A. C. (2014). The apparatus of repression: Washington state's order of battle. Retrieved from www.scribd.com/doc/245314943/The-Apparatus-of-Repression.

Hocke, D. (1999). Determining the selection bias in local and national newspaper reports on protest events. In D. Rucht, R. Koopmans, & F. Neidhardt (Eds.), *Acts of dissent: New developments in the study of protest* (pp. 131–163). Lanham, MD: Rowman & Littlefield.

Hutter, S. (2014). Protest event analysis and its offspring. In D. Della Porta (Ed.), *Methodological practices in social movement research* (pp. 335–367). Oxford, UK: Oxford University Press.

Keen, M. F. (1992). The freedom of information act and sociological research. *The American Sociologist, 23*(2), 43–51.

Klandermans, B., & Staggenborg, S. (2002). *Methods of social movement research.* Minneapolis, MN: University of Minnesota Press.

Larsen, M., & Walby, K. (2012). Power, politics and freedom of information process in Canada. In M. Larsen, & K. Walby (Eds.), *Brokering access: Power, politics and freedom of information process in Canada* (pp. 1–34). Vancouver: University of British Columbia Press.

Lee, R. M. (2001). Research uses of the U.S. Freedom of Information Act. *Field Methods, 13*(4), 370–391.

Luscombe, A., & Walby, K. (2017). Theorizing freedom of information: The live archive, obfuscation, and actor-network theory. *Government Information Quarterly, 34*(3), 379–387.

Luscombe, A., Walby, K., & Lippert, R. K. (2017). Brokering access beyond the border and in the wild: Comparing freedom of information law and policy in Canada and the United States: FOI law in Canada and the USA. *Law & Policy, 39*(3), 259–279.

Maney, G. M., & Oliver, P. E. (2001). Finding collective events: Sources, searches, timing. *Sociological Methods & Research, 30*(2), 131–169.

Marx, G. (1972). *Muckraking sociology; research as social criticism.* New Brunswick, NJ: Transaction Books.

Marx, G. (1984). Notes on the discovery, collection, and assessment of hidden and dirty data. In J. Kitsuse, & J. Schneider (Eds.), *Studies in the sociology of social problems* (pp. 78–113). Norwood, NJ: Ablex.

McAdam, D. (1983). Tactical innovation and the pace of insurgency. *American Sociological Review, 48*(6), 735–754.

McCarthy, J. D., & Mayer, N. Z. (1977). Resource mobilization and social movements: A partial theory. *American Journal of Sociology, 82*(6), 1212–1241.

McCarthy, J. D., & McPhail, C. (1998). The institutionalization of protest in the United States. In D. S. Meyer, & S. Tarrow (Eds.), *The social movement society: Contentious politics for a new century* (pp. 83–110). New York: Rowman & Littlefield.

McCarthy, J. D., McPhail, C., & Smith, J. (1996). Images of protest: Dimensions of selection bias in media coverage of Washington demonstrations, 1982 and 1991. *American Sociological Review, 61*(3), 478–499.

Meyer, D. S., & Minkoff, D. C. (2004). Conceptualizing political opportunity. *Social Forces, 82*(4), 1457–1492.

Michener, G. (2011). FOI laws around the world. *Journal of Democracy, 22*(2), 145–159.

Noakes, J., & Gillham, P. (2007). Police and protestor innovation since Seattle. *Mobilization, 12*(4), 335–340.

Noakes, J. A. (1995). Using FBI files for historical sociology. *Qualitative Sociology, 18*(2), 271–286.

Rappert, B. (2012). States of ignorance: The unmaking and remaking of death tolls. *Economy and Society, 41*(1), 42–63.

Roberts, A. (2006). *Blacked out: Government secrecy in the information age.* Cambridge, New York: Cambridge University Press.

Sadurni, L. F. (2016, June 30). President Obama signs FOIA reform bill into law on 50th anniversary. *Reporters Committee for Freedom of the Press.* Retrieved from www.rcfp. org/browse-media-law-resources/news/president-obama-signs-foia-reform-bill-law-50th-anniversary.

Savage, A., & Hyde, R. (2014). Using freedom of information requests to facilitate research. *International Journal of Social Research Methodology, 17*(3), 303–317.

Seattle Police Department. (2015). Seattle police department manual. Retrieved from www.seattle.gov/police-manual.

Snow, D. A., & Anderson, L. (1991). *Researching the homeless.* Chapel Hill, NC: University of North Carolina Press.

Snow, D. A., & Trom, D. (2002). The case study and the study of social movements. In B. Klandermans, & S. Staggenborg (Eds.), *Methods of social movement research* (pp. 146–172). Minneapolis, MN: University of Minnesota Press.

Theoharis, A. G. (2011). *Abuse of power: How cold war surveillance and secrecy policy shaped the response to 9/11*. Philadelphia, PA: Temple University Press.

Tilly, C. (1978). *From mobilization to revolution*. Reading, MA: Addison-Wesley Pub. Co.

Uldam, J., & McCurdy, P. (2013). Studying social movements: Challenges and opportunities for participant observation. *Sociology Compass, 7*(11), 941–951.

U.S. Department of Justice. (2014). *Department of justice guide to the Freedom of Information Act*. Washington, DC: Department of Justice – Office of Information Policy. Retrieved from www.justice.gov/oip/doj-guide-freedom-information-act-0.

Walby, K. (2009). 'He asked me if i was looking for fags.' Ottawa's National Capital Commission Conservation Officers and the policing of public park sex. *Surveillance & Society, 6*(4), 367–379.

Walby, K., & Larsen, M. (2012). Access to information and freedom of information requests: Neglected means of data production in the social sciences. *Qualitative Inquiry, 18*(1), 31–42.

Walby, K., & Luscombe, A. (2017). Criteria for quality in qualitative research and use of freedom of information requests in the social sciences. *Qualitative Research, 17*(5), 537–553.

Walby, K., & Luscombe, A. (2018). Ethics review and freedom of information requests in qualitative research. *Research Ethics, 14*(4), 1–15.

Wood, L. J. (2014). *Crisis and control: The militarization of protest policing*. New York: Pluto Press.

Woolley, J. T. (2000). Using media-based data in studies of politics. *American Journal of Political Science, 44*(1), 156–173.

# Appendix A

Protest Events in Seattle, by data source, January 1, 2014 to January 1, 2016

| Date | Protest | SPD | Seattle Times |
|------|---------|-----|---------------|
| 1/2/14 | Machinists Union Rally | No | Yes |
| 1/11/14 | Protest firing of HS teacher | No | Yes |
| 1/12/14 | Minimum Wage | No | Yes |
| 1/20/14 | MLK Day | No | Yes |
| 2/20/14 | Minimum Wage | No | Yes |
| 2/22/14 | Venezuela | No | Yes |
| 3/15/14 | Minimum Wage | No | Yes |
| 3/25/14 | DUI Awareness | No | Yes |
| 4/11/14 | Prison Privatization | No | Yes |
| 5/1/14 | May Day 2015 | Yes | Yes |
| 5/1/14 | Heal the Hood | No | Yes |
| 5/30/14 | Anti-Violence Against Women | No | Yes |
| 6/26/14 | Teachers vs. Gates Foundation | No | Yes |
| 7/24/14 | Anti-Oil Train | No | Yes |
| 8/9/14 | Pro-Palestinian Rally | No | Yes |
| 11/24/14 | Ferguson | No | Yes |
| 11/25/14 | Ferguson | No | Yes |
| 11/28/14 | Black Lives Matter | No | Yes |
| 11/29/14 | Protest Against Police | Yes | Yes |
| 12/1/14 | Ferguson | No | Yes |
| 12/2/14 | Ferguson | Yes | No |
| 12/3/14 | Ferguson | No | Yes |
| 12/3/14 | Ferguson | Yes | Yes |
| 12/4/14 | Ferguson | Yes | No |
| 12/6/14 | Ferguson | Yes | Yes |
| 12/7/14 | Ferguson | Yes | Yes |
| 12/8/14 | Ferguson | Yes | No |
| 12/12/14 | Ferguson | Yes | No |
| 12/13/14 | Ferguson | Yes | No |
| 12/14/14 | Black Lives Matter | Yes | Yes |
| 12/15/14 | Ferguson | Yes | No |
| 12/27/14 | Pro-Police | No | Yes |
| 1/10/15 | Police Accountability | No | Yes |
| 1/19/15 | MLK | Yes | Yes |
| 2/7/15 | Walking While Black Protest | Yes | No |
| 2/13/15 | March Against Police State | Yes | No |
| 2/25/15 | UW Black Lives Matter | Yes | Yes |
| 2/25/15 | Seattle U Adjunct Walkout | No | Yes |
| 3/7/15 | March Against Capitalism | Yes | No |
| 3/10/15 | Anti-Minimum Wage Increase | No | Yes |

(*Continued*)

(Cont).

| Date | Protest | SPD | Seattle Times |
|------|---------|-----|---------------|
| 3/15/15 | Police Brutality March | Yes | No |
| 4/6/15 | Marijuana Safety | No | Yes |
| 4/10/15 | LGB TQ Homeless Youth March | No | Yes |
| 4/14/15 | Black Lives Matter | Yes | No |
| 4/15/15 | Minimum Wage | Yes | Yes |
| 4/25/15 | Black Transgender Lives Matter | Yes | No |
| 4/25/15 | UW Animal Rights Protest | Yes | Yes |
| 4/26/15 | Shell No! Anti-Oil Rig | Yes | No |
| 4/29/15 | Black Lives Matter – Baltimore | Yes | Yes |
| 5/1/15 | May Day 2015 | No | Yes |
| 5/2/15 | Black Lives Matter | Yes | No |
| 5/9/15 | Black Lives Matter | Yes | No |
| 5/14/15 | Shell No! Rig Move In | Yes | No |
| 5/15/15 | Justice for Oscar Perez | Yes | No |
| 5/16/15 | Shell No! | No | Yes |
| 5/18/15 | Shell No! Rig Move Out | Yes | Yes |
| 5/19/15 | Teacher Walkout | No | Yes |
| 5/26/15 | Justice for Bryson Chaplainand Andre Thompson | Yes | No |
| 5/30/15 | Check Your Privilege Rally | Yes | No |
| 6/1/15 | UW Animal Lab Protests | No | Yes |
| 6/5/15 | June Against Doom – Anti-Shell | Yes | Yes |
| 6/6/15 | June Against Doom – Anti-Shell | Yes | No |
| 6/8/15 | June Against Doom – Anti-Shell | Yes | No |
| 6/9/15 | Ragin' Grannies – Anti-Shell | No | Yes |
| 6/13/15 | Queer Nation: Protest Against Violence | Yes | No |
| 6/15/15 | Shell No! Rig Move Out | Yes | No |
| 6/19/15 | United Gang Members March | Yes | Yes |
| 7/1/15 | SEIU Healthcare Picket/Rally | Yes | No |
| 8/8/15 | Black Lives Matter at Bernie Sanders Rally | No | Yes |
| 8/9/15 | Ferguson Anniversary Rally | No | Yes |
| 8/14/15 | Hempfest | Yes | No |
| 8/22/15 | Planned Parenthood Rally | Yes | No |
| 9/10/15 | Charter School Support Rally | No | Yes |
| 9/22/15 | Chinese President Visit | No | Yes |
| 10/2/15 | Animal Rights at UW | Yes | Yes |
| 11/27/15 | Black Lives Matter – Black Friday | Yes | Yes |
| 12/7/15 | Coal Train/Fossil Fuel Protest | No | Yes |
| 12/11/15 | Justice for Hazma | Yes | Yes |
| 12/13/15 | End Gun Violence | No | Yes |
| 12/31/15 | YSC Protest | Yes | No |

## PART 3

# Freedom of Information

Triangulation, data analysis
and exposition

# 8

# PIECING IT TOGETHER, STUDYING PUBLIC–PRIVATE PARTNERSHIPS

## Freedom of Information as oligoptic technologies

*Debra Mackinnon*

## Introduction

Owing to the difficulty in gathering qualitative and quantitative data about surveillance, security and intelligence, scholars have pioneered new methods and adapted existing ones.[1] In particular, Access to Information (ATI) and Freedom of Information (FOI) mechanisms[2] are progressively being used by social science researchers to supplement traditional data collection practices. By exercising quasi-constitutional rights, these mechanisms enable individuals and organisations to request information from federal, provincial and municipal levels of government, which thereby provides a means of compelling a somewhat limited form of transparency (Epp, 2000). These mechanisms are often useful for addressing internal dynamics, historical contexts, knowledge production and representations of government bodies (Larsen & Walby, 2012). Cast as a form of "smart mixed methods" (Lather, 2010), ATI/FOI can be used to guide exploratory research, highlight longitudinal trends and establish disjunctures between official, experiential and ATI/FOI produced data (Savage & Hyde, 2014; Walby & Larsen, 2011). Furthermore, this access to the "live archive" produces insights into surveillance societies, the interoperability of government agencies, as well as challenges, conceptions or insertions of the "state" (Larsen & Walby, 2012). Government agencies and the records that are produced by them are rarely the domain of a single organisation (Walby & Larsen, 2011). Rather than a monolithic, homogenous entity, these mechanisms lend credence to analysis that shows the multitude of networked agencies enacting "the state." For example, much research has used FOI to explore the role of the corrections (Larsen & Piché, 2009), policing (Luscombe & Walby, 2014; Monaghan & Walby 2012) and national security (Monaghan, 2017).

However, in all of these instances, "the state" and its actions are never wholly "public." Nowhere is this more apparent than with respect to Public–Private Partnerships (PPPs), and in particular public–private policing[3] partnerships. As established by Bayley and Shearing (1996), these policing projects are often made up of a network of public and private actors. Noting intensification and variegated corporate structures, recent work on networked policing has primarily focused on private contract firms (Huey & Rosenberg, 2004; Lippert & O'Connor, 2006; Lippert & Walby, 2012) as well as community-based methods models (Johnson & Shearing, 2003). Entangled with broader trends of neoliberalisation, outsourcing/agentification, entrepreneurialism, privatisation and austerity, this work depicts a shift from direct and public state control to private and quasi-entities. Referred to as New Public Management (NPM), since the 1980s, many democratic nations have dramatically restructured their private sector in these ways (Roberts, 2000). However, as noted by Roberts in 2000 – while this shift to NPM has been criticised for undermining democratic control, putting public interest at odds with entrepreneurialism and weakening chains of responsibility – little attention has been paid to how NPM restructuring and the rise of these quasi-entities has weakened FOI mechanisms.

In this chapter, I review methods for studying private policing and offer critical reflections on methods and methodology. This chapter is guided by the following key question: What does it mean to do FOI research on public–private information? Heeding calls for more empirical cases detailing networked policing, this chapter focuses on the use of ATI and FOI mechanisms in the context of public–private partnerships and policing, specifically focusing on the surveillance and security initiatives of Business Improvement Areas (BIAs). Through a review of normative and sustained methods for inquiry, I argue that when studying these public yet private enterprises, FOI mechanisms can be an effective tool for exploring these contingent and continuously enacted processes. Grounded in a case of the creation of a public–private information sharing network, I trace entry points into this surveillance network and offer a reflexive account of the multiple ways in which these mechanisms can help provide insights into surveillance societies. Specifically, by presenting a case of an actor network, I argue that the enactment of FOI mechanisms are oligoptic technologies, that, when pieced together with documents, interviews and participant observation, are a valuable means of *gathering* insights into the creation and nature of public–private partnerships and interoperability of para-governmental agencies. Continuing in the vein of emerging research that has studied FOI as an actor network (Luscombe & Walby, 2017), I suggest that the promise of data triangulation needs to be tempered with notions of object fragments, the "problem of multiplicity" and the process of gathering. Too often as researchers we sanitise accounts in attempting to declutter and make sense of mess (Law, 2004). Reflecting on the quantity and quality of objects and representations that I have gathered in this tracing exercise, I suggest that by thinking about the FOI collection and request process as oligoptic, we can wade our way through these fragmented objects and better account for the constitutive influence of our gathering practices.

## Privately policing the urban

Private policing across North America has rapidly expanded over the past three decades (Cunningham, Strauchs, & Van Meter, 1990; Leclair & Long, 1996). In Canada, the growth of private security has consistently outpaced public forces 3-to-1 (Easton & Furness, 2012; Rigakos & Greener, 2000). This expansion has further blurred the distinction between public police and private security. However, these leaky containers (Lyon, 2001) of public and private security infrastructures are increasingly coming into contact with one another. Cooley (2005) notes that while privatisation characterises the shift in the nature of policing, it is a simultaneously limiting concept, as the broader tasks of policing are increasingly performed by a network of private and public police. Normatively, discussed as a nodal governance, Johnston and Shearing (2003) argue that while this multiscalar and context-based approach may advance democratic outcomes, it may also reproduce power inequalities. The production of security is an inherently plural and unstable process comprised of internal and environmental forces (Dupont, 2014). This security regime, while not only sharing many institutional, technological and practical characteristics (Kempa, 2011), also shares in the production and exchange of data and information. Boyle (2011) argues that "these diffuse alliances seek to insinuate themselves within state and non-state networks, by monopolizing capital, or context specific resources" (p. 176).

BIAs, as the further neoliberalisation of public–private partnerships, represent a "new" and contentious form of privatised local governance, and in many instances policing. Often established in consultation with other BIAs, local law enforcement and security experts, BIAs have increasingly added crime control policies and practices to their organisational mandates. While primarily concerned with varying levels of broken windows policing – the promotion of beautification projects, street cleaning, façade regeneration and graffiti removal – some BIAs have also opted for CCTV and private security personnel. Attempting to maintain safety and security in these areas, BIAs have become integral actors responsible for privately policing cities.

In Canada, those studying BIAs and private policing have challenged traditional conceptions of BIAs as simply forms of entrepreneurial urbanism, friendly commercial spaces or grass-roots business communities. Instead, they have been conceptualised as vehicular ideas spreading and mutating across the globe (McCann & Ward, 2012; Ward, 2005, 2006), purveyors of private policing (Huey, Ericson, & Haggerty, 2005), agents of urban pacification (Kempa, 2011; Rigakos, 2015), brandscapes of control and consumption (Bookman & Woolford, 2013; Lippert & Sleiman, 2012) and producers of "clean and safe rationalities" (Lippert, 2012, 2014; Sleiman & Lippert, 2010). These studies have primarily relied on a range of mixed methods, including interviews, surveys, ethnographies, work shadowing and reviews of planning and BIA-produced documents. While yielding in-depth and instructive cases, which temper a lot of the hype and normative discourses surrounding BIAs, following the other recommendations of this volume, I suggest work in this area could be further supplemented through the use of FOI and ATI mechanisms. However, to do so when studying PPPs, service providers and third parties, requires navigating practical questions of custody and control. Are BIAs public or private entities, and what is the reach of FOI mechanisms into their inner workings?

## Public or private partnerships? Custody and control

Usually established in areas with high levels of existing commercial space, businesses in a district may petition their municipal government to create an autonomous authority for the marketing and management of local issues. BIAs are formed and maintained through both provincial and municipal legislation. In British Columbia, the British Columbia Local Government *Act* outlines a BIA's incorporation, governance and organisation; however, its business plan, financial requirements and budget must be approved at the municipal level (City of Vancouver, 2014). With a traditional board governance structure, businesses determine the BIA's budget and request that the funds be collected as a levy against its property taxes. Depending on the needs of the area, this budget may include activities such as promotion, placemaking, community safety and governance and administration (City of Vancouver, 2018). The levy, recoverable grant structure, as well as their relationships to local government and various liaison points, challenge their quasi-corporate structure, imbricating them in various FOI processes – but only in part. As Walby and Larsen (2011) note,

> It is difficult to inquire into the texts that one government agency produces or the work that is done with texts in one government agency without understanding how that work and those texts are organized in a network with other agencies within the government sphere – and often with private sector and nongovernmental interests.
>
> *(p. 34)*

Under the *Freedom of Information and Protection of Privacy Act* (FIPPA) and other analogous acts,[4] individuals and organisations have the right to access any record in the "custody" or under the "control" of a public body. Since these terms are not defined in the *Act*, there are various orders that consider whether a record is in the custody and control of a public body, and this includes records created by service providers and third parties. While precedence and guidance is mixed in terms of outcomes (2002 BCIPC; 2010 BCIPC 5; 2015 BCIPC 71), directive policy suggests that:

> custody (of a record) means having physical possession of a record, even though the public body does not necessarily have responsibility for the

record. Physical possession normally includes responsibility for access, managing, maintaining, preserving, disposing, and providing security.

*(Government of British Columbia)*

However, possession of a record is not enough to establish custody. As determined in Ontario Order P-239, rather than physical possession, custody concerns a public body having "some right to deal with the records and some responsibility for their care and protection" (1991 OIPC 33). In other words, the public body must have some legal right or obligation to the record in order to establish custody over it (2013 BCIPC 30). Beyond custody of a record, a public body must also have authority over that record. Since control is not a defined term in the *Act*, plain meaning definitions as well as various legal tests have been used to determine its meaning. Guidance suggests that "control [of a record] means the power or authority to manage the record throughout its life cycle, including restricting, regulating and administering its use or disclosure" (Government of British Columbia, 2018).

Control, Commonly understood as having power over, courts have also considered and distinguished between "ultimate," "immediate," "partial," "full," "transient," "lasting," "de jure" and "de facto" control (2015 BCIPC 71). In other words, rather than a persistent feature, control is contextual, situational and often session based. In order to establish if a public body has control over a record, various factors are considered including: who created the record and was it in the course of their duties; was the record created by a consultant; does a contract specify, control or permit the public body to inspect, review, possess or copy the record; could a public body reasonably expect to maintain a copy of the record; does the content of the record pertain to the mandate and functions of the public body; does the public body have authority to regulate the use and disposition of the record; does the public body rely on the record to a substantial extent; and is the record integrated with other records held by the public body (Government of British Columbia 2015 BCIPC 71).

While not an exhaustive list (see Larsen, 2013 for further discussions of exemptions), factors like these are considered by an institution when determining whether to release or redact records. As with the use of ATI and FOI mechanisms more generally, success in acquiring records can be a complicated and ineffective task and some of these questions may only arise through a challenge or decision. Third-party processes are common when dealing with issues of custody and control. This would likely involve the public body contacting the service provider or partner to determine how the release of a record might impact them. In a negotiation process that could result in delays and extensions, files would be sent off to the third party for review, at which point they can request that a record be redacted or omitted. While many governments are turning towards open data practices, especially for matters concerning taxation and public spending (see Savage & Hyde, 2014), generally, FOI requests concerning PPPs result in fractured views determined not only by the parameters of the request, but also by relations of custody and control.

## Piecing it together: tracing a BIA information communication network

To illuminate this discussion of navigating FOI mechanisms and PPP, I will recount an exploratory research project; specifically, tracing and following the involvement of one Downtown Vancouver BIA through major Vancouver events – The Stanley Cup Riot and Occupy Vancouver (OV). As two events in the contemporary Vancouver imaginary, they are frequently drawn upon and recontextualised in order to justify and legitimise the increase in surveillance and neoliberal governance. By viewing methods as a bricolage, I highlight various vantage points or keyholes into studying this PPP policing network. These additive and cascading methods, when overlaid, help make sense of the mess, multiplicity and practice of FOI data production and gathering.

On October 15, 2011, the Vancouver, British Columbia branch of the Occupy Movement assembled in front of the downtown art gallery (VAG). Initially bringing together people from "all walks of life" (Doc11, November 6, 2011),[5] the tent city in the heart of Vancouver's art and entertainment district challenged the spatial boundaries of the Downtown Eastside; within two weeks of its construction, the City, backed by local business, called for its closure. By November 21, the courts imposed steep sanctions, and the Vancouver Police Department (VPD), with the help of other agencies, forcibly removed Occupiers from the art gallery lands.

Several FOI requests and many months later, I found myself sifting through hundreds of emails between Vancouver City Hall, the VPD and various stakeholders, including the Downtown Vancouver Business Improvement Association (DVBIA). Piecing together participant observation, interviews and various documents including police board minutes, presentation docks from City Hall, numerous BIA publications and newspaper articles, I was able to explicate the role of the DVBIA in the policing of OV and other events, and uncover the activities of the public–private surveillance networks.

As extensively documented (see Wolf, December 29, 2012), multiscalar interoperability was a key factor in the criminalisation of OV, as well as the Occupy Movement as a whole. Multiscalar interoperability refers to non-linear correspondence, intelligence gathering and coordinated administrative decisions between and within governing bodies, as well as similar practices with those outside of the governing bodies. The VPD, on behalf of the City of Vancouver, sought additional resources from the provincial government, namely the Royal Canadian Mounted Police (RCMP) Tactical Troop and the Provincial Police force (Doc4, October 14, 2011). In his request, Vancouver Chief Constable Chu listed the DVBIA, the Canadian Bankers Association and various property owners as key stakeholders in the management of this protest event (Doc4, October 14, 2011). Cited as potential targets of OV, the relationship between these organisations, as city partners, was detailed in further correspondence.

In particular, one heavily redacted chain between the City and the VPD concerning the estimated costs of OV caught my attention. A November 1, 2011

Council Briefing stated that the DVBIA was working closely with the business community, adjacent hotels and the Vancouver Art gallery to mitigate the impacts of OV (Doc 14). The nature of this mitigation was further elaborated upon in a December 19, 2011, internal correspondence from City Manager's Office to Council. The then Vancouver City Manager Ballem stated,

> During the occupation, the local business community was extremely supportive of [the City's] efforts to manage the occupation. As an example, local hotels provided [the City] with access to their business centre to enable access to computers and printers for some of the legal and regulatory work involved in the Occupy issue. They also provided intermittently through the situation access to a hotel room to allow us to monitor events and deploy staff when required. Both VPD and VFRS used these facilities intermittently for their 24/7 oversight of the situation.
>
> *(Doc 15)*

But the role of the DVBIA was not limited to the lending of printers, or free hotel rooms for the 24/7 surveillance of the tent city. As detailed in a presentation dock, the cooperation of businesses surrounding the VAG lands was key to the City's statutory and regulatory framework for managing OV. The gradual creation of this framework was set forth throughout internal correspondence. In an October 24 internal memorandum, which was officialised at the October 27 meeting, the DVBIA along with Vancouver Coastal Health, VAG, TransLink, the Government of BC, BC Ambulance Service and E-COMM were named as key external partners of the City Large Events Oversight Committee (CLEOC)[6] (Doc7, October 24, 2011; Doc13, October 27, 2011). On a recommendation from the June 2011 Stanley Cup riots inquiry, the CLEOC was created as the body overseeing the regulation and enforcement of bylaws. Based on this briefing, as well as DVBIA publications, the Business Improvement Association assumed a prominent leadership role in liaising with the CLEOC and local business.

Initially presented as part of the guiding principles of managing OV, the creation and administration of this framework involved various members of the CLEOC, the external partners of the CLEOC and consultations with other jurisdictions. For instance, the City of Vancouver drew on discourses and strategies previously deployed in Victoria, Calgary, Ottawa, Edmonton, Toronto and Montreal[7] (Doc13, October 27, 2011). The City and Department of Justice legitimised the use of surveillance in its framework by constructing the strategies of other jurisdictions as "monitor and wait" approaches (Doc13, October 27, 2011; Doc17, n.d.). Specifically, this framework included the *Public Health Act*, the *Fire By-law*, the *Street and Traffic By-law*, the *Criminal Code*, the *City Land Regulation By-law* and the *Trespass Act*.

While the City primarily managed OV, the creation and utilisation of the CLEOC blur the roles and responsibilities of administration and enforcement. The social control of protest is not limited to the actions of municipal or state officers, but instead it is an organisational means of maintaining security that is increasingly reliant on the interoperability of security and surveillance networks, as well as the connections between the "public" and "private" network (Earl, Soule, & McCarthy, 2003; Monaghan & Walby, 2012). As OV challenged representations of space, various levels and forms of governance established reciprocal information sharing relationships (as well as free hotel rooms; Doc15, December 19, 2011). Charles Gauthier, executive director of the DVBIA, claimed that OV necessitated the creation of a "robust network for disseminating information about critical incident matters" (DVBIA, 2012, p. 1). In order to help members manage the protest,

> [the] DVBIA gathered its own intelligence and obtained tips from the VPD, such as names of businesses that were at risk of being targeted, and protest march routes. Updates were sent out around the clock. Throughout Occupy Vancouver, the DVBIA solicited advice and perspectives from fellow BIAs in Canada and the United States. Going forward, the Vancouver Police Department and the City Large Event Oversight Committee have both agreed to share information about the future of public gathering with the DVBIA.
>
> *(DVBIA, 2012, p. 1)*

By viewing "public gatherings" as potential riots and revenue losses for the downtown core, the DVBIA further legitimised its administrative role. The DVBIA "leveraged relationships with the police, security experts and hotel operators" to gather information on strategies employed by police officers and other business owners (DVBIA, 2012, p. 1). While sharing information about "future public gatherings," none of the organisations clearly defined what constituted a "public gathering."

The VPD in its *Public Demonstrations Guidelines* (2012) states, "[it] manages approximately 250–300 public gatherings a year. These range from large planned congregations such as the [Honda, HBSC] Celebration of Light to gatherings which ultimately become demonstrations, such as Occupy Vancouver…" (p. 2). This differentiation between public gatherings and public demonstrations was recontextualised by the DVBIA. In *Downtown Matters* (2012), the DVBIA noted that OV's "tent city" forced the relocation of the "Coast Capital Christmas Square" and shortened the "Rogers Santa Claus Parade." It is evident that "public gatherings" for the DVBIA are not those attended by the public, but rather those that are not organised by private business. Private interests bring with them insurance, economic sponsorship and the promise of profit.

In this early illustrative instance, the creation of this information sharing network highlights the actors involved in the increasing interoperability and alignment of public and private bodies responsible for urban governance and policing. Five years later, I found myself sitting across the table from a DVBIA representative following up on their crime and security initiatives. Drawing on this insider knowledge and playing the acronym game, I asked about the CLEOC and the companion programme Operation Cooperation. I disclosed my familiarity with the programme and asked how it had changed. Unfazed, the Safety Manager responded:

Operation Cooperation. We're going to close it down and we're going to start fresh. We have our main people, but we want to see as I mentioned, the different level of access…. We are at the stage where we had a meeting with VPD yesterday to get their input and what they think. They can't directly advise us, and we can't be an agent to the VPD, or however you want to phrase it, but for it to be successful, we need their support behind it. Or for it to be useful to them.

Noting the blurred, yet clearly distinguishable boundaries between the DVBIA and the municipal police, the coordinator stressed the importance of functionality and buy-in:

We are gathering ideas and trying to do something different. We want to find a more effective network, it's more about the communications of working together. For example, I talked about a push-alert system for businesses. Say there is a protest Downtown, a road closure, a riot, or a natural disaster – you want something that is going to be able to reach out to a huge membership and area.

Once again, drawing upon these shared histories of protests and riots, the manager explicated an intended use case. He compared and critiqued a local high-end retail group's information system, stating:

They receive information on protests or road closures [from the City and VPD], but that's not all that specific to them, and how much of that information is then given down for the retailers and business owners? That information should be available to everyone if needed. So, if you have a system that sends people notifications whether it be by email, or thinking big, text messages – it will be pretty effective. I go back to the Vancouver Riots and ask what could we have had then technology-wise that would have helped us? I think they did a great job, especially with the clean up after. But should we ever have anything like that again, this will make it easier, and that's where I see the need for more information sharing.

By piecing together ATI and FOI releases, public documents and interviews, the role of the DVBIA in policing the downtown area was highlighted. The recurring involvement of city officials and private organisations over the course of three key events – the installation of CCTV with the 2010 Olympics, the creation of anti-masking legislation days after the 2011 Stanley Cup Riots and Occupy Vancouver – helped formalise an information communication network between these and other public and private agencies (Mackinnon, 2018). A network that continues to be made and remade. However, only by approaching this network via different institutional nodes and forms of information I was able to trace these relations altogether gather a picture. A cascading and complicating process, without initial

FOI mechanisms, I would not have had insights into the nature of these relationships or the basic organisational structure of the PPP. Similarly, without overlaying
this information with BIA-produced documents, I may not have been able to
broker interviews or draw upon insider knowledge in order to ask for additional
information. So, while offering a particular vantage point, like any method, using
FOIs when studying PPPs serves to produce compelling narratives that may not
otherwise be traced through conventional means.

## Oligopticism and looking through keyholes: partiality, multiplicity and gathering

Much research has noted the power as well as the problems of FOI as either the
"live archive," "obfuscation" or an "actor network" (Luscombe & Walby, 2017).
Recent work on the latter has theorised FOI as an actor network, full of hetero-
geneous actors and actants, contingency, obligatory passage points, messiness and
black boxes. Interested in questions of how, rather than why (Savage & Hyde,
2014), studying FOI actor networks focuses on the processes of the making,
production, collection and gathering of objects and representations. While not dis-
missing contending and often co-existing views, theorising in this vein challenges
preconceived understandings of the state, citizens, compliance, users, records and
power (Luscombe & Walby, 2017). Rather, these relations are enacted. In order
to extend this discussion, I temper these conceptions of FOI and complicate
the above polished case with a reflexive account of FOI mechanisms as oligoptic
technologies by examining notions of partiality, multiplicity and gathering.

FOI mechanisms offer researchers a particular means of exploring what PPPs
are doing, that a researcher might not have been able to access (Savage & Hyde,
2014). Although these tools may provide access to the "live archive," researchers
must remember that actor networks and methods assemblages – as well as the
records and objects that are collected – are co-constructed. Notions of spins, stalls
and shutdowns endemic to policing and security research can be juxtaposed with
brokering access, law in the wild and feral law (Lippert, Walby, & Wilkinson,
2015; Luscombe, Walby, & Lippert, 2017).

Collection processes and the mechanisms used to access them are oligoptic in
nature, in that they afford partial and selected views – what I have referred to
throughout as vantage points, or keyholes. As nodes of calculation, through
which arithmetic control is fractured and contested, multiple spaces and subjectivities are co-constructed. These nodes "see too little to feed the megalomania
of the inspector or the paranoia of the inspected, but what they see, they see it
well" (Latour, 2005, p. 181). While the clarity offered by these mechanisms may
be contested, through creative brokering practices and varied and cascading
channels, they enable actors to gaze in some directions and not others (Amin &
Thrift, 2002). However, rather than see the multiple rays that these oligoptic
tools may trace as flaws, the multiplicity they enact is powerful.

Those using FOI mechanisms have stressed their power, but also their limitations in terms of data triangulation (Lippert et al., 2015; Savage & Hyde, 2014). The integration, or triangulation, of different methods is a common and highly productive practice that often requires critical reflection on the research questions and the methodological foundations of the project. In studies that pursue a multi-faceted understanding of social phenomena, data triangulation adds "rigor, breadth, complexity, richness and depth to any inquiry" (Denzin, 2012, p. 82). While Denzin's conception of triangulation has positivist and modernist overtones that assume a fixed, singular reality, others have borrowed and expanded his term to consider multiplicity and complexity. As argued by Cook and Crang (1996),

> the power of a text which deals with these knowledges comes not from smoothing them out, but through juxtaposing and montaging them… so that audiences can work their way through them and, along the way, inject and make their own critical knowledges out of them.
>
> *(as cited in Cook 2004, p. 642)*

In this sense, the bricolage of competing representations and antagonisms enables a richer, more nuanced tracing (see also Pich, this volume). In the above case, method and mechanism were path-dependent. However, layering them and tracing convergence and divergence created almost an additive effect. For instance, combining the city hall presentation with internal communications sheds light on the CLEOC. And by attempting to trace it through FOI mechanisms and the various records of stakeholders, parts of its organisational structure were enacted. These partial records, or fractional objects, overlap and interfere with each other, highlighting the messiness and multiplicity, as they enact different perspectives and realities (Law, 2004). Framed by Mol (2002) as the "problem of multiplicity," social science, rather than trying to seek truth out of these partial sightlines and multiple realities, should try to know realities that are vague, as "much of the world is enacted in that way" (Law, 2004, p. 14).

Understanding FOI as an actor network emphasises processes and enactments. Beyond accentuating FOI users' proficiency in knowing, enrolling and navigating (Luscombe & Walby, 2017), these methods assemblages highlight the active role of the researcher in the "gathering" process (see Bracken-Roche, this collection). Rather than understanding these oligoptic mechanisms as revealing a particular truth, gathering is the active role of the researcher in bringing together, relating, picking, meeting, building up or flowing together. This case highlights brokering strategies used throughout the FOI and research process as well as my role in the process as a gatherer, and how I navigated and made sense of the mess – or how records can be used to understand these oligoptic processes. By making knowledge public through the FOI process, researchers not only enact particular realities through "data production" (Walby & Larsen, 2011), but also afford the ability to place readers and others in the thick of it.

The publicness of FOI data is powerful in that it allows and even fosters multiplicity. In doing so, it is a useful tool in the methods assemblage that allows us to enact and depict multiple realities, amplifying and detecting resonance. However, as warned by Roberts (2000), this "publicness" has long been under fire. As once public services continue to be transferred or contracted to private and quasi-public entities, accountability and transparency have been devalued and/or lost. In other words, what was once entailed by the "public" in previous incarnations of NPM organisations and PPPs, has been eclipsed by the "new" and the "private," and so too have mechanisms for public resource. Recognising the shift to NPM, why haven't we seen a shift in legislation to account for the new nature of governance? Notions of competitive advantage and trade secrets need to be tempered with accountability, transparency and the protection of public interests. Law is malleable, and FOI mechanisms should reflect the changing nature how public services are being distributed. Under NPM, accountability and transparency are paramount; broader, nuanced understandings of the nature of these quasi-public entities need to be reflected in the law. Given precedent in other jurisdictions to include quasi-public and para-governmental entities in FOI mechanisms (Moe, 2001; Savage & Hyde, 2014), efforts to expand the scope of policy and legislation should be taken to the Office of the Information Commissioner. Otherwise, as we continue to see neoliberalisation take hold, the keyholes and partial views we currently have may continue to be narrowed and obscured, further limiting transparency and democratic principles.

When studying PPPs, FOI mechanisms act as oligoptic technologies, and, when overlaid rather than triangulated, help trace actor networks. While researchers need to be critical of how much one can trace with these fragmented objects and representations, their power to reveal complex networked relationships is an underutilised method (see Warren, this collection). As both oligoptic collection and production technologies, researchers can reveal these networks through gathering processes, thereby creating multiple subjectivities, spaces and truths. Although traditional FOI research has been primarily concerned with how truth claims are made and shed light on the surveillance state, I argue that the study of PPPs through FOI and the partiality and mess of it is something we need to embrace.

## Notes

1 For example, Marx (1984) explores archival analysis as an institutionalised discovery method in order to access hidden official records. Larsen, Walby, Monaghan, and others have furthered this search for dirty data using Access to Information and Freedom of Information releases (Brownlee & Walby, 2015; Walby & Larsen, 2011, 2013). Similarly, Savage and Hyde (2014) note the power of FOI to amass large data sets that a single researcher would not normally be able to collect. As well, Walby (2005) has argued that institutional ethnography is a useful method for studying circuits of human surveillance agents, texts and human surveillance subjects.
2 Hereafter referred to as FOI mechanisms, or mechanisms more simply.
3 Policing is hereon understood as "any activity that is expressly designed and intended to establish and maintain (or enforce) a defined order within a community" (Hermer et al., 2005, p. 23).

4  See Walby and Larsen (2012) for a detailed list of federal, provincial and municipal ATI and FOI mechanisms.

5  For consistency across work drawing upon these ATI and FOI documents, I have employed the following codes: Doc6-15= File number 04-1000-20-2013-312 City of Vancouver and Doc16-17=File number A-2013-01302 Department of Justice; Doc18-19=File Number 1–3 2947A Vancouver Police Department.

6  A recommendation of the Stanley Cup Riot Review; the CLEOC is chaired by the deputy City Manager, and is made up of key City of Vancouver departments as well external partners including Vancouver Coastal Health, DVBIA, TransLink, Government of BC, Solicitor General, BC Ambulance Service, E-COMM and other partners as necessary (Doc 16, Oct 14, 2011).

7  Based on the October 27, 2011 Council Briefing, internal members of the CLEOC included the City Manager, Deputy General Manager, Community Services Group, Chief Building Official, City Homeless Advocate, City Engineer, Director of Transportation, Special Events Office Manager, Director/AD Communications, Directors Facilities Manager, Directors OEM, Fire Chief/Deputy and Chief Constable/Deputy Chief (Doc13).

## References

Amin, A., & Thrift, N. (2002). *Cities: Reimagining the urban*. Malden, MA: Polity Press.

Bayley, D. H., & Shearing, C. D. (1996). The future of policing. *Law and Society Review*, *30*, 585–606.

Bookman, S., & Woolford, A. (2013). Policing (by) the urban brand: Defining order in Winnipeg's exchange district. *Social & Cultural Geography*, *14*(3), 300–317.

Boyle, P. (2011). Knowledge networks: Mega-events and security expertise. In *Security Games: Surveillance and Control at Mega-events* (pp. 169–184). New York, NY: Routledge.

British Columbia Order F13-23, 2013 BCIPC No. 30 (CanLII).

Brownlee, J., & Walby, K. (Eds.). (2015). *Access to information and social justice: Critical research strategies for journalists, scholars, and activists*. Winnipeg: ARP Books.

City of Vancouver. (2014). Business Improvement Areas. Retrieved from http://vancouver.ca/doing-business/business-improvement-areas-bias.aspx.

City of Vancouver. (2018). Approval of 2018-19 Business Improvement Area (BIA) budgets. Retrieved from http://council.vancouver.ca/20180313/documents/a2.pdf.

Cook, I. (2004). Follow the thing: Papaya. *Antipode*, *36*(4), 642–664.

Cooley, D. (Ed.). (2005). *Re-imagining policing in Canada*. Toronto: University of Toronto Press.

Cunningham, W., Strauchs, J. J., & Van Meter, C. W. (1990). *The Hallcrest report II: Private security trends 1970–2000*. Stoneham, MA: Butterworth-Heinemann.

Denzin, N. (2012). Triangulation 2.0. *Journal of Mixed Methods Research*, *6*(2), 80–88.

Downtown Vancouver Business Improvement Association. (2012). Communications network helps members manage Occupy Vancouver protest. *Downtown Matters*, 40110389. Retrieved from www.downtownvancouver.net/files/newsletters/2012WinterNewsletter.pdf.

Dupont, B. (2014). Private security regimes: Conceptualizing the forces that shape the private delivery of security. *Theoretical Criminology*, *18*(3), 263–281.

Earl, J., Soule, S. A., & McCarthy, J. D. (2003). Protest under fire? Explaining the policing of protest. *American Sociological Review*, *68*, 581–606.

Easton, S., & Furness, E. (2012). *Canadian policing*. Unpublished manuscript, Department of Criminology, Simon Fraser University, Burnaby, Canada.

Epp, C. (2000). Exploring the costs of administrative legalization: City expenditures on legal services, 1960–1995. *Law and Society Review*, *34*, 407–430.

Government of British Columbia. (2018). FOIPPA policy definitions. www2.gov.bc.ca/gov/content/governments/services-for-government/policies-procedures/foippa-manual/policy-definitions#c.

Hermer, J., Kempa, M., Shearing, C., Stenning, P., & Wood, J. (2005). Policing in Canada in the twenty-first century: directions for law reform. In D. Cooley (Ed.), *Re-imagining policing in Canada*. Toronto: University of Toronto Press.

Huey, L., & Rosenberg, R. (2004). Watching the web: Thoughts on expanding police surveillance opportunities under the cyber-crime convention. *Canadian Journal of Criminology and Criminal Justice*, *46*(5), 597–606.

Huey, L., Ericson, R., & Haggerty, K. (2005). Policing fantasy city. In D. Cooley (Ed.), *Re- imagining policing in Canada* (pp. 140–208). Toronto: University of Toronto Press.

Johnston, L., & Shearing, C. (2003). *Governing security*. London, UK: Routledge.

Kempa, M. (2011). Public policing, private security, pacifying populations. In M. Neocleous, & N. Rigakos (Eds.), *Anti-Security* (pp. 85–106). Ottawa, ON: Red Quill Books.

Larsen, M. (2013). *Access in the academy: Bringing ATI and FOI to academic research*. Vancouver, BC: The British Columbia Freedom of Information and Privacy Association.

Larsen, M., & Piché, J. (2009). Exceptional state, pragmatic bureaucracy, and indefinite detention: The case of the Kingston Immigration Holding Centre. *Canadian Journal of Law and Society*, *24*(2), 203–229.

Larsen, M., & Walby, K. (Eds.). (2012). *Brokering access: Power, politics, and freedom of information process in Canada*. Vancouver, BC: UBC Press.

Lather, P. (2010). *Engaging science policy: From the side of the messy*. New York, NY: Peter Lang.

Latour, B. (2005). *Reassembling the social: An introduction to actor-network-theory*. Oxford, UK: Oxford University Press.

Law, J. (2004). *After method: Mess in social science research*. New York, NY: Routledge.

Leclair, C., & Long, S. (1996). *The Canadian security sector: An overview, report*. Toronto: Industrial Adjustment Committee on the Security Sector.

Lippert, R. (2012). 'Clean and safe' passage: Business improvement districts, urban security modes, and knowledge brokers. *European Urban and Regional Studies*, *19*(2), 167–180.

Lippert, R. (2014). Neo-liberalism, police, and the governance of little urban things. *Foucault Studies*, *18*, 49–65.

Lippert, R., & O'Connor, D. (2006). Security intelligence networks and the transformation of contract private security. *Policing & Society*, *16*(1), 50–66.

Lippert, R., & Walby, K. (2012). Municipal corporate security and the intensification of urban surveillance. *Surveillance & Society*, *9*(3), 310–320.

Lippert, R., & Sleiman, M. (2012). Ambassadors, business improvement district governance and knowledge of the urban. *Urban Studies*, *49*(1), 61–76.

Lippert, R. K., Walby, K., & Wilkinson, B. (2015). Spins, stalls, and shutdowns: Pitfalls of qualitative policing and security research. *Forum Qualitative Sozialforschung/Forum: Qualitative Social Research*, *17*(1).

Luscombe, A., & Walby, K. (2014). Occupy Ottawa, conservation officers, and policing networks in Canada's capital city. *Canadian Journal of Criminology and Criminal Justice*, *56*(3), 295–322.

Luscombe, A., & Walby, K. (2017). Theorizing freedom of information: The live archive, obfuscation, and actor-network theory. *Government Information Quarterly*, *34*(3), 379–387.

Luscombe, A., Walby, K., & Lippert, R. K. (2017). Brokering access beyond the border and in the wild: Comparing freedom of information law and policy in Canada and the United States. *Law & Policy*, *39*(3), 259–279.

Lyon, D. (2001). *Surveillance society: Monitoring everyday life*. London, UK: McGraw-Hill.

Mackinnon, D. (2018). Surveillance ready subjects: The making of Canadian anti-masking law. In J. Monaghan, & L. Melgaco (Eds.), *Protests in the information age: Social movements, digital practices and surveillance* (pp. 151–168). London, UK: Routledge.

Marx, G. (1984). Notes on the discovery, collection, and assessment of hidden and dirty data. In J. Schneider, & J. Kitsuse (Eds.), *Studies in the sociology of social problems* (pp. 78–114). Norwood, NJ: Ablex.

McCann, E., & Ward, K. (2012). Assembling urbanism: Following policies & "studying through" the sites and situations of policy-making. *Environment & Planning A, 44*(1), 42–51.

Moe, R. C. (2001). The emerging federal quasi government: Issues of management and accountability. *Public Administration Review, 61*(3), 290–312.

Mol, A. (2002). *The body multiple: Ontology in medical practice.* Durham, NC: Duke University Press.

Monaghan, J. (2017). *Security aid: Canada and the development regime of security.* Toronto: University of Toronto Press.

Monaghan, J., & Walby, K. (2012). Making up 'terror identities': Security intelligence, Canada's Integrated Threat Assessment Centre and social movement suppression. *Policing and Society, 60*(5), 653–671.

Ontario Order P-239, 1991 O.I.P.C. No. 33.

Rigakos, G. (2015). Urban pacification: The rise of the business improvement district. Paper presented at the Socialist Studies Conference, University of Ottawa, 2 June.

Rigakos, G. S., & Greener, D. R. (2000). Bubbles of governance: Private policing and the law in Canada. *Canadian Journal of Law and Society, 15*(1), 145–185.

Roberts, A. S. (2000). Less government, more secrecy: Reinvention and the weakening of freedom of information law. *Public Administration Review, 60*(4), 308–320.

Savage, A., & Hyde, R. (2014). Using freedom of information requests to facilitate research. *International Journal of Social Research Methodology, 17*(3), 303–317.

Sleiman, M., & Lippert, R. (2010). Downtown ambassadors, police relations and 'clean and safe' security. *Policing & Society, 20*(3), 316–335.

University of British Columbia (Re), 2010 BCIPC 5 (CanLII), http://canlii.ca/t/280d0.

Vancouver (City) (Re), 2015 BCIPC 71 (CanLII), http://canlii.ca/t/gmpx4.

Vancouver Police Department. (2012). *Public demonstration guidelines.* Retrieved from http://vancouver.ca/police/assets/pdf/reports-policies/public-demonstration- guidelines.pdf.

Walby, K. (2005). Open-street camera surveillance and governance in Canada. *Canadian Journal of Criminology and Criminal Justice, 47*(4), 655–684.

Walby, K., & Larsen, M. (2011). Getting at the live archive: On access to information research in Canada. *Canadian Journal of Law and Society, 26*(3), 623–633.

Walby, K., & Larsen, M. (2012). Access to information and freedom of information requests: Neglected means of data production in the social sciences. *Qualitative Inquiry, 18*(1), 31–42.

Ward, K. (2004). Entrepreneurial urbanism and the management of the contemporary city: The examples of business improvement districts. Paper presented at the American Association of Geographers Conference, Philadelphia, March.

Ward, K. (2006). Policies in motion: Urban management and state restructuring: The trans-local expansion of business improvement districts. *International Journal of Urban and Regional Research, 30*(1), 54–75.

Wolf, N. (2012, December 29). Revealed: How the FBI coordinated the crackdown on occupy. *The Guardian.* Retrieved from www.theguardian.com/commentisfree/2012/dec/29/fbi-coordinated- crackdown-occupy.

Workers' Compensation Board, Re, 2002 CanLII 42462 (BC IPC), http://canlii.ca/t/1gdcn.

# 9

# RESEARCHING THE COMPLEXITIES OF KNOWLEDGE CONTESTATIONS AND OCCUPATIONAL DISEASE RECOGNITION

## FOI requests in multi-method qualitative research design

*Christine Pich*

## Introduction

An understanding of knowledge contestations about a particular social problem can be strengthened through the development of a research design that draws on multiple sources of data and incorporates methodological tools to allow the researcher to delve beneath formal texts. This is particularly so as public documents produced by governmental agencies – such as annual reports, press releases and corporate strategic plans – aim to present a cohesive discussion that smooths over contestations, tensions and negotiations about the issue at hand. Walby and Larsen (2011) identify these formal documents as "front-stage texts that represent 'official discourse'" (p. 624). The choices made in the production of these formal documents, the divergent perspectives amongst social actors, and the discussions that ultimately lead to final decisions about what information to present and how to frame that information are not easily identifiable by reading these official discourses. Further methodological difficulties are encountered when researching agencies characterised by their "bureaucratic ambiguity" (Best, 2012) where institutional decision-making processes, such as those on policy development, are largely closed off from public audiences.

In this chapter, I discuss the usefulness of a multi-method qualitative research design that combines Freedom of Information (FOI) requests with other qualitative methods. In doing so, I draw on my doctoral research on knowledge contestations and occupational disease recognition in the context of the workers' compensation system in Ontario, Canada. Although not initially incorporated into the research design, FOI requests became a valuable data collection method and were used to access a large volume of restricted records from the Archives of

Ontario (AO) and a draft copy of a report from the Workplace Safety and Insurance Board (WSIB). I suggest that research on competing knowledge claims could benefit from the addition of FOI requests as a qualitative method, as using these requests may provide researchers access to publicly unavailable data that could offer revealing insights into the complexities of knowledge contestations.

The structure of this chapter is as follows. First, I offer a conceptualisation of knowledge contestations which incorporates consideration not only of competing knowledge claims, but also claims to unknowns. Second, I provide some background on the research project, as well as on occupational disease in relation to Ontario's workers' compensation system. Third, I focus on the use of FOI requests in multi-method qualitative research by reflecting on my methodological experiences of submitting FOI requests, combining FOI methods with other qualitative methods, how FOI requests can provide further insight into the complexities of knowledge contestations, and the limitations I encountered in using FOI requests. I conclude with consideration to the significance of FOI requests in relation to sociological qualitative research on occupational disease and workers' compensation.

## Knowledge contestations and the complexities of unknowns

The understanding of knowledge contestations that guides my analysis contains three central points. First, knowledge about occupational disease and how the problem of occupational disease should be responded to are socially and politically contingent (McIvor, 2012; Murphy, 2006; Phillips, 2015; Rosner & Markowitz, 2006). The recognition of occupational diseases is not simply a matter of obtaining "more knowledge" in a linear manner through further medical and scientific research. Rather, how knowledge about occupational disease becomes mobilised and contested is closely connected with the organisation of social interests and values and the political will to address occupational health concerns. In my research, the issue of occupational disease was sometimes described by participants and other data sources as a "political football" with reference to how shifting political climates are accompanied by changing approaches to occupational disease problems.

Second, knowledge contestations about occupational disease can occur between different social groups, as well as within them. In other words, social groups are multi-dimensional; they do not constitute monolithic entities with homogenous knowledge claims. Phillips' (2015) research on the contestations over whether Multiple Chemical Sensitivities (MCS) constitute a legitimate disease identifies divergent perspectives amongst medical and legal practitioners. More specifically, Phillips situates sympathetic experts (those who tend to side with, and advocate for, individuals affected by MCS) as having different interests and approaches from mainstream experts (who are more firmly situated in the orthodoxy of their profession), even though the former tend to become marginalised in their fields for advancing such positions. Therefore, when referring to social groups such as "labour," "capital," "legal" and "medical," it is important to avoid over-simplifying and over-stating knowledge claims, as such perspectives are not necessarily shared by a social group as a whole.

Third, although attention to questions of knowledge (such as how certain knowledge gains legitimacy and authority at the expense of other forms of knowledge) is useful in examining the dimensions and stakes of knowledge contestations, broadening the analysis to consider the role of unknowns can provide fruitful and nuanced insights into these contestations. Furthermore, what is unknown or claimed not to be known is not simply the binary of knowledge that can be overcome by developing or advancing further knowledge. As McGoey (2012) elaborates, unknowns should be conceptualised "not as a precursor or an impediment to more knowledge, but as a productive force in itself, as the twin and not the opposite of knowledge" (p. 3).

In focusing on the component of unknowns, I draw attention to two central points. First, there are always unknowns in knowledge practices and decision-making processes, and these unknowns are multi-dimensional and dynamic. The inevitability of unknowns recognises that there will always be some element or level of complication in making a decision about an occupational health issue. Second, how these unknowns are attended to in relation to knowledge constitutes a prominent feature in decision-making processes. This point acknowledges that while unknowns are inherent in knowledge practices, they do not have to take the current form they are in. In other words, while there is a regularity to unknowns in the sense that not everything can be known (Gross & McGoey, 2015), unknowns are also actively produced (Proctor, 2008). How unknowns become mobilised can be advantageous to one social group over another, and it is important to consider the strategic usefulness of unknowns in relation to the social and political dimensions of knowledge contestations (McGoey, 2009, 2012).

## Occupational disease recognition and workers' compensation

My research identifies occupational disease recognition as one context where various types of knowledge claims and claims to unknowns are made and mobilised as a way to evade sufficient legitimation of, and response to, social justice issues, especially when there is a lack of political will to address such issues. I take as my starting point the challenges that workers and their advocates face in trying to obtain recognition for diseases that are occupationally related. To focus my research, and to produce concrete and context-dependent knowledge (Flyvbjerg, 2001), I examine occupational disease recognition through Ontario's workers' compensation system while simultaneously being attentive to broader processes, practices and debates (such as international classifications of carcinogens) that feed into and interconnect with how occupational diseases are addressed and understood at the provincial level. My research questions ask how unknowns complicate knowledge contestations surrounding the recognition of occupational diseases, how various types of knowledges and unknowns become mobilised into decision-making processes, what counts as evidence and what role does evidence play in supporting various knowledge claims, and how do social and political factors influence the recognition of occupational diseases.

The term occupational disease may bring to mind specific kinds of diseases, such as asbestos and silicosis, commonly associated with industrialised and masculinised labour processes. However, defining what constitutes an occupational disease is a complex matter as there is not a singular or definitive answer. What becomes accepted as an occupational disease depends both on how "occupation" and "disease" are defined and classified in a particular social and historical context, and by whom. The challenges of defining and classifying occupational disease is intensified due to the difficulties of recognising occupational contributors to the development of one's disease. In contrast to more immediately perceivable occupational health and safety issues, such as a falling from a high ledge and breaking a leg, many diseases have long latency periods where the ill-health effects from an occupational exposure can take decades to manifest in terms of symptoms in the worker's body. Coupled with other factors, such as multifactorial disease etiologies and synergistic effects between exposures, the recognition of occupational diseases is filled with numerous obstacles.

Occupational diseases are also challenging to recognise because determining whether or not there is a sufficient linkage between an occupation and a disease brings questions of "causality" into decision-making processes. Causality is a highly contested term in itself as different epistemological viewpoints may conflict with one another when attempting to establish what counts as evidence, and how much evidence is enough to demonstrate a connection between an occupation and a disease. Competing economic interests and the multiplicity of social actors involved in decisions about occupational disease (such as the legal, medical and scientific fields; workers' compensation boards and appeals tribunals; workers and their advocates; organised labour; employers; and community, national and international organisations) further complicate decision-making processes. These challenges and barriers make occupational disease recognition an illuminating site in which to study knowledge contestations.

Prior to delving into a discussion about FOI requests and multi-method qualitative research design, it is important to briefly note how occupational disease is adjudicated through workers' compensation in Ontario. In using the term "workers' compensation system," I refer to the legislation (*Workplace Safety and Insurance Act*, WSIA), the Board responsible for administering the *Act* (Workplace Safety and Insurance Board, WSIB) and the independent appeals tribunal (Workplace Safety and Insurance Appeals Tribunal, WSIAT). In Ontario, there are currently three main routes through which a disease may be recognised as occupationally related and eligible for compensation: (1) Schedule 3 (presumptive legislation) or Schedule 4 (irrebuttable legislation), (2) WSIB policies or (3) on a case-by-case basis. The principles upon which occupational disease should be adjudicated on have been a key area of discussion and debate (see Ison,

1989). While there is a general understanding that specific standards of legal, rather than scientific, principles should guide decision-making processes, how these principles are applied in practice has been fraught with difficulties and there is a reoccurring tendency to import scientific principles about probability and thresholds of proof into occupational disease decisions (see, for example, the discussion in 2016 SCC 25).

## FOI requests and multi-method research design

In Ontario, FOI legislation may be understood as fulfilling the dual purpose of "provid[ing] a right of access to information under the control of institutions" and "protect[ing] the privacy of individuals with respect to personal information about themselves held by institutions and to provide individuals with a right of access to that information" (FIPPA, R.S.O., 1990, s. 1). In other words, individuals can submit requests for general information and/or personal information. Canadian scholars from various disciplines played a pivotal role in advocating for access legislation in the latter half of the twentieth century (Kazmierski, 2011). Central to this push were concerns about the lack of government transparency and accountability, issues of government secrecy and how such information was deemed to be essential for more meaningful participation in democratic decision-making processes (Clement, 2015; Kazmierski, 2011). At the federal level, Canada first enacted Access to Information (ATI) legislation in 1983 through the *Access to Information Act* (ATIA), while provinces and territories varied in their adoption of this legislation. In Ontario, FOI requests fall under the *Freedom of Information and Protection of Privacy Act* (FIPPA), which was enacted in 1988. Currently, FIPPA "applies to over 300 provincial institutions such as ministries, provincial agencies, boards and commissions, as well as community colleges, universities, local health integration networks, and hospitals" (Information and Privacy Commissioner of Ontario, 2017, p. 9). The Office of the Information and Privacy Commissioner of Ontario (IPC) was established in 1987 with a mandate to work independently of the government and provide oversight of the province's access to information and personal privacy legislation.

More recently, academic researchers have brought heightened attention to how ATI/FOI requests could be used as a research tool to study governmental institutions, as well as the value of using such requests to develop more in-depth analysis of social and historical phenomena (Clement, 2015; Savage & Hyde, 2014; Walby & Larsen, 2011; Walby & Luscombe, 2016). Using these requests provides academic researchers the opportunity to delve beneath the top layer of formal governmental texts, which are constructed and framed with the intention of being presented to public audiences, and into the messiness of texts that are not deliberately packaged for public purposes (Walby & Larsen, 2011). In doing so, researchers are able to gain access to data that would otherwise not be available (Walby & Luscombe, 2016). Although increasing academic attention to ATI/FOI requests has contributed to methodological insights about the ways in which these requests could be used as a data collection method in qualitative research designs, these requests continue to constitute "an under-used means of producing data in the social sciences" (Walby & Luscombe, 2016, p. 2).

In exploring knowledge contestations in relation to the recognition of diseases as occupationally related through Ontario's workers' compensation system, I developed a multi-method qualitative research design that included the use of FOI requests (see also Bracken-Roche, this volume on multi-method research). The methods used were fourteen in-depth interviews with individuals working with issues of occupational disease in a professional capacity (from the legal, medical, scientific, academic and professional advocacy fields), participation in events on occupational disease in the role of an observer, archival methods, extensive document analysis and FOI requests. In the discussion that follows, I will first identify how I came across FOI requests as a research method and the types of FOI requests that I submitted. Second, I discuss how I incorporated FOI requests into a multi-method qualitative research design and the methodological approach utilised in relation to FOI requests. Third, to illustrate the usefulness of FOI, I highlight how documents accessed through FOI requests provided insight into the dynamics of knowledge contestations by looking at occupational disease in relation to the medical–scientific–legal nexus. Fourth, I reflect on the limits I experienced in using FOI requests in my research.

## Submitting FOI requests

My introduction to FOI requests was serendipitous. I initially came across these requests when I encountered access restrictions to the archival records I wanted to review at the Archives of Ontario (AO). To obtain more information about accessing archival records, I located a Customer Service Guide about FIPPA available on the AO website which, in reference to FIPPA, notes that "the *Act* applies to most records created and/or used by the Government of Ontario. This means that the *Act* applies to not only records created by the Government and its agencies, but also any records that they receive" (AO, 2015, pp. 1–2). The records of interest for my research fell across various provincial agencies, such as the Ministry of Labour, Ministry of Natural Resources and the Workmen's Compensation Board/Workers' Compensation Board (currently named the Workplace Safety and Insurance Board). As the documents located in these files were either created (e.g., internal memos) or received (e.g., letters) by provincial agencies, they had access restrictions on them.

In accordance with the information provided in the AO's Customer Service Guide on how to create and send in a FOI request for archival records, I submitted my first request to AO's Coordinator of the Information and Privacy Unit in October 2014 for ten archival files. I located these files through a search on their online database using the keyword "occupational disease." Within the 30-day period that an agency is legislated to make an access decision within, I was contacted via email by an Information and Privacy Unit Analyst informing me that they were finalising my request and asking whether I would make arrangements to visit the AO in Toronto to view the files or have the records reproduced and mailed to me. In consideration of costs (photocopying fees at the AO are $0.20 per page) and not knowing exactly what, or how many, documents would be in each archival file, I opted to visit the AO and examine the records on-site. Shortly after, I received a formal letter in the mail informing me that I was given partial access to the records requested. In December 2014, two months after submitting the FOI request, I went to the AO to view the records.

My first FOI request ended up being one of three requests that I submitted in the span of a 10-month period to the AO for access to a total of fifty-nine files and two large groupings of files. This was because my initial searches and review of records led me to identify further keywords and locate additional records relevant to occupational disease. Knowledge about the research topic constitutes an important component of the FOI request process as the researcher is able to better specify what they are looking for and use relevant language to identify the records (Clement, 2015). Occupational disease was a relatively new object of sociological inquiry for me, and while my methodological strategy included researching as much as possible about occupational disease and workers' compensation before getting into the phases of research that involved human participants, I realised how important background knowledge about the research topic is for fine-tuning FOI requests as well. For example, temporal changes of keywords are of pivotal significance. In the context of my research, "occupational disease" is a more recent term; "industrial disease" was the common term used in historical records. Once I plugged in "industrial disease" to my database search, I was able to locate numerous additional files that I would not have found if I limited my search to the contemporary terminology of occupational disease. Overall, the types of documents accessed included memorandums, letters, correspondences, news articles, draft copies of various types of texts, internal reports, handwritten notes, conference proceedings, brochures, meeting minutes and roundtable discussions.

Subsequent to the three FOI requests to the AO, I submitted a request for one document to the WSIB, the *Draft Report of the Chair of the Occupational Disease Advisory Panel*. One component of my document analysis took place at the publicly accessible WSIB reference library, located at their Head Office in Toronto. At the reference library, I reviewed submissions to a public inquiry that took place in 2004 in response to this draft report. The final report and some of the supplementary documents related to it are publicly available online but the draft report is not, and I wanted to examine the similarities and differences between the draft report and the final report. At this point in my research, I was gaining familiarity with literature on FOI and I was aware that some agencies, including the WSIB, are identified as less likely to informally provide information that is not publicly accessible (Roberts, 2008). Being aware that I might encounter obstacles if I informally inquired about this document, and keeping in mind temporal considerations and the research project timeline, I decided to submit a formal FOI request to the WSIB for the draft report. Initially, the Privacy Analyst called me to inform this document did not exist. However, I was able to provide additional information about the document and was then told that this would be further looked into. Within the 30-day legislated period, I was mailed a copy of the draft report without any information redacted.

In contrast to submitting FOI requests without knowing what types of documents exist, an advantage experienced in the context of my research was the ability to request clearly identified documents and records. In other words, I had a relatively good idea of what types of files existed before making my requests and this permitted me to request specific items by name, while avoiding potentially costly search fees. For example, when searching keywords in the archival database, the results identify a record group number, series number and file name. For the FOI requests to the AO, I provided a list of records that included the record information. For the request to the WSIB, I filled out a FOI form available on their website and jotted down the exact name of the document of interest. In this way, I was able to gain access to a variety of texts from multiple governmental institutions that I would otherwise not be able to examine due to access barriers.

## FOI requests as a method in multi-method qualitative research

When designing the research project, I had not proposed to use FOI requests as a method nor was I aware of methodological discussions about using FOI requests for the purpose of social scientific research. Although FOI requests were not originally identified as a method in my research design, adding FOI requests at a subsequent phase of the research process is compatible with a qualitative approach to knowledge production. In contrast to quantitative and positivist-oriented research designs where the components of the research project are firmly determined before the data collection process commences, qualitative research designs allow for openness and flexibility in how the research will be carried out (van Den Hoonard, 2015). Insight gained during the research process can be used to inform further data collection procedures as a way to gain a more in-depth understanding of the social phenomenon of interest, thereby strengthening the quality of the research. In this regard, methodological adaptations made during research process should not be perceived as an indicator of poorly designed research. As Schwartz-Shea and Yanow (2012) elaborate:

> Rather than a matter of lack of thought or planning, or even simple convenience, flexibility is essential to intelligent maneuvering in the field so as to pursue the situated, contextualized meaning-making of those whose lives, interactions, situations, visual records and visual images, and so on are being studied.

*(p. 57)*

As previously identified, in developing a research design to study knowledge contestations about occupational disease recognition, I utilise a multi-method approach that draws on and integrates five types of qualitative methods: (1) in-depth semi-structured interviews; (2) participant observation; (3) archival methods; (4) document analysis and (5) FOI requests. The research progressed through three different phases: (1) document search and analysis, (2) strategic interviews and participant observation and (3) data analysis and writing. It is important to mention that this progression was not linear and the phases were not mutually exclusive; rather, they overlapped with one another. For example, although I began constructing and submitting FOI requests in the first phase of the study, I continued to do so throughout the second phase as well. My initial searches, as well as data obtained through my sources, provided assistance in identifying further documents to examine.

FOI requests are particularly suitable for a multi-method qualitative approach. Due to the partiality of documents made available through FOI requests and the limitations of using FOI requests as a research method (which will be elaborated on in the subsequent section), FOI requests should be considered in combination with other methods (Savage & Hyde, 2014). For example, Savage and Hyde (2014) identify that using FOI requests alongside other methods allows researchers to gain more depth into their research topic and to be better situated to ask further questions about the topic. Indeed, I experienced this in the context of my research. While the majority of documents accessed through the FOI requests were archival documents, by further adding methods such as in-depth interviews, a richer and more nuanced understanding was developed about shifting historical processes and their contemporary relevance. This is further strengthened by the sampling criteria used when identifying potential interview participants. Since the interview participants had considerable experience working with occupational disease issues, many were also well positioned to speak about the history of occupational health in Ontario. Their perspectives and experiences, including what historical moments they identify as pivotal and how they discussed these moments, allowed greater clarity and context into historical events such as the wildcat strike of 1974 by miners in Elliot Lake that occurred in response to health and safe issues (see also MacDowell, 2012). I came across archival records that made references to this event, but by speaking with individuals through open-ended interviews, I was better situated to delve deeper into the significance of this moment, the knowledge contestations that led up to the strike, and how this historical moment instigated subsequent occupational health and safety reforms. In addition, the data obtained through FOI requests was fruitful in making adaptations to the interview guide. For instance, I had not initially included any questions specific to historical moments. As qualitative semi-structured interview guides permit flexibility in terms of questions asked, I subsequently added a question about historical moments in light of the data I was reviewing from the archival records and the discussions that were emerging from my early interviews.

The conceptualisation of depth that I draw on differs from one that is entangled with common notions of triangulation. Triangulation generally refers to the process of combining multiple methods in order to generate data about an object of inquiry with the intention of cross-checking the sources for consistency to validate the research results (Savage & Hyde, 2014; Schwartz-Shea & Yanow, 2012). With a focus on the use of FOI requests in both quantitative and qualitative research, Savage and Hyde (2014) argue that by combining FOI requests with methods such as questionnaires and semi-structured interviews "data is bolstered [ ... ] in a bid to provide deeper, more triangulated explanations of the phenomena under investigation" (p. 313). This, in turn, is attributed to a stronger validity of the research conducted (Savage & Hyde, 2014). However, qualitative researchers often encounter tension over the suitability of applying quantitative criteria (validity, reliability, generalisability) to assess the quality of qualitative research (Walby & Luscombe, 2016). The epistemological notion that researchers can cross-check multiple sources in order to obtain congruency has also been problematised due to "the multiple ways in which humans can make sense of the same event, document, artifact, etc." (Schwartz-Shea & Yanow, 2012, p. 88). In this regard, different perspectives on, and narratives about, the same issue should not necessarily be perceived as diminishing the quality of the study. Rather, variances between sources are expected due to the various positionalities and experiences that people have in relation to the topic of focus (Schwartz-Shea & Yanow, 2012).

Rather than incorporating multiple methods to obtain triangulation, a key purpose of using multiple methods research design was to acknowledge the complexity of knowledge about occupational diseases due to the various perspectives between, and within, social groups. This is not to say that all perspectives are equally valid and that certain positions should not be problematised; indeed, I explicitly approached my research topic from the standpoint that occupational disease and workers' compensation is a social justice issue. Instead, it draws attention to the messiness of the social problem and how there may be numerous interpretations and meanings that are not necessarily in congruence with one another. In studying knowledge contestations, an acknowledgement of a multiplicity of perspectives also recognises that such perspectives may vary in relation to epistemological positions, such as between (and within) medical, scientific and legal approaches to the problem of occupational disease.

Furthermore, combining unobtrusive methods with research involving human participants recognises the inevitable partiality of data sources. My methodological approach in using FOI requests is in alignment with my approach to unobtrusive methods more generally, which recognises that texts have the potential to provide useful insights while acknowledging that they do not simply represent factual or complete information (Ashforth, 1990; Bowen, 2009; Schwartz-Shea & Yanow, 2012). The meaning of texts is not one-dimensional; rather, texts are situated in, and influenced by, particular social and political contexts (Ashforth, 1990), and are also open to multiple interpretations and meanings (Schwartz-Shea & Yanow,

2012). In terms of archival methods, positivist claims to objectivity and historical truths have been contested as literature stresses the importance of considering how archival records are historically, socially and politically situated (Burton 2005; Ghosh, 2005; Tamoukou, 2014). The acknowledgement that archival records are contextually contingent has led to the general recognition that historical knowledge will always be limited to some extent. As Tamoukou (2014) argues,

> Archival research is fragmented through and through: there is always something missing, because not everything found a place in the archive, because of serendipity, because of intentional selections and deselections as well as because of specific rules of taxonomy and classification that allow certain documents to be preserved and others to become obscure or marginalized.
>
> *(p. 631)*

Research using FOI requests is "fragmented" as there will inevitably be "something missing." The types of documents accessed may vary based on the records located by the Privacy Analyst, the researcher's background knowledge of the topic and of using FOI requests, how well the researcher is able to negotiate access to documents, intentional or unintentional decisions by government workers as to what information becomes textually preserved, how much information becomes redacted for records granted partial access, and so on (Clement, 2015; Luscombe, Walby, & Lippert, 2017). However, in recognising the partiality of data sources and arguing for the potential usefulness of combining multiple qualitative methods in a research project, this is not to suggest that a "complete picture" could be obtained through the use of multiple methods, nor that it would be epistemologically possible to do so. Even with multiple methods, knowledge about the object of inquiry will always be partial but by combining methods, there is enhanced opportunity for more in-depth analysis and greater appreciation of the complexity of the phenomenon.

## FOI requests to access data on knowledge contestations

To illustrate the insights about knowledge contestations obtained from records that had access restrictions on them, I spotlight a key area of contestation in occupational disease recognition, that is, how legal, medical and scientific knowledges become mobilised into decision-making processes in relation to standards of proof (see also Jasanoff, 1995). A particularly contentious issue is how "certainty" is defined and what level of certainty is required to make a probable connection between an occupation and a disease. The scientific definition of certainty rests on the meaning of statistical significance, which is often based on a 95 percent confidence interval (i.e., a 0.05 percent probability value). In other words, the likelihood that the association between an occupational factor and a disease is by chance would be less than five percent. Due to this high threshold for establishing certainty, science is characterised by unknowns due to the regularity of uncertainty in scientific knowledge and practice (Messing, 2014). The legal standard of certainty diverges amongst different types of law. In Canada, the standard of proof for criminal law is based on "beyond a reasonable doubt," which entails more certainty than the standard of the "balance of probabilities" which is used in civil and administrative law. The WSIA is encompassed in the framework of administrative law, and in principle, the level of certainty in determining linkages between an occupation and a disease is based on a balance of probabilities, which means that certainty is defined as being more than 50 percent (50 + 1). However, the threshold for certainty in workers' compensation decisions is slightly lower due to the benefit-of-doubt principle which refers to situations when the evidence is equally for and against the worker. In these cases, the benefit of doubt should go to the worker and they should be granted compensation.

Contestations over which standard of proof should be used, as well as how they are used in theory versus in practice, is a central theme that emerged from the data collection process. The use of FOI requests provided another point of access into these contestations, especially in examining issues over legal, scientific and medical definitions of certainty through a historical lens and identifying dynamic shifts in the positions of social actors over time. For example, in the submissions to the 2004 public inquiry about the Occupational Disease Advisory Panel (ODAP) draft report, labour representatives argued for the proper use of legal standards of proof where "significant contribution" is used as the causal test. In other words, occupational factors should constitute a significant, but not necessarily primary, contribution to the development of disease. In contrast, employer representatives were more likely to support scientific standards of proof and argue for occupational factors to be the primary contribution to the development of disease, especially with regard to any diseases being incorporated into Schedule 3 or Schedule 4 of the WSIA. Interestingly, this suggests a shift in positions from the early 1990s. One of the archival documents I viewed, and which was accessed using an FOI request, was notes based on an Occupational Disease Task Force roundtable discussion (AO, RG 7-168, B817706). In this discussion, divergent perspectives between labour and employer representatives were noted in relation to the level of certainty that should be required when making linkages between an occupation and a disease. Labour representatives argued for a less stringent and more general requirement based on whether or not a connection could be established. Employers contested this by arguing for an increased level of certainty through the utilisation of the causal test of significant contribution. These discussions suggest changing positions in terms of what standard of proof is perceived most appropriate to use, and by whom, as well as a gradual shift towards the normalisation of higher thresholds of certainty.

For the most part, the records reviewed contained relatively brief glimpses into some of the contestations occurring about the scientific–medical–legal nexus. There would be a few letters addressed to and from individuals, for example, without much, or any, additional documents to develop more clarity about the exchanges. Nevertheless, accessing these records was useful to develop further insight into knowledge contestations and how they were framed. This included exploring how claims to unknowns were made, and the various ways in which unknowns were strategically used (whether intentional or not). One example of this was in response to the Exposure Criteria Project being carried out by the Ministry of Labour in the 1990s. Employers contested the development of exposure criteria for dusts such as limestone and calcium carbonate by making the claim that no medical evidence existed to suggest that the inhalation of these dusts would cause ill-health effects, and further, that reducing worker exposure in adherence to such criteria would be economically unfeasible (AO, RG7-1, b221114). Making claims to unknowns to suggest an absence of evidence about a connection between a product and/or labour process and a health problem is a common industry strategy to diffuse responsibility and minimise threats to business practices (Michaels 2008), and such strategies could also be seen in knowledge contestations over occupational disease issues in the context of Ontario.

## Limitations to using FOI requests as a research method

FOI requests are useful in accessing governmental records that are not publicly available, but it is important to acknowledge the methodological limitations in using these requests as a research tool. As Kazmierski (2011) states, "access legislation does not always guarantee access to information" (p. 614). Key barriers and limitations include temporal delays, financial costs, issues with the administration of the legislation, issues in appealing decisions, arbitrariness and inconsistencies with what information becomes released, researcher experience and skill in identifying the existence of records (especially when being told that they do not exist) and, if records are released, issues around how much information was released and how heavily redacted the documents may be (e.g., Clement, 2015; Larsen & Walby, 2012). As Hameed and Monaghan (2012) argue, "[t]he greatest concern facing ATI users is that the adjudication of requests has become an institutional process that is, according to a host of critics, reliably unreliable" (p. 142). There is also an unevenness in how FOI requests are processed between different agencies, which contributes to varying experiences when attempting to obtain access to information (see, for example, IPC Annual Reports on processing times and the types of access decisions made amongst different governmental institutions).

My methodological experience of using FOI requests encountered limitations of temporal delays and costs. The first two groups of archival files that I requested to view went through smoothly, with minimal costs (under $50 each) and a decision for partial access made within the required 30-day time frame. For the files in the third group, there was a significant amount of material and the Privacy Analyst at the AO contacted me with three options: (1) paying a high processing fee for the processor to go through all the materials and redact personally identifying material; (2) reducing the number of files on my list or (3) submitting a research agreement, the *Request for Access to Personal Information for Research Purposes*, so that I could view all these files without having to pay a high processing fee. As a high fee would make access unobtainable due to budgetary constraints, and as I did not want to reduce my list since this would limit the amount of data available, I opted for the third option. This entailed filling out and submitting a form outlining how I was to protect and not disclose personal information when going through the files and when referring to the files in my research.

While selecting the option to submit a research agreement allowed me to view all the material I had initially requested, I nevertheless encountered further limitations. Although there is a legislative requirement for agencies to make a decision in response to a FOI request within 30-days, agencies also have the option to give an official notice of extension thereby granting them a longer period to respond. While the length of these extensions varies, it is not unheard of to experience delays that extend over a year (Clement, 2015), and these delays can impact project timelines and even the overall feasibility of being able to undertake or continue doing the research. For this request, I was notified that due to the volume of files the AO would be filing, a 75-day extension period was applied. As I initially made the request in July 2015, this meant that I did not receive the decision until November 2015 and I still had to make travel arrangements to go to the archives so that I could examine the records on-site. Although I was able to reduce costs associated with processing fees (due to being informed of the research agreement option) and reproduction fees (as I elected to view documents on-site), there were still charges ($165.00) in addition to the five-dollar request fee to access the documents requested through this FOI submission.

In addition, a notable limitation in using FOI requests is whether or not the researcher can identify the existence of records. As previously mentioned, an advantage of my research was that I could identify specific files when submitting requests to the AO and I identified the exact name of the draft report for the FOI request to the WSIB. Nevertheless, I encountered the necessity of having to verify the existence of the document with the WSIB, as I was initially told that the requested document did not exist. Fortunately, I discussed this with the Privacy Analyst over the phone and provided additional information about the document, such as where the draft report was referenced to in other publicly available documents and how a public inquiry took place in 2004 specifically in response to the draft report. This conversation led to the document being successfully located and a copy mailed to me within the 30-day required period.

The lack of initial familiarity I had with both the research topic and using FOI requests also constituted a limitation in my research. It was only in having to submit an FOI request to access restricted archival records did I begin delving into literature on using FOI requests as a research method. I was unclear on how to use FOI requests when I did not know the name of specific files or documents, or what type of information about occupational disease I could potentially request from agencies such as the WSIB. It was only later on in the research process did I gain better clarity of how to use FOI requests to obtain restricted information. For example, earlier on in the research process, I could have submitted a larger request (or multiple smaller requests) to the WSIB for information about the ODAP and/or historical records in order to gain access to a greater number of documents.

The unique limitations of FOI request as a research method make these requests a suitable tool to use in conjunction with other methods. Barriers such as temporal delays and costly fees may jeopardise the feasibility of a research project that solely relies on FOI requests. Such limitations, however, should not sway researchers away from using FOI requests as there are numerous strategies individuals could use to access information through the submission of these requests. These strategies include "brokering access" by learning how to efficiently negotiate with Privacy Analysts (Larsen & Walby, 2012; Luscombe et al., 2017), thoroughly researching the topic beforehand and making multiple smaller requests to avert extension delays and high fees (Clement, 2015). For example, although I did not initially realise the strategic usefulness of submitting multiple requests, if I had waited to group all the archival files into one large request later on in the research process, this may have resulted in a longer temporal delay to obtain access.

## Conclusion

Knowledge contestations, including claims to unknowns, are multi-dimensional, dynamic and complex. Using FOI requests as a research method in a multi-method qualitative design provides an opportunity for researchers to gain enhanced insight into the behind-the-scenes texts which are more likely to reveal contestations, tensions, negotiations, as well as relatively mundane governmental processes. In this way, combining FOI requests with other methods allows researchers to gain richer, more detailed data which could lead to further appreciation of the complexity of the social problem that is being studied.

The importance of identifying and using FOI requests as a qualitative method is that they offer the possibility of additional access to conduct academic research on governmental institutions that remain largely closed-off to public inquiry and which are characterised by their ambiguity. Workers' compensation is an institution that encounters notable public scepticism due to its contentious organisational practices, and its overall lack of openness and transparency. Although accessing information about institutional processes does not simply equate with enhanced transparency or a democratisation of decision-making procedures, using FOI requests as a research method acknowledges the necessity of obtaining additional points of access to study governmental institutions. The use of FOI requests averts positioning important social justice issues, such as how workers' compensation deals with the problem of occupational disease, as an inaccessible research topic for qualitative sociological inquiry.

# References

Archives of Ontario. (2015, October). *Freedom of information and protection of privacy: 109 customer service guide.*

Ashforth, A. (1990). Reckoning schemes of legitimation: On commissions of inquiry as power/knowledge forms. *Journal of Historical Sociology, 3*(1), 1–22.

Best, J. (2012). Bureaucratic ambiguity. *Economy and Society, 41*(1), 84–106.

Bowen, G. A. (2009). Document analysis as a qualitative research method. *Qualitative Research Journal, 9*(2), 27–40.

Clement, D. (2015). "Freedom" of information in Canada: Implications for historical research. *Labour/Le Travail, 75,* 101–131.

Flyvbjerg, B. (2001). *Making social science matter: Why social inquiry fails and how it can succeed again* [S. Sampson, Trans.]. Cambridge, UK: Cambridge University Press.

Ghosh, D. (2005). National narratives and the politics of miscegenation. In A. Burton (Ed.), *Archive stories: Facts, fiction, and the writing of history* (pp. 27–44). Durham, NC and London: Duke University Press.

Gross, M., & McGoey, L. (2015). Introduction. In M. Gross, & L. McGoey (Eds.), *Routledge international handbook of ignorance studies* (pp. 1–14). Oxon and New York: Routledge.

Hameed, Y., & Monaghan, J. (2012). Accessing dirty data: Methodological strategies for social problems research. In M. Larsen, & K. Walby (Eds.), *Brokering access: Power, politics, and freedom of information process in Canada* (pp. 142–166). Vancouver and Toronto: University of British Columbia Press.

Information and Privacy Commissioner of Ontario. (2017). *Third years of access and privacy services: 2017 annual report.* Retrieved from: www.ipc.on.ca/wp-content/uploads/2018/06/ar-2017-e-web.pdf.

Ison, T. G. (1989). *Compensation for industrial disease under the workers' compensation act of Ontario.* Toronto and Ontario.

Jasanoff, S. (1995). *Science at the bar: Law, science, and technology in America.* Cambridge and London: Harvard University Press.

Kazmierski, V. (2011). Accessing democracy: The critical relationship between academics and the access to information act. *Canadian Journal of Law and Society, 26*(3), 613–622.

Larsen, M., & Walby, K. (2012). Introduction: On the politics of access to information. In M. Larsen, & K. Walby (Eds.), *Brokering access: Power, politics, and freedom of information process in Canada* (pp. 1–32). Vancouver and Toronto: University of British Columbia Press.

Luscombe, A., Walby, K., & Lippert, R. K. (2017). Brokering access beyond the border and in the wild: Comparing freedom of information law and policy in Canada and the United States. *Law & Policy, 39*(3), 259–279.

MacDowell, L. S. (2012). The Elliot Lake uranium miners' battle to gain occupational health and safety improvements, 1950 – 1980. *Labour/Le Travail, 69,* 91–118.

McGoey, L. (2009). Pharmaceutical controversies and the performative value of uncertainty. *Science as Culture, 18*(2), 151–164.

McGoey, L. (2012). Strategic unknowns: Towards a sociology of ignorance. *Economy and Society, 41*(1), 1–16.

McIvor, A. (2012). Germs at work: Establishing tuberculosis as an occupational disease in Britain, c.1900 – 1951. *Social History of Medicine, 25*(4), 812–829.

Messing, K. (2014). *Pain and prejudice: What science can learn about work from the people who do it.* Toronto: Between the Lines.

Murphy, M. (2006). *Sick building syndrome and the problem of uncertainty: Environmental politics, technoscience, and women workers.* Durham, NC and London: Duke University Press.

Phillips, T. (2015). *Law, environmental illness and medical uncertainty: The contested governance of health*. New York: Routledge.

Proctor, R. N. (2008). Agnotology: A missing term to describe the cultural production of ignorance (and its study). In R. N. Proctor, & L. Schiebinger (Eds.), *Agnotology: The making and unmaking of ignorance* (pp. 1–33). Stanford, CA: Stanford University Press.

Roberts, A. (2008). Retrenchment and freedom of information: Recent experiences under federal, Ontario and British Columbia law. *Canadian Public Administration, 42*(4), 422–451.

Rosner, D., & Markowitz, G. (2006). *Deadly dust: Silicosis and the ongoing struggle to protect workers' health*. Ann Arbour, MI: University of Michigan Press.

Savage, A., & Hyde, R. (2014). Using freedom of information requests to facilitate research. *International Journal of Social Research Methodology, 17*(3), 303–317.

Schwartz-Shea, P., & Yanow, D. (2012). *Interpretive research design: Concepts and processes*. New York: Routledge.

Supreme Court of Canada. (2016 SCC 25). *British Columbia (Workers' Compensation Appeal Tribunal) v. Fraser Health Authority*.

Tamoukou, M. (2014). Archival research: Unraveling space/time/matter entanglements and fragments. *Qualitative Research, 14*(5), 617–633.

van Den Hoonard, D. (2015). *Qualitative research in action: A Canadian primer* (2nd ed.). Don Mills: Oxford University Press.

Walby, K., & Larsen, M. (2011). Getting at the live archive: On access to information research in Canada. *Canadian Journal of Law and Society, 26*(3), 623–633.

Walby, K., & Luscombe, A. (2016). Criteria for quality in qualitative research and use of freedom of information requests in the social sciences. *Qualitative Research, 17*(5), 537–553.

# 10

# REPERTOIRES OF EMPIRICAL SOCIAL SCIENCE AND FREEDOM OF INFORMATION REQUESTS

## Four techniques for analysing disclosures

*Kevin Walby and Alex Luscombe*

## Introduction

The use of freedom of information (FOI) requests to produce empirical material is growing in popularity among social scientists. In the United States (US), the United Kingdom (UK), Canada and more than one hundred other countries (Hazell & Worthy, 2010; Holsen, 2007; Jiwani & Krawchenko, 2014; Roberts, 2006; Savage & Hyde, 2014; Worthy, 2017), FOI laws allow researchers to request information that would not otherwise be released from government agencies. Many FOI users are journalists (Cribb, Jobb, McKie, & Vallance-Jones, 2015), lawyers or government opposition staffers (Worthy & Bourke, 2011), but academics increasingly see the benefits of and insight to be obtained from accessing government texts that have not been proactively released into the public domain. While there are works on the history of FOI (e.g., Birkinshaw, 2010; Schudson, 2015; Worthy, 2017), and texts in journalism that reflect on basic techniques of its use (e.g., Burgess, 2015; Cuillier & Davis, 2010), the methodological and disciplinary implications of FOI are only beginning to be explored.

As FOI becomes a more popular approach to producing empirical material for social science research, literature on the methodological dimensions of FOI has started to emerge. Methodological interventions reflecting on FOI requests and social research have so far focused on research design, data collection, establishing rapport with FOI coordinators and ethics (Jiwani & Krawchenko, 2014; Lee, 2005; Savage & Hyde, 2014; Walby & Luscombe, 2018). The issue of data analysis in relation to FOI disclosures has not yet been developed in any lengthy methodological discussion.

In this chapter, we describe four approaches to data analysis that can be used to help interpret and make sense of FOI disclosures. We argue that content analysis, discourse analysis, metaphor analysis and social network analysis can be used together or on their own by researchers analysing the results of FOI requests. There is value in comparing and contrasting data analysis techniques (also see Burck, 2005; Starks & Trinidad, 2007) not just for FOI researchers, but for social scientists more broadly. To illustrate these techniques, we draw from the results of some of our own analyses and the research of others.[1] We do not mean to suggest that these are the only four approaches with merit (see for example, Greenberg, this volume for a discussion of other approaches). Rather, inspired by Honan, Knobel, Baker, and Davies (2000), we show that different techniques for analysing the same data can result in qualitatively different claims and arguments that enrich an account and extend an inquiry in novel ways. For these reasons, social researchers must be open to using multiple tools to make sense of empirical material.

By explaining how content analysis, discourse analysis, metaphor analysis and social network analysis can be used to make sense of FOI disclosures, we add to literature on FOI use in the social sciences, and to literatures on these four approaches to data analysis. However, we also engage with what Savage and Burrows (2007) call the "coming crisis in empirical sociology." In response to the waning validity of traditional survey and interview research, Savage and Burrows (2007, p. 895) call on scholars to rethink the repertoires of knowledge production in the social sciences. Haggerty (2004) has similarly lamented the decline of politically engaged and ethically "edgy" research that often provides the deepest insights into authority, relations of power and domination, and inequality. As a means of accessing government data, some of which is politically sensitive and potentially contentious, we conceive of FOI requests in research as a means of helping rethink the repertoires of empirical social science. It is the promise of revelation, its power as an investigative tool and the credibility and trustworthiness of FOI disclosures as the "raw" stuff of bureaucratic governance that makes FOI such a powerful and exciting research technique. Elsewhere, we have argued that FOI data, when obtained systematically, can be considered as credible and trustworthy as the results of established research methods (Walby & Luscombe, 2017). Building on this argument, and on the grounds that no data speaks for itself (Mauthner & Doucet, 2003; Yanow, 2000), here we discuss four approaches to analysis of FOI data.

This chapter has four parts. First, we situate FOI use and disclosures in literature on research design and overview some of the key aspects of FOI in practice. Second, we provide an overview of four methods of analysis and how they can be used to make sense of FOI disclosures. The four techniques we discuss are content analysis, discourse analysis, metaphor analysis and social network analysis. In conclusion, we reflect on what our arguments mean for the growing literature on FOI research methodology and to literatures on these four approaches to data analysis more broadly.

## Freedom of information and research design

Before turning to analysis of FOI disclosures, an outline of the process of using FOI requests to produce datasets is warranted. Like other approaches to data collection, there is no how-to guide for using FOI requests to produce data. Similar to ethnography or interviewing, FOI is a research "craft" (Tracy, 2010) that one gains a tacit knowledge of and knack for over time. It is easier to demonstrate in practice than to write out the steps and wrinkles involved in incorporating it into a project's research design. Previous research has used FOI requests in a nested sequential design prior to interviews (Monaghan, 2017; Walby, Lippert, & Wilkinson, 2014), after interviews, in conjunction with archival materials (Clement, 2015), and in combination with news media, political speeches and other open-source materials (see Monaghan, 2014).

To make an FOI request, the researcher submits a written letter (sometimes with an initial processing fee) to a government agency's FOI unit, where it is subsequently assigned to a coordinator. The FOI coordinator locates any texts relevant to the researcher's request and prepares them, in accordance with FOI legal requirements (e.g., protection of privacy or sensitive proprietary information, national security, etc.), for whole or partial disclosure. Some records do not have to be released and are exempt from FOI disclosure requirements (e.g., cabinet confidences in Canada, security intelligence records in the UK). An FOI request is completed once the requester receives a disclosure package and/or legal explanation for why some or all of the records were withheld from disclosure.

Only a fraction of the texts that government workers create are ever publicly disclosed (Galison, 2004), and those texts which are proactively released (i.e., without FOI) are typically manicured by public relations and communications specialists. To better understand government practices, researchers can use FOI to access those circulating texts that actually inform and bring into being the process of governing. Internal government texts that order and inform civil servant's actions and decision-making, communicate rationales, make calculations, or provide rules for organisation can all to some extent be accessed using FOI. FOI can produce useful insight into government conduct that can be generative for theorising (Swedberg, 2016) as well.

There are five steps involved in filing a successful FOI request (Jiwani & Krawchenko, 2014; Savage & Hyde, 2014). First, some preliminary research identifying the relevant agency (or agencies), programme, file type, etc. is required. Second, the request must be submitted. This can require a paper letter submission, but increasingly the submission process is moving online. Third, once the request is received, the FOI coordinator will be in contact with the researcher/requester in order to clarify, negotiate and broker the scope and meaning of the request. In more egregious cases, the FOI coordinator may try to stealthily steer the FOI user away from certain topics or dates (Sheaff, 2016). Fourth, usually after some period of waiting, the requester will receive a written explanation with a possible disclosure package containing the requested information (sometimes the information may be withheld outright, depending on the nature of the records, specific FOI law, etc.). The letter iterates what was requested and explains (if applicable) why information was redacted and under what section of law. Finally, and usually outlined at the end of the letter, there will be an option to appeal the agency's decision. Though not always warranted, the appeal process is an important phase in the FOI process and can be an effective means of correcting erroneous decisions made by coordinators. When multiple disclosures from different agencies are combined, these data can have what Monaghan and Hameed (2012) call a mosaic effect; that is, the sum of FOI records released in portions can reveal more than its parts in isolation.

We understand use of FOI as part of an ethical obligation of researchers to study up (Nader, 1974) and to investigate powerful, authoritative organisations that may be secretive or resistant to outside scrutiny (Lee, 2005; Monahan & Fisher, 2015). Although shadowing can be used (McDonald, 2005), access is difficult to come by and often only provides a glimpse at one part of any organisation. Expert interviewing (Meuser & Nagel, 2009) likewise can provide partial insights into government practices and processes, but government workers are often restricted in what they can say, calling the validity of such data into question (e.g., Brodeur, 2010, p. 36 on police as "deceptive objects"). Yet these more conventional research approaches are not immune from recent critiques of traditional methodological repertoires in social science (Greiffenhagen, Mair, & Sharrock, 2015; Savage & Burrows, 2007). Government workers, notably those in more guarded agencies and ministries, can come to operate as "cloistered communities" (Wichroski, 1996). One way to peer into the everyday worlds of these insulated communities and organisations is to use FOI requests.

In our view, FOI disclosures should be conceived of differently from "secondary data" in the traditional sense (Tarrant, 2017). There are two reasons for this. First, the multiple, complex and variegated processes that the researcher becomes embroiled in when filing an FOI request means that they play an active role in producing a disclosure (Luscombe, Walby, & Lippert, 2017). Two researchers seeking records on the same general subject are unlikely to produce identical disclosure packages. The researcher files and frames the initial request, brokers and negotiates with the coordinator over its meaning, appeals the agency's decisions and redactions and can even subsequently sue the organisation. An FOI disclosure package is "produced" for the user, not "found" data produced for secondary purposes. Second, data generated through FOI can describe existing and ongoing government practices. A report disclosed through FOI may be still actively circulating in government and being discussed by bureaucrats at the same time as the researcher obtains a copy. Based on this temporal element, analysing secondary data seems to have much more in common with archival research than data produced by FOI for social scientific research.

In sum, we understand academic inquiry as a "reticular process" (Brownstein, 1990, p. 163) that unfolds in a non-linear manner and that demands the continual use of reflexivity (Berger, 2015; Guillemin & Gillam, 2004). Incorporating FOI into one's research design could be considered what Altheide, Coyle, DeVriese, and Schneider (2008) refer to as emergent document analysis. Though it is difficult and challenging to mix approaches to data collection and analysis (Mclellan, Macqueen, & Neidig, 2003; Moran-Ellis et al., 2006), we advocate for research designs that include FOI requests, surveys, interviews, archival documents, news media and other available sources. Elsewhere, for example, we advocate nested sequential interviewing before and after use of FOI requests (Walby & Luscombe, 2017). When combined with multiple different research techniques and used in accordance with criteria for quality (Tracy, 2010), FOI requests can have a major impact on the design and results of social inquiry. Focusing on data analysis rather than design *per se*, below we reflect on four ways of analysing the results of FOI requests. Developing themes (Ryan & Bernard, 2003) and patterns is a key goal of any research technique, and the four approaches we discuss below each provide a unique yet complementary approach to identifying, analysing and making sense of the information contained in FOI documents.

## Four approaches to analysing Freedom of Information disclosures

### Content analysis

Content analysis allows researchers to extract manifest and latent trends from documents (Fields, 1988; Grimmer & Stewart, 2013). Content analysis can be used to determine the character and substance of a text by identifying, for example, how frequent the use of specific words or phrases is. Content analysis, often conducted with the aid of computer software, can be performed on both large and small datasets (Nelson, 2017; Nelson, Burk, Knudsen, & McCall, 2018). The categories used for coding can be derived both inductively (from the data) or deductively, using themes from relevant literature (Cho & Lee, 2014).

There are a number of examples of using content analysis strategies to analyse FOI data. Using records obtained through FOI, Young (2015) calculated that, for the past four decades, at least one pipeline every day had ruptured and created an oil spill in the province of Alberta. In their research on the representation of ethnoracial groups in Canada's prisons, Owusu-Bempah and Wortley (2014, p. 292) conducted FOI requests with provincial and territorial prisons across the country. Unlike at the federal level, Canadian provincial and territorial prisons do not proactively disclose information on the ethnoracial makeup of their prisoner populations, making FOI a necessary means of access. The data Owusu-Bempah and Wortley (2014) gained access to under FOI showed clear evidence of Indigenous and African Canadian overrepresentation in provincial and territorial prisons. In their analysis of racial disparities in marijuana misdemeanour arrests in New York City, Geller and Fagan (2010) used FOI to gain access to New York City Police Department stop activity logs, which recorded every time a citizen was stopped by an officer along with other relevant sociodemographic (including race) and contextual information. Geller and Fagan combined this information with other sources and analysed their dataset using content analysis alongside more sophisticated statistical techniques to measure disparities resulting from flawed "broken windows" and racist war on drugs policies in New York City.

Content analysis can also be more qualitative. Frequency of occurrences is an important and often used insight of content analysis, but it is not everything. As Fields (1988) points out, it is necessary to go beyond an analysis of frequency count alone if content analysis is to explain the more complex and variegated meaning that words take on in combination. While traditional methods of content analysis are more concerned with frequency, translating words into numbers, qualitative approaches to content analysis tend to use tools of mapping and diagramming to show how "codes, categories, and accompanying memos appear to relate or fit together" (Finfgeld-Connett, 2014, p. 346). This approach goes by different names depending on the discipline. In communication studies, Altheide (1987) uses the term ethnographic content analysis, the use of purposive and theoretical sampling to investigate how "a message is assumed to be reflected in various modes of information exchange ..." (p. 68; also see Altheide & Schneider, 2013). In qualitative health research, Hsieh and Shannon (2005) refer to it as "summative content analysis."

Combining quantitative and qualitative styles of content analysis, Roziere and Walby (forthcoming) conducted a content analysis of police files on militarisation of public police and special weapons and tactics (SWAT) teams in Canada. In official discourse, police in Canada typically claim their SWAT teams are for emergency (mass public casualty) purposes only. However, a content analysis of records disclosed through FOI revealed a different picture. Analysing the frequency and type of SWAT team deployment in Canadian cities, Roziere and Walby (forthcoming) found that municipal SWAT teams across Canada are now used for routine policing activities, including traffic stops, community policing, response to mental health and domestic violence calls, and execution of warrants. They found that SWAT teams were used for non-serious routine warrant executions in addition to more serious drug warrants. Not only did the content analysis reveal a portrait of SWAT team deployment that contrasted starkly with what the police publicly claimed, but the study provided the first empirical overview of frequency and type of SWAT team deployment in Canada. This research illustrates both the power of FOI to access police records not typically made a matter of the public record, and the utility of content analysis as a unique method of analysis for revealing frequencies and patterns of police conduct.

## Discourse analysis

Discourse analysis is a second strategy useful for making sense of FOI disclosures. Discourse and content analysis are sometimes mistakenly used interchangeably, but in our understanding, there are three main differences between the two. First, while content analysis tends to be more descriptive, identifying "emergent" themes through recurrence in the dataset, discourse analysis has a more critical theoretical foundation, influenced variably by the very different works of Foucault (1980) and Fairclough (2003). Second, discourse analysis is more likely to move outside the text, broadening the analysis by engaging with specific theoretical-constructs like Foucault's "discursive formation" or Fairclough's conceptions of power and hegemony. Third, content analysis and discourse analysis vary in terms of their deeper ontological and epistemological assumptions and the types of data sources they analyse (also see Hardy, Harley, & Phillips, 2004).

Though it is impossible to craft any one "formula" for discourse analysis, Waitt (2005) has usefully broken up the more Foucaultian approach to discourse analysis into five major "moments." First, the researcher must try to suspend pre-existing categories and classification by taking as agnostic a relation to the data as possible. Second, the researcher should immerse themselves into the texts they select by doing their best to understand them in their own terms and against their own frames of reference. Third, the researcher should examine the texts for its taken-for-granted assumptions and what sort of "truth" is it proposing to the reader. This is a reading for how the text's producer is situated in a discursive formation or regime of truth. Fourth, the researcher should examine the text for inconsistencies, non-sequiturs, logical leaps of faith, incoherent arguments and silences (also see Huckin, 2002). Finally, the researcher should analyse and reproduce the most persuasive and detailed excerpts that illustrate key and underlying trends in the text (Van Dijk, 1996).

Monaghan (2014) used this style of discourse analysis to show how government records of surveillance and policing – obtained through FOI – used racialising and stereotyping claims, arguments and classifications to portray Muslim Canadians as criminogenic and therefore targets of heightened surveillance and policing. His dataset included a wide range of internal record types, such as threat reports from an anti-terror working group comprised of members from 20 government agencies. Monaghan's (2014) painstaking research demonstrates how the discourse used by these government workers is indexed to a discursive formation generated by the ongoing "war on terror" that portrays Muslim persons as a global threat. Monaghan provides a compelling example of not only how to code FOI disclosures using discourse analysis, but also how to make the broader connection between data and theoretical constructs. Monaghan and Walby (2012) have likewise used discourse analysis to demonstrate how security intelligence agencies in Canada have devised classifications such as "multi-issue extremism" to categorize social and political advocacy groups as dangerous "extremists" in need of surveillance and repression.

Mackinnon (2014) used discourse analysis on FOI disclosures in order to analyse how the police in Vancouver, Canada responded to that city's Occupy Movement. To analyse these FOI records, she drew from Fairclough's more politically "critical discourse analysis" (CDA) (Fairclough, 1995). Like the more Foucaultian approach to discourse analysis noted above, Fairclough's CDA involves four major stages. The first involves the analyst searching for a social injustice depicted in a text. Next, the researcher searches for barriers to fixing or solving this injustice. Third, the researcher decodes the extent to which the existing political order may benefit from this social wrong or injustice. Finally, the analyst seeks ways of moving past or resisting the injustice through the use of "immanent critique." Using CDA, Mackinnon (2014) showed how the police framed and justified their crackdown on Occupy Vancouver, why this framing of the intervention was supported by broader publics, how the intervention served to support the existing order and proposed ways that policing in response to the Occupy Movement could been executed differently.

## Metaphor analysis

The third technique underscores the use of metaphors in talk and text. While approaches to metaphor analysis vary (Lakoff & Johnson, 1980; Ritchie & Zhu, 2015), a metaphor can be broadly defined as a word or phrase applied to an action or object to which it is not directly applicable. The word or phrase might have a literal meaning, but that meaning is stretched to apply to another general area or issue (Schmitt, 2005). Culturally, it is important to study and understand metaphors as they can build shared social meanings and group cohesiveness (Owen, 1985). Metaphors are central to all discursive practices, from the work of organisations (Manning, 1979) to this very chapter (DiCicco-Bloom & Gibson, 2010; Brown, 1976). Government agencies use metaphors to create and reinforce shared meanings that help rationalise and inform their programmes and actions. Numerous scholars have stressed the importance of studying how metaphors are used in organisations and their implications for practice (Koch & Deetz, 1981; Manning, 1979; Spencer, 2015; Yanow, 1992). As central "actors" in the insider discourse and decision-making practices of government (Luscombe & Walby, 2017), texts disclosed through FOI provide a fertile ground for the analysis of metaphors and their broader consequences for action.

Monaghan and Molnar (2016) used metaphor analysis to examine a passage they encountered in documents obtained through FOI on Royal Canadian Mounted Police (RCMP) anti-terrorism efforts. The specific metaphor was found in training files for RCMP and partnering police agencies aimed at teaching frontline officers to recognise potential terror suspects during their work. To do this, the training document employs the metaphor of officers "walking in the shoes of your enemy" (Monaghan & Molnar, 2016, p. 407). The documents analysed by Monaghan and Molnar describe how to "become" an imagined terrorist as a way of identifying and tracking the whereabouts of suspects as part of the broader governmental project of predicting terrorist activity. According to these training files, participating officers were organised into two groups, some role playing what they understand to be terrorists, while the others were instructed to observe patterns in their behaviour and assess them based on "clustered" indicators of suspicion in mock interactions. In this case, the RCMP deployed the metaphor to help enact an overarching approach that they encouraged officers to use, one where Muslim Canadians are at greater risk of being profiled as suspected terrorists due to the benign yet culturally specific nature of many of the so-called indicators of "radicalisation" (e.g., travelling to a Middle Eastern or Muslim country, asking too many questions of public officials, training in martial arts). By conflating this kind of blanket profiling based on crude and invalidated indicators of suspicion with a more seemingly nuanced and empathetic model of profiling devised by "walking in the shoes of your enemy," the RCMP's metaphor operates as a legitimating tool that can reinforce shared meanings about the alleged sophistication and sensitivity of anti-terrorism investigation methods in Canada. By applying strategies of metaphor analysis to FOI data, Monaghan and Molnar are able to reveal the underlying meanings and implications of the RCMP's use of metaphoric language, as well as how these metaphors connect to broader stereotypes evident in the war on terror and the unjust and racialised surveillance practices it entails.

## Social network analysis (SNA)

Network analysis can be generally understood as "a means of mapping roles comprehensively, so allowing the 'real' qualities of social structures to be delineated" (Crossley, 2008; Knox, Savage, & Harvey, 2006, p. 117). Social network analysis (SNA) is a specific branch of network analysis concerned with mapping and explaining trends and structures in uniquely "social" (as opposed to, e.g., biological) networks. Some of the major goals of SNA include studying the density, intensity, reciprocity, centrality and multiplexity of nodes in a network, where nodes can be anything from individuals, to organisations, to countries. Density refers to the sheer number of connections in a network as a function of the total number possible. Intensity, or "the strength of the relation" (Tichy et al., 1979, p. 509), is shaped by everything from frequency of contact to the extent to which a single node is willing to "honor obligations or forego personal costs to carry out obligations" (ibid.). Most networks are unevenly configured, and the extent to which two or more nodes report an equivalent or similar "intensity" of relationship as the others defines the network's overall reciprocity. Nodes that have more connections than others and are better strategically located in the network are said to be more "central." Finally, SNA scholars are crucially concerned with how multiple overlapping role requirements can link persons in a network to one another, thereby increasing the intensity of the relationship, bridging distinct networks (Smith, 2014). SNA scholars use these and other network concepts to test hypotheses about the benefits and setbacks of operating according to different network forms.

Most SNA research uses relational data collected from traditional methods like surveys. However, there is a developing trend in SNA toward constructing network matrices from documents and social media metadata (Borgatti, Everett, & Johnson, 2013, p. 30). SNA researchers, for example, have constructed social networks from information gleaned from archival data sources (e.g., Crossley, Edwards, Harries, & Stevenson, 2012; Padgett & Ansell, 1993; Smith & Papachristos, 2016). Many of the archival data sources that have been used to date to conduct SNA research could be obtained through FOI. Smith and Papachristos (2016), for instance, analysed multiplexity in Al Capone's organised crime network between 1900 and 1950. The authors' ambitious "Capone database" was generated by analysing 5,000 pages of "archival and secondary sources" from public bodies like the Chicago Crime Commission, Federal Bureau of Investigation and the Internal Revenue Service (Smith & Papachristos, 2016, p. 651). Though it is not clear how the authors gained access to records from these agencies (i.e., they may have used FOI), it is worth highlighting that these are all public organisations subject to FOI. To analyse the network structure of the UK suffragette movement, Crossley et al. (2012) worked with Home Office records listing suffragette court appearances from 1906 to 1914. The records were older and therefore available in the UK national archives. However, we again highlight that the Home Office is a state agency that is subject to FOI law. Had the records Crossley et al. (2012) were working with been more recent and not yet publicly archived, it is conceivable that they could have used FOI to gain access to them.

Though it is difficult to identify many published works which have formally combined FOI and SNA, there is much potential (as one example, see Reeves-Latour & Morselli, 2017). Many of the record types researchers can gain access to through FOI can easily be translated into network matrices. In our own research on institutional gifts and corporate sponsorship practices, we have used FOI to generate a large database of donations and sponsorships received by police departments throughout North America (Luscombe, Walby, & Lippert, 2018). Often these records are accessed by requesting the excel-format "registries" maintained internally by police agencies. These registries can include information on the identity of the donor/sponsor, the value of in-kind and monetary donations and sponsorships, the terms of the agreement (e.g., what was given back in return) and the name of the department office or unit that received it. Using SNA tools to analyse this information (e.g., UCINET), we have been able to identify central nodes (e.g., donors, sponsors, soliciting staff) in the network that we can subsequently zoom in on for further in-depth analysis. By mapping the in-kind and financial flows moving between police and donors/sponsors, we have also been able to get a sense of intensity and reciprocity of the network and its components. And by merging this FOI data with open-source information on the connections among donors/sponsors and their multiple relationships with the police (e.g., as board members on a police department's non-profit "police foundation," as a bidder for major procurement contracts with the police, etc.), we have been able to partially measure the density and multiplexity of this network.

In future research endeavours, and as the use of documents and other non-survey relational datasets grow in popularity, SNA researchers would benefit from the great deal of potential in FOI. Meeting minutes, email chains and the various kinds of detailed "logs" and "registries" kept by public bureaucracies are some of the more immediately relevant data forms for SNA, but they are only the tip of iceberg. As SNA scholars continue to devise new strategies for extrapolating relational information from documents, the potential fruitfulness of FOI, given the variety of documentary forms it can obtain access to, will also increase.

## Discussion and conclusion

FOI requests enable researchers to produce new datasets that provide powerful insights into the practices and processes of government (Noakes, 1995; Sheaff, 2016). Based on our own work and the work of others, we have shown how content analysis, discourse analysis, metaphor analysis and social network analysis are well-suited techniques for analysing FOI disclosures. We are in strong support of novel ways of combining these approaches in qualitative and mixed-methods research design (e.g., Crossley, 2010). Our main objective has been to illustrate how these approaches can be used on FOI documents in combination with other sources of data, including interview transcripts, surveys, news articles, archival data, or political speeches and other official rhetoric (on multi-methods research using FOI, see Pich, this volume). Our discussion of these four techniques has been short and incomplete. We are not suggesting that other approaches to data analysis (e.g., grounded theory; see Apramian et al., 2017) or variations within these approaches would not be fruitful or worth considering. Indeed, it would be quite possible to use grounded theory in analysis of FOI disclosures but we have not dealt with it here due to issues of space. Our hope is that this discussion will be the start of a larger conversation where the merits and pitfalls of FOI in combination with different analytic methods can be weighed and considered (for a discussion of difficulties with statistical analysis and FOI data, see Bows, this volume). We also hope that this discussion can aid future researchers in investigating government agencies and organisations using FOI requests.

Our discussion of FOI requests, research design and data analysis techniques has two broader implications. First, it provides further evidence that use of FOI requests is an increasingly popular method in the social sciences and is gaining formal legitimacy in the academy. As the use of this approach grows, interventions like this one become more timely and necessary to advance FOI users as a thoughtful and reflexive methodological community. Second, we hope to have encouraged social researchers to adopt some of these four methods of analysis in their own methodological toolkits, regardless of whether they are using FOI.

We should also note that there is incredible potential for collaboration around FOI. First, given the immense task of studying one or more government agencies, and the equally immense task of trying to make sense of these data, we recommend researchers work together in small teams. Second, there is potential for archiving and revisiting FOI disclosures as data and treating disclosures used for previous projects as secondary data (Mauthner, Parry, & Backett-Milburn, 1998). While confidentiality and anonymity remain a pressing issue with archiving and revisiting interview transcripts (Parry & Mauthner, 2004), this is not the case with FOI disclosures which are considered published material. Using FOI disclosures in this way would allow the scholarly community to test new hypotheses and pursue new research questions on existing data, as well as to validate or refute the arguments and claims of others.

## Note

1 It is not our intent to recount how to use FOI requests to produce data, as that issue is already reported on elsewhere (Jiwani & Krawchenko, 2014; Lee, 2005; Savage & Hyde, 2014). Nor is it our intention to go too far into the details of the varieties of these approaches to data analysis. For example, there are multiple forms of content analysis and discourse analysis (Fields, 1988; Hsieh & Shannon, 2005; Magnusson, 2005; Schreier, 2012; Tonkiss, 2004). There are also differences in how the methods are used across disciplines.

## References

Altheide, D. (1987). Ethnographic content analysis. *Qualitative Sociology*, *10*(1), 65–70.

Altheide, D., Coyle, M., DeVriese, K., & Schneider, C. (2008). Emergent qualitative document analysis. In S. Hesse-Biber & P. Leavy (Eds.), *Handbook of emergent methods* (pp. 127–151). New York: Guilford Press.

Altheide, D., & Schneider, C. (2013). *Qualitative media analysis* (2nd ed., pp. 39–74). Los Angeles: Sage.

Apramian, T., Cristancho, S., Watling, C., & Lingard, L. (2017). (Re)Grounding grounded theory: A close reading of theory in four schools. *Qualitative Research*, *17*(4), 359–376.

Berger, R. (2015). Now I see it, now I don't: Researcher's position and reflexivity in qualitative research. *Qualitative Research*, *15*(2), 219–234.

Birkinshaw, P. (2010). *Freedom of information: The law, the practice and the ideal*. Cambridge: Cambridge University Press.

Brodeur, J. P. (2010). *The policing web*. New York: Oxford University Press.

Brown, R. H. (1976). Social theory as metaphor: On the logic of discovery for the sciences of conduct. *Theory and Society*, *3*(2), 169–197.

Brownstein, H. (1990). Surviving as a qualitative sociologist: Recollections from the diary of a state worker. *Qualitative Sociology*, *13*(2), 149–167.

Burck, C. (2005). Comparing qualitative research methodologies for systemic research: The use of grounded theory, discourse analysis and narrative analysis. *Journal of Family Therapy*, *27*(3), 237–262.

Burgess, M. (2015). *Freedom of information: A practical guide for UK journalists*. London: Routledge.

Cho, J. Y., & Lee, E. H. (2014). Reducing Confusion about grounded theory and qualitative content analysis: Similarities and differences. *The Qualitative Report*, *19*(32), 1–20.

Clement, D. (2015). Freedom of information in Canada: Implications for historical research. *Labour/Le Travail*, *75*, 101–131.

Cribb, R., Jobb, D., McKie, D., & Vallance-Jones, F. (2015). *Digging deeper: A Canadian reporter's research guide* (3rd ed.). Toronto: Oxford University Press.

Crossley, N. (2008). (Net)Working out: Social capital in a private health club. *British Journal of Sociology*, *59*(3), 475–500.

Crossley, N. (2010). The social world of the network. Combining qualitative and quantitative elements in social network analysis. *Sociologica*, *4*(1).

Crossley, N., Edwards, G., Harries, E., & Stevenson, R. (2012). Covert social movement networks and the secrecy-efficiency trade off: The case of the UK suffragettes (1906–1914). *Social Networks*, *34*(4), 634–644.

Cuillier, D., & Davis, C. N. (2010). *The art of access: Strategies for acquiring public records*. Washington: CQ Press.

DiCicco-Bloom, B., & Gibson, D. R. (2010). More than a game: Sociological theory from the theories of games. *Sociological Theory, 28*(3), 247–271.

Fairclough, N. (1995). *Critical discourse analysis: The critical study of language.* Harlow: Longman.

Fairclough, N. (2003). *Analyzing discourse: Textual analysis for social research.* New York: Routledge.

Fields, E. E. (1988). Qualitative content analysis of television news systematic techniques. *Qualitative Sociology, 11*(3), 183–193.

Finfgeld-Connett, D. (2014). Use of content analysis to conduct knowledge-building and theory-generating qualitative systematic reviews. *Qualitative Research, 14*(3), 341–352.

Foucault, M. (1980). Two lectures. In C. Gordon (Ed.), *Power/knowledge: Selected interview and other writings 1972–1977* (pp. 78–108). New York: Pantheon.

Galison, P. (2004). Removing knowledge. *Critical Inquiry, 31*(1), 229–243.

Geller, A., & Fagan, J. (2010). Pot as pretext: Marijuana, race, and the new disorder In New York City street policing. *Journal of Empirical Legal Studies, 7*(4), 591–633.

Greiffenhagen, C., Mair, M., & Sharrock, W. (2015). Methodological troubles as problems and phenomena: Ethnomethodology and the question of 'method' in the social sciences. *British Journal of Sociology, 66*(3), 460–485.

Grimmer, J., & Stewart, B. M. (2013). Text as data: The promise and pitfalls of automatic content analysis for political texts. *Political Analysis, 21*(3), 267–297.

Guillemin, M., & Gillam, L. (2004). Reflexivity and 'ethically important moments' in research. *Qualitative Inquiry, 10*(2), 261–280.

Haggerty, K. D. (2004). Ethics creep: Governing social science research in the name of ethics. *Qualitative Sociology, 27*(4), 393–414.

Hardy, C., Harley, B., & Phillips, N. (2004). Discourse analysis and content analysis: Two solitudes? *Qualitative Methods Newsletter,* 19–22.

Hazell, R., & Worthy, B. (2010). Assessing the performance of freedom of information. *Government Information Quarterly, 27*(4), 352–359.

Holsen, S. (2007). Freedom of information in the UK, US, and Canada. *Information Management Journal, 41*(3), 50–55.

Honan, E., Knobel, M., Baker, C., & Davies, B. (2000). Producing possible hannahs: Theory and the subject of research. *Qualitative Inquiry, 6*(1), 9–32.

Hsieh, H., & Shannon, S. (2005). Three approaches to qualitative content analysis. *Qualitative Health Research, 15*(9), 1277–1288.

Huckin, T. (2002). Textual silence and the discourse of homelessness. *Discourse and Society, 13*(3), 347–372.

Jiwani, F. N., & Krawchenko, T. (2014). Public policy, access to government, and qualitative research practices: Conducting research within a culture of information control. *Canadian Public Policy, 40*(1), 57–66.

Knox, H., Savage, M., & Harvey, P. (2006). Social networks and the study of relations: Networks as method, metaphor, and form. *Economy and Society, 35*(1), 113–140.

Koch, S., & Deetz, S. (1981). Metaphor analysis of social reality in organizations. *Journal of Applied Communication Research, 9*(1), 1–15.

Lakoff, G., & Johnson, M. (1980). *Metaphors we live by.* Chicago: University of Chicago Press.

Lee, R. M. (2005). The UK Freedom of Information Act and social research. *International Journal of Social Research Methodology, 8*(1), 1–18.

Luscombe, A., & Walby, K. (2017). Theorizing freedom of information: The live archive, obfuscation, and actor-network theory. *Government Information Quarterly, 34*(3), 379–387.

Luscombe, A., Walby, K., & Lippert, R. (2017). Brokering access beyond the border and in the wild: Comparing freedom of information Law and policy in Canada and the United States. *Law & Policy*, *39*(3), 259–279.

Luscombe, A., Walby, K., & Lippert, R. (2018). Police-sponsorship networks: Benign ties or webs of private influence? *Policing & Society*, *28*(5), 553–569.

Luton, L. S. (2015). *Qualitative research approaches for public administration*. London: Routledge.

Mackinnon, D. M. (2014). The criminalization of political dissent: A critical discourse analysis of occupy Vancouver and Bill C-309. Dissertation, Simon Fraser University, Department of Sociology and Anthropology.

Magnusson, E. (2005). Cultural discourse in action: Interactional dynamics and symbolic meaning. *Qualitative Sociology*, *28*(4), 371–398.

Manning, P. K. (1979). Metaphors of the field: Varieties of organizational discourse. *Administrative Science Quarterly*, *24*(4), 660–671.

Mauthner, N. S., & Doucet, A. (2003). Reflexive accounts and accounts of reflexivity in qualitative data analysis. *Sociology*, *37*(3), 413–431.

Mauthner, N. S., Parry, O., & Backett-Milburn, K. (1998). The data are out there, or are they? Implications for archiving and revisiting qualitative data. *Sociology*, *32*(4), 733–745.

McDonald, S. (2005). Studying actions in context: A qualitative shadowing method for organizational research. *Qualitative Research*, *5*(4), 455–473.

Mcillwain, J. S. (1999). Organized crime: A social network approach. *Crime, Law and Social Change*, *32*(4), 301–323.

Mclellan, E., Macqueen, K. M., & Neidig, J. L. (2003). Beyond the qualitative interview: Data preparation and transcription. *Field Methods*, *15*(1), 63–84.

Meuser, M., & Nagel, U. (2009). The expert interview and changes in knowledge production. In A. Bogner, B. Littig, & W. Menz (Eds.), *Interviewing experts* (pp. 17–42). London: Palgrave Macmillan Limited.

Monaghan, J. (2014). Security traps and discourses of radicalization: Examining surveillance practices targeting Muslims in Canada. *Surveillance and Society*, *12*(4), 485–501.

Monaghan, J. (2017). *Security aid: Canada and the development regime of security*. Toronto: University of Toronto Press.

Monaghan, J., & Hameed, Y. (2012). Accessing dirty data: Methodological strategies for social problems researchers. In M. Larsen, & K. Walby (Eds.), *Brokering access: Politics, power and freedom of information in Canada* (pp. 142–168). Vancouver: UBC Press.

Monaghan, J., & Molnar, A. (2016). Radicalization theories, policing practices, and 'the future of terrorism'. *Critical Studies on Terrorism*, *9*(3), 393–413.

Monaghan, J., & Walby, K. (2012). Making up 'terror identities': Security intelligence and Canada's Integrated Threat Assessment Centre. *Policing & Society*, *22*(2), 133–151.

Monahan, T., & Fisher, J. A. (2015). Strategies for obtaining access to secretive or guarded organizations. *Journal of Contemporary Ethnography*, *44*(6), 709–736.

Moran-Ellis, J., Alexander, V. D., Cronin, A., Dickinson, M., Fielding, J., & Thomas, H. (2006). Triangulation and integration: Processes, claims and implications. *Qualitative Research*, *6*(1), 45–59.

Nader, L. (1974). Up the anthropologist – Perspectives gained from studying up. In D. Hymes (Ed.), *Reinventing anthropology* (pp. 284–311). New York: Vintage Books.

Nelson, L. K. (2017). Computational grounded theory: A methodological framework. *Sociological Methods & Research* online-first.

Nelson, L. K., Burk, D., Knudsen, M., & McCall, L. (2018). The future of coding: A comparison of hand-coding and three types of computer-assisted text analysis methods. *Sociological Methods & Research* online-first.

Noakes, J. A. (1995). Using FBI files for historical sociology. *Qualitative Sociology, 18*(2), 271–286.

Owen, W. F. (1985). Metaphor analysis of cohesiveness in small discussion groups. *Small Group Behavior, 16*(3), 415–424.

Owusu-Bempah, A., & Wortley, S. (2014). Race, crime, and criminal justice in Canada. In S. M. Bucerius, & M. Tonry (Eds.), *The Oxford handbook of ethnicity, crime, and immigration* (pp. 281–320). New York: Oxford University Press.

Padgett, J. F., & Ansell, C. K. (1993). Robust action and the rise of the medici, 1400–1434. *American Journal of Sociology, 98*(6), 1259–1319.

Parry, O., & Mauthner, N. S. (2004). Whose data are they anyway? Practical, legal and ethical issues in archiving qualitative research data. *Sociology, 38*(1), 139–152.

Reeves-Latour, M., & Morselli, C. (2017). Bid-rigging networks and state-corporate crime in the construction industry. *Social Networks, 51*(1), 158–170.

Ritchie, L., & Zhu, M. (2015). Nixon stonewalled the investigation: Potential contributions of grammatical metaphors to conceptual metaphor theory and analysis. *Metaphor and Symbol, 30*(2), 118–136.

Roberts, A. (2006). *Blacked out: Government secrecy in the information age.* Cambridge: Cambridge University Press.

Roziere, B., & Walby, K. (Forthcoming). Police militarization in Canada: Media rhetoric and operational realities. *Policing: A Journal of Policy and Practice.*

Ryan, G. W., & Bernard, H. R. (2003). Techniques to identify themes. *Field Methods, 15*(1), 85–109.

Savage, A., & Hyde, R. (2014). Using freedom of information requests to facilitate research. *International Journal of Social Research Methodology, 17*(3), 303–317.

Savage, M., & Burrows, R. (2007). The coming crisis of empirical sociology. *Sociology, 41*(5), 885–899.

Schmitt, R. (2005). Systematic metaphor analysis as a method of qualitative research. *The Qualitative Report, 10*(2), 358–394.

Schreier, M. (2012). *Qualitative content analysis in practice.* Los Angeles: Sage.

Schudson, M. (2015). *The rise of the right to know: Politics and the culture of transparency, 1945–1975.* Harvard: Harvard University Press.

Sheaff, M. (2016). Constructing accounts of organisational failure: Policy, power and concealment. *Critical Social Policy, 37*, 1–20.

Smith, C. M., & Papachristos, A. V. (2016). Trust thy crooked neighbor: Multiplexity in Chicago organized crime networks. *American Sociological Review, 81*(4), 644–667.

Smith, S. (2014). Social network boundaries and tricky to access populations: A qualitative approach. *International Journal of Social Research Methodology, 17*(6), 613–623.

Spencer, A. (2015). Metaphor analysis as a method in terrorism studies. In P. Dixit, & J. Stump (Eds.), *Critical methods in terrorism studies* (pp. 91–107). London: Routledge.

Starks, H., & Trinidad, S. B. (2007). Choose your method: A comparison of phenomenology, discourse analysis, and grounded theory. *Qualitative Health Research, 17*(10), 1372–1380.

Swedberg, R. (2016). Before theory comes theorizing or how to make social science more interesting. *British Journal of Sociology, 67*(1), 5–22.

Tarrant, A. (2017). Getting out of the swamp? Methodological reflections on using qualitative secondary analysis to develop research design. *International Journal of Social Research Methodology, 20*(6), 599–611.

Tichy, N. M., Tushman, M. L., & Fombrum, C. (1979). Social network analysis for organizations. *Academy of Management Review, 4*(4), 507–519.

Tonkiss, F. (2004). Analysing text and speech: Content and critical discourse analysis. In C. Seal (Ed.), *Researching society and culture* (pp. 368–382). London: Sage.

Tracy, S. J. (2010). Qualitative quality: Eight 'big-tent' criteria for excellent qualitative research. *Qualitative Inquiry, 16*(10), 837–849.

Van Dijk, T. A. (1996). Discourse, power and access. In C. R. Caldas-Coulthard, & M. Coulthard (Eds.), *Texts and practices: Readings in critical discourse analysis* (pp. 83–104). London: Routledge.

Waitt, G. R. (2005). Doing discourse analysis. In I. Hay (Ed.), *Qualitative research methods in human geography* (2nd ed., pp. 163–191). New York: Oxford University Press.

Walby, K., Lippert, R., & Wilkinson, B. (2014). "The right people to do the right job …": Legitimation work of municipal corporate security personnel. *Australian & New Zealand Journal of Criminology, 47*(2), 259–275.

Walby, K., & Luscombe, A. (2017). Criteria for quality in qualitative research and use of freedom of information requests in social research. *Qualitative Research, 17*(5), 537–553.

Walby, K., & Luscombe, A. (2018). Ethics review and freedom of information requests in qualitative research. *Research Ethics, 14*(4), 1–15.

Wichroski, M. A. (1996). Breaking silence: Some fieldwork strategies in cloistered and non-cloistered communities. *Qualitative Sociology, 19*(1), 153–170.

Worthy, B. (2017). *The politics of freedom of information: How and why governments pass laws that threaten their power.* Manchester: Manchester University Press.

Worthy, B., & Bourke, G. (2011). *The sword and the shield: The use of FOI by parliamentarians and the impact of FOI on Parliament.* London: Constitution Unit.

Yanow, D. (1992). Supermarkets and culture clash: The epistemological role of metaphors in administrative practice. *American Review of Public Administration, 22*(2), 89–109.

Yanow, D. (2000). *Conducting interpretive policy analysis.* Newbury Park: Sage.

Young, L. (2015). The power of numbers: Holding governments accountable with the own data. In J. Brownlee, & K. Walby (Eds.), *Access to information and social justice: Critical research strategies for journalists, scholars and activists* (pp. 34–53). Winnipeg: Arbeiter Ring Publishing.

**PART 4**

# Freedom of Information and research design

## Challenges and dilemmas

# 11

# ANALYSING PUBLIC POLICY IN THE UK

## Seeing through the secrecy, obfuscation and obstruction of the FOIA by the Home Office

*John R. Campbell*

### Introduction

Implementation of the United Kingdom's Freedom of Information Act (FOIA) was delayed five years due in large part to Prime Minister Blair's concern that the Act would have a "chilling" impact on the conduct of government business. Worthy and Hazell's (2017) review regarding how the Act has been used concluded that "the effects of access to information laws are nuanced and changeable" and that the impact of the Act is shaped by complex and contradictory processes. They argue that the use of the FOIA has been relatively high and that the members of the public have made the most use of FOIA (to obtain personal information), followed by journalists, businesses and academics. The authors concluded that the Act has made "government more transparent and [it had] increased accountability" though it "has not had any significant impact on the decision-making processes" (p. 36).

While researchers are using their rights under the FOIA to obtain information on government policy and policy implementation, this task is complicated by the volume of government publication, by "open government" initiatives that release vast amounts of information of varying value into the public domain and by the tendency of officials to refuse to disclose politically significant information. Ultimately the effective use of the FOIA is also limited by the narrow focus of much research and by the failure of researchers to co-operate and work together. The problems encountered since it became possible to use FOI for research purposes mean that the task of moving "beyond official discourse" to understand the nature and impact of government policy (Walby & Larsen, 2012, 2011; Wedel, Shore, Feldman, & Lathrop, 2005) remains as elusive as ever.

This paper examines two cases in which FOI requests played a critical role in an attempt to go "beyond official discourse." The first case concerns official claims involving the use of "expert knowledge" to analyse the spoken language of asylum seekers to determine their "nationality" (and refuse them asylum). The second case illustrates how a government can cite "national security interests," etc. to justify non-disclosure, and how ineffective appeals to the Information Commissioner, the principle regulator, can be (on appeals, see also Bows, this volume). Nevertheless, both cases also illustrate how research can "see through" the policy claims made by officials even when they fail to disclose critical information.

## UK Border Agency's reliance on "scientific knowledge" to assess asylum applicant's language

In 2007, I began a two-year research project to ethnographically map and analyse the various institutions and actors operating in the United Kingdom's "asylum field" in order to understand how they influence asylum policy and decisions on individual asylum claims. It was clear from the outset that analysing a representative sample of asylum applicants – approximately 25,000 asylum application were made in 2006 (UK, 2016: chart 2.1) – was beyond the scope of the project. We focused our efforts and resources on following a limited number of asylum claims working their way through the "asylum system." While this empirical focus provided detailed information about individual cases, it was evident that we would also need to interview individuals (e.g., asylum applicants, lawyers, officials, NGOs, etc.), analyse documents and policy statements, and make FOIA requests[1] to understand the work of the key government departments directly engaged in asylum-related policy work, e.g., the Home Office, the Ministry of Justice and the Government Legal Department (Campbell, 2017; Savage & Hyde, 2014).

One strand of this project focused on "language analysis" (hereafter LA) which was authorised under sec. 19 of the *Race Relations Act* (1976).[2] The Act was amended in 2000[3] to allow government to suspend anti-discrimination laws to "investigate" and take action to prevent foreign nationals from entering or seeking asylum in the UK. There rapidly followed a number of "Ministerial authorisations" – which take the form of making a brief statement either to Parliament or the House of Lords – setting out the exemption being sought. Authorisations were initially made for a specific period, e.g. 4 months[4]; however, Ministers have authorised language analysis continuously since 2000.

What is "language analysis" and how is it implemented? According to published Asylum Policy Instructions, the purpose of LA was to provide "expert evidence" to identify the place of origin of asylum seekers who were believed to be making false claims. The policy instruction sets out a step-by-step procedure which officials are supposed to follow in examining the spoken language of individuals who claim to be from specific countries. The process required officials to identify suspect asylum applications and to set up a 20–30-minute phone interview between the asylum applicant and an "expert linguist." Immediately following the interview, the "expert" sends the official a preliminary analysis, followed 3–5 days later by a detailed report setting out the "probability" that the asylum applicant speaks language "X" (expressed with varying degrees of certainty). Officials were required to use the test result, together with other information available to them, to decide an asylum claim.

My research on this policy was based on the analysis of asylum appeals where LA evidence was submitted by the Home Office, analysis of case files, discussions with immigration barristers and material disclosed by the Home Office through FOI requests.[5] I concluded (Campbell, 2013) that: (a) contrary to policy statements, officials did not follow their own policy guidelines which set out how the policy was supposed to be implemented (e.g., the criteria for selecting the individuals to be tested was too broad); (b) an applicant's spoken language was not analysed by "experts" (because analysts were "native speakers" who were "supervised" by trained linguists and because in certain cases applicants were not interviewed in their "native language"); and (c) officials relied on LA reports to the exclusion of other information available to them to (unlawfully) refuse an individual asylum.

Decisions based on LA evidence alone were problematic because, contrary to an unequivocal statement endorsed by professional linguists, LA is not able to conclusively determine the nationality of individual asylum applicants (LANOG, 2004). The best that it could do, if appropriate procedures were meticulously followed, was to establish the region from which an asylum applicant came. This limitation is important for two reasons. First, individuals who come from the same country cannot be assumed to speak the same language or speak a standard dialect of a language. Second, when individuals are displaced outside their country of origin by war/violence, their spoken language(s) is gradually modified to include elements from their "new" social environment. Displacement has two implications for refugees. First, residence in a second country does not invalidate an individual's fear of persecution and right to claim asylum. Second, such individuals would need to have his/her entire "linguistic biography" (i.e., all their spoken languages) examined which cannot be done in the 20–30-minute interview relied upon by the Home Office.

The four pieces of information disclosed by the Home Office in response to my FOI requests provided little empirical justification for the policy. The first item disclosed was a 15-page summary of a 2003 "evaluation of Language Analysis Pilot" that used four different commercial firms to provide LA. The pilot sought to evaluate the operational usefulness of LA in assisting UKBA to detect false claims, the extent to which it assisted officials to decide claims, the extent to which it created evidence that would influence the outcome of legal appeals to the Asylum & Immigration Tribunal and therefore its usefulness to the Home Office in deporting applicants from the UK. A total of 100 individuals were tested (51 from Afghanistan, 63 from Somalia and 39 from Sri Lanka). Despite the limited number of individuals tested and the lack of independent evidence supporting the operational value of LA, the Home Office awarded a contract to

Sprakab, a Swedish commercial firm, to undertake LA. A purported reason to adopt LA was that this evaluation indicated that 30% of applicants claiming to be from Somalia were falsely "posing" as Somali nationals. It is important to note that professional linguists were not asked about the methods used for LA or about the reliability of LA findings.

The second document disclosed was a table listing the number of individuals who had been tested between 2007 and 2009 and the results of LA testing. The list indicated that 2,628 individuals from 39+ countries were tested (the five largest nationalities in declining order were Somalia, Afghanistan, Palestine Authority, Kuwait/Bidoon and Sudan). The document did not provide any information about the usefulness of LA in official decision-making or how LA evidence was viewed in the courts. If anything, the document strongly suggests that individuals were indiscriminately selected to be tested for language (which indicates the subjective nature of the criteria used to select individuals for analysis).

The third document that was disclosed was a four-page "Eritrean intake report" written in 2008 summarising LA tests and the outcome of 146 Eritrean cases. LA determined that 44% of the individuals tested spoke "Amharic" which was identified as an "Ethiopian" language.[6] The report concluded that "it cannot be said that LA is helping case-owners to achieve their performance targets, neither does it appear to be a factor in the decision-making processes."[7]

The fourth document disclosed was a three-page "overview" of 785 Somali cases that was written in 2008. This document summarised limited information about LA tests and while it waxes lyrical about detecting fraudulent claims – primarily by Kenyans (51%) – it cites no reliable data to support the validity of LA or how LA evidence was evaluated in appeals heard in the Tribunal. However, the document underlines the pre-occupation of the Home Office with detecting fraud, influencing the outcome of asylum appeals and removing failed applicants.

On the basis of all of the evidence available to me at that time, I concluded that "the language of science" adopted by the Home Office to justify language analysis was used "to obfuscate flawed assumptions about language use and capricious bureaucratic practices" (Campbell, 2013, p. 686). In effect, the Home Office was attempting to transform a political problem, namely border enforcement, into a technical problem "by recasting it in the neutral language of science" which could only be addressed by "experts" (i.e., not officials). LA reports would, it was hoped, be accepted as scientifically valid evidence by the courts thereby justifying official decisions to refuse individuals asylum.

Legal appeals to the Tribunal involving claims where LA evidence was used to refuse an individual asylum sought to challenge the validity of the procedures used by Sprakab, the Swedish firm contracted to analyse an asylum applicant's spoken language. Barristers successfully argued that the "experts" used to interview and analyse an asylum applicant's spoken language lacked the training and the competence to carry out LA (Campbell, 2013, p. 682-f). However, in 2010, this line of attack was undermined by the Asylum & Immigration Tribunal when it decided the case of RB *(Linguistic Evidence – Sprakab) Somalia [2010]*

*UKUT* 329 *IAC*.[8] Rather than looking at the key issues raised by the case – i.e., dialect, "language mixing," claims about deficiencies in linguistic knowledge, and the failure of Sprakab to interview the applicant in her "native" language – the Tribunal focused on the need to maintain the anonymity of Sprakab's analysts despite the fact that none of the firm's "native speakers" possessed professional linguistic qualifications and despite the firm's failure to comply with IAFPA guidelines in conducting language analysis (Language and National Origin Group, 2004).

The 2010 case emboldened the Home Office's to continue its LA policy. However, new issues have emerged which undermine the validity of LA. First, there is virtually no published research that examines the techniques relied upon by language analysis to determine the country of origin of asylum seekers. Indeed, the two commercial firms which are contracted by the Home Office for this purpose – Sprakab and Verified – have not published any material about their methods or the reliability of their research.

Interestingly OCILA, which undertakes LA for the Dutch Immigration and Naturalisation Service, has addressed this issue. Cambier-Langeveld (2016), an advisor and linguist who works for OCILA, observes two key limitations of LA which are relevant to the way that the Home Office use LA. First, before a language can be analysed, it needs to be adequately documented. However, many of the languages spoken by asylum applicants are not documented. OCILA have no problems in analysing what they refer to as "clearly audible and well described differences between northern Somalia and southern Somalia language varieties" (p. 29). However, many of the individuals who were tested by the Home Office, including "RB" whose case was examined in 2010 by the Tribunal, were not Somali speakers; they claimed to be speakers of "Kibajuni" (a dialect of Kiswahili; Canada, 2005). Furthermore, these individuals were not interviewed in their "mother tongue," as claimed in the Home Office Asylum Policy Instruction, but in Kiswahili (see Campbell, 2013, pp. 682–683). This practice violated the basic assumptions of LA. If individuals are not interviewed in their "native language," they tend to "accommodate" their speech to conform with the language of the interviewer, a situation which can easily result in a finding by an "analyst" that the individual did not speak their claimed language. Furthermore, because of decades-long conflict in Somalia, many Kibajuni speakers have been displaced into Kenya where Kibajuni, their "native language," would have been affected by interaction with speakers of a different dialect of Swahili. This means that their entire "language profile" should have been tested (Cambier-Langeveld, 2016, p. 30-f).

Second, OCILA argues that LA on Eritrean nationals is not warranted because of difficulties in distinguishing between speakers of Tigrinya who reside in Ethiopia and in Eritrea. Analysis is difficult "because of the shared history of these countries and the patchy geographic backgrounds of many people in that area" (p. 30). For this reason, OCILA does not undertake LA on Eritreans.[9] In short, to the extent that the Home Office refused asylum to some Eritreans and to Somali

Kibajuni speakers on the basis of LA alone, that decision was wrong and may have resulted in individuals being wrongly denied asylum.

Since LA was initiated in 2000, only one case has reached the UK's Supreme Court. In *Secretary of State for Home Department v MN and KY (Scotland) [2014] UKSC 30 (March 6, 2014)*,[10] the Justices set out guidance which the Tribunal should use to decide cases which rely upon language analysis reports submitted by the Home Office. The Justices made it clear that, contrary to *RB (Linguistic Evidence – Sprakab) Somalia [2010] UKUT 329 IAC*, evidence critical of LA reports should be made available and that the Tribunal should carefully assess all the evidence to determine "the strength of the reasoning and the expertise used to support them" (¶48). In short, and not before time, "expert" LA evidence was finally subject to the same requirements as all other types of expert opinion-based evidence.[11]

Nevertheless, the Home Office has continued to make use of LA in deciding asylum claims. A recent FOI request[12] to the Home Office disclosed the current version of the Asylum Policy Instruction on LA and a heavily redacted 2012 report which purports to analyse the costs and benefits of LA testing and which provides statistics on the number and nationality of individuals tested between 2011 and 2016 (summarised in Table 11.1).

If we compare the Asylum Police Instruction published in 2010 with the 2017 version (Home Office, 2017a), the recent version acknowledges the statutory requirement placed on the Home Office to "safeguard and promote the welfare of children"[13] (including the need for a "responsible adult" to attend the LA

**TABLE 11.1** Language Analysis tests conducted between 2011 and 2016: Total number by year and by largest nationality tested

|  | 2011 | 2012 | 2013 | 2014 | 2015 | 2016 | Total |
|---|---|---|---|---|---|---|---|
| Kuwait/ Bidoon | 9 | 57 | 155 | 8 | 373 | 16 | 618 |
| Palestine Authority | 7 | 25 | 37 | 4 | 40 | 12 | 125 |
| Somalia | 4 | 29 | 30 | 5 | 16 | 8 | 92 |
| Syria Arab Republic | 1 | 31 | 333 | 46 | 947 | 982 | 2,340 |
| Eritrea | 1 | 6 | 21 | 0 | 33 | 3 | 64 |
| Afghanistan | 0 | 3 | 22 | 3 | 52 | 18 | 98 |
| Iran | 0 | 10 | 20 | 7 | 40 | 101 | 178 |
| Iraq | 0 | 0 | 4 | 0 | 10 | 20 | 34 |
| Total number tested | 31 | 186 | 665 | 94 | 1,650 | 1,180 | 3,806 |
| Estimated cost of LA | £12,400/ £21,700 | £74,400/ £130,200 | £266,000/ $465,500 | £37,600/ £65,800 | £660,000/ £1,155,000 | £472,000/ £826,000 | £1,522,400/ £2,664,200 |

interview with the child), the need for officials to obtain "consent"[14] from individuals before they can be tested, and the need to recognise medical/disability grounds which may prevent an individual from attending and/or completing LA.[15] The new API partially reflects the 2014 Supreme Court decision (discussed above) by stating that Home Office officials and the Tribunal must not rely solely on language analysis in determining an asylum claim. Other than these changes, the procedure in the 2017 API mirrors earlier guidance. Even so, there are good reasons to be sceptical about the "scientific" "expert" basis of Home Office LA because, as my earlier research found, neither officials nor the commercial firms which are contracted to provide language analysis necessarily adhere to the procedures set out in the API. In short, policy guidance on and the use of LA does not appear to have changed since 2010.

A brief look at the Home Office's analysis of the cost/benefit of using LA shows that it relies on limited data for the period of 2008 and 2009 when, at most, less than five percent of asylum applicants were subjected to LA (LA was used primarily to examine Afghan, Eritrean, Kuwaiti, Palestinian and Somali claims). Despite redacting nearly all the statistical data in the original report, it is clear that the analysis is methodologically flawed. At no point are questions raised about the criteria used by the Home Office to select individuals to be tested, nor do the authors of the report question the reliability of LA testing. Instead, various data are provided in the form of tables which (a) purport to compare the results of LA tests against the total number of applicants from a specific country and against the "asylum grant rate" for that country; (b) compare initial decisions where LA was used as against initial decisions in cases when LA was not used; (c) demonstrate the usefulness of LA for case workers in arriving at a timely decision and (d) show the usefulness of LA in preventing "abusive" asylum claims and "nationality swapping."

The simple fact is that the number and type of claims that were tested do not provide a large enough sample to arrive at valid conclusions. Indeed, a careful reading of the report clearly shows that the Home Office has insufficient empirical data to conduct a cost–benefit analysis. For example, in summarising its conclusions, the report states that "changes to asylum intake over time are not easy to explain" (which means that LA could not have been a deterrent) and that "Tribunals and courts did not give significant weight to LA" (Home Office 2011). Or, "[t]his comparison will not provide a full picture because it was not able to take into account other differences in case types that could affect asylum case outcomes ..." (p. 15). Or, "[a] comparison of case outcomes is not possible but the results could be skewed" and "findings should be treated as indicative" (p. 16). Indeed, the report states that "LA does not seem to be associated with any difference in appeal outcomes" (p. 17). While it is possible that after 2010 LA evidence was more widely accepted as a valid form of evidence by the Tribunal, this report does not examine data for this period. In short, the report fails to provide any evidence that would support the continued use of LA.

Home Office disclosure of the total number of individuals tested between 2011 and 2016 (see Table 11.1, below) indicates that 3,806 individuals were tested and that most of those tested came from five countries. However, a comparison of Home Office statistics on language testing with official statistics on asylum applications by year and nationality[16] suggests there is no clear correlation between LA (i.e., as a means of deterring fraudulent claims) and changes in the number of asylum applicants from the top five countries from which applicants claim to have originated from. Indeed, the variation over time in the number of people tested and the nationalities of those tested suggests that individuals were randomly chosen.[17]

What can we conclude from the recent information disclosed by the Home Office? First, it should be clear that the language tests relied upon by the Home Office lack a scientific basis: there are no independent analyses of the methodologies used to analyse language, nor are there studies which indicate that the procedures produce reliable and accurate findings (UK, 2015). Equally important, and unlike forensic language analysis in the criminal courts, LA is not subject to statutory regulation by the UK's Forensic Science Regulator.[18] Internal Home Office reports and analysis have consistently failed to establish the value of LA in determining the country of origin of asylum seekers, and the firms contracted to do this work consistently failed to follow professional guidelines. On a final note, it is possible to estimate the financial cost of using LA to the public purse. Based on information in disclosed documents,[19] for the period 2011–2016, between £1.5 million and £2.6 million pounds have been paid to private firms to undertake language analysis. This estimate does not include the time spent by Home Office officials making use of LA, nor does it include litigation costs when Home Office decisions are appealed to the Tribunal or appellate courts. Finally, the human cost to asylum seekers of being refused protection because of LA is not included.

## Secret meetings and asylum policy

In 2015, and following several years in which the UK recognised that human rights abuses in Eritrea provided sufficient grounds to grant asylum to Eritrean nationals, the Home Office suddenly announced a new policy which stated that Eritrean nationals could safely be "returned" to Eritrea without contravening their human rights (Home Office, 2015a, 2015b). In arriving at this decision, the Home Office relied on a report produced by the Danish Immigration Authority (2014) which was the subject of ongoing disputes in Denmark that led to the policy being withdrawn by the Danish government in 2015.

Home Office case officers, who had been warned in advance of an impending change to asylum policy, delayed their decisions on Eritrean claims. However, with the announcement of the new policy in March 2015, case workers summarily rejected the majority of Eritrean asylum applications. Their decisions transformed asylum applicants into destitute "failed" asylum seekers who were subject to deportation. The situation led to an enormous increase in the number of appeals to the Tribunal against Home Office decisions, of which 87 percent[20] were eventually overturned by the Immigration and Asylum Tribunal (see Table 11.2, below, though there remains a large backlog of claims which have still not been heard). Since each appeal costs the taxpayer approximately £3,300[21], the cost of litigation caused by the Home Office change of policy was estimated at £5.5 million.

In mid-2015, an FOI request was made by Mr. X to secure information from the Home Office and the Foreign Office about meetings which officials had held with Eritrean, Somali, Ethiopian and Egyptian officials in late 2014 to discuss migration. The Home Office failed to reply to this request. Mr. X appealed to the Information Commissioner who required the Home Office to respond. Arguing that disclosure would "prejudice to effective conduct of public affairs" and would "violate personal information," the Home Office confirmed that it held such information but refused to disclose it. In April 2016, and under the threat of litigation, the Home Office confirmed the names of three senior officials who met with senior Eritrean officials, but it refused to disclose additional information. Mr. X appealed to the Office of the Information Commissioner who upheld the Home Office's decision not to disclose information on the basis of a public interest test. In mid-2016, Mr. X unsuccessfully appealed against the decision by the Information Commissioner, the Foreign Office and the Home Office not to disclose "notes of those meetings."

In late 2016, Mr. X asked me to provide a *pro bono* "expert report" that reviewed information in the public domain about Eritrean international relations, the human rights situation in Eritrea and the history of UK–Eritrea relations. In October 2016, my report together with further legal argument, was submitted in an appeal to the General Regulatory Chamber Information Rights Tribunal. This appeal initiated a slow process of disclosure by the Home Office[24] in their attempt to avoid litigation.

Disclosure revealed that on November 27, 2014, a meeting was held in Asmara between the Eritrean Foreign Minister and the Immigration and Security Minister of the UK to discuss "migration related issues." A second meeting was held in early December 2014 in Asmara between the Eritrean Foreign Minister and a UK delegation that consisted of the British ambassador and officials from the Foreign and Home Office. The focus of the first meeting was to re-establish

**TABLE 11.2** Asylum appeal statistics on Eritrean claims, 2014–2016[22]

| Year | Number of appeals | Appeals allowed | Percentage of appeals allowed[23] |
|------|-------------------|-----------------|------------------------------------|
| 2014 | 172 | 50 | 29% |
| 2015 | 1737 | 459 | 26% |
| 2016 | 722 | 1,206 | 167% |

an agreement with Eritrea to facilitate the return of failed asylum seekers; the focus of the second meeting was to discuss how to control irregular migration "between Eritrea and the UK."[25]

The Home Office also disclosed short "notes" taken by British officials during these meetings which indicate either an incredible naivety about Eritrea or a willingness to suspend judgement in order to pursue pre-determined policy objectives aimed at stopping Eritrean migration to the UK. The key points made by Eritrean officials at these meetings, which were accepted by UK officials,[26] were:

1. That Eritrean officials were "taking the fingerprints of the entire population, although not all will get a new ID card for some time. We have details of every Eritrean ..."

2. "If someone has an Eritrean ID card <u>or</u> passport they are free to come back into Eritrea ..."

3. "People who have left illegally as children or [were] born abroad will have no problems on return – they need to prove their citizenship and get documents from the embassy."

4. "Everyone (all ages, including young children) requires an exit visa to leave the country ..."

5. "To get one [an exit visa] someone should apply to the ministry with a demobilization certification (available from the Ministry of Defence) and 100 Nakfa."

6. "There are no extra-judicial retributions on people who return having left illegally without doing national service. There is no clemency, but no harsh measures against them." Finally,

7. "From November 2014 national service is reverting to duration of 18 months ..."

On the basis of these meetings, a "Diptel"/diplomatic telegram was sent from the British High Commission in Asmara to the Foreign & Commonwealth Office, London on December 15, 2014 and was quickly followed by an email to the FCO on 16 December affirming information contained in the "notes." These communiques reiterated that Eritrean officials showed "clearer political will to tackle migration" but in return they requested development assistance that would help reduce migration[27] (discussion included agreeing a Memorandum of Understanding with the UK enabling the UK to return failed asylum seekers; Eritrean officials apparently stated that the UK was "offering 'preferential treatment' to Eritreans'). The note also made it clear that British officials needed clarification about how failed asylum seekers would be treated on return to Eritrea.

This information, and possibly other undisclosed material, was passed to the Home Office in late 2014 and, together with the 2014 Danish Immigration Report, was used to issue a new Country of Information Guidance (CIG) Report in September 2015 (Home Office 2015a, 2015b). This report concluded that Eritreans should not be granted asylum in the UK because they would not be persecuted for a Convention reason on return to Eritrea.

Back in the UK, there was some disquiet concerning the 2015 change of policy because it was known that the Danish authorities had withdrawn their Eritrea policy (which UK policy was supposedly based upon) and because the new policy did not reflect a balanced assessment of all the objective evidence available on Eritrea. In late 2015, during a period when many Eritrean claims were being appealed to the Immigration and Asylum Tribunal, I was commissioned by the UK's Chief Inspector of Borders and Immigration to review Home Office policy on Eritrea (Campbell, 2015). I concluded that the Home Office had selectively cited "objective" evidence which it approved of, including the flawed report by the Danish Immigration Authority, but failed to consult or cite other evidence which did not support their conclusion. I concluded that the Home Office report was a biased and partisan evaluation of Country of Origin Information which violated the UK's adherence to European reporting standards (EASO, 2012). I also concluded that the report represented a clear attempt to influence the Tribunal to refuse asylum to Eritreans.

Between December 2015 and May 2016 – i.e., from the publication of my review of Home Office policy and the first appeal scheduled to be heard by the Upper Tribunal (Immigration and Asylum Chamber) which was to examine current Home Office policy – the Home Office continued to refuse Eritreans asylum. In February 2016, the Home Office mounted a "fact-finding mission" to Eritrea which relied on the support of the Eritrean government to identify individuals to speak to and government translators to enable the "team" to gather information. Unsurprisingly, the fact-finding mission supported its 2015 policy (Home Office, 2016). In May 2016, the Upper Tribunal convened to hear the case called "*MST & Others.*"[28] It took evidence about Home Office asylum policy on Eritrea as well as other objective evidence (including my review of Home Office policy) and evidence submitted by UNHCR. When the Upper Tribunal published its decision on this case in October 2016, the Home Office was forced to withdraw its 2015 policy and issue new guidance (Home Office, 2017c; in effect, it reverted to its 2014 position). Even so, many Eritreans whose claims were wrongly refused are still filing fresh asylum claims to secure protection.

What can we conclude about this particular case? First, following its 2015 report, the Home Office violated the UK's commitment to the Refugee Convention by unfairly refusing Eritrean asylum applications. Second, attempts to use the FOIA to obtain information about what government officials do in secret meetings and how they use secret information are nearly impossible. Officials argue that disclosure of information would "prejudice the conduct of public affairs," etc. and they refuse to disclose relevant information. Official obstruction makes it very difficult to successfully appeal to the courts to secure the right to information guaranteed under the FOI Act 2000 especially when the Information Commissioner, whose office is responsible for overseeing the

Act, blithely supports officials (this situation needs to be reviewed).[29] Disappointingly the disclosure of secret meetings between UK and Eritrean officials attracted limited media attention and had no impact on official decision-making[30] or on Home Office policy. Not even prolonged and costly litigation in the Tribunal affected asylum policy until the 2016 Country Guidance decision on "MST & Others" was published. Then, and only then, did the Home Office withdraw its iniquitous policy and replace it with appropriate guidance.

## Conclusion

It seems that the *FOI Act* is relatively little used by researchers looking at asylum or the work of the UK's Home Office. For instance, Burridge and Gill (2016) in their work on asylum-related legal aid and Connolly (2015) and Humphris and Sigona (2016) in their work on migrant/unaccompanied children in the UK have only used FOI requests to obtain basic information from the Home Office and local government. In each case, researchers ran up against a wall of indifference characterised by delays in responding to requests, not infrequent refusal to comply (citing the cost of disclosure) and, as Burridge and Gill (2016, p. 30) noted, "bureaucratic inconsistency and chaotic self-contradiction" in terms of the information that was released (cf. Campbell, 2017, pp. 10–12). Seen in this light, it is not surprising that, pace Worthy and Hazell (2017) the FOIA has had a limited impact on government transparency, accountability or decision-making. Certainly, the case studies examined in this chapter illustrate how difficult it can be to exercise a right to information using the FOIA.

With regard to UK asylum policy which requires asylum seekers to undergo "language analysis," it should be clear that there is no evidence to support the claims made by the Home Office that LA can determine the country of origin of asylum seekers. There is no scientific evidence to support the use of LA for this purpose, and the Home Office's own internal reports provide no empirical evidence to support its continued use to deter/prevent fraudulent claims or to assist officials to make timely (much less correct) decisions on asylum applications. Furthermore, an analysis of the financial costs and benefits (however calculated) of using LA provides no evidence that might support the continuing use of the policy. Perhaps, the key value of its policy on LA has been to convince the Tribunal to accept LA evidence. In any case, it should be evident that the Home Office has used the language of "science" to obfuscate flawed assumptions about language use and obscure its own capricious bureaucratic practices to refuse individuals' asylum.

The second case concerning the Home Office's refusal to comply with FOI requests, and the apparent unwillingness/inability of the Information Commission/Tribunal to force compliance, raises equally troubling issues. This case reveals how easy it is for officials to cite "prejudice to the conduct of public affairs" to refuse FOI requests but it also reveals how British officials made use of information from secret meetings to alter government policy and how they are able to conceal their actions. The information discussed in secret meetings with Eritrean officials was twisted and combined with information from a discredited Danish report in an attempt to convince the Asylum and Immigration Tribunal that political conditions in Eritrea had changed and that Eritreans applying for asylum should be refused protection and "returned" to their country of origin.

If we step back and compare the two UK cases with similar research elsewhere, we find strong similarities in the manner in which officials deal with FOI requests. There is clear evidence in Canada, Mexico, Brazil, India and elsewhere that governments attempt to undermine the perceived threat to their interests by altering key legislation and centralising control to prevent or "minimise the disruptive potential" of FOI law (Michener, 2011; Roberts, 2005; Roberts & Roberts, 2010). The measures adopted range from outright refusal to comply with FOI requests, deliberate attempts to delay a reply to requests, withholding some or all of the information requested, citing exemptions to justify why data should not be supplied and delaying compliance[31] until disclosure will have minimal impact of government decisions and policy. As Luscombe and Walby (2017) have noted, the political control of information can also be achieved by a lack of depth in the information that is eventually disclosed, by poor document archiving and retrieval practices – which is sometimes a deliberate tactic of FOI officers – and by redacting data that is disclosed. These practices ensure that disclosure, and any research which relies upon FOI disclosure, will be incomplete, partial and that publication will be delayed thereby ensuring that independent research becomes "yesterday's news" and that it attracts limited media or public attention.

It is worth, however, making four final points. First, it is time to rethink how researchers use the FOI Act. As is apparent, FOI requests are primarily an add-on to other methods in an attempt to get information from a government department (e.g., Dembour, 2017). This is hardly an innovative use of FOI at a time when mixed-methods research has long been a standard of good quality social research. Second, new forms of collaborative[32] academic research are clearly required to deal with the restrictions of information imposed by government departments at a time when researchers are facing growing resource constraints. Third, researchers need to share the FOI data they obtain with others to foster more comprehensive research on government practices and policies. Finally, and regardless of the ways that governments stymie and prevent access to information and despite the gaps and problems with the data that is disclosed, good quality research does allow us to "see through" government policy statements. Social science research which incorporates the use of FOI is able to document how officials operate, how little respect they can have for the public, and that policy implementation is frequently very different to what officials claim. As the cases in this chapter demonstrate, Home Office policy can have a very deleterious impact on specific social groups and it shows that the Home Office deliberately contravened the UK's international legal obligations under the Refugee Convention, the EU Qualification Directive and national legislation which requires the Home Office to fairly assess asylum applications.

## Notes

1 Between 2007 and 2010, five attempts to appeal against the refusal of FOI officers to disclose information (including three appeals to the Information Commissioner) were unsuccessful.
2 See: www.legislation.gov.uk/ukpga/1976/74/pdfs/ukpga_19760074_en.pdf.
3 See: www.legislation.gov.uk/ukpga/2000/34/notes/division/4/4.
4 See: https://publications.parliament.uk/pa/cm200708/cmhansrd/cm080205/wmstext/80205m0002.htm.
5 Disclosure was in response to the following FOI request on August 20, 2009 (Home Office Ref. 11,560) and on July 28, 2010 (Home Office Ref. 15,403).
6 Amharic was the official language in Eritrea between the late 1950s and 1991 because Eritrea was an Ethiopian province (Woldemikael, 2003). Between 1998 and 2000, Ethiopia deported approximately 100,000 ethnic Eritreans to Eritrea whose first language was Amharic (Campbell, 2014).
7 In part because there was other evidence negating the importance of LA.
8 See: www.refworld.org/cases,GBR_UTIAC,4ca36a1b2.html.
9 OCILA does not undertake LA for individuals who claim to live on or near a national border because the distribution of a language is not coterminous with national boundaries nor does it test individuals who claim to have left their area of origin at an early age (Cambier-Langeveld, 2016: 30). After a protracted 30-year insurgency, Eritrea gained its independence from Ethiopia in 1991.
10 See: www.supremecourt.uk/cases/uksc-2013-0202.html.
11 At paragraph 51 the Supreme Court identified a number of limitations of LA reports which needed to be explicitly addressed in appeals including: information about the expertise and methods used; the geographical distribution of dialects (based on verifiable sources); the need to make a language recording available for independent experts to examine; information on the limitations of the analysts undertaking LA; whether the identity and qualifications of analysts need to be identified; and an assessment of the extent to which LA does/does not comply with published guidelines (i.e., LANOG (Language and National Origin Group), 2004).
12 Home Office reply to my FOI Request no. 46,586 dated January 4, 2019.
13 This requirement stems from the incorporation of the UN Convention of the Rights of the Child into sec. 55 of the Immigration Act 2009. However, in England and Wales, and probably in Scotland and Northern Ireland, the Home Office does not comply with the policy (Campbell, n.d.).
14 The consent form was disclosed to me in 2010. The form states: "The purpose of the language analysis interview was explained to me. I understand that the analysis will be used to determine whether I am from the place I claim. I understand that a copy of the tape may be sent to me/my representatives and the Immigration Appellant Authority. I do not agree/agree to have a language analysis interview and to have my statements recorded and the tape passed to an expert for analysis." Given linguistic and cultural differences between officials and asylum applicants, this procedure does not adequately explain the test to asylum seekers nor can it secure "informed consent" (see, for example, www.esrc.ac.uk/funding/guidance-for-appli cants/research-ethics/frequently-raised-questions/what-is-freely-given-informed- consent/ (accessed on March 16, 2017).
15 On September 4, 2017, I made an FOI request to the Home Office requesting information about whether a responsible adult had attended interviews with children, whether officials had always obtained informed consent from the individuals tested, the extent to

which applicants with a medical/disability were interviewed (or not). That request was refused on the basis of the cost of retrieving the relevant information. In January 2018, I sent four separate FOI requests (one for each issue) in the hope that this might assist FOI officers by narrowing the work required. Instead, the four requests were treated as a single request and were refused on the grounds of costs.

16  See: Home Office (2017b).

17  The API sets out only two criteria which officials should use to identify individuals for LA, namely if there are doubts about an individual's claimed country of origin and if a claim is "inadequately documented." However, nearly all asylum claims are undocumented and Home Office officials do not possess the language/linguistic skills which might enable them to identify applicants involved in "nationality swapping."

18  See: www.gov.uk/government/organisations/forensic-science-regulator. In email correspondence with the regulator, I have confirmed that LA evidence relied upon by the Home Office is not regulated and that procedures used by the commercial firms it subcontracts for the tests are not standardised, etc.

19  The redacted 2012 cost/benefit analysis (Home Office 2011) states that the Home Office spent £400 per test, although the National Audit Office estimated the cost at £700 per test.

20  See: "Home Office Eritrea guidance softened to reduce asylum seeker numbers" (*The Guardian*, 22/1/2017).

21  See: Kate Lyons "Hundreds of Eritrean asylum applications still 'incorrectly' refused" (*The Guardian*, July 28, 2016). Note that the information she relied upon came from an FOI request.

22  Source: UK (2016).

23  The large percentage of successful appeals in 2016 reflects, in part, the backlog of appeals that had been built up in 2015.

24  The Foreign Office and the Home Office provided signed statements by two senior British officials in October 2016, which attempted to argue that disclosure would undermine the UK's relation with Eritrea. The central reasons given by both officials was the need to maintain trust with Eritrean officials in order to encourage them to participate in a bilateral agreement with the UK to facilitate the return of nationals "with no right to remain in the UK" and to encourage officials to participate in the Khartoum Process to manage regional migration. Mr. X continues to seek further disclosure of related matters.

25  The Home Office disclosed a witness statement by Anne Brewer, Country Returns Operator and Strategy Team, Home Office, dated 26/2/2015. The second visit involved additional meetings with Eritrean immigration officials, legal professionals and members of the diplomatic community.

26  Note 1 is titled "Meeting with three officials ... 10 December 2014" and note 2 is titled "Meeting with Yemane Gebreab, President's Advisor and UK delegation ... December 9, 2014." Both take the form of quotes and/or bullet points.

27  In fact, Eritrea was in negotiation with the European Union to secure development assistance. A €200m development grant to Eritrea was announced in December 2015. See: www.tesfanews.net/eu-approves-new-development-package-to-eritrea/. Indeed, the Eritrean government continues to insist that international co-operation to control illegal migration must be premised on receiving development assistance ("Should Europe Pay to stop refugees from fleeing oppressive Eritrea?" *The Guardian*, 28/4/2016).

28  This case was "*MST and Others (national service – risk categories) Eritrea CG [2016] UKUT 00443 (IAC),*" see: www.refworld.org/cases,GBR_UTIAC,57fc91fc4.html.

29  As a recent review into how government departments deal with FOI requests reveals (Randall, 2015, 3), the Home Office withholds information in 45% of requests.

30  See: "Home Office Eritrean guidance softened to reduce asylum seeker numbers" (*The Guardian*, January 22, 2017).

31 The use of information technology enables governments to tag, track and control disclosure in ways which prevent or reduce the impact of adverse publicity on officials; see Roberts (2005).
32 Including, perhaps, with journalists. Perhaps, the best examples of collaborative research comes from the persistent attempt by journalists to investigate how governments treat asylum seekers (C. Knaus "Details of Australia's asylum seeker boat turnbacks released in FOI battle" (*The Guardian*, April 3, 2017) and from the collaboration between the Evening Standard Newspaper and the Chair of the Treasury Select Committee of the House of Commons to obtain information about "Brexit-related" spending by the Home Office ("Revealed: How the embattled Home Office is spending our money on handling Brexit," *Evening Standard*, May 2, 2018).

## References

Burridge, A., & Gill, N. (2016). Conveyor-belt justice: Precarity, access to justice, and uneven geographies of legal aid in UK asylum appeals. *Antipode, 49*(1), 23–42.

Cambier-Langeveld, T. (2016). Language analysis in the asylum procedure: A specification of the task in practice. *The International Journal of Speech, Language and the Law, 23*(1), 25–41.

Campbell, J. R. (2013). Language analysis in the United Kingdom's refugee status determination system: Seeing through policy claims about 'expert knowledge. *Ethnic & Racial Studies, 36*(4), 670–690.

Campbell, J. R. (2014). *Nationalism, law and statelessness. grand illusions in the horn of Africa.* NY & Oxford: Routledge.

Campbell, J. R. (2015). Review of UK home office country information and guidance – eritrea: national (incl. military) 'service' (version 2.0e, September 2015) and eritrea: illegal exit' (version 2.0e, September 2015. Prepared for the Chief Inspector of Borders and Immigration and the Independent Advisory Group on Country Information (IAGCI).

Campbell, J. R. (2017). *Bureaucracy, law and dystopia in the united kingdom's asylum system.* NY: Routledge.

Campbell, J. R. *Why the 'best interests' of Unaccompanied Asylum-Seeking Children are Left at the Border: Structural Violence and British Asylum Policies.* Unpublished paper.

Canada. (2005, November). *Immigration and refugee board of Canada.* SOM100785.E. Retrieved from www.refworld.org/docid/45f1480520.html

Connolly, H. (2015). Cut off from justice. The impact of excluding separated migrant children from legal aid. *Children's Society.* England: University of Bedfordshire.

Danish Immigration Authority. (2014). Eritrea: Drivers and root causes of emigration, national service and the possibility of return. Retrieved from www.nyidanmark.dk/ NR/rdonlyres/B28905F5-5C3F-409B-8A22-0DF0DACBDAEF/0/EritreareportEnde ligversion.pdf

Dembour, M.-B. (2017). Surely Not! Procedurally lawful age assessments in the UK. In M. Sedmark, B. Sauer, B. Gornik, & S. Hernandez (Eds.), *Unaccompanied children in European migration and asylum practices: In whose best interests?* (pp. 149–180). London & NY: Routledge.

EASO (European Asylum Support Unit) (2012). Country of origin report methodology. Luxembourg. Retrieved from http://ec.europa.eu/dgs/home-affairs/ what-we-do/policies/asylum/european-asylum-support-office/coireportmethodology finallayout_en.pdf

Home Office. 2011. Language analysis testing of asylum applicants: Impacts and economic costs and benefits. UK Border Agency. London. At: https://www.gov.uk/government/uploads/system/uploads/attachment_data/file/257177/language-analysis.pdf.

Home Office. (2015a, March). Country information and guidance eritrea: Illegal exit. Retrieved from www.refworld.org/country,ERI,5507fe424,0.html

Home Office. (2015b, March). Country information and guidance eritrea: National (incl. military) service. Retrieved from www.refworld.org/publisher,UKHO,COUNTRY POS,ERI,552779c34,0.html

Home Office. (2016). Report of a home office fact finding mission eritrea: Illegal exit and national service. Conducted 7–20 February 2016. Retrieved from www.gov.uk/govern ment/uploads/system/uploads/attachment_data/file/565637/Report-of-UK-FFM-to-Eritrea-7-20-February-2016.pdf

Home Office. (2017a, February). Language analysis API. V. 20. Retrieved from www. gov.uk/government/uploads/system/uploads/attachment_data/file/591701/Lan guage-analysis-v20.pdf

Home Office. (2017b). Immigration statistics, asylum tables as 01 to as02. Retrieved from www.gov.uk/government/publications/immigration-statistics-october-to-december-2016/asylum

Home Office. (2017c, October). Country policy and information note: Eritrea- national service & illegal exit. Retrieved from www.gov.uk/government/uploads/system/uploads/attachment_data/file/565635/CPIN-Eritrea-NS-and-Illegal-Exit-v4-October-2016.pdf

Humphris, R., & Sigona, N. (2016). Becoming adult. Mapping unaccompanied asylum-seeking children in England. *Researching Young Migrant's uncertain futures*. Retrieved from https://becomingadultproject.files.wordpress.com/2016/07/research-brief-series-01_2016.pdf

LANOG (Language and National Origin Group). (2004). Guidelines for the use of language analysis in relation to questions of national origin in refugee cases. *Speech, Language and the Law, 11*(12), 261–266.

Luscombe, A., & Walby, K. (2017). Theorizing freedom of information: The live archive, obfuscation, and actor-network theory. *Government Information Quarterly, 34*, 379–387.

Michener, G. (2011). FOI laws around the world. *Journal of Democracy, 22*(2), 145–159.

Randall, J. (2015, September). FOIA fighters: How departments dealt with FOI requests in the first quarter of the new government. *Institute for Government*. Retrieved from www. instituteforgovernment.org.uk/blog/foia-fighters-how-departments-dealt-freedom-information-requests-first-quarter-new-government

Roberts, A. (2005). Spin control and freedom of information: Lessons for the United Kingdom and Canada. *Public Administration, 83*(1), 1–23.

Roberts, A., & Roberts, N. (2010). A great and revolutionary law? The first four years of India's Right to Information Act. *Public Administration Review, 70*(6), 925–933.

Savage, A., & Hyde, R. (2014). Using freedom of information requests to facilitate research. *International Journal of Social Research Methodology, 17*(3), 303–317.

UK. 2015. *Forensic language analysis* September). Postnote no. 509. Houses of Parliament. Parliamentary Office of Science and Technology: London.

UK. (2016, August). *Asylum statistics*. House of Commons Briefing Paper SN01403. London.

Walby, K., & Larsen, M. (2011). Getting at the live archive: On access to information research in Canada. *Canadian Journal of Law and Society, 26*(3), 623–633.

Walby, K., & Larsen, M. (2012). Access to information and Freedom of Information requests: Neglected means of data production in the social science. *Qualitative Inquiry, 18*(1), 31–42.

Wedel, J., Shore, C., Feldman, G., & Lathrop, S. (2005). Towards an anthropology of public policy. *American Academy of Political and Social Science, 600,* 30–51.

Wilson, J. (2011). Freedom of information and research data. *Research Ethics, 7*(3), 107–111.

Woldemikael, T. (2003). Language, education and public policy in eritrea. *African Studies Review, 46*(1), 117–136.

Worthy, B., & Hazell, R. (2017). Disruptive, dynamic and democratic? Ten years of FOI in the UK. *Parliamentary Affairs, 70,* 22–42.

# 12

# A DOUBLE-EDGED SWORD?

## Freedom of Information as a method in social research

*Hannah Bows*

## Introduction

Despite legislation introduced more than a decade ago providing citizens with the right to request data from public authorities in the UK, researchers have been slow on the uptake. Recently, a number of studies have identified the opportunities and challenges in using Freedom of Information (FOI) legislation and documented the utilisation of FOIs as a data collection tool across health, social and criminological research. However, few papers have discussed the process of analysing this data. This chapter draws on three criminological studies, which have all used FOI requests to collect data from police forces in the UK, to outline how data was collected, negotiated and analysed. The major challenges in analysing this data is the inconsistent responses from police forces and managing large volumes of data (see also Walby and Luscombe, this volume). To some extent, these challenges can be addressed through careful wording and designing of requests; it is important that the terminology adopted in requests reflect that which is used by the public body, and that requests are written in simple, clear language. Moreover, providing tables can help to convey to the public body the nature of the data being requested and improve the consistency in responses, simplifying the data analysis. However, there remain significant problems with delays in responses, partial/incomplete responses and refusals to provide data by engaging the exemptions contained in the legislation. This chapter closes with a brief discussion on how these challenges can be overcome and the implications for both researchers and public authorities.

## Background

Access to information is relatively new in the UK, compared with other European countries. As far back as 1766, Sweden introduced a *Freedom of the Press*

*Act*, providing access to public documents and the right to publish written documents. By 2006, over eighty countries across the globe had some provision for access to information (Banisar, 2006). The UK introduced rights to access data held by public data through two statutes: *The Freedom of Information Act* (2000) (England, Wales and Northern Ireland) and the *Freedom of Information Act* (2002) (Scotland). Under these acts, individuals and organisations (including those who are not citizens or residents in the UK) have the right to make requests to public bodies to access data held by them. As Shepherd and Ennion (2007, p. 33) point out, the FOI acts place "significant duties and responsibilities on public authorities to give access to the information they hold."

Public bodies incorporate a range of organisations and institutions, including government departments, local council, health trusts, schools, colleges, universities, police forces and other criminal justice agencies. This chapter will mainly focus on the FOI Act 2000 (England, Wales and Northern Ireland) unless stated otherwise.

There is a positive obligation on behalf of public bodies to release the data requested unless it comes under one or more of the exemptions contained within the Act. In England and Wales, there are twenty-three exemptions. These exemptions comprise seven "absolute exemptions" which relate to information that is either already available, is prohibited by another piece of legislation or information which relates to security matters (including information held by courts). For these exemptions, the public body can refuse all requests without providing any further information on the reasoning. The remaining sixteen "non-absolute" exemptions are subject to a public benefit test; the public body must consider whether the information requested would come under one of the exemptions and, if it does, whether it is in the public benefit to release the information anyway. The reasons for engaging the exemption and the outcome of the public benefit test must be provided to the applicant. Additionally, Section 12 of the legislation provides that a public body can refuse any request which exceeds the appropriate cost and time limit set by the legislation.

Requests must be made in writing (most commonly by email) and public bodies have twenty working days in which to respond, either providing the data as requested or with a refusal notice based on one of the exemptions contained in the Act. If the public body is unable to respond within the timeframe, they must contact the applicant to advise them of a delay and give an indication of when a response should be expected.

Both FOI Acts have proven to be a useful tool for individual citizens and journalists. According to the Ministry of Justice (2008), there were over 30,000 requests per year to central government bodies alone and the majority came from members of the general public (Brown, 2009, p. 89). FOI requests are widely used by journalists in the UK, particularly for news stories based on crime and criminal justice issues. A quick scan of published new stories in national papers in August 2018 reveals FOI requests were used to access data on violent assaults against older people (*Daily Express*,

August 28, 2018), the number of prisoners being released without stable housing (*Guardian*, August 13, 2015) and the rise in mobile phones in prisons (*Daily Mail*, August 15, 2018). It has been argued that social researchers use a relatively narrow range of data collection techniques (Lee, 2005) and the need to find innovative methods has been of increasing importance in social science and related disciplines. Despite the comparably widespread use of FOI in other jurisdictions, social scientists, and criminologists in particular, are only just beginning to use FOIs as a research method. However, a number of studies have emerged over the last few years which have utilised FOIs. For example, Savage (2016) gained access to whistle-blowing policies held by 39 police forces in the UK; Westmarland, Johnson, and McGlynn (2017) examined how restorative justice and community resolutions had been used by the police in domestic abuse cases; Payne-James, Rivers, Green, and Johnston (2014) explored the use of less-lethal forms of the Use of Force.

Despite the potential of FOIs to provide researchers with quick and free access to previously unpublished data, the challenges in accessing and analysing this data have been highlighted in a number of recent publications which broadly fit within three stages of an FOI request: designing the request, accessing the data and analysing the data. The remainder of this chapter will examine these three stages, drawing on three studies which have utilised FOIs to collect data from police forces in the UK.

## The studies

Research examining policing and security is increasing, yet challenges remain in accessing data on policing policy and practice because such agencies are "particularly secret, secured, or otherwise difficult to access by scholars interested in how they operate" (Lippert, Walby, & Wilkinson, 2015, p. 2). The police hold important data on crimes, victims and offenders which researchers can use to examine patterns, trends and profiles of crimes and are therefore an important source of data for researchers. One of the primary benefits of FOI requests is that they facilitate access to data or information that would otherwise be unattainable (Kingston et al. 2017) and it is therefore unsurprising that the majority of published criminological research using FOIs has made requests to police forces. This chapter provides methodological reflections on the use of FOIs to gain access to police-recorded data in three studies. All three studies have collected quantitative data.

- The first study utilised FOI requests to examine the extent, nature and characteristics of rape and sexual assault by penetration (Sections 1 and 2, *Sexual Offences Act* 2003) of victims aged 60 and over, recorded between January 1, 2009 and December 31, 2013 (Bows & Westmarland, 2017). FOIs were sent to all 49 forces.

- The second study examined the extent, nature and characteristics of stalking. There were two phases in this study. The first utilised FOIs to collect data on recorded offences involving male victims; the second collected data on stranger stalking incidents. Both requests sought data on recorded incidents between January 1, 2014 and December 31, 2015. FOIs were sent to all 49 forces (including those at ports, e.g., Port of Dover police).
- The final study utilised FOI requests to collect data on the characteristics of homicides involving victims aged 60 and over recorded between January 1, 2010 and December 31, 2015. Again, the request was sent to all 49 forces in the UK.

Police forces are a primary source of crime data for the media, researchers and citizens more broadly. Traditionally, police records were "police-created, police-held and police-owned other than through a central government or legal requirement, neither of which openly led to public dissemination" (Johnson & Hampson, 2015, p. 250). However, moves towards intelligent-led policing and the development of police record keeping systems and processes have rapidly changed the crime record from an "administrative feature to a core item of source material for the management and direction of policing activity" (p. 250). Moreover, Johnson and Hampson (2015) argue that the introduction of Freedom of Information legislation in the UK changed the face of crime records again, requiring forces to share data with citizens. However, the same authors note that, whilst the potential of FOIs as a tool to access police data is high, in practice, access is not necessarily straightforward. Among the various issues highlighted in previous work (Bows, 2017; Lippert et al., 2015; Walby & Luscombe, 2017), the major challenges encountered across the three studies I have conducted related to interpretation of the request by the police force; inconsistency in responses (either incomplete/partial responses; inaccurate responses or misunderstandings about the data being requested); the myriad of response styles (forces using spreadsheets, word files, PDFs and some using tables, others providing text answers and so on) and delays in responses by forces. A range of techniques have been utilised to address these challenges and avoid refusals from responding police forces.

## Designing the request

Although the FOI legislation does not stipulate that requests must be presented in a particular way (other than in writing), the formatting and style of the request is important. As Ludwig and Marshall (2015, p. 236) point out, "FOI staff may be disconnected from the operations about which a request is made and are, therefore, reliant on systems of varying quality to interrogate, locate, retrieve and collate the requested information." It is therefore important that a request is carefully drafted. In particular, there are two things to consider when drafting a request.

## Terminology

The first is terminology. When making data requests to any public body, it is important that the FOI officer who handles the request understands what is being requested. One of the most common reasons for delays in providing the data, or refusals to provide the data, is that the FOI officer does not understand what is being requested. Using terminology which matches the terminology of the public body that is receiving the request is important. Often, this involves having sufficient information about the organisation who holds the data and how that data is held (Savage & Hyde, 2014). Moreover, as Johnson and Hampson (2015) point out, the requirement that a request must describe the information that is desired requires the applicant to have some understanding of how information is stored, as well as requiring them to know how to ask for it. For example, the police use terminology which mirrors that used in legislation and associated guidance. Asking the UK police, for example, for data relating to cases of elder abuse, is likely to result in a delay or refusal, since "elder abuse" is a health and social care concept which is not formally recognised in the UK criminal justice system. There is no "offence" of elder abuse and the operating definitions vary across academia, policy and practice. Similarly, there is no agreed definition of "elderly." Furthermore, police forces often hold different information on offenders, victims and incidents on different databases or systems depending on the *stage* of the criminal justice process. For example, different information may be collected and stored by police at arrest stage compared with charge stages (Johnson & Hampson, 2015). Therefore, it is important to draft requests that use the same language as the organisation but also, where possible, to gain an understanding of the different processes and databases used by the public body.

For example, in the homicide study I conducted, examining the extent, nature and characteristics of homicides involving older people, I asked for the following:

> The total number of murder and manslaughter offences, recorded between 2010 and 2015, involving a victim aged 60 and over at the time of the offence.

In other requests, for example in the sexual violence study, more specific language was used. In this study, I asked the police forces for data relating to two specific offences: rape (as per Section 1 of the *Sexual Offences Act* 2003) and sexual assault by penetration (as per Section 2 of the *Sexual Offences Act* 2003). These requests were initially "piloted" with five forces (of differing sizes and locations) to test whether the terminology and nature of the requests were possible. The responses received from the five forces indicated that the type of data requested was held by them and the terminology and language in the request matched their terminology and, importantly, their crime recording methods.

## Format

Under the FOI acts, authorities are required to provide the data in the requested format, wherever possible. However, in relation to police data, using a single template can create difficulties. Police data are collected and stored within each specific force contexts for specific purposes and reflect the particular assumptions, needs and priorities of that particular force. In fact, Magee (2008) estimates the 43 police forces of England and Wales alone have more than 350 different systems. However, to try and ensure consistency in responses and data provided and to make it easier to analyse, pro forma tables were developed for the data requests in the three studies. Initially, a pilot was conducted with three forces, including one force with whom the researcher had an existing relationship. The aim of the pilot was to gain feedback on the data collection materials designed for the FOI requests to measure the suitability and to gain feedback on the ease of completing the request to gauge the time it took and whether this would fall outside of the remit of the act.

The three forces who were sent the pilot materials were not done so under an FOI request. Each study has followed a similar format and the requests have been similar in nature, requesting:

- Part 1: Overall number of recorded incidents over a period of time, broken down by year (for example, the number of homicides recorded between 2010 and 2015)

  - The number of incidents during the same period involving the subject group (for example, the number of homicides involving an adult aged 60 and over).

- Part 2: For all incidents involving the subject group (e.g., older victims), a breakdown (in each case) of the gender, age and ethnicity of victim and perpetrator, the relationship between victim and perpetrator and, in some requests, the nature of the incident and location (for example, where did the homicide occur and what was the method of killing).

A table was provided for the second part of the request, which asked forces to provide a unique case number for each case involving an older victim and then the relevant information for each variable as requested (see Table 12.1).

Designing the request in this way helps to show what information is being requested but also provides a template, which can help analyse the data. This is discussed later in the chapter.

TABLE 12.1 Example of part 2 of FOI request for homicides

| Unique no. | Victim gender | Victim age | Victim ethnicity (self-defined) | Offender gender | Offender age | Offender ethnicity (self-defined) | Relationship between victim and offender | Location | Method |
|---|---|---|---|---|---|---|---|---|---|
| E.g. 1 | Female | 60–69 | | Female | 16 and under | | Partner | Victim home | Sharp instrument |
| | Male | 70–79 | | Male | 17–19 | | Friend | Care home | Firearm |
| | Other | 80–89 | | Other | 20–29 | | Stranger | Public home | Assault (with weapon) |
| | | 90–99 | | | 30–39 | | Acquaintance | Public outdoor | Assault (without weapon) |
| | | 100+ | | | 40–49 | | Stranger | Public indoor | Choking/strangulation |
| | | | | | 50–59 | | Family member | Hospital | Asphyxiation |
| | | | | | 60–69 | | Neighbour | Other | Other |
| | | | | | 70–79 | | Other | | |
| | | | | | 80–89 | | | | |
| | | | | | 90–99 | | | | |
| | | | | | 100+ | | | | |

## Accessing data

As described earlier in this chapter, the FOI legislation in the UK provides a number of exemptions which, if engaged, require the public body to either refuse the request (either fully or partially) or to consider whether a refusal should be made following application of the public benefit test. In some cases, the police force(s) have relied on exemptions that are not applicable (non-compliance with the Act); however, the key issue has been the variation in how the police apply the exemptions (Savage & Hyde, 2014).

Whilst some of the exemptions are clear and leave little room for subjectivity, a number of them are vague and open to interpretation and discretion by the force. In the three studies I have conducted using FOIs, the most commonly engaged exemptions have been as follows: exemption where cost of compliance exceeds appropriate limit (Section 12) and the request relates to personal information (Section 40).

The FOI Act sets a maximum limit for the amount of time (and therefore cost) that a request should take the public authority to complete. This is set at £450 for most public bodies (a slightly higher amount of £650 applies to central government, Parliament and armed forces requests). This is calculated based on an hourly rate of £25 per hour of staff time, meaning the maximum time a request should take the public body is 18 hours, or 24 hours.

FOIs can be costly to the public bodies handling the request; for example, in a recent paper by Hammond et al. (2016) who utilised FOIs to gain access to data held by National Health Service (NHS) trusts. They estimate (drawing on previous commentator's calculations) that the cost of complying with this request cost over £75,150 (using the maximum £450/18 hours as a baseline). It is unsurprising, therefore, that in the three studies conducted using FOI requests, several forces in each request refused to provide some or all of the data on the basis that the request exceeded the maximum cost/time threshold. However, the most common reason Section 12 (cost/time) was engaged was due to misunderstandings about what was being requested and incorrect calculations by the FOI officer. In the former, these issues can usually be dealt with via discussions with the FOI officer. In the latter situation, the exemption usually relates to the force incorrectly calculating how much time it will take to retrieve data. In England and Wales, public bodies are required to explain how they reached their calculation and make suggestions about how a request might be refined in order to be feasible within the cost/time threshold. However, across the three studies, several forces did not explain how they had reached the total. In the sexual violence study, one force responsible for a relatively small force area with a small-medium population indicated they had over 100 cases matching the criteria (e.g., victim aged 60 and over recorded between 2009–2013), and had it been calculated on that basis, it would exceed the threshold to examine each case to retrieve the information requested. The majority of other, significantly larger, forces had responded to the request and indicated between 20 and 30 cases each. After several emails questioning the number of cases, it transpired the force actually had less than 15 which met the criteria. The reason for the initial calculation of 100 cases was not provided. This highlights the importance of being clear when requesting data to ensure the public body knows exactly what is being requested, but also the lack of transparency in the handling of some requests.

The second most common exemption engaged by forces in the three studies using FOIs has been that the request relates to personal information which may identify an individual. Given the nature of police data, which relates to crime incidents which, in most cases, involve a victim and a perpetrator, it is unsurprising that the exemption has been engaged by several forces. This exemption is primarily concerned with data protection and ensuring that private, personal information about individuals is not released to the public. The way requests are designed is important in avoiding this exemption being applied. For example, in all three studies, the same template was used (see Table 12.1 earlier in this chapter) which used age categories and broad location categories to minimise the risk of victim or perpetrators being identifiable. However, this exemption was still relied on by several forces. In some cases, negotiations with the forces led to the data being provided; however, in a number of cases, appeals were made to the Information Commissioner (ICO) to deal with complaints about the conduct or response of a public body in relation to an FOI request. All of the appeals were successful.

These inconsistencies in the application of exemptions echo the experiences of previous researchers. Johnson and Hampson (2015) also found that poor interpretation of requests and/or of the legislation and exemptions was a barrier to accessing data held by police forces.

In some cases, they felt police forces were overly defensive in responding to their FOI request. Furthermore, previous research has reported that public body employees are often confused and/or inconsistent in their interpretation and understanding of exemptions (Taylor & Burt, 2010). Clearly, this can have serious consequences for applicants, who may be incorrectly denied access to data. Given the motivation beyond the FOI acts was to increase transparency in public bodies and promote trust by opening up organisational data to the public, inaccurate and inconsistent application of the legislation presents a major barrier to achieving this aim.

## Time delays

Although the Act requires the public body to respond within twenty working days (either with the data or to indicate there will be a delay and give reasons and an estimated date for full response), delays in receiving responses were common across all three studies with some forces taking up to a year to respond to requests. This is partly due to the volume of requests and lack of resources. When the FOI legislation came into force in 2005, public bodies were not given additional funding or resources to manage and respond to requests. Moreover, in the last ten years, austerity measures in the UK have resulted in many public bodies receiving cuts in funding resulting in smaller workforces. At the same time, the number of FOI requests that have been made is increasing; a recent report by the Cabinet Office (2018) revealed a 3% increase in the number of requests received by central government in 2017 compared with the previous year. In real terms, this equated to an increase of 1,266 requests (total 46,681). This can have implications on research timelines and may be particularly important if FOIs are used as a method in research projects that are funded by external research councils or funding bodies.

## Analysing data

As mentioned earlier in this chapter, applicants must request data in writing and public bodies must also respond, with the information, in writing. However, the format that public bodies present the data in is not requested by the Act. Moreover, even where applicants request the data in a particular format, the public body is not obliged to comply with this.

In all three studies I have conducted using FOIs, the template has been used by approximately half of the forces. The other half have provided the data in varying formats; often grouping together the data into aggregated totals. For example, forces have often given overall numbers of victims and offenders falling within particular age groups (so out of 100 homicides, 25 victims were aged 60–69, 25 were aged 70–79 and so on whilst 40 of the offenders were aged 30–39, 25 were aged 40–49 and so on). This creates difficulties in running statistical analysis on the findings, as the relationships between specific variables cannot be tested when data is given in aggregated formats. For example, it is not possible to specifically analyse cases involving victims aged 60–69 because the data provided has not been given on an individual case basis, meaning it is not clear how many of the 40 offenders aged 30–39 committed homicides against victims aged 60–69. This resulted in incomplete analysis in some of the studies, as the forces could not be included in a number of the statistical tests run on the data. Similar issues have been highlighted elsewhere. For example, Johnson and Hampson (2015) concluded that there is uncertainty in relation to the process of producing, recording and disclosing data held by police forces which create analytical barriers. Whilst some forces in their study provided the data in the format requested, others chose to aggregate offences into broad categories and some did not provide the type of data requested.

In some other cases, forces did provide the full data but in varying formats which required additional analysis. For example, rather than just providing the requested data on older victims in the homicide study, some forces provided the data relating to all homicides recorded in the study time period (2010–2015) which required additional analysis to identify the cases which involved an older victim. Some forces provided the exact ages of victims and offenders rather than the categories.

Even where FOI requests were fully complied with, missing data created numerous challenges in analysing the data across the three studies. As others have pointed out, one of the major challenges in analysing police data is the incomplete and unrepresentative data held by forces (Ludwig & Marshall, 2015). In the three studies conducted using FOI requests, data was frequently missing for victim and offender ethnicity, offence location and relationships between victims and offenders. In most cases, this is a result of different recording systems and practices; not all forces capture the same victim and offender demographics or collect them in the same way/using the same systems, leading to data being unavailable in many cases. However, in several cases, the forces did not initially provide data (claiming it was unavailable or not collected) but, when challenged further about this, were able to produce some or all of this data. Echoing the concerns of Johnson and Hampson (2015), this inconsistency casts doubt over the validity of data provided via FOI requests and the extent to which the information disclosed can be considered accurate.

## Discussion and conclusions

This chapter has highlighted some of the challenges in using FOIs for social research and some of the key considerations that researchers should take into account when designing and analysing their requests. FOIs provide a useful tool for researchers to gain access to otherwise hidden information. However, as others have previously noted (e.g., Ludwig & Marshall, 2015; Savage & Hyde, 2014), they come with a myriad of challenges which can make access to data difficult. Despite the FOI legislation placing an obligation on public bodies to comply with requests and provide the data, the exemptions have created a number of barriers to gaining access to data in the studies discussed in this chapter. Furthermore, there have been inconsistencies with the way public bodies have engaged exemptions and responded to requests more generally. This includes time delays, partial or incomplete data, inconsistency in the application of exemptions and data being provided in a range of formats. As well as creating practical difficulties in terms of accessing data, these can also present challenges in analysing the information provided by the public bodies. However, many issues can be prevented by careful design of the request and discussions with FOI officers and in some cases through appealing to information commissioners. In particular, it is important that requests are carefully designed; the use of terminology should reflect that adopted by the public body, requests should be written clearly and simply, and it may help to use tables to show the public body the data you are requesting. A further benefit of using tables is that some public bodies will use these to provide the data, which can help with consistency in responses and help with data analysis. Echoing the points made by Savage and Hyde (2014), researchers should carefully consider whether the data they are requesting falls within the scope of the FOI legislation; requests that are too wide or vague are likely to be refused on cost/time grounds and data that may compromise ongoing investigations or that would identify individuals will be refused in line with the exemptions contained in the statutes. FOI requests provide an important tool for researchers to access data that is otherwise unavailable, and researchers should take advantage of this method in future research.

## References

Banisar, D. (2006). *Freedom of information around the world 2006: A global survey of access to government records law*. Retrieved from www.freedominfo.org

Bows, H. (2017). Researching sexual violence against older people: Reflecting on the use of freedom of information requests in a feminist study. *Feminist Review, 115*(1), 30–45.

Bows, H., & Westmarland, N. (2017). Rape of older people in the United Kingdom: Challenging the "real-rape" stereotype. *British Journal of Criminology, 57*(1), 1–17.

Brown, K. J. (2009). COUNTERBLAST: Freedom of information as a research tool: Realising its potential. *Howard Journal of Criminal Justice, 48*(1), 88–91.

Hammond, S. P., Cross, J. L., Poland, F. M., Patel, M., Penhale, B., Smith, T. O., & Fox, C. (2016). Freedom of Information Act: Scalpel or just a sharp knife? *Journal of Medical Ethics, 43*(1), 60–62.

Johnson, D., & Hampson, E. (2015). Utilising the UK Freedom of Information Act 2000 for crime record data: Indications of the strength of records management in day to day police business. *Records Management Journal, 25*(3), 248–268.

Lee, R. M. (2005). The UK Freedom of Information Act and social research. *International Journal of Social Research Methodology, 8*(1), 1–18.

Lippert, R. K., Walby, K., & Wilkinson, B. (2015). Spins, stalls, and shutdowns: Pitfalls of qualitative policing and security research. *Forum Qualitative Sozialforschung/Forum: Qualitative Social Research, 17*(1).

Ludwig, A., & Marshall, M. (2015). Using crime data in academic research: Issues of comparability and integrity. *Records Management Journal, 25*(3), 228–247.

Magee, I. (2008). *Review of Criminality Information (ROCI)*. London: Home Office.

Payne-James, J. J., Rivers, E., Green, P., & Johnston, A. (2014). Trends in less-lethal use of force techniques by police services within England and Wales: 2007–2011. *Forensic Science, Medicine, and Pathology, 10*(1), 50–55.

Savage, A., & Hyde, R. (2014). Using freedom of information requests to facilitate research. *International Journal of Social Research Methodology, 17*(3), 303–317.

Shepherd, E., & Ennion, E. (2007). How has the implementation of the UK freedom of information act 2000 affected archives and records management services? *Records Management Journal, 17*(1), 32–81.

Walby, K., & Luscombe, A. (2017). Criteria for quality in qualitative research and use of freedom of information requests in the social sciences. *Qualitative Research, 17*(5), 537–553.

Westmarland, N., Johnson, K., & McGlynn, C. (2017). Under the radar: The widespread use of "out of court resolutions" in policing domestic violence and abuse in the United Kingdom. *British Journal of Criminology, 58*(1), 1–16.

# 13

# THE FALLING CURRENCY OF DEMOCRACY

Information as an instrument of control and certainty in the postwar and post-truth eras[1]

*Sean Holman*

## Introduction

"He was a one-man band. Now he's a conglomerate" (Greider, 1971). That is how one reporter described consumer advocate Ralph Nader following the publication of his best-seller *Unsafe at Any Speed*. The book's publication changed American auto safety laws. But it also changed Nader. He went from being described as a "high-minded crackpot" (Anderson, 1967) to the head of a network of organisations that were "probing and assaulting a Naderesque panorama of corporate sin and government sloth" (Greider, 1971). As a result, Nader had become a "brand name, the label of credibility which sells a report or a news item to the media and to the general public" (Greider, 1971). On November 2, 1971, he used this brand name and a speech at the National Press Club in Washington, DC to make another pitch. Nader announced he would be undertaking "the most comprehensive and detailed study of the Congress since its establishment" (Nader, 1971b). Much of that work would be done by a staff of about 80 graduate students and young professionals (Morris, 1971; Washington Bureau of The Sun, 1971). Nader said hundreds of citizens would be enlisted to help them (Morris, 1971). "If information is the currency of democracy, it is time to apply that principle to the sinews of citizenship involvement with their representatives in Congress" (Nader, 1971b), he declared.

Just before the first part of the Congress Project was released, Nader's staff told *The Washington Post* he believed it was the most important thing he had ever done (Russell, 1972b). At least some of those who reviewed the resulting paperback, *Who Runs Congress?*, did not share that belief (Kilpatrick, 1972; Martin, 2002, p. 161; Russell, 1972a). Indeed, the study would come to be seen as Nader's first mistake (Martin, 2002, p. 162). Yet his description of information as the currency of democracy – Nader's first widely reported use of

**TABLE 13.1** Freedom of information laws by year and country, pre-1983

| Date approved | Country |
| --- | --- |
| 1766 | Sweden |
| 1951 | Finland |
| 1966 | United States |
| 1970 | Denmark |
| 1970 | Norway |
| 1974/1976 | United States Freedom of Information Act amendments |
| 1978 | France |
| 1978 | The Netherlands |
| 1982 | Australia |
| 1982 | New Zealand |
| 1982 | Canada |

*Note.* Dates from "Overview of all FOI laws," by Roger Vleugels (2011) and "FOIA legislative history," by National Security Archive (n.d.).

a phrase he would use over and over again[2] – would endure, becoming a rhetorical cudgel for transparency advocates worldwide. It has been used by everyone from African reporters trying to obtain basic data from their governments (Machipisa, 1996) to Australian scientists opposed to censoring information about how climate change is affecting the Great Barrier Reef (Innis, 2016). However, if we accept Nader's metaphorical description of information as the currency of democracy, it begs the question: what instrumental value does it have to individuals within a political and economic context? In other words, to extend Nader's metaphor, what can information buy in a capitalist democracy?

In this chapter, I will use relevant historical examples from Canada and the United States to show how the answer to this question can help explain why there was a "rise of the right to know" in both countries during the postwar period, resulting in the introduction of freedom of information laws (see Table 13.1) and other important transparency measures. I will also identify opportunities for further research, exploring how changes to the value of information might explain the recent attraction of authoritarianism. I will then conclude the chapter by commenting on what that means for anyone who is using freedom of information laws to obtain records from public bodies.

## Valuing and defining information

Government transparency scholarship is an emerging independent field of research (Meijer, 2012) that studies the "prevalence of information pertaining to any number of aspects related to government" (Cucciniello, Porumbescu, & Grimmelikhuijsen, 2017, p. 37). Since much of the demand for information in the postwar period was directed at government, this scholarship is relevant to understanding why it is the currency of democracy. However, using transparency literature to determine the value of information can also be a fraught exercise. It tends to conflate the definition of transparency with the definition of information.[3] As a result, the literature also conflates the value of transparency with the value of information. Moreover, in some cases, it does not strictly delineate the value of transparency to its object (i.e., governments or corporations) versus its subject (i.e., citizens and consumers). Instead, those values are all considered reasons for transparency, with their identification having become "something of a sport among scholars," according to sociologist Tom McClean (2011, p. 13).

That being the case, in the absence of "any collective empirical understanding" (Michener & Bersch, 2013, p. 233) of transparency, I will define it as a condition that lets an observer sense (i.e., see or hear) what would otherwise not be sensed and to do so themselves rather than via an intermediary (Transparency, n.d.; Transparent, n.d.).[4] In doing so, this condition permits access to information, which classical democratic, traditional economic and psychological theories tell us has two instrumental values for individuals who possess it: the first being cognitive and the second being emotional. Seen from the former perspective, information is supposed to allow individuals to make decisions about things they might not otherwise know about. It also allows individuals to make "better decisions, because their ability to predict the consequences of their actions increases."[5] With that cognitive value, individuals are believed to be able to purchase a panoply of public and private goods.

Classical democratic theory, for example, assumes citizens can use information to make what behavioural scientist Bernard Berelson called "wiser decisions" (1952, pp. 317–318; see also Dahl, 1989, pp. 99–100; Davis, 1964, pp. 37–39) about government. Those wiser decisions often take the form of votes to elect representatives that "best serve the citizen's interests" (Dahl, 1989, p. 99) and hold those representatives to account. Traditional economic theory makes a similar assumption (Friedman, 1967, p. 13; Katona, 1953, pp. 308–309; Stigler, 1961, p. 213). It supposes that "economic man" can use information to attain a better pay-off, reaching what Nobel Prize and Turing Award winner Herbert A. Simon described as the "highest attainable point" on his "preference scale" (Simon, 1955, p. 99). The founders of the consumer and modern environmental movements also shared such sentiments. That is why, in their 1927 book *Your Money's Worth*, Stuart Chase and Frederick Schlink claimed that shoddy or dangerous products might be avoided if shoppers could be "armed with the findings of impartial analysis and test" (1932, p. 120). That is also why biologist Rachel Carson, the author of the 1962 book *Silent Spring*, liked to quote French philosopher and scientist Jean Rostand, who declared "the obligation to endure gives us the right to know," (Carson, 2002, p. 14; Rostand, 1960, p. 1491; Tower, 1981) shortly after his country conducted its second atomic weapons test (Blair, 1960; Holman, 2018). And that is perhaps why the first Earth Day, initiated by American Senator Gaylord Nelson, was not characterized as a march or demonstration but rather a teach-in ("Environmental Teach-In Planned," 1969).

However, it was the founders of the modern transparency movement who were perhaps the most ardent believers in the cognitive value of information. In its first report, the influential United States House of Representatives Special Subcommittee on Government Information, which undertook an early study of unnecessary government secrecy, stated:

> Concealment and control of information have been the traditional hallmark of despots. The Iron Curtain countries of today, the dictators of recent history, the political bosses whose rule of corruption once controlled some cities and States in our Nation, prove the truth of this comment. In each case the ruling people grasped control because of the lack of information to the people. Could Hitler and his storm troopers have taken over Germany in the 1930's and maintained their control if they did not suppress the true facts and distort them in their own propaganda mill? Would Stalin have been able to commit the crimes being exposed in Russia today if the people had not been ignorant of his schemes and deeds? Would the corrupt political boss have been able to continue his reign of graft if the people in the city he controlled were not ignorant of his corruption? The inherent right of people to control their government rests solidly on the foundation of information.
>
> *(H.R. Rep. No. 2947, 1956, p. 2)*

In other words, for the committee, information had such enormous cognitive value that German and Russian citizens could have used it to stop two of the twentieth century's greatest crimes against humanity. Such a claim may be as hyperbolic as it is contestable. However, it and the examples cited above illustrate that information was not just seen as a means to make decisions and make better decisions. It was ultimately seen as a means for individuals to exert personal, economic or political control, especially over powers that threatened to control them. I believe this is why Nader (1970, p. 1), who claimed information allows citizens "access to a more just governmental process," described it as the currency of democracy.[6]

That said, this is not information's only value. According to behavioural economist George Loewenstein's information gap theory, it also has an instrumental emotional value. This theory states that individuals are motivated to acquire information "when attention becomes focused on a gap in one's knowledge" (Loewenstein, 1994, p. 87). Individuals can be alerted to such gaps by situational factors, such as "the violation of expectations," "the possession of information by someone else," and "past attainments" of information that serve as a "reference point" against what they do not know about but should (Loewenstein, 1994, p. 91). Once that happens, these gaps "produce the feeling of deprivation labeled curiosity. The curious individual is motivated to obtain the missing information to reduce or eliminate the feeling of deprivation" (Loewenstein, 1994, p. 87). That is because individuals "desire clarity or dislike uncertainty" (Golman & Loewenstein, 2016,

p. 19) with the resolution of these feelings being the instrumental emotional value of information. As such, that theory could be seen as consistent with Nobel Prize-winning economist Kenneth Arrow's (1963, p. 856) view that "when there is uncertainty, information or knowledge becomes a commodity."

Early transparency advocates sometimes directly and sometimes indirectly acknowledged this value. For example, in a seminal paper arguing for more openness in Canada, Carleton University political science professor Donald C. Rowat (1965, p. 480) wrote that "if one does not have full access to the facts one can easily imagine the worst." Similarly, the introduction to *The People Right's to Know*, the first comprehensive "scholarly, legally documented presentation of the subject" (Pope, 1953, p. ix) in the United States, began with an epigram warning that if the public does not have the facts, they might begin to imagine the "face of the age" as "endlessly emitting nightmare monsters from a womb-like cave" (Cross, 1953, p. 3).[7] However, it was Toronto lawyer Heather Mitchell and Simon Fraser University social psychologist Jocelyn Calvert who provided one of the most articulate early accounting of the emotional value of information within the context of the transparency movement.

In a report on access to information that was prepared for the Consumer Research Council and submitted to the Canadian government, Mitchell included a section on the social psychological effects of information deprivation. That section, which relied on research prepared by Calvert, reminded readers that one of humanity's "primary motivating drives" (1975, p. 15) is to understand the meaning of events – even if that understanding is flawed or false. As an example, the report stated, "It has been suggested that the rise of Hitler was possible because he provided a clear and unambiguous solution under conditions of anxiety generated by defeat in war and extreme social and economic stress" (1975, p. 16). That means, from an emotional standpoint, information does not have to be defined as something that is truthful, which would be the case when we discuss its cognitive value. After all, if information was not "in accordance with fact or reality" (Truth, n.d.) we would not be able to make better decisions with it. Instead, from an emotional standpoint, information can simply be something that provides certainty (Mock, 1999, p. 1072).[8] Finally, it is worth mentioning that making better decisions – and the control that it supposedly provides over political and economic institutions – could reasonably be said to create a feeling of certainty. So that means there is an emotional aspect to information's cognitive value too.

## The size, power and authority of government

These instrumental valuations of information – the cognitive and the emotional, control and certainty – and their interplay between seven key developments in politics, the economy, technology and education can help explain why there was a demand for information in Canada and the United States in the postwar period. The first of those developments was an expansion in the size, power and authority of the American and Canadian governments (Crozier, Huntington, & Watanuki, 1975, p. 65, 206; Gwyn, 1974). In part, this expansion (see Table 13.2) represented an enlargement of the welfare state to destroy what Sir William Beveridge called the "five giant evils" of "Want, Disease, Ignorance, Squalor and Idleness" (1943, p. 42). This enlargement included the creation of social safety net programmes, such as old age pensions, unemployment insurance and health insurance, helping government catch those who would have otherwise fallen into the perdition of poverty and infirmity. However, this was not the only part of government that was growing.

The regulatory state expanded to protect workers, consumers, citizens and the environment from the excesses of corporations, as well as scientific and technological progress (see Tables 13.3 and 13.4). The national security state also expanded in response to the threat posed by domestic unrest and terrorism, as well as the West's Cold War adversaries. At the same time, the American president was being described as imperial (Lehmann-Haupt, 1973; Schlesinger, 1989; Wicker, 1972), while the Canadian prime minister was being described as presidential (Stevens, 1969; Westell, 1970). Abusive government behaviour, such as the Watergate scandal and the Vietnam War in the United States and the use of the War Measures Act in Canada, resulted in concerns about what the state could do with this newfound and newly recognised capacity for action (see Tables 13.5 and 13.6). And bestriding all these developments was the power of the atom. Whether it came in the form of a bomb, a missile or an electric plant, it was government that ultimately controlled or regulated this power and, in doing so, posed an existential threat to human existence (Michael, 1950).

As a result, there was a cognitive demand for information about what those governments were doing, so citizens could better control them.[9] That demand was on display during the Special Subcommittee on Government Information's first set of hearings. New York University law professor Bernard Schwartz told the committee that the "overriding peril of the present century" was "that of the superstate with its omnipotent administration, unrestrained by any checks on its all-pervasive regulatory activities" (H.R. Rep. No. 2947, 1956:75). However, he said that peril could be prevented if "the elected representatives of the people assert their right to lay bare all that goes on within the executive" (H.R. Rep. No. 2947, 1956, p. 76). After all, "an executive whose abuses and inadequacies are exposed to the public eye can hardly become a menace to constitutional government" (H.R. Rep. No. 2947, 1956, p. 76). In fact, during those same hearings, James S. Pope, the executive editor of *The Courier-Journal* and *The Louisville Times*, characterised the fight against government secrecy as being a "fight against the enormous size of the Federal Government in 1955" (*Availability of Information*, 1956, p. 6).

Nor were concerns about that size confined to committee rooms and other chambers along the corridors of power. They also appeared in the news media. For example, in an op-ed published in *The Toronto Daily Star* in 1968,

**TABLE 13.2** Government expenditure as a percentage of GDP, 1938–1982

| Year | Canada | United States |
|------|--------|---------------|
| 1938 | 10.49 | 7.86 |
| 1939 | 12.11 | 9.61 |
| 1940 | 18.61 | 8.94 |
| 1941 | 22.76 | 10.46 |
| 1942 | 42.74 | 21.04 |
| 1943 | 48.15 | 40.00 |
| 1944 | 44.27 | 43.23 |
| 1945 | 43.30 | 44.08 |
| 1946 | 22.16 | 27.14 |
| 1947 | 16.30 | 15.93 |
| 1948 | 14.03 | 12.22 |
| 1949 | 14.58 | 14.75 |
| 1950 | 14.99 | 13.44 |
| 1951 | 16.56 | 12.95 |
| 1952 | 17.03 | 18.21 |
| 1953 | 16.16 | 19.51 |
| 1954 | 15.93 | 18.60 |
| 1955 | 14.98 | 16.50 |
| 1956 | 14.57 | 16.09 |
| 1957 | 14.59 | 16.63 |
| 1958 | 14.86 | 17.65 |
| 1959 | 14.88 | 18.15 |
| 1960 | 14.93 | 28.29 |
| 1961 | 30.63 | 29.62 |
| 1962 | 30.63 | 29.71 |
| 1963 | 30.27 | 29.52 |
| 1964 | 29.66 | 28.94 |
| 1965 | 29.81 | 28.44 |
| 1966 | 30.76 | 29.41 |
| 1967 | 32.87 | 31.33 |
| 1968 | 33.79 | 31.63 |
| 1969 | 33.94 | 31.27 |
| 1970 | 36.03 | 32.30 |
| 1971 | 37.30 | 32.47 |
| 1972 | 37.53 | 32.26 |
| 1973 | 36.00 | 31.33 |
| 1974 | 37.59 | 32.71 |
| 1975 | 41.11 | 35.13 |
| 1976 | 40.20 | 33.96 |
| 1977 | 41.43 | 33.07 |
| 1978 | 41.62 | 32.29 |
| 1979 | 40.04 | 32.29 |
| 1980 | 41.55 | 34.29 |
| 1981 | 42.47 | 34.65 |
| 1982 | 47.26 | 36.99 |

*Note.* Data from International Monetary Fund (n.d.).

**TABLE 13.3** Pages of federal government regulation in the United States, 1938–1982

| Year | Federal Register[a] | Code of Federal Regulations[b] |
|------|--------------------|-------------------------------|
| 1938 | 3,194 | – |
| 1939 | 5,007 | – |
| 1940 | 5,307 | – |
| 1941 | 6,877 | – |
| 1942 | 11,134 | – |
| 1943 | 17,553 | – |
| 1944 | 15,194 | – |
| 1945 | 15,508 | – |
| 1946 | 14,736 | – |
| 1947 | 8,902 | – |
| 1948 | 9,608 | – |
| 1949 | 7,952 | – |
| 1950 | 9,562 | 9,745 |
| 1951 | 13,175 | 15,932 |
| 1952 | 11,896 | 19,232 |
| 1953 | 8,912 | 18,464 |
| 1954 | 9,910 | 16,502 |
| 1955 | 10,196 | 17,989 |
| 1956 | 10,528 | 21,651 |
| 1957 | 11,156 | 19,589 |
| 1958 | 10,579 | 20,643 |
| 1959 | 11,116 | 21,760 |
| 1960 | 14,479 | 22,877 |
| 1961 | 12,792 | 25,242 |
| 1962 | 13,226 | 22,863 |
| 1963 | 14,842 | 25,828 |
| 1964 | 19,304 | 31,584 |
| 1965 | 17,206 | 34,783 |
| 1966 | 16,850 | 43,118 |
| 1967 | 21,088 | 50,375 |
| 1968 | 20,072 | 53,513 |
| 1969 | 20,466 | 52,863 |
| 1970 | 20,036 | 54,834 |
| 1971 | 25,447 | 56,720 |
| 1972 | 28,924 | 60,632 |
| 1973 | 35,592 | 64,872 |
| 1974 | 45,422 | 67,860 |
| 1975 | 60,221 | 71,224 |
| 1976 | 57,072 | 72,740 |
| 1977 | 65,603 | 84,729 |
| 1978 | 61,261 | 94,151 |

(*Continued*)

**TABLE 13.3** (Cont).

| Year | Federal Register[a] | Code of Federal Regulations[b] |
|------|------|------|
| 1979 | 77,498 | 98,032 |
| 1980 | 87,012 | 102,195 |
| 1981 | 63,554 | 107,109 |
| 1982 | 58,494 | 104,938 |

*Note.* Data from Office of the Federal Register (n.d.).

a According to George Washington University's Regulatory Studies Center, the size of the Federal Register – the daily journal of the federal government in which all newly proposed rules are published – "provides a sense of the flow of new regulations issued during a given period and suggests how the regulatory burden will grow as Americans try to comply with the new mandates" (n.d.). This column accounts for the total number of pages in the register.

b According to George Washington University's Regulatory Studies Center, the size of the Code of Federal Regulations – which codifies all rules and regulations promulgated by federal agencies – "provides a sense of the scope of existing regulations with which American businesses, workers, and consumers must comply" (n.d.).

**TABLE 13.4** Number of federal statutory orders, regulations and statutory instruments in Canada published in the *Canada Gazette: Part II*, 1951–1982[a]

| Year | Statutory Orders and Regulations | Statutory Instruments | Combined |
|------|------|------|------|
| 1951[b] | 609 | – | – |
| 1952 | 573 | – | – |
| 1953 | 531 | – | – |
| 1954 | 748 | – | – |
| 1955 | 463 | – | – |
| 1956 | 469 | – | – |
| 1957 | 504 | – | – |
| 1958 | 503 | – | – |
| 1959 | 488 | – | – |
| 1960 | 578 | – | – |
| 1961 | 549 | – | – |
| 1962 | 489 | – | – |
| 1963 | 474 | – | – |
| 1964 | 506 | – | – |
| 1965 | 565 | – | – |
| 1966 | 575 | – | – |
| 1967 | 621 | – | – |
| 1968 | 571 | – | – |
| 1969 | 638 | – | – |
| 1970 | 540 | – | – |
| 1971 | 689 | – | – |
| 1972[c] | 466 | 110 | 576 |
| 1973 | 649 | 107 | 756 |
| 1974 | 623 | 130 | 753 |
| 1975 | 640 | 136 | 776 |

(*Continued*)

**TABLE 13.4** (Cont).

| Year | Statutory Orders and Regulations | Statutory Instruments | Combined |
|------|------|------|------|
| 1976 | 747 | 153 | 900 |
| 1977 | 905 | 200 | 1,105 |
| 1978 | 876 | 176 | 1,052 |
| 1979 | 838 | 162 | 1,000 |
| 1980 | 831 | 148 | 979 |
| 1981 | 967 | 128 | 1,095 |
| 1982 | 1,037 | 175 | 1,212 |

*Note.* Data from Queen's Printer for Canada (1951-1982).

a  Unlike the Government of the United States, the Government of Canada does not track the number of pages of regulation published in the *Canada Gazette: Part II* or the number of regulations enacted each year (Queen's Printer for Canada, personal communication, June 28, 2018). That latter limitation means this table only includes data for regulations published in the *Canada Gazette: Part II*. It does not include data for so-called "unpublished regulations," statutory orders and statutory instruments exempted by law from publication (Library and Archives Canada, personal communication, August 16, 2019).

b  In 1951, the Regulations Act "required all regulations be published in English and French within 30 days of being made" (Queen's Printer for Canada, 2001, p. 38).

c  In 1972, the Statutory Instruments Act expanded the definition of the regulations required to be published in the *Canada Gazette: Part II* (Queen's Printer for Canada, 1972, p. 1).

**TABLE 13.5** Percentage of respondents who think big business, big labour or big government will be the biggest threat to Canada in the future

| Year | Big business | Big labour | Big government |
|------|------|------|------|
| October 1968 | 23.3 | 44.9 | 31.8 |
| May 1972 | 27.5 | 36.0 | 22.2 |
| August 1975 | 23.3 | 42.6 | 34.1 |
| November 1976 | 18.1 | 42.5 | 32.8 |
| September 1977 | 18.6 | 38.5 | 31.3 |
| July 1978 | 18.8 | 40.4 | 40.8 |
| January 1979 | 18.1 | 33.5 | 36.9 |
| January 1980 | 20.3 | 36.2 | 29.1 |
| January 1981 | 25.8 | 35.1 | 39.1 |
| October 1981 | 16.3 | 27.6 | 43.9 |
| February 1982 | 17.6 | 33.9 | 48.6 |
| July 1982 | 13.0 | 29.4 | 45.6 |
| November 1982 | 13.9 | 30.3 | 44.4 |

*Note.* Data from Canadian Institute of Public Opinion (1968, 1972, 1975, 1976, 1977, 1978, 1979, 1980, 1981a, 1981b, 1982a, 1982b, 1982c).

Progressive Conservative MP Alvin Hamilton wrote, "With the government so large a force in the life of the modern capitalist state a way has to be found to bring more administration activities into public view" (1968). That is why *The Globe and Mail* urged the government to pass Canada's first freedom of

**TABLE 13.6** Percentage of respondents who think big business, big labour or big government will be the biggest threat to the United States in the future

| Year | Big business | Big labour | Big government |
|---|---|---|---|
| February 1965 | 17 | 29 | 35 |
| December 1966 | 14 | 21 | 48 |
| July 1968 | 12 | 26 | 46 |
| November 1969 | 19 | 28 | 33 |
| January 1977 | 23 | 26 | 38 |
| September 1978 | 19 | 19 | 47 |
| May 1979 | 28 | 17 | 43 |
| September 1981 | 22 | 22 | 46 |

*Note.* Data from Fishman & Davis (2017).

information bill when it was introduced by New Democratic Party MP Barry Mather in 1965. According to the editorial, that bill could help "restrain" government officials "from arbitrary acts which they would not care to have become the subject of public discussion. There is nothing like the spotlight of publicity to improve a man's democratic manners" (1965) – the implication being that information about ill-mannered acts would be the subject of public decisions that might result in judgement, censure or punishment.

However, citizens were not just looking to control the machinery of government and its operators. The government's increasingly innumerable cogs and wheels also violated expectations of what the state should be doing and how it should be doing it. This created what the Canadian Task Force on Government Information called a "crucial paradox of the times" (1969, p. 1). According to its final report,

> in the interests of improving the personal welfare of the individual citizen, [governments in Western democracies] have grown so huge and so complex that the individual is no longer able to feel that he personally matters to them. Moreover, a Federal Government may appear not merely impersonal and remote but increasingly intrusive and imperative.
>
> *(1969, p. 1)*

The impersonal and remote nature of government was increased by its automation (Penn, 1966). Even the steel, glass and concrete civic buildings of this period, built in more modernist styles (Foell & Robinson 2003, pp. 44–55; Wright, 1997, pp. 262–271), could be described using these adjectives. However, as more and more outrageous and outlandish scandals came to the public's attention, words such as threatening and frightening would also come to be associated with government.

Those scandals included illegal domestic spying by law enforcement and intelligence agencies – activities that were investigated by the Church Committee, the Pike Committee and the Rockefeller Commission in the United States, as well as the McDonald Commission, the Keable Commission and the Laycraft Inquiry in Canada. They also included even stranger stories, such as the CIA's mind control experiments on unwitting Americans and Canadians (The Canadian Press, 1977, 1979a, 1979b, 1980a; Crewdson, Horrock, Rensberger, Thomas, & Treaster, 1977; Horrock, 1977; Martin, 1979) and United States Army chemical warfare testing above Minneapolis, St. Louis and Winnipeg (Martin, 1980; The Canadian Press, 1980b; United Press International, 1980). Meanwhile, other changes to government seemed straight out of science fiction magazines. Just a year before the United States dropped its atomic bomb on Hiroshima in 1945, a short story about just such a weapon was published in *Astounding Science Fiction* (Silverberg, 2003a, 2003b). Such increases in the size, power and authority of government were so destabilizing and alienating that, in 1970, Carleton University political scientist Jon Alexander observed that the state's technological paternalism had left some people feeling that "they are in the hands of a power beyond their control, an unknowable God" (1968, p. 21).

These feelings identified for citizens a gap in their knowledge about what government used to be versus what it had become, something Canadian Progressive Conservative MP Gerald Baldwin articulated in a 1977 speech prepared for the Canadian Association for Information Science. In that speech, Baldwin said that citizens in most democratic countries have "somewhat reluctantly" accepted that there are few areas of society where they were not "involved in the machinery of government, and the activities of government and what government is doing to them" (1977, p. 4). Nevertheless, Baldwin, the "father and grandfather" (The Governor General of Canada, n.d.) of Canada's Access to Information Act, said many of those citizens were

> very concerned because they don't know why it is being done. And I think it is important for people that they be made aware of the facts and that they be given the opportunity of finding out the basis of actions.
> 
> *(1977, p. 4)*

That emotional demand for certainty through information could even be heard at the United States Department of Defense. John S. Foster, Jr., the department's director of defense research and engineering, asked its civilian defense science board to address "specific questions" (Defense Science Board 1970, p. iv) related to the classification of scientific and technical information by the military. The board's task force on secrecy did just that, submitting a report that noted "more might be gained than lost if our nation were to adopt – unilaterally, if necessary – a policy of complete openness in all areas of information" (1970, p. 1). The task force acknowledged such a policy might not be practical. However, it also noted the classification of information "creates areas of uncertainty in the public mind on policy issues" (1970, p. 1).

## The size, power and authority of corporations

However, individuals were not just worried about what government was and was not doing during this period. They were also worried about what corporations were doing with their size, power and authority. Senator Nelson gave voice to those worries when the United States Senate Select Subcommittee on Monopoly, which he chaired, started its second set of hearings on corporate secrecy. "Not only States and industries but even nations are now dwarfed by the giant corporations," he said.

> It is interesting – and not especially comforting – to note that in 1960, there were 59 countries and 41 corporations on the list (of the 100 largest 'money powers' of the world). In 1965, there were 57 countries and 43 corporations. In 1970, there were 49 countries and 51 corporations. Plainly, the corporations are growing faster than the nations.
>
> *(The Role of Giant Corporations 1972, p. 1043)*

The preponderance of mergers and acquisitions during the postwar period drew attention to that growth (see Table 13.7), especially when such activity resulted in the formation of conglomerates – companies that produced unrelated products and delivered unrelated services – or multinational corporations.

Big businesses were also increasingly seen as exerting that power and authority in public life – so much so that, in 1972, *The New York Times* published an Independence Day editorial suggesting that "special interests" were "frustrating the democratic process," potentially resulting in the creation of a "corporate state" (Editorial, 1972). As an example of that influence, Willard Fitz Mueller, the former chief economist of the Federal Trade Commission, warned Nelson's committee that

> corporate annual reports increasingly read like a state of the Nation address, and in some cases like a state of the world address. Indeed, the tone and scope of a recent ITT annual report are not unlike what one might expect of a Prime Minister's characterization of the British Empire in its days of glory. ITT proudly proclaimed to its stockholders that its

**TABLE 13.7** World's top 100 national and corporate economic entities, 1960–1970

| Year | Number of countries | Number of corporations | Corporate sales as percent of GDP |
|------|---------------------|------------------------|-----------------------------------|
| 1960 | 59 | 41 | 8.34 percent |
| 1965 | 57 | 43 | 8.66 percent |
| 1970 | 49 | 51 | 8.9 percent |

*Note.* Data from *The Role of Giant Corporations* (1972, pp. 1195–1198).

vast international organization: 'is constantly at work around the clock – in 67 nations on six continents, in activities extending from the Arctic to the Antarctic and quite literally from the bottom of the sea to the moon'.

*(The Role of Giant Corporations 1972, p. 1097)*

Such proclamations came as consumer, environmental and workplace safety concerns about large and small businesses were making headlines and bestseller lists. Nader's *Unsafe at Any Speed* and Carson's *Silent Spring* were among the most prominent examples, publicising the dangers of automobiles and pesticides. But there were countless others. There were stories about how cyclamates and saccharin, two kinds of artificial sweeteners, could cause cancer (Burns, 1969; Schmeck, 1969, 1972) – allegations that were later disproven. There were stories about how asbestos was also putting consumers and workers at risk for cancer (Brody, 1966; Schmeck, 1964; Seniuk, 1974). And there were stories about how thalidomide had caused birth defects (Dowd, 1962; Plumb, 1962; The Ottawa Bureau of The Globe and Mail, 1962). Like the abuses of government during the postwar period, these reports heightened concerns about what corporations were doing with their power and authority, as well as their potential costs to society and the environment. Such concerns may not have been as widely or strongly held in Canada as they were in the United States (see Tables 13.5 and 13.6). However, those concerns were prevalent enough for Prime Minister Pierre Trudeau to publicly worry that big corporations had too much economic power (Royal Commission on Corporate Concentration 1978, p. 6) – a concern a majority of Canadians at least partially agreed with (see Table 13.8). And, again, information was seen as a means of providing individuals with both control and certainty about these institutions.

An exemplar of these cognitive and emotional demands for information can be found in the Royal Commission on Corporate Concentration's final report. The commission was struck following Argus Corporation's attempted takeover of Power Corporation of Canada in 1975. That attempt was unsuccessful. However, criticism of that takeover paralleled what the commission described as an increasing unease over the "economic, political, and social impact of large firms

**TABLE 13.8** Prime Minister Trudeau has said that "he believes big unions and big corporations have too much economic power, and that this power will have to be curbed if Canadians want an economy with low unemployment and stable prices. Do you think this is true or not, of either unions or corporations, or of both?" (percentage of respondents)

| Year | Big unions only | Big corporations only | Both | Neither | Can't Say |
|------|-----------------|------------------------|------|---------|-----------|
| 1971 | 15.7 | 5.0 | 65.6 | 13.7 | 18.9 |
| 1976 | 19.1 | 9.3 | 61.5 | 10.1 | 16.0 |

*Note.* Data from Canadian Institute of Public Opinion (1971, 1976).

in Canada" (1978, p. 2). Indeed, many of the commission's witnesses felt those firms should be "made to account" (1978, p. 318) for their use of material and human resources. Such accountability was "impossible unless an adequate base of information, different from that now disclosed to investors and shareholders, is available" (1978, p. 319). From this, the commission concluded "the public does have a right to know more than it does now" – in part, because "openness is fundamental to confidence, and it would be in the public interest if there were more understanding of our major business enterprises. That is often lacking. We do not suggest that openness guarantees confidence, but we do think that lack of openness inhibits it" (1978, p. 322).

## Supply of information

At the same time, the supply of information was growing, so much so that talk of a knowledge explosion had become common (Delahaye, 1968, p. 1). Information held by governments and corporations was part of that explosion, triggering a desire to know. In part, this growth was simply the result of the increasing size, power and authority of those institutions. As they did more, they knew more (French, 1978, p. 3; Lewis, 1975, pp. 12–13). It was estimated that, between 1966 and 1971, the total data generated by the United States' Medicare program would exceed the total paperwork produced by the American government's executive branch in 1820 (Alexander, 1968, p. 10). Knowing was also especially important for the state's regulatory bodies. After all, regulations could not be enforced if the state was ignorant about what was happening in the economy and the environment. That is why the Canadian government, in 1968, encouraged citizens to register their complaints about products or services by writing to "The Consumer, Box 99, Ottawa" (Department of Consumer and Corporate Affairs, 1968). Knowing was important for the state's national security bodies too, since espionage, subversion and terrorism could not be prevented if those bodies were ignorant about such activity. That is why the United States Army, by 1970, had "nearly 1,000 plainclothes investigators, working out of some 300 offices from coast to coast" to "keep track of political protests of all kinds" (Pyle, 1970, p. 4). And knowing was vital to public administration practice, as engineers, scientists, social scientists and their techniques became part of government's policy-making processes (Alexander, 1968, p. 3; Perl, 1971, p. 1211).

The resulting supply of information grew even larger, thanks to government and corporate use of information gathering technologies. That trend was described in the bestselling 1959 book *The Eavesdroppers* (Hochman, 2016). It was then summarised by *The New York Times* with the headline "the Bugged Society" (Bishop, 1969), a phrase Canadian Justice Minister John Turner would use in a major speech on the need for privacy and freedom of information legislation (1969, p. 3). The surveillance technologies those three words referred to included everything from lie detectors, parabolic microphones ("big ears") and concealed microphones ("bugs") to wiretaps, closed circuit television cameras and spy satellites. And the resulting supply of information grew larger still, thanks to the increasing use of computers (Delahaye, 1968, pp. 4–5; see also Tables 13.9 and 13.10). That meant the gap between what citizens and consumers knew and what governments and corporations knew became wider and ever more apparent, heightening the emotional demand for information.

That emotion was palpable in a speech Baldwin prepared for the Canadian Computer Conference. During that speech, he said it was a "well-known fact that in order not to be on someone's computer somewhere, you would have to be a total recluse. You would have to forego not only credit but also insurance, employment, medical care, education, and all forms of government services to individuals" (1978, p. 8). That is because "many of these services are necessities and we have to submit to whatever demands for personal information an organization may make. Furthermore, many organizations want quite a bit of personal information because they wish to make rather fine-grained decisions about us. Are we eligible for welfare? Are we cheating on our income tax? Will we be

**TABLE 13.9** Computer installations in Canada, 1964–1982

| Year | Estimated number[a] |
| --- | --- |
| March 1964 | 502 |
| June 1965 | 710 |
| June 1966 | 948 |
| May 1967 | 1,279 |
| May 1968 | 1,613 |
| May 1969 | 2,037 |
| May 1970 | 2,700 |
| May 1971 | 3,548 |
| May 1972 | 4,406 |
| May 1973 | 5,736 |
| May 1974 | 3,897[b] |
| May 1975 | 4,940[b] |
| May 1976 | 5,937[b] |
| May 1977 | 6,799[b] |
| May 1978 | 8,251[b] |
| May 1979 | 8,598[b] |
| December 1980 | 10,395 |
| December 1981 | 13,434 |
| December 1982 | 15,154 |

*Source*: Data from Chambers and Chiovitti (1983, p. 20).
a Does not include computers that the *Canadian Computer Census* described as "very small" or "midgets." These would come to be known as personal or desktop computers.
b Does not include computers that rented for less than $1,000.

**TABLE 13.10** Cumulative number of computers made by American manufacturers in use in the United States, 1955–1982

| Year | Estimated number |
|------|------------------|
| 1955 | 244[a] |
| 1956 | 745[a] |
| 1957 | 1,500[a] |
| 1958 | 2,550[a] |
| 1959 | 3,810[a] |
| 1960 | 5,400[a] |
| 1961 | 7,550[a] |
| 1962 | 9,900[a] |
| 1963 | 12,850[a] |
| 1964 | 18,200[a] |
| 1965 | 23,200[a] |
| 1966 | 31,100[b] |
| 1967 | 37,000[b] |
| 1968 | 46,500[b] |
| 1969 | 56,800 |
| 1970 | 68,300 |
| 1971 | 83,200 |
| 1972 | 104,000 |
| 1973 | 133,250 |
| 1974 | 172,740[c] |
| 1975 | 212,640[d] |
| 1976 | 261,580[e] |
| 1977 | 355,000[f] |
| 1978 | 564,900[g] |
| 1979 | 832,500[h] |
| 1980 | 1,268,100[i] |
| 1981 | 1,967,300[j] |
| 1982 | 4,729,700[k] |

*Source*: Data from McGovern (1969–1973), Geyer (1974), Peacock (1975–1979), Upton (1980–1982), and Moschella (1983).

a  The figures presented in this table are from *EDP Industry Report*, a computer-industry newsletter that compiled a running census estimating the number of computers shipped by American manufacturers, as well as how many of those computers were in use. In 1969, the newsletter introduced changes to its census that meant its figures for the years 1955–1968 could not be compared to those for subsequent years (McGovern, 1970, p. 14).

b  In 1973, Telex sued IBM for using monopolistic practices ("Trial Begins," 1973). As a result of the documents made public during this trial, as well as other data, *EDP Industry Report* revised its historic estimates for the number of computers made by American manufacturers (Geyer, 1974, p. 2). In 1970, the newsletter had estimated those numbers as being 29,800 in 1966, 40,100 in 1967, and 47,100 in 1968 (McGovern: 15).

c  In 1976, EDP had estimated this figure at 168,800 in 1974 (Geyer, 1976, p. 7). In 1977, EDP Industry Report changed its definition of computers. As a result, the newsletter advised readers that "care must be exercised in comparing charts or figures and forecasts from previous issues of the EDP/IR" (Geyer, 1977, p. 2). That also resulted in its 1974 estimate being changed to 179,900 (Peacock, p. 4). In 1978, that estimate was changed again to 167,100 to avoid double-counting mini- and small business computers (Peacock: 6, 9). It was then changed without explanation to 171,240 in 1979 (Peacock: 9) and 172,240 in 1980 (Upton, 1980, p. 7).

d In 1977, EDP estimated this figure as being 220,200 (Peacock: 4). That estimate was changed to 207,100 in 1978 to avoid double-counting mini- and small business computers (Peacock: 6, 9). It was then changed without explanation to 208,640 in 1979 (Peacock, p. 9), and 212,640 in 1980 (Upton: 12) and 1981 (Upton: 11).

e This figure was estimated at 253,580 in 1979 (Peacock: 9), 264,580 in 1980 (Upton: 12), 261,680 in 1981 (Upton: 11) and 261,580 in 1982 (Upon: 13).

f This figure was estimated at 322,320 in 1979 (Peacock: 9), 361,820 in 1980 (Upton: 12), 355,120 in 1981 (Upton: 11), 356,420 in 1982 (Upton: 13) and 355,000 in 1983 (Moschella: 13).

g This figure was estimated at 401,460 in 1979 (Peacock: 9), 575,380 in 1980 (Upton, p. 12), 563,550 in 1981 (Upton, p. 11), 566,150 in 1982 (Upton, p. 13), and 564,900 in 1983 (Moschella: 13).

h This figure was estimated at 862,440 in 1980 (Upton: 12), 849,560 in 1981 (Upon: 11), 836,760 in 1982 (Upon: 13) and 832,500 in 1983 (Moschella: 13).

i This figure was estimated at 1,283,750 in 1981 (Upton: 11), 1,269,610 in 1982 (Upton: 13), and 1,268,100 in 1983 (Moschella: 13).

j This figure was estimated at 1,952,520 in 1982 (Upton: 13) and 1,967,300 in 1983 (Moschella: 13).

k This figure was estimated at 3,178,555 in 1982 (Upton: 13) and 4,729,700 in 1983 (Moschella: 13).

a reliable employee? This leads not only to a fear of what effect erroneous or misleading information may have on our welfare and livelihood but also to fears that a complete personal profile can be accumulated and then, unfortunately, used" (p. 8). As a result, Baldwin (1978, p. 12) argued that the electorate needs to have access to their own personal information, as well as the "diverse technical and factual information collected by governments."

## Higher education

This emotional demand for information was also driven by an increasingly educated citizenry in Canada and the United States (see Table 13.11). The eminent sociologist Michael Schudson (2015, pp. 174–175) makes this argument in his recent book *The Rise of the Right to Know*, writing, "The changes in higher education undergird every postwar development in greater openness, greater criticism, freer dissent, and a presumption that there is a right to know in democratic culture, if not in the U.S. Constitution."

Loewenstein's information gap theory supports Schudson's proposition. As we know more, we come to know more about what we do not know, identifying gaps that need to be filled. Indeed, the Task Force on Government Information highlighted this exact relationship between education and the emotional demand for information by individuals. In its final report, the task force noted, "People as a whole are better educated than they used to be. They know more than their fathers did, and knowing more things often makes people want to know more still" (1969, pp. 1–2). As a result, it quoted a "distinguished Canadian industrialist" as saying, "The government must recognize that, and extend it to its own processes. It can no longer decide without explanation, introduce programmes without defending them, or adopt policies without justifying them" (1969, p. 2).

**TABLE 13.11** Total number of students enrolled in higher education per million population, 1945–1982

| Year | Canada (Total Students) | United States (Total Students) | Canada (Students Per Million Population) | United States (Students Per Million Population) |
|------|------------------------|-------------------------------|----------------------------------------|-----------------------------------------------|
| 1945 | – | 1,676,851 | – | 11,984 |
| 1946 | 166,538[a] | 2,616,262[h] | 13,548 | 18,504 |
| 1949 | 69,022[b] | 2,659,021[h] | 5,133 | 17,823 |
| 1950 | 74,273 | – | 5,417 | – |
| 1951 | 67,631 | 2,301,884[i] | 4,828 | 14,863 |
| 1952 | – | – | – | – |
| 1953 | – | 2,054,481 | – | 12,826 |
| 1954 | – | 2,283,718 | – | 14,008 |
| 1955 | 69,404[c] | – | 4,421 | – |
| 1956 | 75,993[d] | – | 4,726 | – |
| 1957 | 84,498[e] | 2,742,250 | 5,087 | 15,945 |
| 1958 | – | – | – | – |
| 1959 | 87,303[f] | 3,042,200 | 4,994 | 17,107 |
| 1960 | – | 3,224,000 | – | 17,845 |
| 1961 | 160,535 | 3,726,114[j] | 8,802 | 20,285 |
| 1962 | – | – | – | – |
| 1963 | 256,217 | 4,234,092 | 13,534 | 22,374 |
| 1964 | 283,907 | – | 14,717 | – |
| 1965 | 323,625 | 5,526,325 | 16,474 | 28,442 |
| 1966 | 372,275 | 6,389,872 | 18,600 | 32,508 |
| 1967 | 449,902 | 6,911,748 | 22,078 | 34,783 |
| 1968 | 477,967 | 7,513,091 | 23,089 | 37,433 |
| 1969 | 562,648 | 7,916,991 | 26,791 | 39,062 |
| 1970 | 642,013 | 8,498,117 | 30,146 | 41,444 |
| 1971 | 652,176 | 8,945,645 | 29,696 | 43,078 |
| 1972 | – | – | – | – |
| 1973 | 692,430[g] | 9,602,123 | 30,786 | 45,313 |
| 1974 | 706,652[g] | 10,223,729 | 30,983 | 47,807 |
| 1975 | 818,153 | 11,184,859 | 35,352 | 51,788 |
| 1976 | – | 11,012,137 | – | 50,506 |
| 1977 | 826,263 | 11,285,787 | 34,825 | 51,243 |
| 1978 | 831,263 | – | 34,689 | – |
| 1979 | – | – | – | – |
| 1980 | 888,444 | 12,096,895 | 36,240 | 53,238 |
| 1981 | 924,445 | 12,371,672 | 37,246 | 53,915 |
| 1982 | 988,334 | – | 39,349 | – |

*Note.* Data for total students from Department of International Economic and Social Affairs Statistical Office (1948-1985). Data for Canadian population from Statistics Canada (n.d.-a, n.d.-b). Data for American population from United States Census Bureau (2000).
a  Including preparatory courses at colleges and universities.
b  Including preparatory courses at colleges and universities. Data refer to full-time students.
c  Data refer to reporting institutions only; there was an estimated total of 71,600 students enrolled.
d  Data refer to reporting institutions only; there was an estimated total of 78,100 students enrolled.
e  Data refer to reporting institutions only; there was an estimated total of 102,000 students enrolled.

f  In the United Nations' 1960 Statistical Yearbook, it was reported there were 102,000 higher education students in Canada in 1959. This data was amended the following year.
g  Data exclude part-time students enrolled at non-university institutions.
h  Including universities, junior colleges, teachers' colleges and normal schools, colleges and higher
   technical schools.
i  Including teacher-training.
j  In the United Nations' 1963 Statistical Yearbook, it was reported there were 3,860,643 higher education students in the United States in 1961. This data was amended the following year.

## Government and corporate secrecy

If there had been such a recognition, Canada and the United States might never
have needed to pass freedom of information laws. But instead, there was significant resistance by government to these demands for information. It is beyond
the brief of this chapter to examine the perennial reasons for that resistance.
However, during the postwar period, there was a belief among transparency
advocates on both sides of the border that the increasing size of government was
partially to blame for this secrecy. Virgil Newton Jr., the managing editor of
*Tampa Tribune*, articulated that belief during his testimony before the Special
Subcommittee on Government Information. Newton said the tendency toward
secrecy in the American government began when it "mushroomed immensely
and reached down into the lives of private individuals during the depression and
war years" (*Availability of Information* 1956, p. 14). This mushrooming meant it
became impossible to properly report on government. As a result, "ignored by
the press and left largely on his own in Federal office, the politician began to
develop the philosophy new in American government, that the public servant,
once elected or appointed, possesses the office as his private domain; that he
and only he has the right to give out or withhold information of Government
as he sees fit" (*Availability of Information* 1956, p. 15). Even in Canada, where
the political system had always been opaquer, it was felt that the growth of
government had further cultivated such secrecy. For example, *The Globe and
Mail* wrote,

> One bad side effect of the prodigious growth of government in this cen-
> tury is that it has become exceedingly difficult to keep track of … Accom-
> panying this governmental growth has been a disinclination on the part of
> governments and their creatures to keep the public informed about what
> they are doing.
>
> *(Editorial, 1965)*

This growing government secrecy paralleled a growing secrecy among
corporations. In Canada, a background report for the Royal Commission on
Corporate Concentration crudely quoted one commentator as saying the country's businesses had always "exhibited a 'maidenly reluctance' to expose their
innermost corporate details" (Kazanjian, 1978, p. 27). And when the United

States Senate Select Subcommittee on Monopoly began its hearings on the "role of giant corporations in the American and world economies" its chairman, Nelson, criticised them for claiming a "'right' to keep almost all of their financial and operating data a close secret of their top managements" (*The Role of Giant Corporations*, 1969, p. 16). However, their increasingly diversified activities meant corporate financial statements had become less revealing than they had once been. That is because those reports did not include detailed financial information about their many different lines of business. As a result, in a statement made to a House of Representatives subcommittee investigating food prices, Mueller told its members, "Our economic intelligence about many aspects of business organization is worse today than it was around 1900, when Roosevelt made his plea for opening to public view the 'mammoth' corporations of his day" – which "were pigmies compared to today's giants" (*Food Price Investigation*, 1973, p. 339). Mueller saw such secrecy as "the great enemy of the market economy," since "a market functions properly only in an atmosphere of extensive knowledge concerning financial and other aspects of corporate behaviour" (*Food Price Investigation*, 1973, p. 338). It was also contrary to what Huntly W.F. McKay, vice-president of public relations, statistics and research for the Toronto Stock Exchange, described as the era of "glass pockets for business" (Lutsky, 1967) – with corporations having a responsibility to let the public know what they were doing and demonstrate the ethics of their activities.

In other words, both governments and corporations were violating expectations of how politics and economics in a capitalist democracy should function. After all, individuals could not make good decisions about government, either during or between elections, unless they knew what it was doing, how it was doing it and why it was doing it. Nor could they make decisions about corporations, their products and services unless they were similarly informed. Such secrecy also identified a gap between what citizens and consumers knew about governments and corporations and what governments and corporations knew about themselves. This contributed to a cognitive and emotional demand for information.

## Government propaganda and corporate advertising

Moreover, even when governments and corporations did provide information to the public, there was a belief that it was somehow compromised, being either incomplete or outright inaccurate. Among transparency advocates, the government's expanding propaganda apparatus was at least partially blamed for this behaviour. In 1961, it was estimated that the American government had recruited an army of approximately 50,000 press agents at an annual cost of approximately $100 million – significantly more than the $28 million that had been spent just 20 years earlier (Newton, 1961, p. 19). But even though the public was picking up the bill for those press agents, they certainly weren't being served by them. Instead, according to one journalist, every line an agent wrote was "designed to reflect glory upon his government agency and to prolong the political life of his boss, regardless of whether it is the truth, half truth or no truth" (Newton, 1961, p. 20). A 1974 Privy Council Office study quietly acknowledged the same criticism in Canada. It stated that, "The complaint most often made and most intensely expressed concerning the provision of government information was that the practice of the Canadian government (although enshrined neither in principle nor policy) was to release only that information which was considered advantageous or harmless, and automatically to withhold the rest" (Wall, 1974, p. 16). The study also admitted objectivity was often found lacking in government press releases and speeches, so much so that "credibility was serious strained" (Wall, 1974, p. 9).

Nor was government alone in only releasing information that was considered advantageous or harmless. In the postwar period, there was also concern that corporations were creating false or misleading advertisements. That concern was reflected in American public opinion polls (Calfee & Ringold, 1994, pp. 228, 232–234). And it was seen in Canadian public opinion polls too. For example, 45.6 percent of respondents to a Canadian Gallup Poll survey said they thought advertising was less truthful in 1973 than it had been five years earlier. By comparison, just 27.3 percent said it was more truthful, with another 27 percent saying it was the same. Six years later, when Environics asked Canadians if they could depend on getting the truth in most advertising, 77.7 percent of respondents said they were not very confident or not at all confident in being able to do so. And, two years after that, 72.4 percent said the same thing.

This lack of trust in advertising was voiced by senior government officials, consumer advocates, retailers and advertising executives in both countries. For example, in 1953, the departing chairman of the Federal Trade Commission warned his successor that there would be an increase in deceptive advertising because of keener competition in the economy (Wall Street Journal Staff Reporter, 1953). A year later, when *The Wall Street Journal* checked Better Business Bureaus in 16 American cities, it found an "upswing in shady selling tactics" due to "fiercer competition" (Wall Street Journal News Roundup, 1954). Concerns about those tactics were also aired north of the border, with David A. Gilbert, national manager of the Retail Merchants' Association of Canada, advising a convention of his Calgary colleagues that "false advertising and misrepresentations" were prevalent to the point where "they are getting out of hand" (The Canadian Press, 1958). Such concerns were heightened by the increased breadth and depth of advertising that came from television commercials, as well as the use of social science techniques to manipulate consumers, the latter of which was sensationally described in the bestselling 1957 book *The Hidden Persuaders*.

This propaganda and advertising made consumers and citizens uncertain about the information governments and corporations were providing. It also violated expectations about how politics and the economy should theoretically function, in the same way government and corporate secrecy had – impairing decision-making about these institutions. As a result, propaganda and advertising also contributed to emotional and cognitive demands for information – something that was even recognised by the president of the United States. In a special message to Congress, John F. Kennedy observed that consumer choice was increasingly "influenced by mass advertising utilizing highly developed arts of persuasion" (1962, p. 2). That meant consumers did not know "whether drug preparations meet minimum standards of safety, quality, and efficacy," "how much he pays for consumer credit" or "whether one prepared food has more nutritional value than another" (1962, p. 2). As a result, Kennedy said government had a responsibility to safeguard Americans' "right to be informed – to be protected against fraudulent, deceitful, or grossly misleading information, advertising, labelling, or other practices, and to be given the facts he needs to make an informed choice" (1962, p. 2). Such behaviour, when practiced by government, also violated a "basic tenant of democracy," according to Tom Riley, an associate of Baldwin's who campaigned for freedom of information in both Canada and the United States (Riley, n.d.). Writing in *Content* magazine, Riley stated, "To make a rational decision it is necessary to have all the facts, not what the government decides one should have. To hope to marshal all the facts, persons in a society must have free access to information. Information freely given is one thing. Information carefully selected and channeled by the government is propaganda" (1976, p. 2).

## Feelings of uncertainty and uncontrollability

I would remiss if I did not recognise the overall tenor of the times as heightening these demands. In the postwar period, there seems to have been a feeling in Canada and the United States that the world was uncertain and uncontrollable – in part, because of the forces identified in this chapter. This feeling can be seen in some of the political polling from that period, which shows many Americans and Canadians believed they could not control their own governments (see Table 13.12). Americans also felt increasingly uncertain about whether their government would do the right thing (see Table 13.13). As is too often the case, comparable data does not appear to exist for Canada. However, when Environics asked Canadians if they felt they could depend on what they were told by the country's political leaders, 69.9 percent of respondents said they were not very confident or not at all confident in 1979, with 72.6 percent providing the same response in 1981. And those same feelings of uncertainty and uncontrollability seem to have extended beyond politics and into other forums.

Richard Goodwin, the former American presidential advisor who penned Lyndon Johnson's "Great Society" speech, captured these feelings in a *New Yorker* article that was later quoted in the Canadian Task Force on Government Information's final report (1969, p. 2). In the article, Goodwin painted a morose picture of the "non-poor citizen's" public life: "The air around him is poisoned, parkland disappears under relentless bulldozers, traffic stalls and jams, airplanes cannot land,

**TABLE 13.12** Percentage of respondents who agree people like themselves don't have any say about what the government does[a]

| Year | Americans | Canadians |
|------|-----------|-----------|
| 1952 | 31 | – |
| 1956 | 28 | – |
| 1960 | 27 | – |
| 1964 | 29 | – |
| 1965 | – | 52.0 |
| 1966 | 34 | – |
| 1968 | 41 | 49.0 |
| 1970 | 36 | – |
| 1972 | 40 | – |
| 1974 | 40 | 53.9 |
| 1976 | 41 | – |
| 1977 | – | 53.9 |
| 1978 | 45 | – |
| 1979 | – | 56.2 |
| 1980 | 39 | – |
| 1981 | – | 54.7 |
| 1982 | 45 | – |

*Note.* Data for Americans from The American National Election Studies (n.d.). Data for Canadians from the *Canadian Election Study* and *Social Change in Canada* surveys (Atkinson, Blishen, Ornstein, & Stevenson, 1979, 1983a, 1983b; Clarke, Jenson, LeDuc, & Pammett, 1975; Converse, Meisel, Pinard, Regenstreif, & Schwartz, 1966).

a The Canadian Election Study and Social Change in Canada surveys asked respondents if they agreed if people like themselves "don't have any say" about what the government does. By comparison, the American National Election Studies asked respondents if people like themselves "don't have a say" about what the government does.

and even his own streets are unsafe and, increasingly, streaked with terror. Yet, he cannot remember having decided that these things should happen, or even having wished them. He has no sense that there is anything he can do to arrest the tide. He does not know whom to blame. Somehow, the crucial aspects of his environment seem in the grip of forces that are too huge and impersonal to attack" (1969, p. 40). Such concerns were also aired in the Canadian Royal Commission on Corporate Concentration's final report, which described "an overall and growing feeling of individual helplessness in a society increasingly dominated by large power blocs" (1978, p. 7).

However, it was not just members of government and the news media who were voicing such opinions. They were also being voiced in popular culture. Perhaps, the most famous example is the "Mad as Hell" speech that was such a memorable part of the 1976 movie *Network*. In that speech, which became so emblematic of the seventies that a history of the decade would be named after it (Sandbrook, 2011), fictional news anchor Howard Beale told his audience, "We know things are bad – worse than bad. They're crazy. It's like everything

**TABLE 13.13** Percentage of respondents who think the government in Washington can be trusted to do what is right[a]

| Year | None of the time | Some of the time | Most of the time | Just about always | Don't know, depends |
|------|------|------|------|------|------|
| 1958 | 0 | 23 | 57 | 16 | 4 |
| 1964 | 0 | 22 | 62 | 14 | 1 |
| 1966 | 2 | 28 | 48 | 17 | 4 |
| 1968 | 0 | 36 | 54 | 7 | 2 |
| 1970 | 0 | 44 | 47 | 6 | 2 |
| 1972 | 1 | 44 | 48 | 5 | 2 |
| 1974 | 1 | 61 | 34 | 2 | 2 |
| 1976 | 1 | 62 | 30 | 3 | 3 |
| 1978 | 4 | 64 | 27 | 2 | 3 |
| 1980 | 4 | 69 | 23 | 2 | 2 |
| 1982 | 2 | 62 | 31 | 2 | 3 |

*Source*: Data from The American National Election Studies (n.d.).
a The Canadian Election Study asked respondents, "How much of the time do you think you can trust the government in Ottawa to do what is right?" in 1965 and 1968. In 1979, the study asked whether they strongly agreed, agreed, disagreed or strongly disagreed with the statement, "Most of the time we can trust people in government to do what is right." But only half the sample was asked that question. The question wasn't asked in 1974 or 1980.

everywhere is going crazy, so we don't go out anymore ... I don't want you to protest. I don't want you to riot. I don't want you to write to your congressman, because I wouldn't know what to tell you to write. I don't know what to do about the depression and the inflation and the Russians and the crime in the street. All I know is that first you've got to get mad" (Gottfried & Lumet 1976). Echoes of that despair can be heard in the thrillers and satires of the sixties and seventies. We can hear it in *Seven Days in May*, when United States President Jordan Lyman warns that a "nuclear age" has "killed man's faith in his ability to influence what happens to him" (Lewis, 1964). We can hear it in *The Candidate*, when California senatorial contender Bill McKay, worries that people may lose the power to "shape their own lives," which are "more and more determined by forces that overwhelm the individual" (Coblenz & Ritchie 1972). And we can even hear it in the protest music of the period. For example, on his classic album *What's Going On*, Marvin Gaye sings about how everything from "trigger happy policing" to inflation and taxes, makes him "wanna holler and throw up both my hands" (Gaye & Nyx, 1971). These feelings that the world had become more uncertain and uncontrollable resulted in demands for information, with John Lennon's 1971 double-platinum selling album *Imagine* giving voice to that desire. In one song, Lennon complains about being "sick and tired of hearing things" from "pig-headed politicians" and "narrow-minded hypocrits [sic]" who have tried to "soft soap" him with a "pocketful of hope." Instead, he pleads, "All I want is the truth. Just gimme some truth."

## The demand for information and transparency in the post-truth era

The rejection of these demands for information resulted in leaks (Nader, 1971a, p. 10; Robertson, 1972, p. 150), as well as calls for transparency measures. After all, if those demands had been met, there would not have been a need for whistle-blowers. Nor would there have been a demand for such measures – most of which were directed at government, since it was seen as the paramount source of information about both the public and private sector during the postwar period (Jacobs, n.d.; Rock, 1976, p. 1). Freedom of information laws, which were approved in 1965 in the United States and 1982 in Canada, are perhaps the ultimate example of those transparency measures. As a result of their passage, Americans and Canadians were given the power to legally request access to records that public bodies had not already released. Such laws are often seen as being the foundation for any transparency regime (Ruijer & Meijer, 2016, p. 896). However, other transparency policies and programmes were also introduced during the postwar period, such as food labelling rules and guidelines (Gray, 1960; Ross, 1973; The Associated Press, 1973; Wall Street Journal Reporter, 1973), pollution indexes (Haseltine, 1964; "Index of Air Pollution" 1965; Koprowski, 1967; Stevens, 1970) and requirements to record and report work-related injuries and illnesses (The Associated Press, 1971; United Press International, 1974; Wall Street Journal Staff Reporter, 1971, 1974). Yet many of the forces that contributed to the creation of those measures continue to persist today.

After years of cutbacks and rollbacks, our governments may no longer be seen as the "unknowable" gods Alexander once claimed they were. However, much of their size remains, with the Canadian and American governments comprising 39.32 and 31.09 percent of their countries' gross domestic product in 2017 (International Monetary Fund, 2018). Big businesses are also getting even bigger, so much so that 69 of the world's top 100 economic entities are corporations rather than countries (Global Justice Now, 2016; Woolridge, 2016). And the abuses and potential abuses of governments and corporations remain just as frightening as they have ever been. The 2008 financial crisis showed how government and corporate mismanagement could put livelihoods at risk. Meanwhile, the threat of nuclear weapons, accompanied by the threat of climate change, continues to put the lives of every species on the planet at risk (Bulletin of Atomic Scientists Science and Security Board, 2018).

At the same time, Americans and Canadians continue to be more educated than they have ever been before. During the beginning of the 2015/16 academic year, there were 56,793 postsecondary students per million population in Canada (Statistics Canada, n.d.-b, n.d.-c) and 63,569 in the United States (National Center for Education Statistics, 2017; United States Census Bureau, 2018). Yet, no matter how educated they are, governments and corporations continue to have more information than individuals do, thanks to the use of

sophisticated surveillance, information storage and information retrieval technologies. National Security Agency whistle-blower Edward Snowden and the
Cambridge Analytica scandal have drawn dramatic attention to these vast sup-
plies of information (Channel 4 News Investigation Team, 2018; Greenwald
et al., n.d.). Despite their supposed commitment to the open government movement (Orszag, 2009; Treasury Board of Canada, 2014), the Canadian and
American governments continue to be reluctant to share what they know
(Howard, 2016; LeBlanc, 2018). And corporations often seem to be just as
reluctant. Instead, their propaganda and advertising poisons the public square,
choking off debate and dissent.

Yet, are we seeing the same cognitive demand for information and transparency now that we saw in the postwar period? If we aren't, I believe that may be
because information does not appear to be able to purchase the kind of citizen
and consumer control we thought it would or should. As a result of partisanship,
the permanent campaign and the influence of special interests – especially big
businesses – elected and non-elected government officials often seem impervious
to the truth, being unable to make informed, reasoned and empathetic decisions
that are in the public interest. The decisions they make are then further con-
strained by the prevailing expectations about what government can and cannot
do, which began to significantly diminish in the eighties. Even more pernicious,
though, are the officials and citizens whose beliefs and behaviours seem
unmoored from reality. President Donald J. Trump is perhaps the ultimate
example of such an official. But he is merely representative of large portions of
the public who repeatedly fail to make decisions that are in their own long-term
best interest. Nor do they seem capable of making decisions that are in the
long-term best interests of others: from family, friends and neighbors to fellow
citizens, non-citizens and the multitude of species living on this fragile planet
we all share. It is against this backdrop that we see spectacles such as the March
for Science, where the demonstrators' pleas for evidence-based decisions can
perhaps be more clearly heard as pleas to empower truth in politics (March for
Science, n.d.). Yet those pleas are so often ignored that the impotence of truth
has become a punchline, with one *Saturday Night Live* skit mocking the idea
that even an admission of guilt by Trump that he obstructed the Russia investigation wouldn't matter (Kelly, Schneider, Tucker, & Sublette, 2017).

As a result, the cognitive demand for information and control may be receding in favour of an emotional demand for certainty. And, in this demand for
certainty, we can see the seduction of authoritarianism, as well as the spurning
of democracy. Even those who prize information's cognitive and controlling
value may welcome such a change, if government would actually act in accordance with the truth. So, what does this mean for anyone who cares about information – for social scientists, humanities scholars, educators and journalists,
whose careers are premised on its cognitive value? What does it mean for
anyone who uses freedom of information laws to obtain that information? It
means we should not simply be advocating for transparency. It means we should

also be advocating for the value of information. It means we need to do more to teach our children how to use that information to make reasoned, empathetic decisions. And we need to do more to ensure those decisions matter within the context of politics and the economy. Because, when those decisions do not matter, information ceases to be the currency of democracy, providing a means of controlling our governments and corporations. And if we cannot control those governments and corporations, we no longer live in a democracy.

## Notes

1 A version of a paper presented at Mount Royal University and Medicine Hat College's second annual Liberal Education conference on May 3, 2018. I have benefited from comments by conference attendees, my dissertation supervisor Steve Hewitt, as well as Ian Bron, Jacquelyn Holman, David Taras and Mark Weiler.

2 This quotation is often spuriously misattributed to Thomas Jefferson, according to the foundation that owns and operates his former plantation. The foundation describes Nader's "earliest recorded usage" (Thomas Jefferson Foundation, n.d.) of it as the press conference announcing his Congress Project. However, I have found Nader used that phrase a month earlier, on October 11, 1971, while testifying before a Senate subcommittee. During that testimony, Nader told its members, "If we believe, as I think we should, that information is the currency of democracy, you can appreciate just how much emphasis industry committees place on blocking these questionnaires and surveys" that are used by government to obtain information about corporate activities (*Advisory Committees*, 1971).

3 Political scientists Greg Michener and Katherine Bersch make a similar observation, stating that transparency is often "undifferentiated from 'information'" (2013, p. 234).

4 This is similar to Michener and Bersch's definition of transparency, which describes it as a condition that makes visible information that is inferable. For them, information that is inferable has three qualities. First, it does not include explicit conclusions, in the way a news release or propaganda would. Instead, conclusions can be drawn from it, with examples being transcripts and raw data. Second, that information has been vetted by third party to assure it's trustworthy. And, third, that information must be simplified so, for example, it can be understood by a layman. As a result, this quality of inferability means Michener and Bersch could also be seen as conflating the definitions of transparency and information.

5 In this quote, public administration professor Anoeska Buijze refers to the value of transparency rather than the value of information (2013, pp. 8–9). However, I otherwise concur with her valuation.

6 Transparency scholars ascribe the cognitive or controlling value of information to transparency (Cucciniello et al., 2017, p. 40; Meijer, 2013, p. 432; Meijer, Curtin, & Hillebrandt, 2012, p. 21).

7 In full, the epigram reads: "It is the presentation of the facts that matters, the facts that put together are the face of the age; the rise in the price of coal, the new ballet, the woman found dead in a kimono on the golf links, the latest sermon of the Archbishop of York, the marriage of a Prime Minister's daughter. For if people do not have the face of the age set clear before them they begin to imagine it; and fantasy, if it is not disciplined by the intellect and kept in faith with reality by the instinct of art, dwells among the wishes and fears of childhood, and so sees life either as simply answering any prayer or as endlessly emitting nightmare monsters from a womb-like cave." It is taken from writer Rebecca West's 1947 book *The Meaning of Treason*.

8  Transparency scholars have studied the relationship between transparency and trust in government. However, the findings of those studies "differ according to the method of analysis – experiments and case studies tend to turn back negative or mixed findings, whereas studies drawing on survey data uncover more positive relationships" (Cucciniello et al., 2017, p. 40). Perhaps that is because the certainty provided by information can facilitate trust but does not necessarily guarantee it? Indeed, this dynamic was suggested by Canada's Royal Commission on Corporate Concentration (1978, p. 322).

9  Political scientist Colin Bennett argues "'big government' and a general perception of 'big government' are apparently necessary conditions" for the airing of arguments in favour of freedom of information laws (1997, p. 222). Big government is also central to public administration scholar Alasdair Roberts' (2015, pp. 6–7) explanation of how transparency measures emerge, which argues they are often a response to a build-up of state capacity.

# References

*Advisory committees: Hearings before the Subcommittee on Intergovernmental Relations of the Committee on Government Operations on S. 1637 to establish uniform standards and procedures for government advisory committees, s. 1964 to authorize the office of management and budget to establish governing the creation and operation of advisory committees throughout the federal government which are created to advise officers and agencies of the federal government, and s. 2064 to authorize the office of management and budget and the domestic council to establish standards and procedures governing the operation of existing government advisory committees and the creation of new ones; to provide consumer representation on certain federal advisory committees; to expand public access to advisory committee deliberations, and for other purposes*, Senate, 92nd Congress, 1 (1971) (testimony of Ralph Nader).

Alexander, J. (1968, June 6). *Technological politics or political science in the hands of an angry god.* Paper presented at the Annual Meeting of the Canadian Political Science Association. Calgary, AB.

Arrow, K. (1963). Uncertainty and the welfare economics of medical care. *The American Economic Review, 53*(5), 851–883.

Atkinson, T., Blishen, B. R., Ornstein, M. D., & Stevenson, H. M. (1979). *Social change in Canada, 1977* [Data file and code book]. Retrieved from https://search2.odesi.ca/#/.

Atkinson, T., Blishen, B. R., Ornstein, M. D., & Stevenson, H. M. (1983a). *Social change in Canada, 1979* [Data file and code book]. Retrieved from https://search2.odesi.ca/#/.

Atkinson, T., Blishen, B. R., Ornstein, M. D., & Stevenson, H. M. (1983b). *Social change in Canada, 1981* [Data file and code book]. Retrieved from https://search2.odesi.ca/#/.

*Availability of information from federal departments and agencies, part 1 – Panel discussion with editors et al.: Hearings before a Subcommittee of the Committee on Government Operations*, House of Representatives, 84th Cong. 2 (1956).

Baldwin, G. (1977, May 16). [Speech to the Canadian Association for Information Science]. *Gerald Baldwin fonds (Box 3, Folder Canadian Association for Information Science).* Library and Archives Canada, Ottawa, ON.

Baldwin, G. (1978, May 15). Privacy and computers. *Gerald Baldwin fonds (Box 3, Folder Canadian Information Processing Society). Library and Archives Canada.* Ottawa, ON.

Bennett, C. J. (1997). Understanding ripple effects: The cross-national adoption of policy instruments for bureaucratic accountability. *Governance: An International Journal of Policy and Administration, 10*(3), 213–233.

Berelson, B. (1952). Democratic theory and public opinion. *The Public Opinion Quarterly, 16*(3), 313–330.

Beveridge, W. H. (1943). *The pillars of security and other war-time essays and addresses.* London, UK: George Allen & Unwin.

Bishop, J. W., Jr. (1969, June 8). Privacy vs. protection – The bugged society. *The New York Times Magazine*, pp. 30–31, 117–122.

Blair, G. W. (1960, April 2). Compact a-bomb closer in France: Sizable step taken toward operational device with second Sahara blast. *The New York Times*, p. 6.

Brody, J. E. (1966, March 2). Asbestos dust called a hazard to at least one-fourth of U.S. *The New York Times*, p. 83.

Buijze, A. (2013). The six faces of transparency. *Utrecht Law Review*, *9*(3), 3–25.

Bulletin of Atomic Scientists Science and Security Board. (2018, January 25). It is now 2 minutes to midnight. *Bulletin of Atomic Scientists*. Retrieved from https://thebulletin. org/sites/default/files/2018%20Doomsday%20Clock%20Statement.pdf

Burns, J. (1969, October 22). Canada to ban cyclamates; Nov. 30 deadline for most: Diabetic drugs, sucaryl excepted. *The Globe and Mail*, p. 1, 4.

Calfee, J. E., & Ringold, D. J. (1994). The 70% majority: Enduring consumer beliefs about advertising. *Journal of Public Policy and Marketing*, *13*(2), 228–238.

Canada, Department of Consumer and Corporate Affairs. (1968, May 21). Consumer complaint? Don't know what to do? Write to us – We'll do something (Advertisement). *The Globe and Mail*, p. 31.

Canada, Royal Commission on Corporate Concentration. (1978). *Report of the Royal Commission on Corporate Concentration.* Ottawa, ON: Author.

Canada, Task Force on Government Information. (1969). *To know and be known.* Ottawa, ON: Author.

Canadian Institute of Public Opinion. (1968). *Canadian Gallup Poll, October 1968, #332* [Data file and code book]. Retrieved from https://search2.odesi.ca/#/.

Canadian Institute of Public Opinion. (1971). *Canadian Gallup Poll, February 1971, #349* [Data file and code book]. Retrieved from https://search2.odesi.ca/#/.

Canadian Institute of Public Opinion. (1972). *Canadian Gallup Poll, May 1972, #353* [Data file and code book]. Retrieved from https://search2.odesi.ca/#/.

Canadian Institute of Public Opinion. (1975). *Canadian Gallup Poll, August 1975, #379* [Data file and code book]. Retrieved from https://search2.odesi.ca/#/.

Canadian Institute of Public Opinion. (1976). *Canadian Gallup Poll, November 1976, #394* [Data file and code book]. Retrieved from https://search2.odesi.ca/#/.

Canadian Institute of Public Opinion. (1977). *Canadian Gallup Poll, September 1977, #404* [Data file and code book]. Retrieved from https://search2.odesi.ca/#/.

Canadian Institute of Public Opinion. (1978). *Canadian Gallup Poll, July 1978, #414* [Data file and code book]. Retrieved from https://search2.odesi.ca/#/.

Canadian Institute of Public Opinion. (1979). *Canadian Gallup Poll, January 1979, #420* [Data file and code book]. Retrieved from https://search2.odesi.ca/#/.

Canadian Institute of Public Opinion. (1980). *Canadian Gallup Poll, January 1980, #433a* [Data file and code book]. Retrieved from https://search2.odesi.ca/#/.

Canadian Institute of Public Opinion. (1981a). *Canadian Gallup Poll, January 1981, #445_1* [Data file and code book]. Retrieved from https://search2.odesi.ca/#/.

Canadian Institute of Public Opinion. (1981b). *Canadian Gallup Poll, October 1981, #454_1* [Data file and code book]. Retrieved from https://search2.odesi.ca/#/.

Canadian Institute of Public Opinion. (1982a). *Canadian Gallup Poll, February 1982, #458_1* [Data file and code book]. Retrieved from https://search2.odesi.ca/#/.

Canadian Institute of Public Opinion. (1982b). *Canadian Gallup Poll, July 1982, #463_1* [Data file and code book]. Retrieved from https://search2.odesi.ca/#/.

Canadian Institute of Public Opinion. (1982c). *Canadian Gallup Poll, November 1982, #467_1* [Data file and code book]. Retrieved from https://search2.odesi.ca/#/.

Carson, R. (2002). *Silent Spring.* New York, NY: Mariner Books. (Original work published in 1962).

Chambers, J., & Chiovitti, M. J. (1983). *Canadian Computer Census.* Toronto, ON: Canadian Information Processing Society.

Channel 4 News Investigation Team. (2018, March 17). Data, democracy and dirty tricks. *Channel 4 News.* Retrieved from www.channel4.com/news/data-democracy-and-dirty-tricks-cambridge-analytica-uncovered-investigation-expose.

Chase, S., & Schlink, F. J. (1932). *Your money's worth: A study in the waste of the consumer's dollar.* New York, NY: The Macmillan Company. (Original work published 1927).

Clarke, H., Jenson, J., LeDuc, L., & Pammett, J. (1975). *Canadian Election Study, 1974* [Data file and code book]. Retrieved from https://search2.odesi.ca/#/.

Coblenz, W. (Producer), & Ritchie, M. (Director). (1972). *The candidate [Motion picture].* United States: Warner Bros.

Converse, P., Meisel, J., Pinard, M., Regenstreif, P., & Schwartz, M. (1966) *Canadian election study, 1965* [Data file and code book]. Retrieved from https://search2.odesi.ca/#/.

Crewdson, J. M., Horrock, N. M., Rensberger, B., Thomas, J., & Treaster, J. B. (1977, August 2). Private institutions used in C.IA. effort to control behavior: $25-year, 25 million program. *The New York Times,* p. 1, 16.

Cross, H. L. (1953). *The people's right to know: Legal access to public records and proceedings.* New York, NY: Columbia University Press.

Crozier, M. J., Huntington, S. P., & Watanuki, J. (1975). *The crisis of democracy: Report on the governability of democracies to the Trilateral Commission.* New York, NY: New York University Press.

Cucciniello, M., Porumbescu, G. A., & Grimmelikhuijsen, S. (2017). 25 years of transparency research: Evidence and future directions. *Public Administration Review, 77*(1), 32–44.

Dahl, R. A. (1989). *Democracy and its critics.* New Haven, CT: Yale University Press.

Davis, L. (1964). The cost of realism: Contemporary restatements of democracy. *The Western Political Quarterly, 17*(1), 37–46.

Delahaye, A. N. (1968, March). The information explosion (Freedom of Information Center Report No. 197). Columbia, MI: University of Missouri School of Journalism.

Dowd, E. (1962, March 31). Withdraw drug after 3 months of investigation. *The Globe and Mail,* p. 3.

Editorial. (1965, April 16). It is the public's business. *The Globe and Mail,* p. 6.

Editorial. (1972, July 4). The corporate state. *The New York Times,* p. 16.

Environmental teach-in planned: National effort set for spring. (1969, November). *The Gaylord Nelson Newsletter.* Retrieved from www.wisconsinhistory.org/Records/Image/IM99088.

Fishman, N., & Davis, A. (2017, January 5). *Americans still see big government as top threat.* Washington, DC: Gallup. Retrieved from. http://news.gallup.com/poll/201629/americans-big-government-top-threat.aspx.

Foell, S. S., & Robinson, J. H. (2003). *Growth, efficiency and modernism: GSA buildings of the 1950s, 60s, and 70s.* Washington, DC: U.S. General Services Administration, Office of the Chief Architect, Center for Historic Buildings.

*Food price investigation: Hearings before the Subcommittee on Monopolies and Commercial Law of the Committee on the Judiciary,* House of Representatives, 93d Cong. 1 (1973).

French, R. D. (1978). *Legislation on public access to government documents.* Ottawa, ON: Secretary of State of Canada.

Friedman, M. P. (1967). Quality and price considerations in rational consumer decision making. *The Journal of Consumer Affairs, 1*(1), 13–23.

Gaye, M., & Nyx, J., Jr. (1971, Inner city blues [Recorded by Marvin Gaye]). *On What's Going On [mp3]*. Detroit, MI: Tamla Records.

Geyer, T. (1974, April 19). Industry fundamentals finally look good as courts cast a cloud. *EDP Industry Report, 9*(13), 1–13.

Global Justice Now. (2016, September 12). *10 biggest corporations make more money than most countries in the world combined.* London, UK: Author. Retrieved from www.globaljustice. org.uk/news/2016/sep/12/10-biggest-corporations-make-more-money-most-countries-world-combined.

Golman, R., & Loewenstein, G. (2016, January 2). An information-gap theory of feelings about uncertainty. *Carnegie Mellon University Department of Social and Decision*. Retrieved from www.cmu.edu/dietrich/sds/docs/golman/Information-Gap%20Theory%202016.pdf.

Goodwin, R. N. (1969, January 4). Sources of the public unhappiness. *The New Yorker*, pp. 38–58.

Gottfried, H. (Producer), & Lumet, S. (Director) (1976). *Network [Motion picture]*. Unites States: Metro-Goldwyn-Mayer.

Gray, W. (1960, June 1). Food labels to list names of ingredients. *The Globe and Mail*, p. 9.

Greenwald, G. et al. (n.d.). The NSA files. *The Guardian*. Retrieved from www.theguardian. com/us-news/the-nsa-files.

Greider, W. (1971, December 5). Institutional 'lone ranger:' Ralph Nader strives to inspire 'public citizens'. *The Washington Post*, p. A1, A22.

Gwyn, R. (1974, March 30). The biggest boss is growing even bigger. *The Toronto Star*, p. B4.

H.R. Rep. No. 2947 (1956).

Hamilton, A. (1968, September 14). 'Secret government' could harm country if Trudeau tries it. *Toronto Daily Star*, p. 8.

Haseltine, N. (1964, April 11). Daily report on index of air pollution urged. *The Washington Post*, p. D10.

Hochman, B. (2016, February 3). Eavesdropping in the age of *The Eavesdroppers*; or, the bug in the olive. *Post45*. Retrieved from http://post45.research.yale.edu/2016/02/eavesdropping-in-the-age-of-the-eavesdroppers-or-the-bug-in-the-martini-olive/.

Holman, S. M. (2018, March 12). *Freedom of information and the French atom bomb.* Retrieved from https://seanholman.com/2018/03/12/freedom-of-information-and-the-french-atom-bomb/.

Horrock, N. M. (1977, August 3). Drugs tested by C.I.A. on mental patients: Documents disclose use in '58 of LSD in Canadian hospital. *The New York Times*, p. A1, A9.

Howard, A. (2016, November 10). What the Trump administration means for open government. *Sunlight Foundation*. Retrieved from https://sunlightfoundation.com/2016/11/10/what-the-trump-administration-means-for-open-government/.

Index of air pollution to be printed in Times. (1965, March 3). *The New York Times*, p. 82.

Innis, M. (2016, May 27). Australia gets some bad news cut from U.N. study. *The New York Times*, p. A3.

International Monetary Fund. (2018). *Fiscal monitor (April 2018)* [Data file and code book]. Retrieved from www.imf.org/external/datamapper/GGR_G01_GDP_PT@FM/ADVEC/FM_EMG/FM_LIDC.

International Monetary Fund. (n.d.). *Government expenditure, percent of GDP* [Data file and code book]. Retrieved from www.imf.org/external/datamapper/exp@FPP/USA/CAN.

Jacobs, T. J. (1975, March 8). Knowing and knowing. *The New York Times*, p. 25.

Katona, G. (1953). Rational behavior and economic behavior. *Psychological Review, 60*(5), 307–318.

Kazanjian, J. A. (1978, April). *Corporate disclosure: A background report.* Ottawa, ON: Royal Commission on Corporate Concentration.

Kelly, C., Schneider, S., Tucker, B. H., & Sublette, K. (Head writers). (2017, May 13). Episode 828 [Television series episode]. In L. Michaels (Producer), *Saturday night live.* New York, NY: National Broadcasting Company. Retrieved from www.youtube.com/watch?v=OT2UNv0C-V0.

Kennedy, J. F. (1962, March 14). *Special message on protecting the consumer interest to the Congress of the United States.* Papers of John F. Kennedy (Presidential papers, President's office files, Speech files). John F. Kennedy Presidential Library and Museum, Boston, MA. Retrieved from www.jfklibrary.org/Asset-Viewer/Archives/JFKPOF-037-028.aspx.

Kilpatrick, J. J. (1972, November 4). What's good for Ralph Nader … *Human Events,* p. 22.

Koprowski, C. (1967, April 21). Area board adopts air pollution alert. *The Washington Post,* p. A24.

LeBlanc, D. (2018, February 21). Information watchdog blasts Liberals ahead of her retirement. *The Globe and Mail.* Retrieved from www.theglobeandmail.com/news/politics/information-watchdog-blasts-liberals-ahead-of-her-retirement/article38060282/.

Lehmann-Haupt, C. (1973, November 16). Historical and polemical: Books of *The Times. The New York Times,* p. 39.

Lennon, J. (1971). Gimme some truth. On *Imagine* [mp3]. London, UK: Apple Records.

Lewis, A. (1975). Introduction. In N. Dorsen, & S. Gillers (Eds.), *None of your business: Government secrecy in America* (pp. 3–24). New York, NY: Penguin Books. (Original work published in 1974).

Lewis, E. (Producer), & Frankenheimer J. (Director). (1964). *Seven days in may* [Motion picture]. Unites States: Paramount Pictures.

Loewenstein, G. (1994). The psychology of curiosity: A review and reinterpretation. *Psychological Bulletin, 116*(1), 75–98.

Lutsky, I. (1967, May 24). Public relations men drop press-agentry for professionalism. *The Globe and Mail,* p. B5.

Machipisa, L. (1996, July 29). Africa-Media: Information is the currency of democracy. *Inter Press Service News Agency.* Retrieved from www.ipsnews.net/1996/07/africa-media-information-is-the-currency-of-democracy/.

March for Science. (n.d.). The march: Our history. Retrieved from www.marchforscience.com/our-history.

Martin, J. (2002). *Nader: Crusader, Spoiler, Icon.* New York, NY: Perseus Publishing.

Martin, L. (1979, January 29). Canadians used as CIA 'guinea pigs,' ex-patient says: Psychiatrist worked at McGill. *The Globe and Mail,* p. 1, 2.

Martin, L. (1980, May 12). U.S. chemical testing got Canada's approval. *The Globe and Mail,* p. 1, 2.

McClean, T. (2011). *Shackling Leviathan: A comparative historical study of institutions and the adoption of freedom of information* (Doctoral dissertation). Retrieved from http://etheses.lse.ac.uk.

McGovern, P. J. (1969, March 25). A history, projection, and analysis of the computer industry through 1975. *EDP Industry Report, 4*(14), 8–13.

McGovern, P. J. (1970, March 12). Mature product lines … and unbundling result in level computer shipments but significant increase in revenues. *EDP Industry Report, 5*(9), 1–15.

McGovern, P. J. (1971, March 12). Shipments plateau for third straight year as U.S. feels economic pinch; industry revenues up 15%; new product directions set by IBM, other mainframers. *EDP Industry Report, 6*(9), 1–14.

McGovern, P. J. (1972, March 30). Shipments turn upward as new industry growth pattern emerges. *EDP Industry Report, 7*(10), 1–11.

McGovern, P. J. (1973, March 30). Shipments up 24% as teleprocessing growth phase begins. *EDP Industry Report, 8*(11), 1–14.

Meijer, A. J. (2012). Introduction to the special issue on government transparency. *International Review of Administrative Sciences, 78*(1), 3–9.

Meijer, A. J. (2013). Understanding the complex dynamics of transparency. *Public Administration Review, 73*(3), 429–439.

Meijer, A. J., Curtin, D., & Hillebrandt, M. (2012). Open government: Connecting Vision and Voice. *International Review of Administrative Sciences, 78*(1), 10–29.

Michener, G., & Bersch, K. (2013). Identifying transparency. *Information Polity, 18*, 233–242.

Mitchell, H. (1975). *A Report on Access to Information*. Toronto, ON: Consumer Research Council.

Mock, W. (1999). On the centrality of information law: A rational choice discussion of information law and transparency. *Journal of Computer and Information Law, 17*(4), 1069–1100.

Morris, J. D. (1971, November 3). Congress facing inquiry by Nader: 1,000 people expected to take part in study. *The New York Times*, p. 19.

Moschella, D. (1983). Value of worldwide computer shipments to grow 17.3% per year over 1982-87 period. *EDP Industry Report, 19*(10&11), 1–16.

Nader, R. (1970). Freedom from information: The Act and the agencies. *Harvard Civil Rights-Civil Liberties Law Review, 5*, 1–15.

Nader, R. (1971a). An anatomy of whistleblowing. In R. Nader, P. Petkas, & K. Blackwell (Eds.), *Whistle blowing: The report of the conference on professional responsibility* (pp. 3–11). New York, NY: Penguin Books.

Nader, R. (1971b, December 23). The underachievements of Congress. *The New York Times*, p. 25.

National Center for Education Statistics. (2017). *Table 301.10. Enrolment, staff, and degrees/ certificates conferred in degree-granting and non-degree-granting postsecondary institutions, by control and level of institution, sex of student, type of staff, and level of degree: Fall 2015 and 2014–15* [Data file and code book]. Retrieved from https://nces.ed.gov/programs/digest/d16/tables/dt16_301.10.asp

National Security Archive. (n.d.). *FOIA legislative history*. Washington, DC: Author. Retrieved from https://nsarchive2.gwu.edu//nsa/foialeghistory/legistfoia.htm.

Newton, V. M. (1961). *Crusade for democracy*. Ames, IA: The Iowa State University Press.

Orszag, P. R. (2009, December 8). *Open government directive*. Washington, DC: Executive Office of the President of the United States. Retrieved from https://obamawhitehouse.archives.gov/open/documents/open-government-directive.

Peacock, J. (1975, April 30). Shipments break records, despite recession, as significant changes approach. *EDP Industry Report, 10*(15&16), 1–15.

Peacock, J. (1976, April 30). After a level 1975, several years of shipment increases forecast. *EDP Industry Report, 11*(18&19), 1–10.

Peacock, J. (1977, April 22). Computer shipments hit $13 billion; new price/performance curves fashioned. *EDP Industry Report, 12*(19&20), 1–9.

Peacock, J. (1978, May 19). Computer shipments jump 20%; similar growth expected this year. *EDP Industry Report, 13*(21&22), 1–12.

Peacock, J. (1979, June 29). 1978 and first half of 1979 meet or exceed forecasts. *EDP Industry Report*, *15*(2&3), 1–13.

Penn, S. (1966, December 20). Shape of the future: Computers will bring problems along with their many benefits. *The Wall Street Journal*, p. 1, 19.

Perl, M. L. (1971). The scientific advisory system: Some observations. *Science*, *173*(4003), 1211–1215.

Plumb, R. K. (1962, April 12). Deformed babies traced to a drug: 'Harmless' tablet given to mothers abroad is cited as infants' crippler. *The New York Times*, p. 37, 58.

Pope, J. S. (1953). Forward. In H. L. Cross (Ed.), *The people's right to know: Legal access to public records and proceedings* (pp. vii–xi). New York, NY: Columbia University Press.

Pyle, C. H. (1970, January). CONUS Intelligence: The army watches civilian politics. *Washington Monthly*, pp. 4–5, 49–58.

Queen's Printer for Canada. (1951-1982). *The Canada Gazette: Part II*. Ottawa, ON: Author.

Queen's Printer for Canada, *Canada Gazette* Directorate (2001). 160 years of the *Canada Gazette*. Ottawa, ON: Author.

Regulatory Studies Center. (n.d.). *Reg stats*. Retrieved from https://regulatorystudies.columbian.gwu.edu/reg-stats.

Riley, T. (1976, October). Time is here for foes of secrecy to push freedom of information law. *Content*, p. 2, 5-7.

Riley, T. (n.d.). [Resume of Thomas B. Riley]. Copy in possession of Cathia Riley.

Roberts, A. (2015, June 4-6). *Too much transparency? How critics of openness misunderstand administrative development*. Paper presented at the Fourth Global Conference on Transparency Research. Lugano, Switzerland.

Robertson, G. (1972). Official responsibility, private conscience, and public information. *Optimum*, *3*, 149–162.

Rock, P. (1976, November 8). Canadian legislative policy report. Gerald Baldwin fonds (Box 3, Folder Canadian Community Newspapers Association). Library and Archives Canada, Ottawa, ON.

*Role of giant corporations: Hearings before the Subcommittee on Monopoly of the Select Committee on Small Business on the role of giant corporations in the American and world economies, part 1 – Automobile industry – 1969*, Senate, 91st Cong. 1 (1969).

*Role of giant corporations: Hearings before the Subcommittee on Monopoly of the Select Committee on Small Business on the role of giant corporations in the American and world economies, part 2 – Corporate secrecy, overviews*, Senate, 92d Cong. 1 (1972).

Ross, N. L. (1973, January 18). Full food labels ordered by FDA. *The Washington Post*, p. A1, A6.

Rostand, J. (1960). Popularization of science. *Science*, *131*(3412), 1491.

Rowat, D. C. (1965). How much administrative secrecy? *The Canadian Journal of Economics and Political Science*, *31*(4), 479–498.

Ruijer, E., & Meijer, A. (2016). National transparency regimes: Rules or principles? A comparative analysis of the United States and the Netherlands. *International Journal of Public Administration*, *39*(11), 895–908.

Russell, M. (1972a, October 8). Nader's book on Congress no eye-opener. *The Washington Post*, p. A16.

Russell, M. (1972b, October 1). Nader takes on Congress: 25,000-page critical study draws outcry. *The Washington Post*, p. A1, A16.

Sandbrook, D. (2011). *Mad as hell: The crisis of the 1970s and the rise of the populist right*. New York, NY: Alfred A. Knopf.

Schlesinger, A. M. (1989). *The Imperial Presidency*. Boston, MA: Houghton Mifflin. (Original work published 1973).

Schmeck, H. M., Jr. (1964, October 7). A rare carcinoma believed on rise: Study of asbestos workers shows a high incidence. *The New York Times*, p. 24.

Schmeck, H. M., Jr. (1969, October 19). Government officially announces cyclamate sweeteners will be taken off market early next year. *The New York Times*, p. 58.

Schmeck, H. M., Jr. (1972, January 29). F.D.A. removes saccharin from list of safe foods. *The New York Times*, p. 27.

Schudson, M. (2015). *The rise of the right to know: Politics and the culture of transparency, 1945–1975*. Cambridge, MA: The Belknap Press of Harvard University Press.

Seniuk, G. (1974, September 27). Years after plants close, cancer still takes its toll. *The Globe and Mail*, p. 1, 2.

Silverberg, R. (2003a, September). Reflections: The Cleve Cartmill affairs: One. *Asimov's Science Fiction Magazine*, pp. 4–7. Retrieved from web.archive.org/web/20130618175748/www.asimovs.com/_issue_0310/ref.shtml.

Silverberg, R. (2003b, October). Reflections: The Cleve Cartmill affairs: Two. *Asimov's Science Fiction Magazine*, pp. 4–9. Retrieved from web.archive.org/web/20141006183638/www.asimovs.com/_issue_0311/ref2.shtml.

Simon, H. A. (1955). A behavioral model of rational choice. *The Quarterly Journal of Economics, 69*(1), 99–118.

Statistics Canada. (n.d.-a). *Estimated population of Canada, 1605 to present* [Data file and code book]. Retrieved from www.150.statcan.gc.ca/n1/pub/98-187-x/4151287-eng.htm.

Statistics Canada. (n.d.-b). *Table 17- 10-0005-01:Population estimates on July 1st, by age and sex* [Data file and code book]. Retrieved from www.150.statcan.gc.ca/t1/tbl1/en/tv.action?pid=1710000501.

Statistics Canada. (n.d.-c). Table 37-10-0011-01: *Postsecondary enrolments, by program type, credential type, classification of instructional programs, primary grouping (CIP_PG), registration status and sex* [Data file and code book]. Retrieved from www.150.statcan.gc.ca/t1/tbl1/en/tv.action?pid=3710001101.

Stevens, G. (1969, October 11). Trudeau moving toward presidential system, professor tells Tory conference: Delegates are uniformly unalarmed. *The Globe and Mail*, p. 10.

Stevens, G. (1970, March 21). Pollution warning system coming soon for Ontario: Could stop industry's operation. *The Globe and Mail*, p. 1, 2.

Stigler, G. J. (1961). The economics of information. *Journal of Political Economy, 69*(3), 213–225.

The American National Election Studies. (n.d.). *The ANES guide to public opinion and electoral behavior* [Data file and code book]. Retrieved from https://electionstudies.org/resources/anes-guide/

The Associated Press. (1971, May 21). U.S. lists rules for employers' record keeping. *The Washington Post*, p. A11.

The Associated Press. (1973, March 14). Consumers will be able to tell what they're buying in 1975. *The Globe and Mail*, p. 13.

The Canadian Press. (1958, July 25). Unfair trade practices said prevalent here. *The Globe and Mail*, p. 17.

The Canadian Press. (1977, August 4). Ex-official confirms Montreal experiments. *The Globe and Mail*, p. 10.

The Canadian Press. (1979a, January 30). Doctor involved in CIA-backed tests on brainwashing lauded for his work. *The Globe and Mail*, p. 10.

The Canadian Press. (1979b, November 17). MP's wife can sue over LSD tests. *The Globe and Mail*, p. 11.

The Canadian Press. (1980a, December 11). Canadians suing U.S. *The Globe and Mail*, p. 16.

The Canadian Press. (1980b, May 14). Winnipeg told 1953 spray was 'smokescreen' testing. *The Globe and Mail*, p. 4.

The Governor General of Canada. (n.d.). Gerald Baldwin, O.C., Q.C., LL.D. Retrieved from https://www.gg.ca/en/honours/recipients/146-

The Ottawa Bureau of *The Globe and Mail*. (1962, February 23). Pill endangers unborn babies, doctors warned. *The Globe and Mail*, p. 2.

Thomas Jefferson Foundation. (n.d.) Information is the currency of democracy (spurious quotation). In *Thomas Jefferson Encyclopaedia*. Retrieved from www.monticello.org/site/jefferson/information-currency-democracy-spurious-quotation.

Tower, S. A. (1981, May 31). Rachel Carson is pictured on new 17-cent issue. *The New York Times*, p. D37.

Transparency. (n.d.). *Oxford English living dictionaries*. Retrieved from https://en.oxforddictionaries.com/definition/transparency.

Transparent. (n.d.). *Oxford English living dictionaries*. Retrieved from https://en.oxforddictionaries.com/definition/transparent.

Treasury Board of Canada. (2014, October 9). *Directive on open government*. Ottawa, ON: Author. Retrieved from www.tbs-sct.gc.ca/pol/doc-eng.aspx?id=28108.

Trial begins in case of Telex vs. I.B.M. (1973, April 17). *The New York Times*, p. 56.

Truth. (n.d.). *Oxford English living dictionaries*. Retrieved from https://en.oxforddictionaries.com/definition/truth.

Turner, J. (1969). *Twin Freedoms: The Right to Privacy and the Right to Know*. An address delivered to the Canadian Bar Association annual meeting in Ottawa.

United Nations, Department of International Economic and Social Affairs Statistical Office. (1948-1985). *Statistical yearbook* [Data file and code book]. Retrieved from https://unstats.un.org/unsd/publications/statistical-yearbook/past-issues.

United Press International. (1974, January 22). Job injuries hit 1 out of 10. *The Washington Post*, p. A17.

United Press International. (1980, May 2). 1953 powdering of Minneapolis in biological war test disclosed. *The New York Times*, p. A22.

United States Census Bureau. (2000). *Historical national population estimates: July 1, 1900 to July 1, 1999* [Data file and code book]. Retrieved from www.census.gov/population/estimates/nation/popclockest.txt.

United States Census Bureau. (2018). *U.S. and world population* [Data file and code book]. Retrieved from www.census.gov/popclock/.

United States, Defense Science Board, Task Force on Secrecy. (1970). *Report of the Defense Science Board Task Force on Secrecy*. Washington, DC: Office of the Director of Defense Research and Engineering.

Upton, M. (1982, September 22). 1982 computer shipments hold firm despite recession; value to rise 15% to $33.9 billion. *EDP Industry Report*, *18*(10&11), 1–15.

Vleugels, R. (2011, October 9). Overview of all FOI laws. *Fringe*. Retrieved from www.right2info.org/resources/publications/Fringe%20Special%20-%20Overview%20FOIA%20-%20sep%2020%202010.pdf/at_download/file.

Wall, D. F. (1974). *The provision of government information*. Ottawa, ON: Privy Council Office.

*Wall Street Journal* News Roundup. (1954, February 9). Hot competition brings an upswing in dubious sales methods too. *The Wall Street Journal*, p. 1, 13.

*Wall Street Journal* Reporter. (1973, January 18). Food label rules will be stiffened under FDA order: More disclosure on nutrition required. *The Wall Street Journal*, p. 9.

*Wall Street Journal* Staff Reporter. (1953, March 30). Mead warns 'false' ads may grow as competition becomes keener. *The Wall Street Journal*, p. 4.

*Wall Street Journal* Staff Reporter. (1971, May 21). Hodgson acts to require employers to keep data on job deaths, injuries. *The Wall Street Journal*, p. 23.

*Wall Street Journal* Staff Reporter. (1974, January 22). One of nine workers had job-related ills in 1972. *The Wall Street Journal*, p. 19.

Washington Bureau of *The Sun*. (1971, November 3). Flaws in Congress are next target for Nader's band of reformers. *The Baltimore Sun*, p. A7.

Westell, A. (1970, April 11). Trudeau called most powerful of all our PMs. *Toronto Daily Star*, p. 1.

Wicker, T. (1972, January 4). The Anderson papers. *The New York Times*, p. 33.

Woolridge, A. (2016, September 17). The rise of the superstars; companies. *The Economist*, pp. S3–S5.

Wright, J. (1997). *Crown assets: The architecture of the Department of Public Works, 1867–1967*. Toronto, ON: University of Toronto Press.

# POSTSCRIPT: ACCESS IN THE ABSENCE OF FOI

## Open-source investigations and strategies of verification

*Giancarlo Fiorella*

I have never worked with Freedom of Information. Not because I do not find the concept or the data that it would provide useful, but because I have yet to do research involving governments that could be compelled to provide me with information upon request. My academic work is centred on civil conflict in Venezuela, namely protest-related violence perpetrated by official state security forces and pro-government armed groups. In my professional life as an investigator for Latin America at the open-source investigation collective Bellingcat, I research cases of state corruption, human rights abuses and conflict. In one recent project, for example, we identified some of the weapons used by pro-government armed groups in Nicaragua and discovered evidence that directly connected these groups with official state security forces (Fiorella, 2019). The work that I do requires information that governments the world over do not want the public to have. This is on top of the fact that in some countries like Venezuela, Freedom of Information legislation is non-existent. There, official data is released only when the government wants to release it. For example, the Banco Central de Venezuela (Venezuelan Central Bank, BCV) has gone years without publishing inflation figures. When it does, it is often after it is compelled to do so by international organisations, not Venezuelan citizens.[1] Whenever there is a protest fatality in Venezuela at the hands of the police, information on the case comes not from the police agency involved in the death, but rather directly from high-ranking government officials who twist facts and alter narratives without consequence. For some governments, like the one in Venezuela today, opaqueness is a defining characteristic.

There are times when I envy my Canadian colleagues who have at their disposal Freedom of Information laws that – albeit imperfect and replete with pitfalls – sometimes offer the promise of results. And yet, I find myself with a curious problem: I have at my disposal too much information. None of it was requested from the governments and institutions that I study. For researchers like me who operate outside of the real of Freedom of Information, there is but one recourse: open-source information.

## Open-source information: going straight to the source

When I first began collecting open-source information (that is, information that is freely available online), I realised neither what it was nor how useful it would become to me. I started collecting data in February 2014 for what would become my doctoral dissertation when I figured out – much later than many – that Twitter could be used to do more than follow celebrities. Venezuelans all over the country were using the platform to share pictures and videos that they themselves had recorded at protests. Thanks to Twitter, by 2014, one no longer needed to wait for the evening news to see images and videos from the world's conflict zones. That material was made available instantly not only on Twitter, but also on other social media platforms like Facebook and Instagram, shared by the very people who were participating in these events. The news anchor, long the mediator between event and audience, no longer had a role to play in the dissemination of information. It was in these conflict zones that the citizen journalist came of age. Anyone on the scene with a cell phone and an Internet connection could reach an audience of millions in just minutes, sometimes before journalists with media giants like CNN or the BBC were even aware that an event was unfolding.

By the hundreds and thousands, citizen journalists across Venezuela used their Twitter accounts throughout the early months of 2014 to share pictures and videos of protest violence with the world. There were videos of National Bolivarian Guard soldiers beating demonstrators, and pro-government armed groups shooting people dead on the streets. Some of these images were captured in places where traditional media outlets had no access, sometimes due to a lack of resources. But the protesters were always, by definition, at the protests. It was through their eyes that we saw many of the worst excesses of the Maduro government's drive to crush dissent. It was in early 2014 that I began to spend most of my time on social media platforms like Twitter looking for videos and images shared by citizen journalists in Venezuela and collecting this information in a blog that I launched that year.

The evaporation of traditional media from the event-audience continuum has a drawback: it leaves the verification of information to the audience. Traditional media outlets like the BBC or the New York Times built their reputations as trustworthy sources of news because they tend to be accurate in their reporting. This is because before publishing a piece of information, they take steps to verify that it is an accurate representation of fact.[2] Was this video really filmed when the person who filmed it says it was? Was it really filmed where the person who filmed it says it was? Does it really show what the person who filmed it says it shows? By circumventing traditional media outlets in the delivery of news, the citizen journalist and other social media users trade the verification processes through which media outlets filtered news to the world for the ability to instantly reach an audience.

Just as my "discovery" of open-source information was accidental, so was my discovery of the verification process that now takes up much of my time. Back in 2014, this process was rudimentary, but the roots of what would become today's sophisticated open-source verification process were there. At the heart of this process was – and still remains – a single fundamental dictum: ask questions. Taking an image or video as accurate simply based on the text from the user who shared it on Twitter is not an option. Luckily for the open-source investigator, there are dozens of free online tools and techniques that allow for the verification of visual information. Google Earth can be used to verify images by matching features in the landscape to those visible on satellite imagery; astronomical calculators can be used to estimate the approximate time that an image was captured based on the shadows visible in the material; flight-tracking websites make short work of verifying whether an aircraft was present at a given location at a given time, while YouTube has millions of hours of footage featuring weapons from small arms to submarines that allow for cross-source comparison. The citizen journalist may have passed on the task of verification to the audience, but the audience is more than equipped to get the job done, given time, patience and practice.

Today, this verification process has developed into a rigorous one with a methodological backbone that has drawn the attention of the International Criminal Court (ICC).[3] This has been partially the result of efforts by Bellingcat, whose open-source investigations have yielded some impressive results, including finding evidence that Russia-linked forces downed Malaysian Airlines Flight 17 over eastern Ukraine on July 17, 2014 (Bellingcat Investigation Team, 2014), and that two supposed tourists on a sight-seeing trip to Salisbury, England were in fact agents with Main Directorate of the General Staff of the Armed Forces of the Russian Federation (more commonly known as the GRU) on a mission to assassinate a man named Sergei Skripal (Bellingcat Investigation Team, 2018). These and other discoveries by Bellingcat investigators were carried out with the use of information that is available on the Internet for anyone to find.

There is arguably no better example of the open-source investigation ethos and its verification process than *Anatomy of a Killing* (BBC Africa Eye, 2018).[4] This investigation began in July 2018 after a video began to circulate on Twitter showing a group of men walking two women and two children down a dusty path somewhere in Africa, blindfolding them and executing them. To the untrained eye, the video offered virtually no information as to the location in which it was filmed, or about the people that it featured. At first glance, the viewer can scarcely make out a path in the savannah, scant vegetation and mountains in the horizon, leaving him/her to discern nothing more than the video was filmed somewhere in Africa at some undetermined point in the past.

Bellingcat alumni Aliaume Leroy and Benjamin Strick led crowdsourcing campaign on Twitter to geolocate the site where the video was filmed,[5] determine when it was filmed and identify the perpetrators. After a month of arduous work, a team of half a dozen contributors had matched the mountains in the background of the video using Google Earth Pro to a location in northern Cameroon, despite affirmations from that country's government to the contrary. They used satellite imagery and one of the men's shadows to calculate that the killings took place between March 20 and April 5, 2015. An analysis of the audio clues in the video led investigators to find the social media profiles of most of the perpetrators. All this information was discerned using open-source information and methods, regardless of the wishes and actions of the government of Cameroon.

The deteriorating situation in Venezuela leads me to believe that I will not live to see the installation of a robust, functioning Freedom of Information regime there. The country has many more challenges to overcome in a post-dictatorship scenario. While I hope to be proven wrong, it may be the case that even if such a regime were to be implemented in Venezuela, open-source researchers like me might not be drawn to it. Not only is the amount of information freely available online increasing by the day, but so are the tools and techniques for verifying that information. Paradoxically, the Venezuelan government's repression of traditional media outlets appears to have created more, savvier citizen journalists who are ever aware of the importance that their work has for open-source investigators across the world. If we see this same pattern develop in other authoritarian countries, then it is likely that the open-source investigator has yet to see his/her finest hour.

The open-source investigation methodology that Bellingcat has helped to pioneer is maturing daily, and its full range of applications has yet to be defined. It may be desirable – or perhaps even advisable – to apply this verification methodology to the data that researchers receive from governments through Freedom of Information requests. In the age of deep fakes and fake news, the open-source information verification process is indispensable to both the researcher and her audience. This process separates truth from mis/disinformation and builds not only trust in the audience but also teaches by example that not all information, no matter how official, is to be believed. If the open-source researcher understands that the data with which he/she works could have been manipulated to mislead him/her, why should the scholar working with Freedom of Information data not consider the same?

## Notes

1 This was the case in November 2018 when the BCV sent inflation data to the International Monetary Fund (IMF) as part of an institutional requirement.
2 One need not look further for an example of this dynamic than CNN's slogan ("The most trusted named in news") for evidence of the importance of the role that traditional media places in the verification of information.

3  On August 15, 2017, the ICC issued an arrest warrant for a Libyan warlord named Mahmoud Mustafa Busayf Al-Werfalli alleging that he had committed war crimes during the most recent conflict in that country. The arrest warrant included open-source information as evidence.

4  As of the writing of this piece, *Anatomy of a Killing* has won several awards, including a Peabody.

5  This feat of geolocation cannot be overstated. Open-source investigators narrowed the site of the atrocity from "somewhere in Africa" (a land mass extending over 30 million km$^2$) to the exact spot on which it was committed: 10°59′34.8″N 13°47′50.6″E.

## References

BBC Africa Eye. (2018). Anatomy of a killing. *BBC Africa Eye*. Retrieved from www. youtube.com/watch?v=4G9S-eoLgX4

Bellingcat Investigation Team. (2014). Caught in a lie – Compelling evidence Russia Lied about the Buk linked to MH17. *Bellingcat*. Retrieved from www.bellingcat.com/news/ uk-and-europe/2014/07/24/caught-in-a-lie-compelling-evidence-russia-lied-about-the-buk-linked-to-mh17/

Bellingcat Investigation Team. (2018). Skripal suspects confirmed as GRU operatives: Prior European operations disclosed. *Bellingcat*. Retrieved from www.bellingcat.com/ news/uk-and-europe/2018/09/20/skripal-suspects-confirmed-gru-operatives-prior-european-operations-disclosed/

Fiorella, G. (2019). Analysis of Nicaragua's paramilitary arsenal. *Bellingcat*. Retrieved from www.bellingcat.com/news/americas/2019/02/12/analysis-of-nicaraguas-paramilitary-arsenal/

# INDEX